Princip
Thr
Dimensio
Compute
Animatio

Principles of
Three-Dimensional Computer Animation

*Modeling, Rendering, and Animating
with 3D Computer Graphics*

THIRD EDITION

Michael O'Rourke

W. W. Norton & Company
New York • London

This book is dedicated to students all around the world. Your talent, energy, and enthusiasm have been a joy to work with. May you use your gifts with wisdom as you move forward in your lives.

For information about permission to reproduce selections from this book, write to Permissions, W. W. Norton & Company, Inc., 500 Fifth Avenue, New York, NY 10110

Composition and book design by Ken Gross.
Manufacturing by Quebecor World Fairfield, Inc.
Production Manager: Leeann Graham.
Jacket illustration: design and direction by Michael O'Rourke; modeling and rendering by Matt Vitalone.

Library of Congress Cataloging-in-Publication Data

O'Rourke, Michael.
    Principles of three-dimensional computer animation: modeling, rendering, and animating with 3D computer graphics / Michael O'Rourke.—3rd ed.
            p.   cm.
    Includes index.
    ISBN 0-393-73083-2
    1. Computer animation. 2. Three-dimensional display systems. 3. Computer graphics. I. Title.

    TR897.7 .O76 2002
    006.6'96—dc21   2002029575

W. W. Norton & Company, Inc., 500 Fifth Avenue, New York, N.Y. 10110
www.wwnorton.com
W. W. Norton & Company Ltd., Castle House, 75/76 Wells St., London W1T 3QT

0   9   8   7   6   5   4   3   2   1

Preface to the Third Edition

This greatly expanded third edition reflects numerous advances in the field and the tremendous growth of the industry in recent years. This edition introduces an abundance of new principles and techniques, including twenty entirely new chapter sections, and over one hundred new illustrations.

The quantity of new material demanded a restructuring of the book. Framed at each end by chapters on preproduction and postproduction, the book now consists of three chapters devoted to the basics of modeling, rendering, and animation, followed by another three chapters addressing the more advanced concepts of these fundamentals.

The result of the expansion is that both beginners and sophisticated users will find useful information on any area of 3D animation they may be pursuing. The reorganization will enable readers to easily locate the material of interest to them. For students and teachers alike, the book should provide grist for at least several focused 3D animation courses.

The field of three-dimensional computer animation has expanded greatly in many areas over the last several years. Currently, virtually all big-budget films make at least some use of 3D computer animation, and many rely on it for their success. The game industry has become one of the largest and fastest growing industries in the world. Additionally, numerous design fields, including architecture, industrial design, package design, and interior design, now rely on 3D computer graphics as a standard part of their toolkit. Internet sites have also begun using 3D graphics and animation.

It is an exciting time to be part of this field. I am happy to be able to make my small contribution to it through this book.

Preface to the Revised Edition

This book is intended for people who work with, or who wish to work with, 3D computer animation. It does not assume any prior knowledge of 3D computer graphics. It does not assume, nor does it present, any of the mathematics or program code that underlie computer graphics. And finally, it does not assume a prior knowledge of animation itself.

Since the book assumes no prior knowledge of the field, it is suitable for readers in the process of learning 3D computer modeling, rendering, or animation. At the same time, since the book is very thorough and covers a wide range of topics, including many advanced topics, it is suitable for readers who have acquired substantial experience and wish to enhance their understanding of the field.

The book is appropriate for both working professionals and students who want to gain a more thorough and systematic understanding of the underlying principles of 3D computer animation. Animators who have worked with traditional animation techniques, art directors who need to understand their animators, industrial and interior designers and architects who may be involved in projects that entail 3D computer animation—any professional with an interest in or a need to understand how this technology works—will find the book valuable.

The book is not, however, a software guide. It makes no attempt to deal with specific software packages. Its subject matter is the general principles common to all 3D computer animation systems, not the implementation of those principles by one software vendor.

It is, nonetheless, a technical book, in that it deals with the *technical* principles of 3D computer animation. These are substantial, and they are also constantly expanding. It is always the case in 3D computer graphics that researchers in laboratories around the world are developing interesting experimental techniques well before these innovations are available in off-the-shelf software packages. This book does not attempt to deal with experimental techniques in early stages of development, but is limited to those techniques found in commercially available software packages.

Finally, I should emphasize that I have made every attempt to illustrate the topics being discussed with numerous drawings, diagrams, and renderings. Animation is a visual art, and I imagine that the readers of this book are visual people, for whom pictures will be worth even more words than usual.

Acknowledgments

I want to thank the many people who have helped me produce this third edition. First, I thank my wife, Gail, for her patience and support as I worked (and worked, and worked) on this very expanded edition. I also want to thank my very capable student assistants who helped with the production of so many new illustrations: Luis Acosta, Bill Burg, Jin Young Doh, Sophia Lin, Christopher Foster, Unju Lee, Sandra Villarreal, and Dejun Wan. Finally, thanks to all of my Pratt animation students, many of whom helped to untangle technical complexities, and all of whom helped me to figure out how to clearly present this material.

This edition builds upon two previous editions, and I want to also thank those who helped make those editions possible. First, all the people from Pratt Institute who helped me while I was working on this book. Some of them helped directly; some helped simply by being friends and keeping me sane. Without their and Pratt's support, this book would not have come into being. Thank you, Rick Barry, Jeremy Gardiner, Sheba Grossman, Maureen Jones, Isaac Kerlow, Lynn Pocock, Sonya Shannon, and others too numerous to name. Thanks also to the following former students, who provided invaluable help with the production of the illustrations: Iris Benado, Chuen Choi, Galen Chu, Jia-Ming Day, Sunmi Kang, Claude Policart, and Chris Shafer.

I also would like to thank all the tremendously talented people at the former New York Institute of Technology Computer Graphics Lab. It was they who taught me computer graphics years ago. Special thanks to Ned Greene, Pat Hanrahan, Peter Oppenheimer, Robert McDermott, Fred Parke, John Schlag, Louis Schure, Jacques Stroweis, David Sturman, Steve Uzzo, Susan Van Baerle, and Lance Williams.

And finally, I would like to thank the people at the University of Pennsylvania who, years ago, helped me so much in my first fumbling attempts to learn this new technology. Thank you, especially, Norm Badler, Dave Bourne, Stan Cohen, and my brother, Joe O'Rourke.

Contents

Introduction

Animation has been around since before the turn of the century, and since then has undergone a tremendous evolution, both technically and artistically. The most recent upheaval in the world of animation has been the development of computer-generated animation. The impact of computer animation, however, goes well beyond what you normally think of as animation, since computer animation techniques also are used to produce such diverse works as movie special effects, video games, scientific simulations, and architectural walk-throughs. Computer-generated animation is changing the face of animation and of cinema in general, and 3D computer animation is among the most sophisticated and stunning of the computer techniques being used to do this.

All moving imagery, whether on film or on video, involves a sequence of still images played back quickly enough for your eye to see them as continuous. When these still images are produced individually, one by one, the process is known as **animation**. The word "animate" means "to give life to." The animator "gives life to" still images.

Animation first appeared in a rudimentary form in the mid-nineteenth century. On one of the first devices for animating still images, the Zoetrope, individual images were placed around the perimeter of a wheel. When the wheel was spun, the viewer looked through a fixed slot at the front of the wheel and saw, in quick succession, each image pass by. If the wheel was spun fast enough, the viewer's eye fused the still images together and saw the sequence as a moving image.

With the advent of film at the turn of the century, animation took a great leap forward. Now individual images, or frames, could be produced and played back with the sophisticated technology being used so successfully for live-action cinema. The wonder of this new technology, which made pictures move, was not lost on people. Whether involving live-action frames or animated frames, the cinema became known by the magical term "the movies."

Animators developed a number of techniques for generating individual frames. The most basic technique, of course, was to draw, and then photograph, each frame one by one. The early animations of Winsor McKay's Gertie the Dinosaur were done in this way and remain, in spite of their relative technical simplicity, delightful.

Walt Disney and the people he gathered around him in the 1930s and 40s took this hand-drawn approach and developed it into a stunningly sophisticated art form. One of the major technical advances made in this period was the use of transparent sheets, called **cels**, onto which were painted different layers of a scene. One cel might contain a stationary background, for example. A second cel might contain only the character intended to move in front of that background. The entire frame was composed by placing the two transparent cels on top of each other and photographing them. This technique became known as **cel animation**. The economies of labor that cel animation permitted were an important factor in making full-length animated films possible.

Other animation techniques developed as well. **Stop-action animation** involves using physical models, positioning them for each frame of the film, photographing them, and then repeating the whole process for the next frame. One of the early geniuses of this technique was Willis O'Brien. One of his earliest successes, *King Kong*, with its unforgettable image of Kong swinging from the Empire State Building and swiping at airplanes, made stop-action animation a standard of the monster-movie genre.

These and other techniques were used by animators with increasing effectiveness over the years to produce films that were purely animations as well as animated segments that were combined with live-action footage. They were used to produce endearing films for children and (most notably outside of the United States) serious films for adults.

In the early 1970s, the first efforts were made to use computers to help produce animation. Much of this initial experimentation was done at the New York Institute of Technology. The first program developed there focused on two-dimensional animation and enabled the animator to produce automatically what are called the "in-between" frames. In traditional animation, it is common for a more experienced, or master, animator to draw the most critical frames of the animation. These are called the "key" frames. The frames that fall between keyframes are called "in-betweens" and normally are drawn by less experienced assistants. The first computer animation programs mimicked this process, substituting the computer for the assistants.

The next step in the development of computer animation entailed applying this same principle—the automatic production of in-between frames—to three-dimensional animation. Once again, the pioneering groundwork was done at the New York Institute of Technology. Programs were developed that allowed the animator to position a three-dimensionally defined computer model in a series of key positions. The computer then automatically generated the in-between positions and rendered each position as a frame of animation.

Recent years have seen an explosive growth in the sophistication of computer animation techniques, and especially of three-dimensional computer animation techniques. Today, three-dimensional computer animation is no longer limited to mimicking the techniques of traditional cel animation. Exciting techniques have been developed that move far beyond the keyframe/ in-between frame concept of traditional animation, and many software packages include techniques that only the computer could have produced, such as procedural animation, motion dynamics, particle systems, motion capture, and nonlinear animation.

The increasing sophistication of computer animation also recently has made it possible to integrate animated three-dimensional imagery with live-action imagery in a seamless way. Herds of computer-generated dinosaurs run with human actors. Contemporary actors talk to and interact with historical figures who exist only on old film footage. Spaceships pass through computer-animated wormholes into other sectors of the universe.

Going even further, entire films can now be shot with computer-generated virtual actors and virtual models moving through virtual spaces.

The applications of 3D computer animation are not limited to big-budget films, however. One of the fastest growing fields is real-time game applications, many of which make heavy use of three-dimensional animation. An increasing number of commercial spots on television are produced with 3D computer animation. Almost all station-ID and company-logo spots on television are produced with 3D computer animation. Architects, designers, medical doctors, and sculptors all make use of 3D computer animation in their professions.

The techniques and principles of this technology are the subject of this book, and all of the material here is relevant for anyone interested in 3D computer animation. Regardless of the specific software package and specific hardware you may be using, the same principles of 3D computer animation apply.

I have organized the material in this book in such a way as to make it easily accessible, even if you consider yourself nontechnical. When a technical term is used for the first time, it is printed in boldface. Alternate terms are frequently provided, since different software packages may use different terminology to refer to the same concept. The principles of 3D computer animation are presented in a step-by-step fashion, with each section building on previous sections. Because of this organization, if you have experience in an area you may find that you can comfortably skip or skim certain sections. If you are a novice, you probably will want to read, in the order presented, each section in detail.

Even though the word "animation" occurs in only two of the chapter titles, the entire book deals with animation. In actual practice, it is impossible to separate "modeling" from "rendering," or either of those procedures from "animation." The process of producing 3D computer animation involves all of these activities, and separating them into individual chapters is a matter of conceptual convenience.

CHAPTER 1
Preproduction

1.1 Introduction

Producing a 3D computer animation is a fascinating and exhilarating process. It can also be a complex process in many respects. In addition to the technical issues on which this book focuses, other important issues must be carefully considered, including the story of the animation, the visual style of the animation, the availability of resources, and the timetable for the production.

Because of the number and variety of issues that must be considered, careful planning of a production is very important, especially when a project is large and involves many people and expensive facilities. Even for a small, personal animation, however, planning is critical. Even if you are working alone, have your own equipment, and are not working against a deadline, there still remain important issues of design, story development, and technical requirements that demand careful planning. The details of production planning vary depending on many factors, including size of the project, output, purpose, resources and so on. But certain issues common to all animation productions are the focus of this chapter.

1.2 Storyboarding

Before you begin working on the production of an animation, you must deal with a number of issues that comprise the **preproduction** phase of the project. One of the most critical parts of this phase is the development of a storyboard.

A **storyboard** is a sequence of images and verbal descriptions describing the intended animation. The "board" part of the term refers to the fact that the images are often mounted on a rigid board for presentation purposes. The "story" part of the term refers to the flow of events in the animation. The concept of **story** is more general than simply "narrative." For example, you need not have characters to have a story. A short station-identification animation or an abstract animation of forms swirling about can have a story in the sense that the events progress in a carefully and effectively developed way, with a clear progression.

In order to successfully communicate what will happen in an animation, typically a storyboard consists of several components, each of which is

Figure 1-1. A preliminary storyboard is a sequence of rough sketches capturing the essence of the concepts, framing, and flow.

Figure 1-2. A presentation storyboard is carefully drawn or painted to convey the design as well as the concepts of the idea. (© Ayako Hayashi.)

designed to convey certain information. The first critical component of a storyboard is the sequence of images, called **panels**, describing the animation. These are arranged in temporal sequence, from the beginning of the animation to its end, and may be produced with a variety of techniques and media, including drawing, painting, or computer graphics. The level of detail and finish in the panels and the actual size of the panels vary depending on the purpose of the storyboard. A **preliminary storyboard** intended to capture a first, fleeting idea may be sketched quickly as a series of small, black-and-white pencil line drawings (Figure 1-1). At this stage it is preferable not to be too elaborate or detailed. The purpose of a preliminary storyboard is to help generate ideas. Spending too much time creating each panel only serves to slow down the idea-generating process. It is also useful in these preliminary stages to draw each panel on a separate piece of paper. This allows you to physically move them about, altering their sequence and that of the animation's events. This is sometimes called a **paper edit**.

At a later stage you may develop a much more elaborate **presentation storyboard** (Figure 1-2). Here, the intended audience is usually a client and the purpose is less the generation of ideas than the exposition of a well-developed idea. Contract decisions frequently are based on a presentation storyboard, which is therefore carefully painted or drawn in full color, frequently by a professional storyboard artist. Color plate 15 is a more complete segment of the same final presentation storyboard illustrated in Figure 1-2. Its panels were meticulously and beautifully painted in watercolor, each panel measuring about 4 by 5 inches.

The first purpose of storyboard panels is to show the story, or progression of events. You should have enough panels to do this effectively, without leaving gaps in the story's progression, but you do not need to illustrate every movement as if you were making keyframe drawings. In the early stages of a preliminary storyboard, fewer panels may be needed to sketch out the overall progression of events; more are added for presentation purposes. A **production storyboard**, used to guide animators in the actual production of the animation, has even more panels, so that details of each scene will be understood clearly by all working on the production.

In addition to telling the basic story, storyboard panels illustrate the **framing** of each scene—that is, what the camera sees. Framing and camera movement have a tremendous impact on the viewer. Is the camera set low and looking up at the towering monster to convey a sense of its power? Has the camera cut to a close shot of the knife to focus our attention on it? Is the camera dollying into the apartment very slowly to create a sense of ominous foreboding? All these camera issues, which affect both what the viewer knows and how the viewer feels, should be conveyed in the storyboard panels. For this reason, it is also important that panels be drawn at the correct aspect ratio of the final medium. For example, if you will be recording to NTSC video, your panels should have the 4 × 3 ratio of that format's frames. If your panels are not drawn at the correct aspect ratio, they cannot properly convey the intended framing.

Another aspect of the animation conveyed through the storyboard panels is the **visual style**, or **look**, of the animation. These terms refer to the visual design elements of the animation, which are in turn determined by the goals of the animation. Is it a light cartoon for children? A ribald short for adults? A disturbing emotional treatment of political suppression? The answers to these questions affect the look of each animation's environments, characters, and lighting and should be conveyed through the panels of a well-developed storyboard.

The visual panels of a storyboard, however, are not enough to convey all the information that is needed. A brief **verbal description** of what is happening at that moment in the animation usually adjoins each panel. The text describes the action represented in the panel, paying special attention to aspects of the action that cannot be gleaned from the picture alone. For example, if a panel shows that a character stands up and the accompanying description says, "She slowly stands up," it tells us something we did not know from the static drawing alone.

Verbal descriptions also are critical to describe the animation of the camera. If one panel shows a long shot of a scene and the next shows a close shot of the same scene, we cannot tell what the camera did to get from the first panel to the second panel. Did the camera cut, or did it dolly into the close shot? Or was there a cross-dissolve between the two cameras? Occasionally, graphic icons are used to help convey this information—for example, an arrow to indicate that the camera pans right. Icons can be ambiguous, however, and concise wording, such as "Cut to close shot," clarifies the situation. Notice in color plate 15 that the verbal description under each panel includes a clear description of the camera transition.

The storyboard's verbal descriptions also must address the **soundtrack**, the collection of sounds, music, and dialogue that accompany the animation. The soundtrack has a profound effect on the viewer's reaction. Imagine a simple scene in which a character walks in from screen left, walks across the empty screen, and continues walking off screen right. Now imagine the same animation with three different soundtracks. In the first, there is silence except for the light clicking of the character's shoes as he walks across an invisible marble floor. In the second version of this same animation, the character walks to the accompaniment of blaring rock and roll music. In the third version, the character walks as a heavy, ominous wind blows through invisible trees. Each of these three soundtracks radically changes how viewers respond to the animation. Describing the soundtrack verbally—for example, "Silence except for clicking of his shoes on marble floor"—clarifies the feel and intention of the animation. Even if there is no sound at all, that fact is significant and should be explicitly stated. Refer once again to color plate 15 and notice that each panel description includes notations on the soundtrack.

A final, critical component of a good storyboard is **timing**. How quickly or slowly do things happen? How long does a scene last? How long is that close-up? Timing is best indicated in seconds and, if the animation is long enough, minutes. For example, one standard representation of time is *02:40*, to indicate "two minutes, forty seconds." Animations of scenes less than a minute long typically represent only seconds, either *:05* or *5 sec.* to indicate "five seconds."

For two reasons it is rare for the timing of a storyboard to be indicated in frames. First, the timing indications of most storyboards are approximations. We probably do not know whether an action will require twenty-two frames or twenty-six frames. (An exception to this would be a final, detailed production storyboard in which frame-accurate timing has been developed for each scene. This might be the case if a dialogue soundtrack has already been recorded and the animators are matching to the existing, and precisely timed, soundtrack.) A second reason not to use frames as timing units is that most people have difficulty translating large frame counts into comprehensible time. Just how long is 1,429 frames, anyhow?

Finally, indicating both the timing in seconds for each panel and the cumulative running time of the animation so far makes it much easier for someone looking at the storyboard to understand quickly how long the animation is. If only the timing for each panel is indicated, a reader of the storyboard has to add up the seconds of each panel to understand the running time of a scene or of the whole animation. There are many ways of showing the individual panel and cumulative running time. In color plate 15, the timing of each panel is indicated above the upper left corner of the panel and the cumulative running time is indicated above the upper right.

1.3 Character and Model Design

At the same time that you are developing your storyboard, you should also develop detailed designs for your principal models and characters. Even if your animation does not involve characters, there will usually be one or a few especially significant models. Whether they are machines, plants, or characters, the **design**, or **look**, of your principal models must be carefully developed as part of your preproduction planning.

Doing so usually begins with a series of quick **pencil sketches**. At this stage, it is best to work quickly and produce lots of different design ideas. Too

Figure 1-3. Detailed sketches of your principal models or characters improve the design process. (Luis Acosta 2002.)

frequently, inexperienced animators do a single drawing and then focus all their energy on developing that one design. If the original design is not strong, no amount of development will fix it; consequently, it is best to start with several design possibilities. Gradually, you eliminate the weaker designs, and begin focusing on the one or two strongest.

As your design develops, your drawings should become more detailed. Drawings from several points of view are very helpful. If you are designing a character, it is common to also produce **character sketches** in a variety of poses—for example, walking, running, or sword fighting (Figure 1-3 and Figure 1-4). Similarly, you should produce drawings of your character in various moods—happy and laughing, sad and crying, worried and fearful. For both the poses and the moods, the choices are based on how the character is expected to act in your animation.

Figure 1-4. The 3D model developed from character sketches captures the design and feel of the sketches. (Luis Acosta 2002.)

It is very common to also develop **physical models** for your main characters or objects (Figure 1-5). This process can be especially useful since your CG models will themselves be three-dimensional. Developing a clay or plasticene model frequently reveals modeling subtleties that might not be apparent in drawings. Very large production companies often have full-time sculptors on staff whose job it is to do just this. In some animations, highly detailed clay models are built, and the CG model is created from a scanned version of this clay model, using the digitizing techniques discussed in section 5.4.

When an animation involves several characters, **size charts** are also developed showing drawings of each of the main characters lined up for size comparison. This becomes especially useful in a production team environment in which a different person may develop each model. The size chart provides each member of the team a consistent reference as they work.

Figure 1-5. Sculpted models are especially helpful and are frequently used in production environments.

1.4 Sound Design

As suggested in the section 1.2, the soundtrack of an animation can have a significant impact on the overall effect of the animation. The design of the soundtrack, therefore, is important and should be considered an integral part of the planning of an animation. The full complexity of this process is beyond the scope of this book, but some of the most significant issues are discussed here.

A soundtrack can be thought of as consisting of several possible components, any or all of which may be present in a given animation. **Sound effects** are such sounds as the closing of a door, the rustling of leaves, the barking of a dog, the shattering of glass, and so on. Recall the simple animation of a character walking across the screen described in the section 1.2. The sound of shoes clicking on a marble floor will create a very different effect than if each footstep is accompanied by the rustle of leaves, and yet another effect if the sound is the clanging of pots and pans. Shoes clicking create a subdued, elegant mood. Leaves rustling create a quiet mood, but suggest a very different physical environment. Pots and pans clanging create a sense of harsh surreality. In planning your animation, you should consider the sound effects of your piece just as seriously and in as much detail as you do the visual actions of the animation. For some animators, in fact, the first ideas for an animation often come in the form of sounds, with the imagery developing out of them. In professional animations, sound effects are considered so important that professional sound designers and sound-effects artists are hired to design and produce them.

The job of one artist, the **foley artist**, is to use various props and gadgets to produce synchronized sound effects in real time while watching the finished animation. For example, if the sound to accompany a character's walk is rustling leaves, the foley artist might push his hand into a small pile of leaves with each of the character's footsteps, while a microphone placed near the leaves records the sounds. If the animation shows a character opening a door and walking down some steps into the backyard, the foley artist would open and close a door and make the sound of footsteps on wood, perhaps by knocking a shoe against a plank of wood. Since each of these sound effects is done in time with the action of the animation, they are both created and synced in one session.

Dialogue is frequently another major component of an animation's soundtrack. Like sound effects, human dialogue can be critical and requires careful planning. If dialogue is to be part of an animation, a detailed script is usually written in the storyboard phases of development. **Voice actors** are then hired to record the dialogue before any work on the animation proper begins. It is much easier for an animator to adjust the timing of an animation to match prerecorded dialogue than it is for an actor to adjust the timing of dialogue delivery to match preexisting animation, especially when the spoken dialogue needs to be synchronized with the animated characters' mouth movements, a process called **lip syncing**, discussed in section 7.14.

Finally, **music** may be a component of an animation's soundtrack. As with the other soundtrack components, music, if it is to be used at all, should be part of the early planning . Recall the example of the character walking across the screen to the sound of rock and roll music described in section 1.2. Now imagine that the music is a very gentle, peaceful classical piece—for example, the beautiful violins of Pachelbel's Canon in D Major. This radically alters the mood of the animation; it may even change the audience's interpretation of the action. If the music is perceived as what is going on inside the head of the character, the two soundtracks portray quite different internal "actions."

Even before specific music is composed or chosen, it is extremely helpful to include detailed notes in the storyboard describing the type and mood of the music. Whether you call for "soft, gentle violins" or "blaring rock and roll" suggests a great deal about the mood of the piece. Vague descriptions such as "background music" convey too little to be useful and should be avoided.

1.5 Technical Tests

Given their technical complexity, almost all 3D computer animations require testing of the technical feasibility of different aspects of the animation. If something is to move in a certain way, how should it be modeled? Should a character be modeled with rigid body parts, or a deformable skin? Will your intended compositing of animation with live-action footage be feasible? These sorts of questions must be answered before you begin production to avoid major problems later on.

Sometimes the answers to these questions are obvious, and the more experience you have, the more frequently this is the case. But if you want to know whether something will work, or the best way to make it work, it is important to test *before* you begin production so you do not spend weeks or months on a project only to discover that something will not work technically and you must throw away the work done. This is a frustration and a waste of time; in a commercial production, it can also be a financial disaster.

Even if you do not have to discard your work entirely, belatedly discovered technical problems may oblige you to modify the animation. Reasonable changes are a normal part of the animation process. One of the most valuable skills of the experienced animator is the ability to find "workarounds"—other approaches that convey the original idea but avoid technical problems. But technically motivated changes are only feasible to the extent that they do not alter the look of the animation. Because of this, it is important to test for technical problems early.

In order to be able to do intelligent technical testing, you must first have a clear idea of what the animation will be—that is, you must have a well-developed storyboard. If you have only a vague idea of the animation, you will be unable to do meaningful technical tests. The more specifically you have storyboarded the animation, the better you will be able to foresee areas that present potential technical difficulties.

You should consider all aspects of an animation—modeling, motion, textures, lighting, final rendering issues, and so on—for potential problems. For example, if a model's shape is to be deformed and that model is also to receive a texture map, how will the texture behave as the model's surface undergoes its shape deformation? Will the texture stretch in undesirable ways? Will it appear to slide across the surface? Different texture mapping methods give different results; testing these mapping techniques early can avoid major problems later.

To take another example: imagine the animation of a snakelike creature. Several techniques might be appropriate, including motion path animation, spline deformation, and various deformers. Which one will give the best results? And depending on which you elect to use, what does that require of your model? It is better to know before you build your model than after.

Anti-aliasing is another example that might merit technical testing . Many narrow parallel lines or objects in a scene may present a severe aliasing problem that can only be solved by using an anti-aliasing algorithm that doubles or triples rendering time. If you know this in advance and test for it, you can decide whether to keep the original design and accept the additional rendering time it requires, or to modify the design and avoid the problem and the long rendering time per frame.

You do not have to wait until your final models, animation, or textures are developed before you can do effective testing. If you know, for example, that thin parallel lines cause aliasing problems, you do not need to model an entire brick building with louvered windows to find out if it is going to present aliasing problems. You can do a simulation—perhaps model a sample window using simplified geometry such as scaled cubes to approximate the final geometry of the intended model. You also do not have to have the final brick texture available to approximate its aliasing problems; you can make a simple texture consisting of repeating rectangles and apply that to a flat surface to simulate the wall. Proceeding in this way, you can very quickly—in perhaps half an hour—build a model that simulates the suspect features of your planned animation and discover early in your planning process any areas of potential difficulty.

The more you know about the technical aspects of 3D computer animation, the more effective the testing can be. If you do not know beforehand that thin parallel lines are problematic, you will not know to test for that. One of the advantages of experience is that your technical testing becomes increasingly effective, allowing you more regularly to avoid significant technical problems.

1.6 Production Scheduling

Any animation project benefits from careful production estimating and sched-uling. In a commercial environment, these are critical and may spell the dif-ference between profit or loss, between a company's survival or bankruptcy. When a client approaches a company with a possible project, the company must bid on the job, specifying what it will do, for how much money, in what timeframe. In order to do this, the company must know specifically what the job entails—what the components are, how long each component will take, who will work on it, and so on. The more specific the estimates, the more accurate the bid. And the more accurate the bid, the better the chance the company will make a profit. This is so crucial in the commercial world that many large companies have a permanent full-time staff member whose sole job is to make **production estimates**.

Good planning and scheduling are important even in a personal animation not being done for profit or against a deadline. By realistically estimating what a project will entail in terms of hardware requirements, the animator's time, additional personnel, and so on, you can determine whether the animation is feasible. If production estimates suggest that it will not be feasible as story-boarded, you can modify the storyboard to make the animation realizable.

As a simple example, imagine a story that takes place in a city. If your production estimates reveal that it will take you three hundred hours to model all the buildings, you might elect to model simple boxes and texture-map pictures of buildings onto them, reducing your modeling time drasti-cally. In order to take advantage of the texture-mapping approach, you might also modify the storyboard to eliminate extreme close-ups of the buildings, or limit the close-ups, and therefore your modeling, to only a few buildings.

It should be clear that any effective production estimates or scheduling require a detailed storyboard. You cannot make intelligent estimates about how long something will take unless you know what it is. The more care-fully developed your storyboard, the more accurate your production esti-mates can be.

The first phase of developing production estimates usually is to develop a **list of tasks** (Figure 1-6). You can organize it in any number of ways, but the goal is to list what needs to be done for the entire animation: modeling, motion tests, texture painting, lighting, rendering tests, final rendering, cred-its, sound effects, working with a composer to develop original music, and so on. The list of specific tasks varies. One animation may involve a great deal of complex character animation but only very simple modeling for the envi-ronment. Another may require sophisticated lighting and subtle camera ani-mation, but no character animation at all.

```
                          List of Tasks

         Modeling, Scene 1
             Cars                                 10 hours
             Buildings                            11 hours

         Lighting, Scene 23                       12 hours

         Character Rigging
             Vampire                              3 days

                                    .
                                    .
                                    .
```

Figure 1-6. A list of tasks is a breakdown of the anticipated tasks of production, including time estimates for each task.

The list of tasks frequently is broken down by scene. Imagine that Scene 1 involves the camera flying through the city; Scene 2 cuts to a close shot of one of the buildings, with a character who peers through a louvered window and turns to leave, long hair swinging behind. The tasks for Scene 1 are quite different than those for Scene 2. For Scene 1, you will model the buildings as simple boxes and develop—perhaps by photographing actual buildings—detailed texture maps for each building. You will do a motion-path animation for the camera. You will collect the sound for Scene 1 from a sound-effects CD and modify it to produce the whooshing sound of flying.

Scene 2's tasks are quite different. Because the camera is very close to the building, you will model the actual geometry of the building, including a detailed model of the louvered window. You also will model the character. There is no camera animation, but there is a complex bit of character animation. You will use a hair modeler to model and animate the character's hair and work with a foley artist to create the sound effects of the character moving away from the window and crossing the room. Both Scene 1 and Scene 2 will require time to set up the lighting, do motion and rendering tests, and render final frames.

Proceeding in this way for each scene as well as for any credits or titles, you develop a detailed list of what needs to be done to produce the entire animation.

Next you assign **time estimates** to each task, as illustrated again in Figure 1-6. How long do you expect it to take to model this building, to photograph those buildings, to select and edit the sound effects? Making realistic time estimates requires experience, and even the most experienced professionals must resist the normal human tendency to underestimate the

Weekly Production Schedule

.
.
.

Week 4 (2/10 - 2/16)
Rigging, vampire (partial)   10 hours
Record soundeffects, Scenes 2,3   11 hours
Total=   **22 hours**

Week 5 (2/17 - 2/23)
Lighting, Scene 23   12 hours
Motion test, Scene 13   8 hours
Total=   **20 hours**

.
.
.

Figure 1-7. To guide the production, a detailed schedule is developed showing tasks, time estimates, and the order in which the work will be done.

amount of work a task will require. But estimating time is important even when you are just a beginner. One of the most common problems of inexperienced animators is undertaking an animation project that is more ambitious than they can actually realize and being faced with the unpleasant choice of either not finishing the animation or cutting back on it so much that it no longer has the original spirit. You can avoid disappointment if you develop realistic time estimates in the early planning stages. If your estimates indicate that the project is too ambitious, you can modify the storyboard to reduce the demands of the animation, while still retaining its core idea and spirit. Rethinking your storyboard in this way is one of the critical skills of the animator. There is always another way to tell the same story. And frequently, rethinking your storyboard and finding alternative solutions results in a *better* storyboard. By forcing yourself to economize, you often find more concise and effective ways to tell the same story.

In a commercial environment, good time estimates are, of course, essential: time translates directly into money. The time an animator spends on a given scene, the time a machine is devoted to rendering frames, the time the director spends consulting with the composer—all must be calculated into the budget and paid for if the production company is to survive.

Once a thorough list of tasks and time estimates has been developed, the next step is to develop a **production schedule** (Figure 1-7). The organization and level of detail in a schedule varies depending on the type of animation and the size of the company (if one is involved), but the purpose of a schedule is always to help you organize your project in such a way that it can be successfully completed. A weekly schedule shows what should be accomplished by whom within each week of the production. A daily schedule is common in some commercial situations. In projects with an extremely short timetable, companies sometimes actually develop hourly schedules specifying that, for example, by 11 A.M. Tuesday the lighting for Scene 4 should be set up.

In a personal animation, schedules normally need not be so rigid. Still, some schedule is extremely useful because it allows you to plan the work flow of your project. This may not be obvious. For example, it is rarely best to proceed through a production in strict sequence from Scene 1 to Scene 2 to Scene 3 and so on. On the contrary, it is frequently more effective to work nonsequentially. To use the example of the city and the character at the window again, imagine that Scene 3 consists of a slow pan of the camera up the length of one building. In this case, you might plan to work on Scene 3 first. Since the camera animation of the scene is very simple, you could quickly get to the point where it is ready for final rendering, so you could have one machine rendering final frames for that scene while you are working on the more time-consuming Scene 1 and Scene 2.

It is also not advisable to work through the production of an animation in the seemingly logical order suggested by "modeling, rendering, animation" (or, if your logic so dictates, "modeling, animation, rendering"). In fact, following this progression is one of most common mistakes of inexperienced animators, and can be disastrous. Modeling, rendering, and animation are interdependent. The way an object is to be rendered may affect the way it should be animated; the way it will be animated may affect the way it should be modeled, and so on.

In scheduling, also keep in mind the undeniable facts of human psychology. Sometimes it is most productive to change tasks deliberately, just to avoid boredom and reinvigorate yourself. Spending a month on textures may actually decrease efficiency. The natural need for variety applies in both small-scale and large production environments. Although large companies commonly hire people to do specific tasks—for example, modeling or lighting—most companies make an effort to give each employee a variety of tasks, even if that variety is within the individual's area of specialization. Small companies often deliberately avoid the categorization of assignments, giving each artist on staff a chance to work on all aspects of an animation—for example, to be responsible for an entire scene.

However it is implemented, a good production schedule is invaluable both for the individual animator working on a small personal animation and for the large production company with scores of employees working on big-budget projects.

CHAPTER 2
Modeling Basics

2.1 Introduction

As soon as you start to think about animating in a three-dimensional space, you by necessity also are thinking about three-dimensional objects in that space. Even if you think simply of rotating a perfectly flat disk in space, that disk has a back side. In other words, it is three-dimensional. In short, if you want to animate things three-dimensionally, you must create, or "model," them three-dimensionally as well.

The very concept of "modeling" something within a computer may be confusing. You usually think of a model as something real, physical and tangible. In working with the computer, however, the models you develop have no physicality. You model an object in the computer in the sense that you *define* it. If you define the object thoroughly enough that the computer can display it on the screen from any number of points of view, then you have developed a workable **model** of the object. In this sense, you use the word "model" in computer graphics in the same way scientists use it when they speak of developing a "model" for the interaction of weather fronts, or a "model" of the behavior of a particle in a magnetic field. Their model is a description of a situation. The computer graphics model of a three-dimensional object is also a description, or a definition, of that object.

In most computer graphics animation, you define an object's shape, or form, using one of three broad approaches.

Imagine that you are holding a brass sphere in your hand. One possibility (Figure 2-1a) is that the sphere is hollow—that it consists of a thin brass surface with empty space inside. If you were to cut such a sphere in half, you would get two brass bowls, into which you could place things. This approach to modeling is called **surface modeling.** In surface modeling, the surfaces that enclose an object define the shape of that object.

On the other hand, the brass sphere could have been fabricated as a solid lump of brass (Figure 2-1b). If you cut this version of the sphere in half, there would be no hollows into which you could place anything. You would have two hemispherical solids. This approach to modeling is called **solid modeling**. In solid modeling, an object is defined as a solid mass—often with density, weight, and other attributes of a solid defined as well.

The distinction between surface modeling and solid modeling is important because the two approaches demand very different things of the animator and

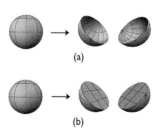

Figure 2-1. A sphere modeled with a surface modeler (a), and with a solid modeler (b).

produce very different kinds of information. Depending on what you want to accomplish, one or the other might be more appropriate for your application. In many engineering applications, for example, solid modelers are used, because that approach makes certain sorts of information about the physical properties (density, mass, inertia, etc.) more readily available to the engineer.

In the great majority of animation applications, however, this kind of information is not needed and the computationally simpler approach of surface modeling is more appropriate. For this reason, in this book you will encounter surface-modeling techniques, with only an occasional reference to solid-modeling techniques when a comparison between the two approaches is helpful.

In addition to surface and solid modeling, a third approach, called **particle-system modeling**, is possible. This approach attempts to deal with such ephemeral phenomena as fire, clouds, and mist, which are composed of neither surfaces nor solid volumes and which do not have a stable "shape" in the same way that a chair has a stable shape. Such phenomena cannot be modeled readily with either a surface modeler or a solid modeler.

Before beginning the discussion of modeling techniques, however, bear in mind the following caveat about the order in which material will be presented here. Sometimes people working with three-dimensional computer animation think of the production process in a "first the modeling, then the animation" way. This seems to make sense from a conceptual point of view, since, as mentioned at the outset, you cannot animate three-dimensionally without some sort of three-dimensional model to animate. While this makes sense conceptually, however, it does not make good sense in practice. Many bad pieces of computer animation have been produced by adhering to a "first the modeling, then the animation" approach. The essence of animation is *movement*, and the person who relegates the animation to a secondary position "after the modeling is finished" risks ending up with a clumsy piece of animation.

In producing animation, the animation and the modeling must develop simultaneously. When you start working on an animation, there is no way of knowing with 100 percent certainty what the animation is going to look like. Consequently, there is no way of knowing exactly what the models should look like. The animation will be influenced by the way the objects are modeled, and the modeling of the objects will be influenced by the demands of the animation.

Nonetheless, I begin with modeling because conceptually it *is* a convenient place to start. Be aware, however, that when you actually make animation, you will not be able to proceed in the conveniently logical order in which material appears in this book.

2.2 Polygonal Modeling

When you use any modeling system, it is important to understand the concepts underlying the techniques. When you work with surface-modeling techniques, understanding the basic concepts means understanding the geometric modeling of all 3D computer graphics systems. Computers are very good at manipulating numbers and quantifiable entities but very bad at dealing with subjective concepts. A computer would have a very difficult time, for example, following your instructions if you told it to make a shape "voluptuous," or to make it "more petal-like." It could easily follow your instructions, however, if you told it to make the shape "twice as long." Because of this, 3D modeling programs are based on numerically quantifiable and manipulable concepts of shape. They are based, in other words, on **geometry**, the mathematical study of shapes.

Telling the computer to make an object "twice as long" is, of course, an extremely simple example. If all you could do to models was make them twice as long, or other equally simple operations, computer graphics modeling would not be of much use. In fact, the techniques of 3D computer modeling are extremely numerous and extremely powerful. All of these techniques remain grounded on geometric principles and concepts.

One basic concept that is involved in all computer graphics modeling is that of a **point**, which is a location in space (Figure 2-2a). Imagine pointing with your finger to indicate that you want something placed "right there." The "right there" that you have indicated ("pointed" to) is a location, or point, in space. It is not a *thing*. It has no size or dimension. In fact, you can say that it is zero-dimensional—it has no width, no height, and no depth.

If you now move that point in exactly one direction (Figure 2-2b), the trace that you produce is a simple straight **line**. Depending on how far you move your original point, the line will be longer or shorter. A line, in other words, does have dimension. It has length. Notice, however, that it has only one dimension. It has no thickness at all (that is, no width or depth), since you produced it by starting with a dimensionless point and moving that point some distance.

Just as you moved a point to produce a line, you can produce the next basic geometric entity in a similar way. Given that you now have a straight, one-dimensional line, you can move that line in any one direction (Figure 2-2c). The trace produced by doing this is called a **plane**, which is simply a flat surface. (Strictly speaking, a plane is not a "surface" in the finite, measurable sense of that term, since a plane continues infinitely in two directions. Nonetheless, this definition is consistent with common usage.) Notice that a plane has two dimensions: the length of the original line, and now the width, or the amount you moved that line in the new direction.

(a)

(b)

(c)

Figure 2-2. A zero-dimensional point, a one-dimensional line, and a two-dimensional plane.

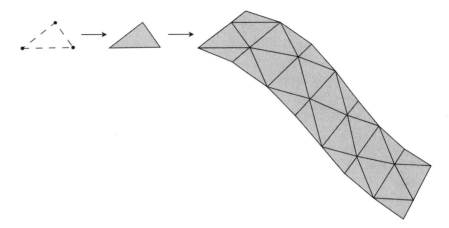

Figure 2-3. Three points define the corners of a triangular plane. Such planes can be combined to form a surface.

Now imagine that you locate three points in space and consider them to be the endpoints of three straight lines, each of which touches the other. These lines define a triangle (Figure 2-3). When points in space define a figure such as this, each point is also called a **vertex**, while several of them are called **vertices**. Instead of thinking of the lines you just defined as infinitely thin lines hanging in space, you can now think of them as the edges of a triangular surface. These edges define a flat triangular plane, also called a face, in three-dimensional space.

Using the same approach and the same three basic elements, you can form many other triangles, each connected to the other, and all at various angles in space. Where you decide to place your points, or vertices, in space determines where the edges are formed and consequently where the planes derived from those edges are formed. Using this approach, you can form any number of differently shaped surfaces (see Figure 2-3). You can then combine surfaces constructed in this way to form "objects."

In the example just given, all the planes defined were triangular planes. There is no reason, however, why a planar surface must be triangular, though there is an advantage to using triangles as your planes. That is, any number of points can define a flat planar surface, but three points in space always define a plane. In Chapter 3 we will discuss the importance of having planar surfaces for rendering. More than three points may or may not, since one or more of them might not lie in the same plane. For example, if you place three points on the surface of a table, and a fourth point suspended above the table, these four points do not describe a perfectly flat surface.

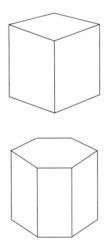

Figure 2-4. Two objects defined by flat planar surfaces composed of varying numbers of points.

The two objects in Figure 2-4 are composed of planar surfaces defined by different numbers of vertices. Any flat planar surface composed in this way can also be called a **polygon**. (The word comes from the Greek and means "many-sided.") The type of three-dimensional modeling that defines surfaces as consisting of flat polygons is therefore called **polygonal modeling**.

The two examples of polygonal modeling in Figure 2-4 have obviously and deliberately flat surfaces. Many objects, however, have surfaces that are curved—for example, the branch of a tree or an automobile tire. In spite of the fact that the individual polygons of polygonal modeling are flat, polygonal modeling can be used effectively for modeling curved surfaces such as these. The technique, called **polygonal approximation**, that accomplishes this uses large numbers of very small polygons to approximate the curvature of the surface (Figure 2-5).

Here the polygonal approximation technique has been used to model three different versions of a cylinder. In Figure 2-5a, where only six polygons approximate the curvature of the cylinder, you get a very rough approximation of a cylinder. This, in fact, looks more like the crystalline structure in Figure 2-4 than like a true cylinder. If you double the number of flat, planar polygons going around the side of the cylinder, as in Figure 2-5b, however, the cylinder begins to look more reasonable. And if you double them yet again, as in Figure 2-5c, the cylinder looks quite smooth.

You must understand, however, that polygonally approximating a curved surface will never yield a *truly* curved surface. No matter how many polygons you use and no matter how close the approximation, the surface is really and always a faceted surface composed of flat polygons. In many applications, this is not a problem, especially because polygons can be rendered to appear smoothly curved (section 3.5). The problem is even less serious if you view the object from far enough away that the edges of the polygons are not discernible. If you move in close enough, however, any polygonally approximated curved surface, no matter how close the approximation or how carefully rendered, will reveal the flat polygons of which it is composed.

For complex objects, it is sometimes necessary to use a great many polygons to achieve a good approximation of the curved surfaces. Models with a lot of polygons are said to have a high **polygon count**. Since the polygon count, or total number of polygons, directly affects the speed with which a computer can process a model, it is usually desirable to keep the polygon count as low as possible. This is especially true in the game industry, where **real-time interaction**—that is, the ability to manipulate the screen image without any visible time delay—is critical. One way of achieving a low polygon count is through **polygon reduction**. This technique, also known sometimes as **polygon thinning** or **polygon culling**, reduces the total number of polygons of a model while retaining as closely as possible the model's original shape. One way to accomplish this is to specify the maximum polygon count of the new, thinned, model. For example, a model that originally had 3,460 polygons might be reduced to only 1,000 polygons, or perhaps to 500 polygons.

Figure 2-5. A cylinder modeled with three different resolutions of polygonal approximation.

Figure 2-6. If adjacent polygons have a small dihedral angle, they can be reduced to a single polygon without significantly changing the shape of the model.

(a) (b)

(a)

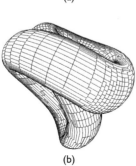

(b)

Figure 2-7. Polygon reduction decreases the total number of polygons while trying to retain the model's original shape.

Another way to reduce the polygon count is to specify the minimum angle allowed between polygons. If adjacent polygons have nearly the same orientation, they can be reduced to a single polygon without significantly altering the shape of the model. If their orientation differs greatly, however, reducing them to a single polygon will not preserve the essential shape of the model (Figure 2-6). The relative orientations of the adjacent polygons is measured by the **dihedral angle**, which is the angle between lines coming perpendicularly off each polygon at the shared vertex. In Figure 2-6a, the two polygons (seen here from the side) have a very small dihedral angle between them, and can be reduced to a single polygon without significantly changing the shape of the model. In Figure 2-6b, however, the two polygons have a larger dihedral angle. Reducing them to a single polygon would substantially change the shape of the model.

Figure 2-7 shows an example of polygon reduction. Here, the original model, Figure 2-7a, has 8,000 polygons. Specifying a minimum dihedral angle of 5 degrees results in reducing the total number of polygons to 2,755 (Figure 2-7b).

The opposite of polygon reduction is **polygon expansion**, which retains the shape of the model while increasing the total number of polygons. One way of doing this is to **subdivide** a polygon into a regular pattern of faces. In Figure 2-8a we see a polygonal cube. In (b), one face of the cube has been subdivided into four smaller rectangular polygons. In (c), one of these has been further subdivided into four more polygons. You can also specify that you want the subdivision process to produce triangular faces, as in Figure 2-8d.

Figure 2-8. A polygonal face can be subdivided into a regular pattern of smaller faces, either rectangular or triangular.

(a) (b) (c) (d)

Figure 2-9. You can split a polygonal face into an irregular pattern of smaller faces or arbitrary shapes.

A second approach to adding polygons is to irregularly **split** a polygon by interactively clicking with the mouse to insert new vertices and edges. In Figure 2-9, the cube face has been split into three irregularly-shaped faces.

Related to polygon expansion is **polygon rounding**, which smooths, or rounds, the sharpest angles of a polygonal model by adding polygons in those areas. Applying successive polygon rounding operations to a cube, for example, gradually changes the cube into a spherelike object (Figure 2-10a, b, c). To control the amount of smoothing, you specify either a total number of polygons, or a smooth-level parameter that gives you more or less of a smooth effect.

In Figure 2-11, we see examples of the effectiveness of polygon smoothing. The original blocky polygon model is seen in (a). In Figure 2-11b the faces on the left end of the model were selected and smoothed. In Figure 2-11c all the faces were smoothed. By controlling which faces get smoothed and by how much, you can greatly extend the usefulness of polygonal modeling.

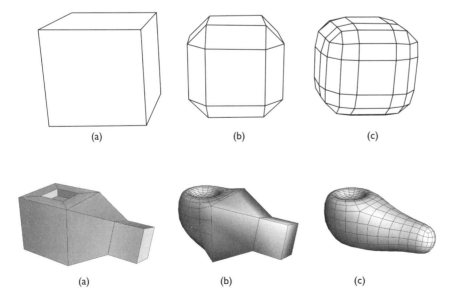

(a)   (b)   (c)

Figure 2-10. Polygon rounding collapses the sharp corners of a model to produce a smoother, rounder version.

(a)   (b)   (c)

Figure 2-11. Individual faces of a polygonal object can be smoothed, producing a new set of faces.

Figure 2-12. Polygons can be added or deleted locally by inserting or deleting individual vertices and edges. (Courtesy, Yukito Kurita)

As with polygon smoothing, polygon reduction and expansion can operate either **globally** on the entire model, or **locally** on individual faces of the model. In the human face model in Figure 2-12 a great deal of polygon data is needed in the areas of the eyes and mouth in order to create the facial expressions of the model. The additional polygons in these areas were created by splitting polygons as described above. This process is also known as **vertex** and **edge insertion**—adding vertices by clicking with the mouse to indicate where each new vertex should be. Once new vertices have been created, edges between them are created by clicking on the vertices that are to serve as the endpoints of the new edge. Since polygons are defined by their edges, creating new edges creates new polygons. All of the additional polygons in Figure 2-12 were created in this way. In fact, the model in this illustration began as a simple polygonal sphere! The artist created a very sophisticated head model by carefully adding vertices and edges and repositioning them. The holes for the eyes and mouth were created with the analogous techniques of **vertex** and **edge deletion**, by clicking and deleting vertices and edges one by one.

One of the most important aspects of polygonal modeling is the possibility of **irregular topology.** Think of topology as the structure of a surface, rather than the shape. If you pull the vertices of a surface this way and that way, you change the shape of the surface, but not the structure. That is, you change the geometry of the object, but not the topology. If, however, you delete a vertex from this structure, you change the topology of the surface.

One of the great strengths of polygonal modeling is that you can build models with very irregular topologies. It is very easy, for example, to create a surface with a hole in it, as well as an extension branching off from one part of it (Figure 2-13). This topological flexibility is one of the great strengths of polygonal modeling. We will see in section 2.3 that such flexibility is not possible with all surface types, some of which require very specific, and sometime restrictive, topologies.

The arbitrary topology possible with polygons allows for a very powerful technique called **face extrusion**. Selecting one face of the model, you pull the face outward from itself. As the face translates outward, it creates new faces connecting itself to the original model. You can optionally rotate or scale the

Figure 2-13. A polygonal surface with an irregular structure (topology) of vertices.

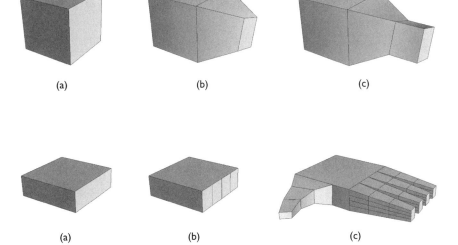

(a)   (b)   (c)   (d)

Figure 2-14. Facial extrusion is one of the most powerful polygon-modeling techniques.

(a)   (b)   (c)

Figure 2-15. Objects with irregular topologies can be modeled with the facial extrusion technique.

face as you extrude it outwards. Because it extrudes new faces as the face translates, the process allows you to quickly create models of very irregular topologies.

In Figure 2-14a we start with a simple polygon cube. In (b), its rightmost polygonal face has been selected and extruded to the right, and simultaneously scaled a bit smaller and rotated. Notice that four additional faces—one for each edge of the polgyon—were created and attached to the side of the extruded face. In Figure 2-14c the face we had extruded in (b) is extruded once again, pulling it straight out to the right and rotating it slightly. Finally, in 2-14d, two successive extrusion operations have been performed. First, the top face of the cube was extruded, this time only with a scaling transformation—that is, leaving it at the same height as the original top face. This newly extruded face was then extruded again, this time translating it straight down. The result is a rectangular depression in the top of the model.

Because the topology of a polygonal model can be so arbitrary, this extrusion process can be repeated forever, creating forms with extremely irregular protrusions and holes. In Figure 2-15, we see the creation of a hand beginning with a scaled cube. Figure 2-15b shows the rightmost face of the box split into four faces. Each of these is then extruded three times to produce fingers. Similar extrusions create a thumb (Figure 2-15c). Smoothing these polygons yields a more naturally curved model. With sufficient skill, you can use this approach to produce a very subtly modeled hand (Figure 2-16).

Figure 2-16. With care, polygonal modeling techniques can produce models of great subtlety. (© Kaori Watanabe 2001.)

Figure 2-17. A complex model illustrating the subtlety possible with polygonal modeling. (Courtesy, Viewpoint DataLabs.)

Figure 2-18. A curve can be represented as a series of straight line segments, yielding a linear approximation of the curve.

Figure 2-17 is a good example of the power of polygonal modeling. In addition to the accuracy of the modeling, note the following two technical issues. First, the topology of this model is extremely irregular. The topological flexibility of polygonal modeling is crucial in this respect. Second, in those areas of the model where the curvature of the surface changes rapidly—for example, in the area around the eyes—the polygons both decrease in size and increase in number. This permits a more accurate approximation of the surface in those areas where it is needed. By contrast, in those areas of the model where the curvature changes only gradually (for example, the thighs), fewer and larger polygons are used without sacrificing any accuracy in the approximation.

2.3 Splines and Patches

SPLINES

In the previous section, you saw how the polygonal approach to modeling uses straight lines and flat planes as basic building blocks. In the real world, of course—especially in the world of nature—curved lines and curved surfaces are much more common than are straight lines and surfaces. Think of a tree branch, the curve of a beautiful neck, a muscular thigh, the hull of a ship, and so on. Polygonal modeling can *approximate* these curves, but it never represents them with perfect accuracy.

Because of this, a second, and very powerful, approach to modeling is common in 3D modeling systems. In these systems, the smoothly curved line, or more simply, the **curve**, is considered another basic geometric building block.

A curve can be two-dimensional or three-dimensional. When you draw a curve on a piece of paper, you draw a two-dimensional curve. When you wave a sparkler about at night, you trace a three-dimensional curve in space with the tip of the sparkler.

Computer graphics uses several approaches to represent curves. One is similar in concept to the polygonal approximation technique you saw in the previous section. When applied to a curve, this technique approximates a curve through a series of straight lines and is consequently known as **linear approximation**. It is also sometimes referred to as a **polyline** technique, because it makes use of many ("poly") lines to represent the curve.

Figure 2-18a shows a crude linear approximation of a curve. Figure 2-18b uses a greater number of line segments, and the approximation of the curve is somewhat less crude as a consequence. In Figure 2-18c, the number of line segments has been increased to give a smoother, more accurate representation of the curve.

The linear-approximation technique has the advantage of being extremely simple conceptually. A curve is represented simply as a series of points, which are connected in a dot-to-dot fashion.

The technique has several disadvantages, however. One is that it can be very awkward to edit the shape of a curve. Changing the shape of a linearly approximated curve can involve laboriously selecting each of many points and moving each point individually. A second disadvantage of the linear-approximation technique is that the number of points required to produce a good approximation of a curve may produce very large quantities of data, which may in turn slow down your interaction with the program. A final disadvantage of the polyline technique is that the "curve" is never truly smooth. It is, in fact, not a curve at all, but only an approximation of a curve. All three of these disadvantages apply equally to the polygonal modeling technique discussed in the previous section.

Most high-end computer modeling systems, therefore, provide a different technique to represent curves. This technique makes use of **splines**. The word derives from the era when ships were built of wood. In order to bend a plank of wood to fit the shape of the hull, shipbuilders would force the wooden plank to bend between several fixed posts, called "ducks." The resulting curved plank was called a "spline" (Figure 2-19). Notice that the placement of the posts determines how much curvature will be given to the plank.

Figure 2-19. A shipbuilder's "spline."

As adapted by mathematicians for computer graphics, the wooden plank of the shipbuilders corresponds to a curve, and the ducks correspond to points in space that control the shape of the curve. Two typical spline curves that might occur in computer graphics appear in Figure 2-20. In both drawings, the solid curved line is the spline curve itself. The points that lie near each curve are the **control points**, which determine the shape of that curve. These points are sometimes called **control vertices**; a single point, a **control vertex**. The dotted straight line connecting each set of points often is known as the **hull** for that curve. The hull is simply the network of straight lines that connects the control points.

As in the original shipbuilding situation, the placement of the control points determines the shape of the spline curve. Moving one of the control points changes the shape of the curve. In Figure 2-20a and Figure 2-20b, the control points are identical, except for the third control point from the left. In Figure 2-20b this control point has been pulled down, changing the shape of the curve. Notice, however, that only a portion of the curve changes. The right end of the curve is unchanged. Each control point affects only a certain region of the curve. Farther away from that point, the curve is unaffected. This example also illustrates another characteristic of spline curves, which may not be obvious. The hull of a spline curve does not necessarily have to stay on only one side of the curve. It may cross over to the other side of the

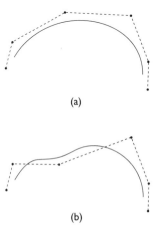

(a)

(b)

Figure 2-20. Two spline curves, each showing the network of control vertices that controls its shape.

curve, and will do so if one control point is pulled far enough, as it is in this example.

Notice that the spline approach to representing a curve answers the three objections raised above about the linear-approximation approach. First, a spline is very easy to reshape. Pulling a single control point can modify an entire section of the curve and do so in a smooth manner. Second, the spline is truly, mathematically curved. No matter how much you magnify a section of a spline, it remains truly curved. And finally, from the programmer's point of view, the spline representation of a curve is very compact and efficient in terms of the amount of data it requires. A handful of control points suffices to define an entire curve.

From a programming point of view, a spline is actually a mathematical formulation of a curve. (The splines of computer graphics are almost always what are called "cubic" splines. The term refers to the fact that the mathematical formulae that define these splines involve a variable raised to the third, or cubic, power.) Depending on what the programmer wants to accomplish, this formulation may differ from one program to the next. One programmer's approach might cause the "control" of the control points to be exerted in one way; another's approach might use the control points to shape the curve in a slightly different way. The exact effect of the control points depends on how the mathematical formulae are written, which in turn depends on what kinds of results the programmer wants to achieve. Over the years, however, a handful of formulations have emerged as the most useful, and these are the varieties of splines most commonly found in computer graphics systems. We will examine several of these, concluding with NURBS splines, the most widely used spline type. Since NURBS splines combine the features of several other spline types, we begin our discussion with these other spline types.

One of two broad categories of splines is the **interpolating spline**. In this form, the spline curve passes directly through each of the control points (Figure 2-21a). A specific type of interpolating spline sometimes found in computer graphics systems is the **Cardinal spline**, in which the curve goes directly through all but the first and last of the control points (Figure 2-21b).

An advantage of all interpolating splines is the direct relationship between the placement of the control points and the final curve they generate. If you want your curve to go "here," you simply place a control point "here." A disadvantage of this direct relationship, however, is that this approach can make it difficult to generate curves having a very smooth and gradual curvature. If a control point is misplaced even slightly, the curvature will not be smooth in that area of the curve, since the spline curve is required to pass exactly through the misplaced control point. The result may be an undesirable little bump in the curve. Imagine, for example, trying to draw a smooth circular

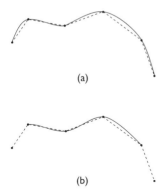

(a)

(b)

Figure 2-21. Two varieties of interpolating splines, in which the curve passes directly through the control points.

arc with an interpolating spline. Unless you precisely and mathematically calculate the location of each control point, you are likely to get some undesirable irregularities in the curvature of your arc (Figure 2-22).

Figure 2-22. Any irregularity in the placement of the control points of an interpolating spline causes a visible irregularity in the curve itself.

The second basic category of spline, the **approximating spline**, addresses this problem of control-point placement by calculating the curve such that it goes *near*, but not directly through, any of the control points. This offers a wider margin of error in the placement of the control points and tends to yield a smoother curve.

One of the most commonly used types of approximating spline is the **B-spline** (Figure 2-23). (The B in the phrase B-spline stands for the word "basis," a mathematical term.) Notice that the B-spline curve does not actually touch any of the control points. This is the nature of the approximating spline. It goes near but not through the control points. Notice also that the curvature of an approximating B-spline is more gradual than the curvature of an interpolating spline that uses the same control points: the control points used for this B-spline are the same points used for the interpolating splines in Figure 2-21. And finally, notice that, like the Cardinal spline, the B-spline curve does not extend all the way to the far ends of the hull. It begins at approximately the second control point and ends at approximately the next-to-last control point.

Figure 2-23. A B-spline curve.

The **Bézier** spline, named after the man who invented it, is another very popular variety of approximating spline. A basic Bézier spline segment is defined by four control points (Figures 2-24a, b). As with the other splines, a dotted line connecting the control points makes the hull of the spline visible.

The Bézier curve introduces a very useful concept in computer graphics. Notice that an arrow appears at each of the two end points of each Bézier curve. Each of these arrows is called a **tangent vector**. A **tangent** is a line that just grazes a curve at one point, while a **vector** is a line that has both direction and length. Each of the arrows is tangent to the curve at the location of an end point and has both direction and length.

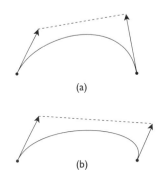

(a)

(b)

Figure 2-24. Two basic Bézier spline curves, showing tangent vectors at the ends. The length and direction of tangent vectors control the shape of a curve.

The significance of these tangent vectors is that the directions and lengths of each vector determine the curvature of the Bézier spline. Changing the direction of a vector changes the direction in which the spline curves, while changing the length of a vector changes the amount of area affected by that vector. In Figure 2-24b, for instance, the second tangent vector has been rotated to the right and shortened, causing the right end of the curve to change shape.

In everyday usage, more than four control points normally define a Bézier spline. In fact, complex Bézier curves consist of many connected simple four-control-point segments (Figure 2-25). In each of these two curves, the total curve consists of three segments, each of which has a tangent vector at the

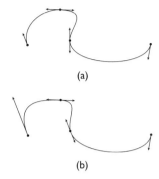

(a)

(b)

Figure 2-25. Two Bézier curves consisting of several curve segments attached. The tangent vectors serve as "handles" for changing the shape of the curve.

Figure 2-26. "Breaking" the pair of tangent vectors at a control point creates a discontinuity in the curve.

Figure 2-27. The control points and the edit points of a NURBS curve.

beginning control point and another at the ending control point. (Because the tangent vectors of a Bézier curve make the structure of control points so clear, the hull of a Bézier curve usually is not explicitly drawn.)

Figure 2-25 also illustrates how you can edit the shape of a Bézier curve. In both of these curves, the locations of all the control points are identical. In Figure 2-25b, however, two of the tangent vectors, or **handles**, as they are often called, have been adjusted. Notice that the length of the handle on the far left has been increased. This causes a larger area of the curve to be affected, and the curve therefore bows outward on the far left. Also notice that the third handle from the left (that is, the pair of arrows at the third control point) has been rotated, causing a change in the direction of the curve in the area of the third control point.

Normally, when two tangent vectors, or arrows, share a control point, they operate as a unit, and are referred to as **locked**. When the third handle of Figure 2-25b rotated, for instance, the two tangent vectors at that point rotated together. This usually is desirable in a Bézier curve, because it assures that the curvature of the spline at that control point will remain smooth, that there will not be a "kink" in the curve.

Sometimes, however, you specifically want a kink (Figure 2-26). In that case you can create a kink, more formally called a **discontinuity** or a **cusp**, by manipulating a pair of tangent vectors so that they do *not* operate as a unit (and do not appear as a continuous straight line). This is referred to as **unlocking** or **breaking** the tangent vectors, and has been done at the third control point of Figure 2-26. The locations of all of the control points for this curve are exactly the same as they were in Figure 2-25. Now, however, the handles at the third control point, broken apart, do not form a straight line. The curve is no longer continuous, or smooth, at that point. Instead, it has a cusp at the third control point.

The most commonly used type of spline employed in 3D computer systems is the **NURBS** curve, or Non-Uniform Rational B-Spline (Figure 2-27). (The terms *non-uniform* and *rational* both refer to specific mathematical properties of this type of B-spline.) A NURBS curve shares many of the best features of a number of spline types. Like an interpolating spline, it goes through the first and last control points. Like an approximating spline, however, it does not go through the intermediate control points. In addition, a set of **edit points**, sometimes called **knots** (represented by the series of small crosses in Figure 2-27), lie exactly on the curve, just as the control points do on an interpolating curve. Thus, you can adjust a NURBS curve by working either with the control points if you are more interested in smoothness, or with the edit points, if you are more interested in precision. This gives you enormous flexibility, effectively combining the best features of both interpolating splines and approximating splines.

These different varieties of spline curve share a critical feature deriving from their mathematical definitions; that is, each curve is defined as having a specific **direction**. A given curve starts here and ends there, with the first control point you specify being the starting point of the curve. You can reverse the direction of the curve if necessary, but the curve always has a direction.

The direction of the curve is significant because it allows you to locate specific points on a spline curve. You do this by indicating that you want to move a certain distance along the curve away from the beginning. Thinking of the curve in these terms is known as **parameterization**, because you use certain parameters—direction and distance—to locate your point. Consequently, spline curves are also known as **parameterized curves**.

For example, many 3D modeling packages make it possible to learn the location of a point that lies 55 percent of the way along a given curve. Usually you specify the distance along a curve as a number between 0.0 and 1.0, and so the distance parameter is 0.55. Either by typing in this number or by interactively moving a cursor along the curve, you position yourself at the location of the point. Having positioned yourself there, you then either inquire as to the precise coordinates of that point, or add a control point, or cut the curve at that point, or perform any number of other operations that the software provides. You will see in later sections of this book that the parameterization of curves is important for a number of other reasons as well.

PATCHES

Because of the ease with which you can generate and edit them, spline curves are extremely powerful tools in any computer graphics package. We will see in section 2.8 that you can use them with many common modeling techniques to generate a variety of forms. But the real power of splines for a 3D modeling package lies in their ability to generate curved surfaces. Remember that a straight line, if pushed through space in some direction other than the direction of the line itself, defines a plane, or flat surface. Similarly, a curve moved through space, either along a straight line or along another curved line, defines a **curved surface** (Figure 2-28).

Figure 2-28. A patch generated from two spline curves. The directions of the two curves are the U and V directions.

The original curve is a heavy line running from left to right. This direction, the direction of the original curve, is by convention called the **U direction.** A second curve, the heavy line extending from top to bottom, runs in a different direction. The direction of this second curve is known as the **V direction**. If you push the original, U curve along the second, V curve, you define a curved surface. A curved surface generated from two spline curves in this way is often referred to as a **patch**. (More technically, since it is formed of two cubic splines, it is called a **bicubic patch**, "bi" meaning "two" and "cubic" referring to the fact that the mathematics of a spline curve involve powers of three.)

Because a patch is generated from two spline curves, different kinds of patches correspond to the different kind of splines. If the original curves are Bézier splines, for example, they generate a Bézier patch. If the original curves are NURBS, they generate a NURBS patch. In most 3D software systems, the two curves used to generate a patch must be of the same type. In a few high-end systems, the two curves may be of different types.

Although Figure 2-28 shows only the two spline curves and the resulting surface, in reality, of course, each spline curve is defined by a set of control points and these control points are connected by a hull. Consequently, when you generate a patch from two splines, you generate a whole network of control points with it, and this network of points is connected by its own hull (Figure 2-29). The number and the direction of the control points in the original U-direction curve determine the number and the direction of control points in the U direction of the patch. In the same way, the number and the direction of control points in the V-direction curve determine the number and direction of control points in the V direction. The type of spline used for the original curves also carries over to the patch. Since the original curves in Figure 2-29 were NURBS curves, the patch generated from them is a NURBS patch.

The network of control points that defines a curved surface is extremely important. Just as you can change the shape of an individual spline curve by moving one of the control points, so you can change the shape of a surface by moving one or more of the control points. In Figure 2-30, several of the control points for the patch, pulled upward, have the effect of bowing the surface upward in the area of those control points.

When working with patches, the amount of control you have in deforming a curved surface depends on how many control points you have in the region you want to deform. If you have only a few control points, as in the previous examples, moving one control point causes a large area of the surface to be deformed. This is very effective for making broad, smooth changes in the shape of the surface, but it is not so effective for small, detailed changes in that shape. In order to make changes to the shape of the surface on a smaller scale, you need to insert additional control points. Most systems allow you to do this. However, because a rectangular grid of control points defines the surface, inserting a single control point in any direction generates an entire row of control points in that direction. In order to model the small spoutlike form at the bottom of the patch in Figure 2-31, you add several additional control points in the U direction. Doing so necessarily creates several new rows of control points, running all the way across the hull in that direction. With these control points in place, however, you pull the appropriate points to adjust the shape as desired.

Figure 2-29. The control points of the generating curves create a network of control points, which in turn define the patch.

Figure 2-30. Moving the control points of a patch changes the shape of the patch.

Figure 2-31. For fine detail, additional control points may be necessary. Adding one control point creates a whole new row of control points.

Figure 2-32. An evocative example of modeling patches by manipulating control points. (Courtesy, Yoshiki Hagihara.)

Manipulating the control points of a patch can yield tremendously complex and subtle modeling. In Figure 2-32, the animator has modeled a strange, sculptural, almost mystical splash of water by manipulating the control points of B-spline patches. This image has been superimposed on a background image that was scanned—that is, digitally copied—into the computer from a photograph.

2.4 Coordinate Systems

In the previous two sections you saw that you can define surfaces either as polygonal approximations or as spline-based patches. You then can combine these surfaces to form objects.

No matter how you define your surfaces and your objects, however, somehow you have to know how to locate these things in space. If you say to yourself, holding your hand up in the air, that you want something located "right there," this is not a very precise form of location. The odds are that tomorrow you won't be able to find that exact spot, or point, in the air. In order to be able to define points in space and to place things accurately in space, you need some clear, precise, and repeatable method of describing where something is.

The method used in nearly all computer graphics systems is analogous to the method you probably used in your high school math classes when you made graphs. If you draw two lines perpendicular to each other, and then

Figure 2-33. A simple two-axis coordinate system.

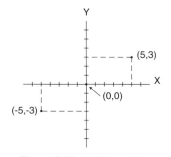

Figure 2-34. An XY coordinate system with both positive and negative directions.

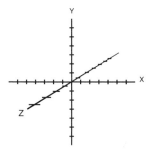

Figure 2-35. A three-dimensional Cartesian coordinate system.

mark off little "tick" marks at certain distances along each line, you have drawn a system that allows you accurately to locate points within the space of those two lines (Figure 2-33). You can say, for example, "Start where the lines cross each other, go over to the right five tick marks, then go straight up three tick marks. That's the point I'm talking about."

In the simple two-dimensional system just described, there is no ambiguity about where your point is located. If you come back tomorrow, you can relocate it exactly within the same system because you can still go over exactly five and up exactly three to define the location of the point.

This sort of numerical location system is called a **coordinate system**, and the numbers that identify where a point is (in this case, five and three) are called the **coordinates** of the point. The coordinates of a point usually are written as a pair of numerals separated by a comma—for example, (5,3). The two lines drawn perpendicular to each other are called the **axes** of the coordinate system; each one is an **axis**. The horizontal axis usually is called the X axis and the vertical axis usually is called the Y axis. The point at which the axes cross and from which you start counting when you move is called the **origin** of the coordinate system. The coordinates of the origin are (0,0).

A more flexible and powerful way of setting up this sort of coordinate system is to draw the two lines so that they continue past each other, forming a cross (Figure 2-34). This gives you the flexibility of moving in either direction away from the origin. In the horizontal direction, for example, you could move either to the right or to the left of the origin. To simplify things, the distances along an axis usually are thought of as being either positive or negative numbers, relative to the origin of the system.

In Figure 2-34, the coordinates (5,3) locate a point in the upper right section, or **quadrant**, of the coordinate system. To locate this point, you move along X (i.e., to the right) positive five and then along Y (i.e., up) positive three. The coordinates (–5,–3), on the other hand, are in the lower left quadrant, because you move along X (i.e., to the left) negative five and along Y (i.e., down) negative 3.

It is very easy to extend this two-dimensional coordinate system into a three-dimensional coordinate system, which allows you to locate points in three-dimensional space. Take a pencil and place the eraser end of the pencil at the origin point of the coordinate system in Figure 2-34. Make sure that the pencil is perpendicular to the paper—in other words, perpendicular to the X and Y axes drawn on the page. In doing this, you have just created a three-dimensional coordinate system (represented, by necessity, as a two-dimensional drawing in Figure 2-35). The pencil you placed on the page is your third axis, for the third dimension. This new, third axis normally is called the

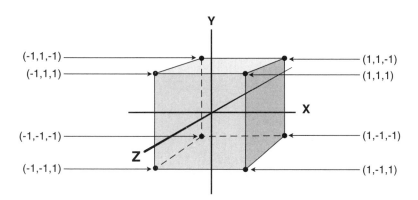

Figure 2-36. The coordinate system permits the precise location of points in space.

Z axis. Like the other two axes, it has positive and negative directions that allow you to move either forward or backward in space. A point in this coordinate system has three coordinate values to define its location. For example, (5,3,1) means "move five units to the right along X, three units up along Y, and one unit closer in Z."

Suppose you want to define a cube in three-dimensional space. If the center of the cube is at (0,0,0), you can define a cube with the following set of eight vertices:

$$(\ 1, \ 1, \ 1)$$
$$(\ 1, \ 1, -1)$$
$$(-1, \ 1, -1)$$
$$(-1, \ 1, \ 1)$$
$$(\ 1, -1, \ 1)$$
$$(\ 1, -1, -1)$$
$$(-1, -1, -1)$$
$$(-1, -1, \ 1)$$

The result is the cube in Figure 2-36.

In addition to thinking about the space of a coordinate system in terms of its three axes, we also sometimes think of it in terms of the three planes defined by those axes. Recall from the section on *Polygonal Modeling* that any three points define a plane. Extending this approach, you can see that any two axes of a coordinate system also define a plane. Thus, the three fundamental planes of a coordinate system are the XZ plane, the XY plane and the YZ plane (Figure 2-37).

Whether two-dimensional or three-dimensional, whether we refer to its axes or its planes, coordinate systems of this type, in which the coordinate system is defined by a set of mutually perpendicular axes, are called **Cartesian coordinate systems**, after the French mathematician René Descartes,

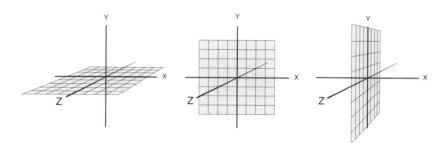

Figure 2-37. The XZ, XY, and YZ planes of a coordinate system.

who first devised them. These sorts of coordinate systems go a long way toward solving the problem of how to accurately and predictably locate a point in space.

Suppose, however, I tell you that I want a point located at (–4,2,7). You start moving to the left along X for a distance of four units. But I start shouting at you, "No, no! Go the other way! Go to the *right* along X. For me, in my system, positive X is to the left and negative X is to the right." When you try to move in the Y direction, the same thing happens. You think you know which direction I mean by "positively in Y," but in my system negative Y is up and positive Y is down. The Z axis presents the same problem: which way is positive and which way is negative?

You may think such reversals are ridiculous. That is, you may be so used to seeing positive X to the right and positive Y up that it seems ludicrous to imagine them any other way. But think of the Z axis, which is not so familiar. Is there any reason positive Z must come "out" of the page, as in Figure 2-35, rather than go "into" the page?

In short, you must decide which direction is positive and which direction is negative, for all three axes, before you start. For three-dimensional Cartesian coordinate systems, there are two standards. And, in spite of the sophistication of the science of computer graphics, these two standards are defined with your fingers.

First take a pen and draw a little X on the tip of the thumb of your right hand. This is the positive X direction of the coordinate system. Now draw a Y on the tip of the forefinger of your right hand. This is the positive Y direction. Finally, draw a Z on the tip of the middle finger of your right hand. This is the positive Z direction. When you hold your right hand in such a way that those three fingers are extended perpendicular to one another, your hand represents a coordinate system with right-handed directionality, or a **right-handed coordinate system** (Figure 2-38b; see also Figure 2-35).

Now go through the same procedure with your left hand: X on the thumb, Y on the forefinger, Z on the middle finger. When you extend your fingers, they describe a **left-handed coordinate system** (Figure 2-38a).

(a)   (b)

Figure 2-38. A left-handed coordinate system, and a right-handed coordinate system.

It is possible to rotate a given coordinate system without changing the definition of its directionality. Hold both of your hands/coordinate systems in front of you, with fingers extended as described above, and with the palms facing towards you. In this orientation, the directionality of the two systems is the same except for the X axes. On your right hand, positive X is to the right, while on the left hand, positive X is to the left. Keep your right hand in this position but rotate your left hand so that you are looking at the back of that hand. Now the X and Y of both systems are going in the same direction, but the Z is reversed.

Notice, however, that while things have changed for the left hand relative to the right hand, *relative to itself* nothing has changed. The middle finger of your left hand didn't suddenly start growing out the other side of your hand. Relative to the rest of your fingers on that hand, it is in exactly the same position as before. The whole system rotated, but within the system nothing has changed. A left-handed coordinate system, whether it is facing toward you or away from you, is still a left-handed coordinate system.

In fact, different industries have different preferences for the way they like to orient a given coordinate system. For example, the aerospace industry likes to orient coordinate systems so that the Z axis is up. This makes the ground plane—that is, what you see from an airplane—correspond to the XY plane. In other words, the ground plane can be plotted using the standard XY axes that you are familiar with. Architects tend to use the same orientation, for the same reason. By contrast, the animation industry usually orients coordinate systems so that the XY plane corresponds to the picture plane. This makes the Z axis serve as the axis that extends back into space.

Figure 2-39a is a left-handed coordinate system, oriented so that positive Z extends back into space. Figure 2-39b is a right-handed system, with positive Z coming out of space toward you. Figure 2-39c is likewise a right-handed coordinate system, but this system is oriented so that positive Y goes back into space and positive Z goes up. All of these different possibilities accomplish the same purpose—to make the location of points and objects in three-dimensional space convenient and unambiguous. None is inherently

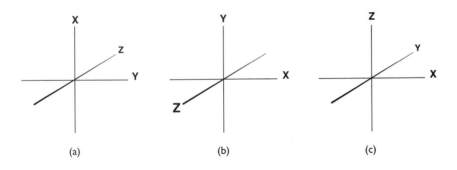

Figure 2-39. Three combinations of coordinate system handedness and orientation.

better than the others. It is important, however, for you to understand very clearly from the outset which coordinate system and which orientation is employed by the software package you use.

2.5 Viewing Windows

Figure 2-40. A typical window configuration consists of several orthographic windows and one perspective window.

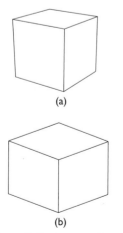

Figure 2-41. A perspective rendering and an orthographic rendering of a cube.

Whichever coordinate system and whichever orientation you use, the purpose is the same—to define the three-dimensional space in which you will be working. Three-dimensional computer modeling systems view this space by means of a set of **windows**, with each window being a particular view into the three-dimensional space (Figure 2-40).

One type of window found on all systems is the **perspective window**. (The concepts of perspective and cameras are discussed in detail in section 3.2). A perspective window, also sometimes called a **camera window**, is one through which you see a scene with the same sort of perspective distortions that you experience with your natural eyes. That is, objects in the distance appear smaller than objects that are close to the viewer, and lines that are parallel converge in the distance. In Figure 2-40a, the perspective window is the window in the upper right. In Figure 2-40b it is the large window on the right.

In addition to a perspective window, most programs also provide several **orthographic windows**. An orthographic rendering of the world does not include perspective. (The root word "ortho" comes from the Greek and means "straight.") In orthographic projection parallel lines do not converge; they remain forever parallel—that is, "straight." And objects in the distance do not get smaller; they remain the same size as they are when seen up close. In Figure 2-40 the windows labeled *Front*, *Top*, and *Right* are orthographic windows showing the model from directly in front, above, and to the right.

Although our eyes do not see the world in this orthographic way, an orthographic representation can be extremely useful because it sometimes allows us to perceive the dimensions of an object more easily. In a perspective rendering such as the one in Figure 2-41a, the lines that represent the rear edges of a cube are not as long as those that represent the front edges of the cube. Figure 2-41b shows the same cube seen from the same angle, but represented orthographically, without any perspective distortion. In this orthographic rendering, all the edges of the cube are represented as being of exactly the same length, as they are in reality.

All 3D software packages provide a default configuration of windows, usually consisting of several orthographic windows and one perspective window. The standard configuration was illustrated in Figure 2-40a. Typically, you can select other combinations and configurations of windows, such as the one illustrated in Figure 2-40b. Most packages also allow you to move and resize any of these windows.

When developing a model or scene, you usually need to work in several of the available windows, using now one and now another depending on what you are trying to accomplish.

2.6 Geometric Primitives

Certain basic geometric shapes are so easily defined mathematically and so widely used in 3D computer graphics that software packages handle them separately, as a set of special entities. These shapes are called **geometric primitives** (Figure 2-42). They include familiar shapes such as the sphere, the cube, the cone, and the cylinder, all of which are so familiar because they are so common, and so common because they are so useful.

A great many man-made objects are composed of some combination of these primitives. A table, for example, might have as the top a very wide and flat cylinder and as the legs, long tapered cylinders. A lamp might consist of a cube-shaped base, a cylinder-shaped column, and a cone-shaped shade. Because so many man-made shapes can be modeled with the geometric primitives, industrial designers and architects make particularly heavy use of them.

When you want to generate a geometric primitive using a computer modeling system, you follow a fairly standard procedure. First, you tell the system which primitive you want to use. Then you provide a few pieces of information to help define the primitive. And finally, you tell the system where in space you want to place the primitive. You may "tell the system," or provide the

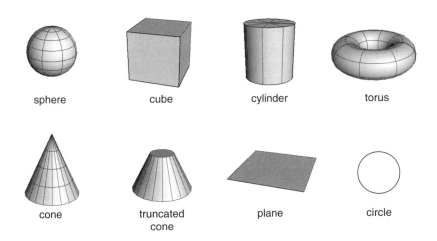

sphere   cube   cylinder   torus

cone   truncated cone   plane   circle

Figure 2-42. Some of the common geometric primitives.

information, by moving a mouse device to make menu selections, by typing at the keyboard, or by using some other input device, such as a joystick or pen.

In order to generate a **sphere**, for example, which is defined as all the points at a given distance from a central point, you must tell the system where the center of the sphere is and what the radius of the sphere is. Many modeling systems, when you request a sphere, ask you to give them these two pieces of information. Informational selections such as these, which affect the outcome of a given procedure, are called **parameters**, as in "defining the parameters of a problem." If you tell the computer, for example, that the center of the sphere is at (10,0,2) and the radius is fourteen, you will get a very different result than if you say that the center is at (0,0,0) and the radius is one.

Many 3D modeling packages do not ask for these parameters. Instead, they provide the necessary values automatically. For example, a software package might generate all spheres at (0,0,0) with a radius of one. If the computer provides its own values for the parameters, those values are called **default** values.

Whether the computer provides default values or whether it asks you to provide at least some of the values, certain predictable parameters are involved for each of the geometric primitives. To create a **cylinder** primitive, the computer needs to know (from you or by default) the center point, the radius, and the height of the cylinder. To generate a **cone**, the computer needs to know the center of the cone, the radius of the circular base, and the height of the cone.

Some software packages condense the cone and cylinder procedures into one by asking you for a total of four parameters: the center, the height, the radius at the bottom, and the radius at the top. If the two radii are the same, you get a standard cylinder. If one of them equals zero, you get a cone, the point of which is at the end where the radius is zero. If the two radii are different, you get a tapered cylinder, also known as a **truncated cone**.

Most systems provide another geometric primitive called the **torus**. For this doughnut-shaped object the parameters usually are the center of the torus, the radius of the circular cross section, and the radius of the whole doughnut from the center to the edge.

Most systems also provide menu selections for two geometric primitives that actually are two-dimensional rather than three-dimensional: the **plane** and the **circle**. When generating a plane as a geometric primitive, you normally are asked to specify the two lengths of the rectangular plane. You also may be asked to specify the orientation of the plane—that is, whether it lies flush with the XY plane, XZ plane, or YZ plane of the coordinate system. When generating a circle, as when generating a sphere, you are asked to provide the center and the radius.

Software systems differ in exactly which set of geometric primitives they provide and which parameters they request. But all systems provide some primitives and request some parameters.

When the software creates, or constructs, a primitive, it initially appears on your screen in a certain orientation. A cone, for example, might appear pointing upward. The initial orientation of any object results from the construction of the object by the software relative to a specific, invisible plane in space. This plane is called the **construction plane**.

Some software packages always create their primitives in the same orientation, so the animator has no control over which construction plane is used. If you want the object to be in a different orientation, you rotate it after it has been constructed. Other software packages, however, give you control over which construction plane to use when generating a geometric primitive. This is done most simply by selecting one of the orthographic windows. (See the section on *Coordinate Systems.*) The plane of that window then becomes the construction plane for the next primitive. For example, in creating a cone primitive, selecting the Top window will activate the XZ plane as the construction plane, giving you the result shown in Figure 2-43a. Selecting the Front window will activate the XY construction plane, producing a cone in the orientation shown in Figure 2-43b. And selecting the Right window will cause the YZ plane to be used as the construction plane for the cone, with the result shown in Figure 2-43c.

Some systems provide additional control over the choice of construction plane by allowing you to use any flat surface, or **face**, in your scene as the current construction plane. In Figure 2-44, the animator has selected the face that is shaded, causing the software to create the cone on a construction plane aligned with that face. As a result the cone exactly coincides with the face. In many animation applications, this kind of accuracy is not necessary, and "eyeballing" an object's rotations after its creation is satisfactory. But in those applications where a more industrial level of accuracy is required, a wise use of construction planes can greatly facilitate modeling.

(a)

(b)

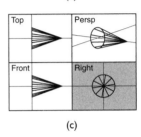

(c)

Figure 2-43. The initial orientation of an object depends on which construction plane was used to generate it.

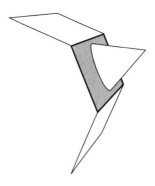

Figure 2-44. A construction plane may be defined to align with the face of an existing object.

2.7 Transformations

If every object you defined in your computer graphics modeling system had to be in exactly the same location and of exactly the same size and oriented in exactly the same way, your modeling capabilities would be very limited and your modeling system of little use. You need at least the same sort of flexibility in modeling that you have in the real world. That is, you need to be able to move an object about in space, rotate it into other orientations, and scale it to change the size. These three operations collectively are called **transformations**.

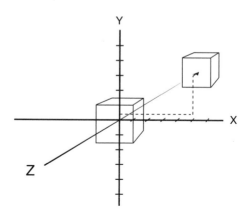

Figure 2-45. A simple translation of a cube.

MOVE

When you relocate an object in space, you **move**, or **translate**, the object. In computer graphics modeling systems, whenever you translate an object in space, you make use of the same three-dimensional Cartesian coordinate system used for locating points in space. That is, you move the object either positively or negatively along any one of the three axes of the coordinate system.

Normally, in order to move an object to its final position, you move it some amount in all three of the axes—X, Y, and Z. Consequently, a translation is written as a set of three numerical values—translation in X, translation in Y, and translation in Z. Typical ways of writing this are *translate x,y,z*, or *translate (x,y,z)*, or *move x,y,z*, or *move (x,y,z)*, where *x,y,z* refer to the three numerical amounts by which the object is being moved. For example, *translate (5,3,–2)* indicates that you want to move in the X direction positive five, in the Y direction positive three, and in the Z direction negative two. The cube in figure 2-45, originally located at (0,0,0), has been translated to the right positive five, up positive three, and back in space negative two.

ROTATE

When you tilt an object or change the direction in which it is facing, you **rotate** the object. This is the second of the basic transformations. In rotating an object, you again make use of the three-dimensional Cartesian coordinate system, which allows you to specify precisely what kind of rotation you have in mind. As an example, imagine a wax statuette of a standing human figure (Figure 2-46a). Now imagine that the Y axis is a skewer going into the top of the head of the statuette and coming out at the bottom of the feet (Figure 2-46b). If you twirl the skewer between your fingers, the statuette rotates around that skewer—that is, around the Y axis; it "rotates about Y."

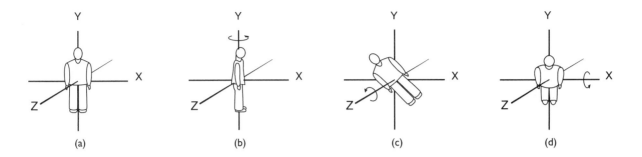

(a)	(b)	(c)	(d)

If the skewer instead goes into the back of the statuette and comes out the stomach, the skewer corresponds to the Z axis of the coordinate system. You then can rotate the figure about the Z axis (Figure 2-46c). If you stick the skewer into one side and out the other side of the statuette, the skewer corresponds to the X axis. A rotation around X tilts the figure forward, almost as if it were bowing (Figure 2-46d).

Figure 2-46. Rotations of an object are described as taking place around the axes of the coordinate system.

You usually specify the amount of a rotation in degrees, 360 degrees being a complete rotation—from a given starting point, all the way around and back to the starting point. (Some systems, designed for more scientific purposes, use radians rather than degrees. One radian equals 57.29578 degrees [$360/2\pi$].) Changing the amount of rotation changes the final orientation of the object. For example, changing the rotation of the statuette to 90 degrees about X rotates the figurine so that it lies flat on its face.

Rotations, like translations, are usually written as a set of three values, one each for the X rotation, the Y rotation, and the Z rotation. *Rotate (90,0,0),* for example, means "rotate 90 degrees around X, nothing around Y, and nothing around Z."

Saying "rotate 90 degrees around X," however, is somewhat ambiguous. Does a 90-degree rotation about X mean rotate "this way" around X, or does it mean rotate "that way" around X? How do you indicate whether the statuette should rotate so that it ends up on its face (a forward rotation) or on its back (a backward rotation)?

As with the directionality of a coordinate system, a standard has to be agreed upon for the directionality of rotations. You need to know whether a 90-degree rotation is 90 degrees in this direction or in that direction. And again, in spite of the high-tech sophistication of computer graphics, your fingers provide the standard.

The accepted way of determining rotational direction is as follows. Using your right hand, consider the tip of your thumb the positive end of some axis. Hold your hand up with the thumb extended and your fingers straight up. Now slowly close the four fingers of your hand. The direction in which your fingers are closing is a positive rotation around the axis described by

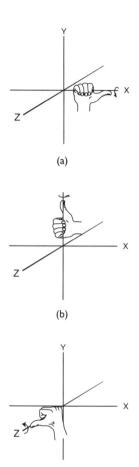

(a)

(b)

(c)

Figure 2-47. The right-handed rule for determining the directionality of rotations.

your thumb. Since you used your right hand, this is a **right-handed rotation**.

Apply this idea to an actual coordinate system. Imagine a right-handed coordinate system—that is, positive X to the right, positive Y up, positive Z coming out of the page. Place your right hand so that the thumb is along the line of the X axis, with the tip of the thumb at the positive X end. Keeping your thumb extended, close the fingers of your right hand. The direction in which your fingers close defines the positive rotation about X (Figure 2-47a). Now place your right hand so that the thumb aligns with the Y axis, with the tip of the thumb at positive Y. Close the fingers of your right hand to see the positive direction of rotation (Figure 2-47b). Finally, place your right hand on the Z axis, with the tip of the thumb at positive Z. Closing your hand shows you the positive rotation about Z (Figure 2-47c). Notice that, for all three axes, if you place your eye at the positive end of the axis and look down the length of the axis, the positive rotation around that axis is in a counterclockwise direction.

It is also possible to apply the right-handed rotation rule to a left-handed coordinate system. The handedness of a coordinate system and the handedness of rotations are completely independent of each other. Try applying the same right-handed rotations you just used to a left-handed coordinate system. If you orient your left-handed coordinate system such that positive X is to the right, positive Y is up, and positive Z is going into the page, you see that the right-handed rotations are the same as they were in the right-handed coordinate system, except for the Z axis. This is because the difference between a left-handed and a right-handed coordinate system is simply a reversal of the Z axis.

Just as it is possible to have a right-handed rule for determining the positive direction of rotation, it is also possible to have a left-handed rule, producing **left-handed rotations**. You can visualize these rotations by placing the thumb of your left hand at the positive tip of each axis and closing your fingers. Again, the direction in which your fingers close indicates the direction of a positive rotation about that axis. Notice that left-handed rotations are in the reverse direction of right-handed rotations. That is, if you look down the length of a given axis, with your thumb near your eyes, each rotation is clockwise about that axis.

There is nothing sacred about these rules for rotational directionality. They are simply convenient ways of setting up a standard that the computer graphics industry can agree upon. Without some standard, there would be confusion about which direction to rotate. It is important, therefore, when you start using a particular three-dimensional software package, to determine which standard is in effect. Are positive rotations in the right-handed direction or in the left-handed direction? And furthermore, is the software using a right-handed coordinate system or a left-handed coordinate system? The most commonly found combination in animation packages is a right-handed coordinate system with right-handed rotations (see Figure 2-47). Because this combination is the most common, it appears throughout this book.

SCALE

The third type of transformation involves changes of size. When you change the size or the proportions of an object, you **scale** the object, and you can scale an object along any one of the three axes.

If you scale an object along only one axis, you change the size in only one direction. In Figure 2-48a a cube is at the original size. In Figure 2-48b, the cube has been scaled along the X axis, making it longer horizontally. In Figure 2-48c the cube has been scaled along the Y axis, making it taller. In Figure 2-48d it has been scaled along the Z axis, making it longer as it goes back in space.

It is also very common, however, for an object to be scaled along more than one axis at a time. In Figure 2-48e the cube has been scaled along the Y axis by three and at the same time along the Z axis by two.

Since the sort of scaling operation just described does not retain the original proportions of the object, it is often called a **nonproportional scale**, or sometimes a **nonuniform scale**. If the scaling factor is the same for all three axes, however, the overall size changes, but the original proportions of the

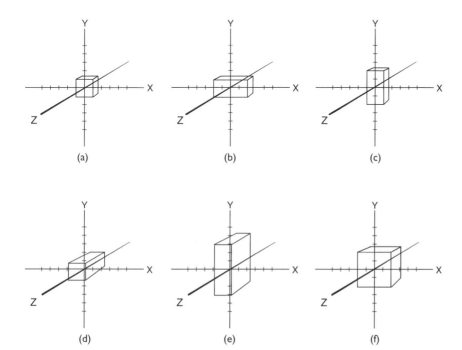

Figure 2-48. Different scaling operations applied to a cube. Scales may be either non-proportional or proportional.

object remain the same. This is called a **proportional scale** or a **uniform scale**. For example, simultaneously scaling the original cube by two in all three axes produces the cube in Figure 2-48f, which is twice as big in each dimension as it was before.

Scale transformations, like the other transformations, are usually written as a series of three numbers, one for each axis. To scale something uniformly by two in all directions, as in Figure 2-48f, you could write *scale (2,2,2)*. To bring about a nonproportional scale of two in the X direction, three in the Y direction and seven in the Z direction, you could write *scale (2,3,7)*.

From a mathematical point of view, scaling is an act of multiplication. Our language reflects this. When you make something twice as big, you make it two "times" as big—that is, you multiply all the numbers that define the object by two. For example, if all the vertices of a cube are at positive/negative one, as they are in Figure 2-48a, then after scaling by two they would all be at positive/negative two, as they are in Figure 2-48f. If you then rescaled the cube by three, all of the new, scaled vertices are at positive/negative six.

This multiplicative aspect of scaling has some interesting consequences. If you scale an object by one in all directions, for instance, the object does not change at all. This is because any number multiplied by one remains the same number. When you scaled the cube by two only in one direction, you effectively scaled it by one in the other directions; the scale operation performed in Figure 2-48b, therefore, is written *scale (2,1,1)*.

If you scale an object by a number less than one (Figure 2-49a), you decrease the size of the object. For example, scaling by 0.5 makes an object half as big (Figure 2-49b), because multiplying those numbers that define the surface of the object by a factor of 0.5 makes all those numbers half of what they were. If a vertex of a cube is located at (6,6,6), scaling the cube by 0.5 causes the vertex to be located at (3,3,3).

If you scale an object by zero, you reduce that object to an infinitesimally small, indeed invisible, point, because any number times zero equals zero. When multiplied by zero, all the points that define an object, no matter the original values, collapse to zero. The effect of this is to make the object disappear (Figure 2-49c).

Finally, if you scale by a negative number, you flip, or invert, the object. Left becomes right, up becomes down, and so on, because multiplication by a negative number reverses the sign of the original number. For example, if one of the points that defines an object is (2,5,8), and you scale (i.e., multiply) it by negative one in the Y direction, the new, scaled point is (2,–5,8). In Figure 2-49d the original head has been scaled negatively along the Y axis, but left unchanged along the other two axes. In other words, *scale (1,–1,1)*. Negating the numbers along the Y axis has the effect of making what was "up" become down and what was "down" become up.

(a)

(b)

(c)

(d)

Figure 2-49. The multiplicative nature of scaling can produce some unusual results.

ABSOLUTE AND RELATIVE TRANSFORMATIONS

Now that you understand the three basic transformations, you want to use them. Immediately, however, you encounter an ambiguity. Imagine the following situation: you are standing at (0,0,0) and I tell you to "move (3,0,0)." You do so. Then I say "move (3,0,0)" a second time. How do you interpret this command? Does it mean "move *to* (3,0,0)"? If it does, you are already there, so you should not move at all. Or does it mean "move *an additional* 3,0,0)"? If so, you should move to the right three more paces.

Often in the real world you want to move *to* a given location, regardless of where you start from. "Go to the corner of Fifty-third Street and Lexington Avenue," for example, means "no matter where you're starting from, go to the corner of Fifty-third and Lexington." This is called an **absolute transformation**. The specific transformation values refer to an absolute location in the three-dimensional coordinate system. Wherever the object begins, it moves to that absolute location. If it begins at that location, it stays there. So if I say "move absolutely (3,0,0)," there is no ambiguity. You move *to* (3,0,0).

In other situations it is more convenient to think in terms of transforming an object relative to the present location of that object, rather than to some absolute location in space. This kind of transformation is called a **relative transformation**. A real-world example would be "go north two blocks and east one block," which means "starting from wherever you are now, go north two blocks and east one block." Thus, if I tell you to "move relatively (3,0,0)," you know that no matter where you are now you must move an additional (3,0,0).

Imagine another example. Start with a cube located at (–2,0,0) (Figure 2-50a). If you request an *absolute* move of (–2,1,0), the cube does not move at all in X, because it is already at x = –2; it moves up one in Y, since it was at y = 0 and must end up at y = 1; and it does not move at all in Z, because it is already at z = 0 (Figure 2-50b). If, however, you return the cube to the original position of (–2,0,0) and request a *relative* move of (–2,1,0), the cube moves an additional (–2,1,0), causing it to end up at (–4,1,0) (Figure 2-50c).

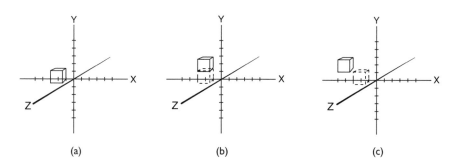

(a) (b) (c)

Figure 2-50. Absolute translations and relative translations.

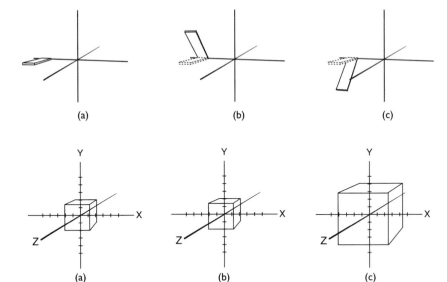

Figure 2-51. Absolute rotations and relative rotations.

(a)　　　　　(b)　　　　　(c)

Figure 2-52. Absolute and relative scaling operations on a cube.

(a)　　　　　(b)　　　　　(c)

Although the examples given so far involved only translations, the distinction between absolute and relative transformations holds true for the other two basic transformations—rotations and scales. Let's look at the other two transformations. When you say "rotate forty-five degrees about X," for instance, you may intend either an absolute rotation or a relative rotation. If you request an absolute rotation, the object ends up rotated exactly forty-five degrees about X, no matter what the original X rotation was. If you request a relative rotation, the object rotates an additional forty-five degrees around X. In Figure 2-51a a "board," rotated ninety degrees around X, lies flat. In Figure 2-51b this same board has been rotated absolutely forty-five degrees around X, and this causes it to pop up. In Figure 2-51c the original board has been rotated relatively forty-five degrees around X, causing it to rotate farther down around the X axis.

A similar thing happens when you apply absolute and relative scaling transformations. If you already have scaled an object by a factor of two in all three axes (Figure 2-52a), and you scale again by a factor of two, there are two possibilities. If the second scaling operation is an absolute scale, the object does not change size (Figure 2-52b). If the second scale is relative, the object doubles in size as a result of the operation (Figure 2-52c).

When working with a 3D computer graphics system, you must know whether you are applying absolute or relative transformations. Most software packages provide you with both alternatives and give you some way of indicating which you want to use. Depending on the individual modeling situation, it may be more convenient to work sometimes with absolute and sometimes with relative transformations.

LOCAL AND GLOBAL TRANSFORMATIONS

Having resolved the possible confusion between absolute and relative transformations, you must resolve one last ambiguity. Imagine a cylinder standing vertically (Figure 2-53a). Suppose you rotate this cylinder negative forty-five degrees around the Z axis by sticking a pin in the front of the cylinder and twirling the cylinder about that pin. The final position of the cylinder depends on where your imaginary pin touches the cylinder; that is, if you insert the pin exactly into the center of the cylinder (Figure 2-553b), or if you insert the pin into the bottom of the cylinder (Figure 2-53c).

The point about which the cylinder rotates is called the **pivot point** or, more accurately, the **local origin** of that object. This second term introduces an idea crucial to the understanding of transformations: every object has a private coordinate system, which resides within the larger coordinate system of the whole world (Figure 2-54a). The **world coordinate system**, or **global coordinate system**, is the one used so far in this book. The "local origin" of an object, in contrast, is the center of the **local coordinate system** of that object.

Transformations of an object take place within the space defined by the local coordinate system of the object. If you define the local origin of a cylinder to be in the center of the cylinder (see Figure 2-54a), then the Z axis of the local coordinate system runs through the center of the cylinder. If, however, you define the local origin of the cylinder to be at the bottom of the cylinder, the local Z axis runs through the bottom of the cylinder (Figure 2-54b).

The importance of the local origin and the local coordinate system of an object is not limited to the rotation transformation, since all three of the transformations can be thought of in terms of a local origin and local coordinate system. When you translate an object, you are moving the object and the local coordinate system together, as a unit. The final numerical location of the object is, in fact, the location within the world coordinate system of the origin of the local coordinate system of the object. Thus, when you say that a

(a)

(b)

(c)

Figure 2-53. The result of the rotation depends on where the "axis" touches the cylinder.

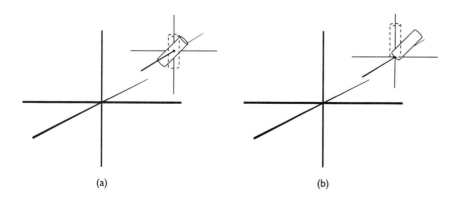

(a)   (b)

Figure 2-54. Each object exists within its own local coordinate system. Here, the local coordinate systems of the two cylinders differ, causing their rotations to differ.

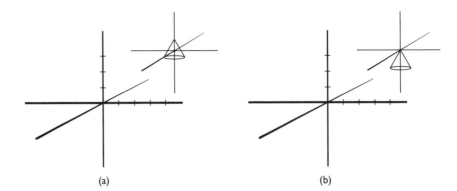

Figure 2-55. The definition of the local coordinate system of an object affects translations applied to that object.

(a)   (b)

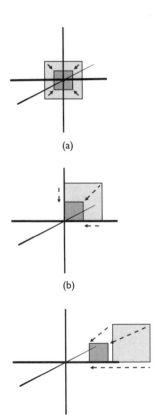

(a)

(b)

(c)

Figure 2-56. Scaling transformations are dramatically affected by the location of the origin of the local coordinate system. (The original cube is represented here in simplified form as the larger and lightly-shaded square.)

cone (Figure 2-55a) is located at (5,3,0), you really are saying that the origin of the local coordinate system of the cone is located at (5,3,0). Suppose, however, that you shift the cone itself so that the local origin is at the *tip* of the cone, rather than in its center (Figure 2-55b). The local coordinate system and the local origin of this cone remain in the same numerical locations—that is, at (5,3,0). Even though you once again have translated the cone to (5,3,0), it ends up looking different because the placement of the cone relative to the local origin is different.

The effect of local origin on scaling can be even more dramatic. Remember that scaling is a multiplicative function. When you scale an object, you multiply the numbers that define the surface of that object. This multiplication takes place within the local coordinate system of the object. Therefore, the placement of the object within that system affects the final visual result of any scaling operation. Depending on where you place the object with respect to the local origin, you get different results from the same scaling operation.

As an example, imagine that you want to scale a cube by 0.5 in all three axes—in other words, make it half as big. If the local origin of the cube is in the center of the cube, scaling the cube by 0.5 makes the cube shrink equally in all directions (Figure 2-56a). This happens because you have multiplied by 0.5 all of the numbers that define the surface of the cube, making them approach by fifty percent the (0,0,0) point, or local origin, which is at the center of the cube.

In Figure 2-56b, however, the local origin of the cube is located at the lower left corner of the cube. A multiplication/scale by 0.5 causes all the numbers that define the surface of the cube to approach *this* (0,0,0) point. As a result, the cube slides down and to the left as it shrinks, approaching the local origin in the corner of the cube.

In Figure 2-56c, the local origin of the cube has been moved even farther to the left. A scale of 0.5 again causes the cube to slide towards its origin, this time actually shifting the new, smaller cube substantially to the left.

THE TRANSFORMATION MATRIX

Although you have been looking at such transformations in isolation from one another, in practice it is more common to apply several transformations to a single object in order to make the object do what you want. For example, if you were going to use a cone to model a lamp shade, you might want to scale the cone to the correct size, move it to the top of the lamp, and then perhaps tilt it a bit off center. Even more realistically, you might translate the cone, translate it again, rotate it, rotate it again, scale it, translate it once more, scale it again, and finally rotate it one last time. All of these transformations end up being compressed by the software of the 3D modeling system into one set of the three basic transformations—that is, into a single translation, a single rotation, and a single scale. This compression of multiple transformations into a single set of transformations is known as the **concatenation of transformations**.

The result of the concatenation of a series of transformations is nine transformation values: the three concatenated translation values (translation in X, translation in Y, and translation in Z); the three concatenated rotation values (rotation in X, rotation in Y, and rotation in Z); and the three concatenated scale values (scale in X, scale in Y, and scale in Z). These nine values are often represented by writing them in a three-by-three rectangular grid. Since a grid is also called a "matrix" (the plural of "matrix" is "matrices"), this representation is known as a **transformation matrix**. (The transformation matrix representation is especially significant from a mathematical point of view, because it permits software developers to easily manipulate transformation values using "matrix arithmetic.") In Figure 2-57a, which is a generic representation of a transformation matrix, the horizontal row at the top contains the three translation values, abbreviated as *tx*, *ty*, and *tz*; the middle row contains the three rotation values; and the bottom row contains the three scale values. In Figure 2-57b, a specific set of transformation values is arranged into a transformation matrix.

Whenever you create an object, the object automatically has a set of transformation values applied to it, even before you deliberately transform it. This default set of transformation values is effectively transparent, in that it doesn't move the object, doesn't rotate the object, and keeps the object at the original scale. This default transformation, in other words, consists of the following transformations: *move (0,0,0); rotate (0,0,0); scale (1,1,1)*. This particular set of transformation values, since it does not alter the object at all, is called the **identity transformation** (Figure 2-58). The identity transformation is also the set of values you return to if ever you want to "remove" all the transformations from an object.

The branch of mathematics that applies the numbers of a transformation matrix to the geometry of a model is called **matrix arithmetic**, or **matrix multiplication**. Imagine that the transformation matrix for a model contains

tx	ty	tz
rx	ry	rz
sx	sy	sz

(a)

translate (-2,1,0)
rotate (90,6,111) ➡
scale (1,-1,1)

-2	1	0
90	6	111
1	-1	1

(b)

Figure 2-57. The nine transformation values can be organized into a transformation matrix.

0	0	0
0	0	0
1	1	1

Figure 2-58. The identity transformation.

a transformation of *tx = 4,* and that a point on the surface of the model is located at (2,2,2). After the matrix arithmetic is applied to this point, the point will appear at (6,2,2). Similar matrix arithmetic would be applied for the rotation and scale transformations.

Although our point appears at (6,2,2), the two original sets of numbers—the transformation matrix and the surface points—are retained as separate entities within the software. That is, the location of our point is not *really* (6,2,2), but remains (2,2,2), with a *tx = 4* transformation applied to it. This concept becomes important in certain operations that require your model to have the identity transformation—that is: 0,0,0; 0,0,0; 1,1,1. At the same time, however, you do not want your model to lose the location, orientation, and scale you have given it. In other words, you want it to be moved, rotated, or scaled, but also to have the identity transformation. This is accomplished with an operation called **identity matrix multiplication**, or in some packages, **freezing** the transformations. This applies the matrix numbers to the surface points in a permanent way. In our example, the point's new location becomes (6,2,2), while its new transformation becomes *tx = 0.* The result of identity matrix multiplication, in short, is that the values of the surface points are all changed while the transformation matrix is reset to identity. Your model appears in exactly the same position, orientation, and scale as before the operation.

Another important application of the transformation matrix concept involves situations in which you find yourself handling a large number of the same object in a scene. Chairs in a large office, for example, might all be of the same style and design—or, to phrase it more technically, the geometry of all the chairs is identical (Figure 2-59). Only the placement and orientation—that is, the transformations—of the chairs vary.

The technique in computer graphics developed to handle this sort of modeling situation is called **instantiation**. With this technique, it is possible to model a single chair and then to create **instances** of that model. An instance is not a "copy" of the model. A copy replicates the geometry of a

Figure 2-59. A scene in which a model is repeated a number of times lends itself to the instantiation technique.

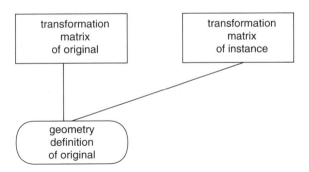

Figure 2-60. An instance has its own transformation matrix, which points to a shared geometry definition.

model. With an instance, the geometry of the model is not duplicated but merely "pointed to," as if the software system were saying, "Give me seven more of those things over there."

You saw earlier that whenever you create a model a transformation matrix is automatically associated with it. When you create an instance, a new transformation matrix is created just for that instance, but again, no new geometry is created. Thus, if you model an original chair and then create an instance of it, there will be one geometry definition with two transformation matrices—the original plus that of the instance—pointing to it (Figure 2-60). Because each instance has its own transformation matrix, you can move the instances around and transform them independently of one another.

A major advantage of instantiation is that it affords tremendous economies of geometric data. In a situation where you have ten identical chairs in a room, you need to create and store the geometry for only one of them. All the other chairs share this same geometry. This means you deal with one-tenth the geometric data you would have dealt with had you duplicated the geometry for each chair.

Another, less obvious advantage of instantiation is that, since all the chairs share the same geometry, you very easily can make changes to the design of the entire collection of chairs. Any change you make to the original geometric definition immediately and automatically changes in each of the instanced chair models. This can be especially useful in large modeling projects such as architectural structures or outdoor scenes.

2.8 Common Modeling Techniques

A number of techniques for modeling surfaces are so simple and so powerful that you find them in almost all 3D modeling programs. These techniques are common to programs based on polygonal modeling and to programs based on patch modeling.

(a)

(b)

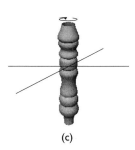

(c)

Figure 2-61. Surfaces of revolution generated by rotating a curve around an axis.

REVOLVE

One such technique was inspired by a standard woodworking technique known as "turning," or "lathing." This woodworking technique involves a machine called a lathe, which clamps a piece of wood into place and then rotates it about the long axis of the piece of wood. As the wood rotates, the woodworker holds a chisel to the wood, cutting the wood symmetrically around the axis of rotation. This technique is used, for example, to form the rounded legs of chairs and tables.

Within computer graphics, you produce a **lathed surface** by drawing a curve in space and rotating it around some axis. The trace left by the curve as it rotates around the axis becomes the surface you are generating. Since rotating the curve around an axis is also referred to as "revolving" the curve around the axis, an object produced in this way is also called a **surface of revolution,** or sometimes simply a **revolve**.

In Figure 2-61a, the straight vertical line in space, represented as the darker line, is revolved around the Y axis a full 360 degrees. The surface that results from this revolution is a cylinder. In Figure 2-62b, a more irregular, S-shaped curve is revolved around the Y axis, producing a vaselike surface. Notice that if the original, or **generating**, curve touches the axis of revolution at some point, then the revolved surface will be closed at that point. This is what happens at the bottom of the vase shape in Figure 2-61b. If the original curve is some distance from the axis of revolution, as at the top of the vase, the surface will be open at that end. In Figure 2-61c, an even more irregular curve, which touches the axis at both ends, is drawn. This curve, when revolved around the Y axis, yields what might be a chair leg, as produced by a wood-turning lathe.

In principle, the generating curve can revolve around any axis. In practice, however, most systems limit the choice of axes. The most common restriction is that the axis of revolution must be one of the three perpendicular axes of the coordinate system—X, Y, or Z. In these systems, you produce a revolved surface along one of these axes, transforming that surface afterward to whatever position and orientation you need. A few software systems allow you to specify any arbitrary axis by indicating the starting and ending points of a straight line. This line is then interpreted as the axis of revolution.

EXTRUSION

Another modeling technique found in almost all 3D packages is equally simple conceptually. In this technique, you draw a generating curve and push it straight back in space. The trace left by the curve as it moves through space becomes the surface. This technique is called **extrusion**. Objects modeled with this technique also are called extrusions or sometimes **extruded surfaces**.

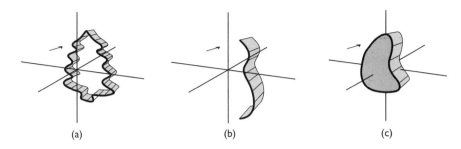

(a)   (b)   (c)

Figure 2-62. Extruded surfaces. If a face is used as the generator, the extruded result has a front and a back.

A real-world example of an extrusion is a cookie cutter. The cutting edge of the cookie cutter corresponds to the generating curve, and the depth into the dough that you push the cookie cutter corresponds to the depth through space that you push the curve. For example, the Christmas-tree-shaped surface in Figure 2-62a was generated by a **closed curve**, which closes upon itself by ending exactly where it begins, like a circle. The surface in Figure 2-62b was generated by an **open**, or **unclosed, curve**.

Notice, however, the difference between a cookie cutter and a computer graphics extrusion. In a computer graphics extrusion, the trace left by the curve when it is extruded through space generates a surface that corresponds to only the *sides* of the cookie . There is no front or back to the extruded surface, whereas cookies, being made of solid material, have fronts and backs in addition to sides.

You can address this problem in one of two ways. Instead of extruding just a curve, some systems allow you to extrude a flat surface in the shape of the generating curve. A flat surface is often called a **face**. When this is done, the generating face produces the front and back of the final extrusion, while the curve that defines the perimeter of the face produces the sides of the extrusion. In Figure 2-62c, the generating face is darkly shaded, while the side surfaces are shaded more lightly. In other systems, you create separate surfaces from the closed generating curve. These serve as top and bottom faces and can be combined with the extruded side surface within a hierarchy (see section 2.9).

Many systems extend the concept of extrusion by allowing you to push the generating curve back into space in a direction other than a straight line. Instead of specifying the distance that you want to extrude your curve, you specify a path along which the curve will be extruded. This path is drawn as a second curve. In Figure 2-63 the circle is the generating curve. The long, snaking curve, rendered here as a dotted line, is the second curve and serves as the path of extrusion. The result is an extruded surface that resembles a snaking garden hose.

Figure 2-63. A circle extruded along a curved path to form a hoselike surface.

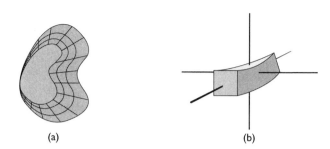

Figure 2-64. Swept surfaces generated by transforming curves as they are extruded through space.

(a)   (b)

SWEEPS

You can extend the extrusion technique further if you transform (see *Transformations*) the generating curve at the same time that it moves along the extrusion path. For example, you might scale or rotate the generating curve as it moves along the extrusion path. (Normally, you can't perform a translation transformation on a generating curve, because the movement of the curve along the path is already bringing about a translation.) When you sweep the curve along the path in this way, the surface is called a **swept surface,** or a **sweep**. For example, look back at the extrusion illustrated in Figure 2-62c. Suppose that, at the same time you push back the kidney-shaped generating curve of that figure into space, you also scale it up—say by a factor of two—to increase the size of the generating curve as it is swept. The result is that the final surface is wider at the back than in the front (Figure 2-64a).

Similarly, you could rotate the generating curve as it is swept along the extrusion path. Suppose the generating curve is a square. If you rotate this square at the same time that you move it along a straight path, you produce a twisted oblong surface (Figure 2-64b).

Combining scaling and rotation transformations with a subtly modeled generating curve and moving that curve along a complex three-dimensional path, you can quickly and easily generate some very complex and beautiful forms.

LOFTS

Figure 2-65. A contour map. Each concentric curve indicates the altitude of the surface of the land.

Another modeling technique found in virtually all 3D software packages was inspired by the contour maps geographers use (Figure 2-65). In these maps, a series of concentric rings indicates the shape of a land mass, with each ring representing an increase in the height, or altitude, of the land.

In computer graphics, using an adaptation of this concept, you draw a series of curves, which may be either open or closed. You then position each curve, lofting it to some height above the previous curve. Finally, you specify the order in which these curves, or contours, are to be connected. The software system then produces a **lofted surface**, or **skin**, connecting the contours.

In Figure 2-66, both the boat hull (a) and the mountainous form (b) were generated as lofted surfaces. When creating a surface like this, the easiest way to fine-tune the model usually is to delete the model if it doesn't look right, adjust the contour curves—either by moving them up or down or by manipulating the control points—and then regenerate the form. You can repeat this process as often as necessary.

Lofting is an extremely powerful technique for generating surfaces that otherwise would be very difficult to model. The success of the technique, however, depends on how carefully you draw the contour curves and how precisely you position them in space. Notice also that the contour curves used to generate a lofted surface are effectively cross sections of the final surface. This fact makes the lofting technique very useful for digitizing physical objects (see section 5.3).

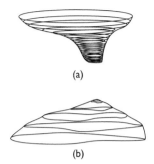

Figure 2-66. Lofted surfaces generated by connecting a series of contour curves.

BOUNDARY SURFACES

A final modeling technique commonly found in 3D modeling packages entails drawing curves to specify the edges, or boundaries, of a surface. With these edges defined, the software then forms a **boundary surface** between the boundary curves.

There are two standard approaches to the boundary-patch technique. The first is simply to draw two **boundary curves**, sometimes called **end curves**, each at an opposite end of the intended patch. You then instruct the system to calculate the surface that connects these two curves. Notice that the two end curves in Figure 2-67a are identical copies of each other, with the same curvature. This produces a surface that is symmetrical from one generating boundary curve to the other. In Figure 2-67b, however, the two end curves have radically different curvatures, and the resulting surface is much more irregularly curved. In both examples, the edges of the surface not defined by end curves are straight lines.

The second standard approach to making boundary patches is to specify four boundary curves, one for each edge of the patch. This approach can yield surfaces with much more complicated curvatures, since none of the edges of the patch need be a straight line (Figure 2-67c).

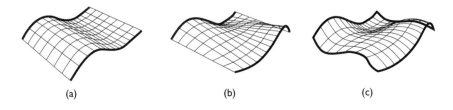

(a)   (b)   (c)

Figure 2-67. Boundary patches formed from either two or four boundary curves.

2.9 Hierarchies

Earlier in this chapter you learned how to move, rotate, and scale objects—that is, to "transform" them. All of the examples in that section dealt with individual objects in isolation from one another. You moved a sphere, you rotated a cube, and so on.

Most objects in the real world, however, and most models that you develop in a computer modeling system, are not that simple and cannot be thought of as single, undifferentiated objects. Many objects consist of several pieces, and models that consist of several parts can present problems when you try to transform them.

A table, for example, consists (at a minimum) of a top and four legs. Figure 2-68a shows a table in a side view, with only two of the legs visible. A cross marks the pivot point, or local origin, of each of the five elements—the top plus the four legs. Suppose you want to rotate the entire table around the Z axis. If you rotate the elements individually, each element rotates about its individual local origin, yielding the result on the right side of Figure 2-68a. Even though you rotate each of the elements the same number of degrees in the same direction, the placement of each element relative to the other elements changes because the local origins, or pivot points, are located at different points in space.

The same sort of thing happens if you try to scale all the elements of the table. Each element scales about its individual local origin, and as a result the legs and the top of the table are no longer positioned correctly relative to one another Figure 2-68b).

Clearly, in a situation like this you want to treat the entire table as a single, unified object. You want to rotate or scale the entire table and retain

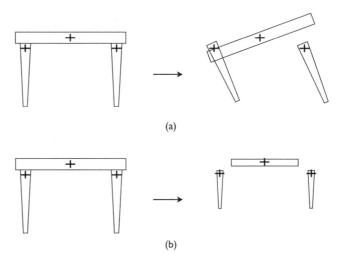

(a)

(b)

Figure 2-68. Transforming several objects around the individual pivot points of each object can cause problems.

the original relationships of the parts to one another. In order for this to happen, the entire table and all of the parts must transform about a single local origin.

At the same time however, since you may need to increase the length of the legs or change the thickness of the top, you still want to be able to operate on each of the elements individually, relative to its individual pivot point.

A possible solution to this problem involves relocating the local origins of all of the elements to exactly the same point—say, to (0,0,0)—which allows you to rotate all the elements of the table uniformly and in the proper orientation. Taking this approach, however, creates other problems. If you later want to adjust the size or shape of one of the elements, you have to return the local origin of that element to the original location. If you still later want to rotate the whole table a second time (as you surely will), you have to make sure that all the pivot points are back at (0,0,0). And so on.

This process becomes very cumbersome very quickly, especially if there are a lot of elements to your model. Imagine, for example, trying to use this approach on a model of an ornate eighteenth-century table. You would have to move, and then move back, and then move back again the pivot point of every piece of molding and every piece of filigree.

The solution is to organize your model into a hierarchical structure. This is called **hierarchical modeling**. In the case of the table, you define the whole table to be the top, or "master" level of the structure. You define the separate elements of the table to be the lower levels of the structure. The mathematics of hierarchical modeling is such that now you can operate on the model as you wish to; that is, you can control the transformations either as a group or individually. If you operate on the top level, you affect the entire table as a unit. If you operate on the lower levels, you affect only the individual elements at those levels.

Remember that when you define an object, it automatically has its own local coordinate system. A similar thing happens with each level of a hierarchical model. When you define the hierarchy for a model, each level of the hierarchy automatically has its own separate local coordinate system and a separate local origin. Transformations applied to each level of the hierarchy thus take place around the local origin of that level. For example, say you define the local origin of the top level of your table hierarchy to be on the floor between the legs. Any transformation to the whole table happens with respect to this local origin. Since you defined the top level to consist of all the various pieces of the table, all of these pieces transform as a unit with respect to this one point in space. Likewise, if you locate the local origin of each leg at the top of the leg (see Figure 2-68), when you operate on one of these lower-level objects, it transforms individually around that one point.

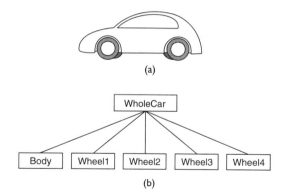

Figure 2-69. A hierarchical
model and a schematic
representation of that model.

To elaborate on this concept: suppose you model a car consisting of a body and four wheels (Figure 2-69a). Each of the four wheels and the body of the car, like any surface, has its own pivot point—that is, a local coordinate system and a local origin. Another way of saying this is that each element has a separate transformation matrix and can therefore be transformed individually as need be. Each of the five elements functions independently of the others. For example, the local origin of each of the wheels is located in the center of the wheel, allowing the wheel to be rotated around an imaginary axle. *Wheel1* rotates without causing any of the other wheels or the body to rotate, and so on.

All five of these elements, however, are grouped hierarchically into a higher-level element, in this case called *WholeCar*. This level has its own local coordinate system and local origin and is controlled by another, separate transformation matrix. Any transformation applied to the *WholeCar* level also affects the lower-level elements, since they are grouped logically within *WholeCar*. The transformations of *WholeCar* "propagate downward" to the lower-level objects. These transformations, however, are always relative to the local origin of *WholeCar*, so that if the entire car is picked up and translated, the wheels translate with it. A simple diagram, or **schematic representation**, makes clear this hierarchy of transformations (Figure 2-69b).

Within such a hierarchy, each element is often called a **node**, and in this instance there are six nodes: one node at the top level and five nodes at the next level down. A node hierarchically just below another node often is called a **child** of the higher node, just as the higher node often is called the **parent** of the lower, child node. *WholeCar*, therefore, is the parent node of the other five nodes. These nodes—*Body*, *Wheel1*, and so on—are children of *WholeCar*.

Suppose that the car is rolling down the road. You want the entire car to translate, and perhaps rotate a bit about Y, as it moves. At the same time, you want each of the four wheels to rotate about its own axis. The structure just diagrammed allows you to do this. To operate on a given wheel—say, *Wheel1*—you put a transformation into the transformation matrix of *Wheel1*

Figure 2-70. A schematic representation showing the presence or absence of geometry at each node of the hierarchy.

on the lower level. The rotation of *Wheel1* has no effect on any other node of the hierarchy, since *Wheel1* is not a parent of any other node. Next, to move the entire car, you transform the *WholeCar* level. Since this *WholeCar* level is a parent of the other nodes, any transformation you apply to it propagates downward and transforms the lower-level nodes as well. For example, if you translate *WholeCar* in X, the wheel and body nodes translate in X with it— that is, all the parts stick together, as they should.

Another possible representation of this same hierarchy of transformations includes some additional, potentially useful information (Figure 2-70). Not only does this diagram illustrate the fact that parent nodes encompass and affect lower-level child nodes; it also illustrates the fact that a given node may or may not include an actual surface. When this happens, the node is called a **null node**, or an **empty node**. Surfaces are often referred to generically as **geometry**, and in this representation an oval (and the abbreviation "geom") indicates the presence of geometry. A rectangle represents the presence of a transformation matrix.

Notice that the five lower-level nodes (*Body*, *Wheel1*, etc.) all consist of both a transformation matrix (a rectangle) and some geometry (an oval). The highest level, *WholeCar*, by contrast, consists of a transformation matrix but no geometry. *WholeCar* is a purely logical construct. There is no "shape" to *WholeCar*, no surface associated with *WholeCar*. *WholeCar* is a logical grouping of several subelements, the grouping accomplished by the definition of a transformation matrix that propagates effects downward to the lower levels of the hierarchy.

Another very common representation of transformation hierarchies is a textual representation, the syntax of which is derived from the *C* programming language, the language most commonly used for writing graphics programs. In this representation, the name of each node is enclosed within an opening and a closing **curly bracket** (Figure 2-71). The levels of a hierarchy are represented by the placement of a lower-level node within the brackets of a higher level node (Figure 2-72). (Indentation improves legibility, but is not necessary.)

Notice that the *WholeCar* node begins with an opening curly bracket, on the first line, and ends with a closing curly bracket, on the last line. Notice

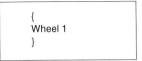

Figure 2-71. Each node of a hierarchy can be represented textually as enclosed within curly brackets.

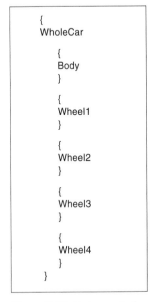

Figure 2-72. Placing a set of curly brackets inside another set indicates that the transformations of the outer set propagate downward to the inner node.

```
{
translate 22, 0, 0
rotate 0, 45, 0
scale 2,2,2
    {
    scale 0.7, 2.1, 1.8
    <geometry of Body>
    }

    {
    rotate 0, 0, 342
    <geometry of Wheel1>
    }

    {
    rotate 0, 0, 222
    <geometry of Wheel2>
    }

    {
    rotate 0, 0, 129
    <geometry of Wheel3>
    }

    {
    rotate 0, 0, -327
    <geometry of Wheel4>
    }

}
```

Figure 2-73. Specific transformations data can be included in the textual representation of the hierarchy.

Figure 2-74. Adding a plate to the stack "pushes" the stack down. Taking one off the stack "pops" the stack up.

also that each of the *Wheel* and *Body* nodes consists of an opening curly bracket, a node name, and a closing curly bracket, and that each of the nodes appears inside the *WholeCar* node. The fact that they are inside the *WholeCar* node indicates that they are influenced by whatever transformations are applied to *WholeCar*.

Such a textual representation becomes particularly useful when you want to see the specific numerical values associated with each transformation, or node (Figure 2-73). (Wherever you see *<geometry of . . . >* would be the actual geometric information defining that particular surface.) From these specific transformation values you can tell that each of the wheels has been rotated some amount around its local Z axis. The *Body* of the car has been scaled, within its local coordinate system, to the desired size. And finally, the *Whole-Car* (which, remember, itself has no geometry—only a transformation matrix) has a translation, a rotation, and a scale, all of which propagate downward through the hierarchy and affect all the lower levels, moving, rotating, and scaling them as a unit relative to the local coordinate system of *WholeCar*.

Representing the hierarchy and the transformations of the model in this way helps make clearer the propagation of the transformations from one level to another. The idea is that any transformation is still in effect as long as it has not been "stopped" by the closing curly bracket that signals the conclusion of that node. Thus, in this example, the translation, rotation, and scale transformations of the upper-level node, *WholeCar*, continue to be in effect (that is, they are propagating downward) all the way to the last line of the text, where they are stopped by the curly bracket that closes the upper-level node. In other words, the transformations on *WholeCar* affect all the subelements (lower-level nodes) of *WholeCar*—which is exactly what you want to happen.

By contrast, the scale transformation applied to the *Body* node (line six of the text) is stopped immediately after the geometry of *Body* (line seven) by the closing curly bracket of the *Body* node (line eight). Again, you want this to happen, because you don't want the scale transformation of *Body* to have any effect on the subsequent wheel nodes.

This starting and stopping of a transformation are referred to in computer science as, respectively, a **push** and a **pop**. The opening curly bracket "pushes"—puts into effect, turns on—the transformation. The closing curly bracket "pops"—turns off—the transformation.

The "push" and "pop" terminology derives from the image of plates stacked on a spring device such as you might find in a cafeteria (Figure 2-74). As you place plates onto the stack, the stack becomes heavier and the plates sink down, so that the topmost plate always stays at the same level, ready for the customer. If you place a plate on such a stack, the stack is *pushed* down. If you take a plate off the stack, the stack *pops* back up a little.

Pushing a plate onto the stack corresponds to turning on a transformation with an opening curly bracket. Popping a plate off the stack corresponds to turning off a transformation with a closing curly bracket. In fact, the term **transformation stack** often is used to indicate the collection of all the transformations currently in effect and how they propagate onto one another. Making even more explicit use of this stack imagery, systems sometimes substitute the words "push" and "pop" for "{" and "}" in the textual representation of a hierarchy of transformations (Figure 2-75).

The examples we have used so far in this section have been deliberately simple. A more complex example of hierarchical modeling is seen in Figure 2-76, with a diagram of its hierarchy in Figure 2-77. With the hierarchy illustrated here, we can operate on the entire machine by selecting and operating on the *All* node. We can independently operate on the *Cab* node, for example, making it rotate right or left. And, we can simultaneously manipulate the arm structure and rotate the wheels.

Notice especially in Figure 2-77 the hierarchical structure of the machine's arm, with each arm section a parent of the adjacent section. The section closest to the cab is at the top of the arm hierarchy. As you move up the arm physically, you move down the arm hierarchically.

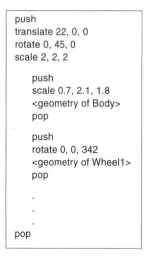

```
push
translate 22, 0, 0
rotate 0, 45, 0
scale 2, 2, 2

    push
    scale 0.7, 2.1, 1.8
    <geometry of Body>
    pop

    push
    rotate 0, 0, 342
    <geometry of Wheel1>
    pop
    .
    .
    .
pop
```

Figure 2-75. The "push"/"pop" terminology can replace the curly brackets to indicate the starting and ending of a transformation node.

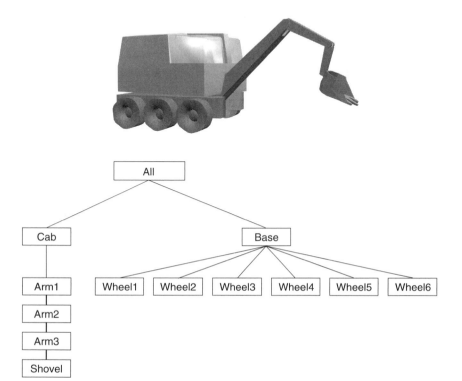

Figure 2-76. The elements of complex objects can be organized into a hierarchical structure.

Figure 2-77. A model's hierarchy can include a number of parent-children-grandchildren relationships.

In structuring the hierarchy of your model, it is important to understand that there is no "correct" way to do it. The hierarchical structure you choose depends on what you want to be able to do with your model—that is, on how you want your model to move. If it moves as needed, it is correct.

In Chapter 4 we will investigate the use of hierarchical structures as they apply to animated models. The hierarchical structure you choose depends on what you want to be able to do with your model; that is, on how you want your model to move.

2.10 Booleans and Trims

In the previous section you saw that it is possible to combine several simple objects into a single, more complex object by structuring the objects into a hierarchy. There are some situations, however, where this technique turns out to be limiting. Suppose, for example, that you want to combine a cylinder and a sphere to form a larger object (Figure 2-78a). If you do this by grouping the two objects hierarchically, the result remains *two* objects. That is, your single object is composed of two distinct pieces. They can be moved about as a unit, since they exist in a hierarchy, but they remain distinct. In Figure 2-78b, "Cylinder" and "Sphere" are grouped under "All" but each retains its own geometry.

Suppose, further, that having joined the two objects, you want to modify in some fashion the surface area where they meet, perhaps producing a smooth, rounded transition between the surfaces. This proves very difficult to do with the two-piece model, since the area where the two objects meet is actually two surfaces, not one. (Another problem might arise if you want to apply a single pattern of color continuously across the whole object as described in section 3.8.) Because you have two distinct objects this technique would not work.

For these and other reasons, sometimes you want to join several objects in various ways and produce a single piece of geometry—a single surface (Figure 2-79a). A **Boolean operation** allows you to do this. Notice that there is only one geometry element in the schematic diagram of this new configuration (Figure 2-79b). The shape of this geometry now includes, within the one geometric definition, both the hemispherical dome and the cylindrical base.

The term "Boolean" honors the British mathematician and logician George Boole, who developed much of the logic on which these operations are based. This logic deals with combining in various ways the contents of different sets, or collections, of things. When Boolean operations deal with spatially defined sets, as in computer graphics, they are also known as **spatial set operators**.

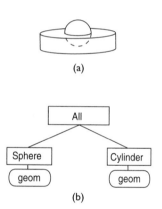

(a)

(b)

Figure 2-78. Combining two objects hierarchically means retaining the original two pieces of geometry.

(a)

(b)

Figure 2-79. Combining two objects with a Boolean operation results in a single, unified piece of geometry.

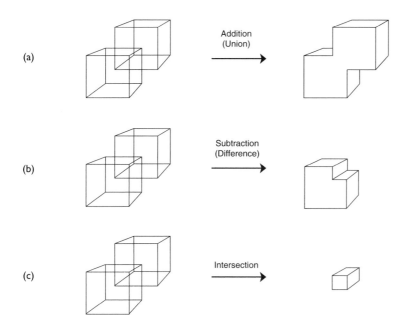

(a)

Addition
(Union)

(b)

Subtraction
(Difference)

(c)

Intersection

Figure 2-80. The three Boolean operations.

These operators, as they are applied to surface models, are actually derived from the Boolean operators used in solid-modeling systems, where they are often referred to collectively as **constructive solid geometry**, or CSG. When adapted for surface modelers, these operations lose some of the precision and exactness they have in the solid-modeling systems. Still, they remain very useful as surface-modeling tools and because of this are found in most high-level 3D animation systems.

There are three distinct Boolean operations. The first is the **addition**, or **union**, of two objects to form a third object. To the right of the two overlapping cubes in Figure 2-80a, for instance, is the result of a Boolean addition. Notice that the overlap—the volume that had been occupied by both of the cubes—has been modified so that only a single object occupies that space. This modified state, of course, corresponds to what happens in the real world, where two objects cannot occupy the same space. The fact that objects *can* do so in computer graphics is one of the great advantages of computer modeling. But if your modeling requires that you eliminate the unrealistic overlapping of two objects, a Boolean addition can do it for you.

The opposite of a Boolean addition is a Boolean **subtraction**, accomplished by the **difference operator**. As the name suggests, a Boolean subtraction takes away from an object the space occupied by another object. Notice, for example, that a piece of the lower cube in Figure 2-80b has been cut out where the upper cube had overlapped it. The upper cube acted, in effect, as a chisel to remove a portion of the lower cube.

There is a difference, however, between performing this Boolean subtraction and simply cutting a hole in the cube. Since the models here are defined by surfaces and are not solid models, cutting a hole in the cube results in an empty space through which something could pass into the lower cube. The Boolean subtraction, on the other hand, closes off this space with new surface area. This happens because the cutting cube, the upper cube, has surface area in that location.

The third Boolean operator is the **intersection operator**. Given two objects, such as the overlapping cubes in Figure 2-80c, the intersection operation finds those parts that are shared by both objects and produces a new object consisting of only those shared areas. In this case the intersection operation saves the space shared by the upper cube and the lower cube.

Among surface modelers, Boolean operators are found most commonly in polygon-based systems. This is because the surfaces that result from Boolean operations are frequently irregularly shaped—that is, they have an irregular topology. Recall from sections 2.2 and 2.3 that polygonal models can have arbitrary topologies, while spline-based patches must have a rectangular (UV) topology. Since polygons do not need to be organized into a UV directional system, an irregular shape such as the cylinder-sphere combination in Figure 2-79a presents no problem to a polygon-based modeler. The same combination does present a problem, however, to a UV-parameterized spline-based modeler.

One solution to this difficulty, presented by some software packages, is to convert all spline-based models to polygon-based models before performing any Boolean operation.

For those systems based solely on splines and patches, there is another—although more limited—solution. Such systems often provide a function, somewhat similar to the Boolean difference operator, usually referred to as **trimming**. This function consists of cutting some pattern into a surface patch.

Figure 2-81a shows a parameterized surface patch. Figure 2-81b shows this patch with a circular hole cut in it by a trim operation, while Figure 2-81c shows the patch with a jagged edge left from trimming. And Figure 2-81d shows the patch with two trim operations—that of (*b*) and that of (*c*)—performed on the same surface.

The first of two techniques for creating a trim on a patch is to draw a curve in space and project it onto the surface you want to be trimmed. Say, for instance, that you want a normal cylinder to be trimmed (Figure 2-82a).

Figure 2-81. Three examples of trimming a surface.

(a)   (b)   (c)   (d)

First you draw a curve, here indicated as a heavy black line. The arrows indicate the direction in which this line projects back in space along the Z axis. Notice that as the curved line projects back along Z, it intersects the cylinder, producing a new curve around the perimeter of the cylinder. This curve is called the **curve of intersection**. Once the curve of intersection has been calculated, the trim operation itself can be performed. The trim operation cuts the original cylinder along the curve of intersection, leaving only a portion of the original surface (Figure 2-82b).

The second method of performing a trim operation is to use two objects, inserting one object into the other in order to calculate the curve of intersection. In Figure 2-83a the surface to be trimmed is the cone. The sphere, placed so that it overlaps the cone, determines the shape of the curve of intersection. That is, the border where the sphere touches the cone marks the curve of intersection. The trim operation cuts the original surface, the cone, along the curve of intersection to produce a new surface—a cone with a hole cut in it (Figure 2-83b).

Although you use some of the same words to describe a trim operation and a Boolean difference operation, and although the results of each look somewhat similar, a trim operation is *not* the same as a Boolean subtraction. A trim operation (see Figure 2-83b) simply cuts a surface. It does not add geometry to a surface, whereas a Boolean subtraction (see Figure 2-81b) does generate new surface area. In the case of the trimmed cone, the hole is just a hole. Because there is no surface in that area, you could stick your hand through the hole into the interior of the cone. If you had cut the cone with a Boolean difference operation instead of a trim operation, you would have produced a surface where the sphere gouged out a portion of the cone.

This limitation of trimming is not insurmountable, however. To address it, you do two trim operations, the first of which is a trim of the cone by the sphere. The second operation is a trim of the sphere by the cone, and this trim produces the orange-peel-shaped surface. If you then hierarchically group this new surface with the surface of the cut cone, you produce a cone with the desired scalloped surface. Software packages that offer this possibility sometimes refer to it as a **Boolean trim**, or a **NURBS Boolean**. It is important to understand, however, that with trim operations like this you still have two surfaces, whereas a true Boolean operation yields a single surface.

(a)

(b)

Figure 2-82. A trim can be produced by projecting a curve through space to calculate a curve of intersection on the original object. The object is then trimmed along this curve.

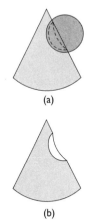

Figure 2-83. The curve of intersection can also be calculated from the intersection of two objects.

2.11 Basic Deformations

So far in this chapter we have presented basic techniques for creating models. It is also possible to change the shape of a model once you have created it using **deformation techniques**. In Chapters 4 and 7 we will discuss a

Figure 2-84. Moving a control vertex smoothly deforms a patch surface.

(a)   (b)

Figure 2-85. Moving a polygon vertex deforms the surface of the model within a more restricted area.

(a)   (b)

variety of these in detail as they apply to animation. Deformations can also be applied at the modeling stage, and we introduce a few basic approaches here.

Recall from our discussion of both polygonal models and patches that any surface is defined by the placement of it surface points. For a polygonal model, these are the vertices of the polygons; for a patch model, they are the control vertices of the patch. Recall also that if any of these points is moved, the shape of the object changes.

In Figure 2-84 we see a torus created as a NURBS patch, along with the structure of its CVs and the connecting hull. In (b), one of those CVs has been translated to the right, causing the shape of the torus to bulge in that direction. Remember that each CV of a patch model controls a certain area of the patch, so moving one point deforms that entire area in a smooth way.

Figure 2-85 shows a similar operation applied to a polygonal torus. Again, when one point is moved to the right, the torus deforms. Here, however, moving one polygon vertex causes a sharply creased deformation since that vertex affects only a restricted area of the surface. To get a smoother deformation of the polygon torus, you would have to move several points.

All surface deformations are based on this simple concept of moving the surface's points. Moving individual surface points can be effective, but it can also become tedious. In some circumstances, it might even be impossible to get the deformation you want. For example, to deform the polygonal torus in Figure 2-85 to have the same smooth deformation we see in Figure 2-84 would require calculating precisely where each of many vertices should be placed.

(a)   (b)   (c)   (d)   (e)

Figure 2-86. Several common shape deformations available in most 3D packages.

To address this problem, a great variety of shape deformation techniques have been developed to simplify the process of moving surface points. Instead of individually selecting and translating a myriad of points, you perform the deformation operation and adjust one or a handful of parameters. These, in turn, move the surface points for you.

One set of deformations found in most 3D packages operates on the entire model to easily change its shape in a few common ways. In Figure 2-86, you see an original, undeformed rectangular box in (a). In Figure 2-86b, this has been deformed with a **bend** deformation. In (c), it has been deformed with a **twist**. In (d), it has been deformed with a **taper**, also called a **flare**. And in (e), it has been deformed with a **sine wave** deformation.

All these deformation techniques allow the animator to simply and usually with one mouse stroke relocate the points that define the surface of an object. (This approach is discussed in more detail in section 4.9.) For a polygon model, these points are the polygon vertices of the surface. For a patch model, they are the control points of the surface. Since deformation techniques such as bending, twisting, and tapering operate on these points, any model that is going to be deformed in these ways must have enough points— either vertices or control points—to permit a smooth deformation. If there are too few points, the model will deform in undesirable ways (Figure 2-87). The cylinder in Figure 2-87a has only three horizontal rows of points. As a result, when it bends, it "creases," rather than bending smoothly. By contrast, the cylinder in Figure 2-87b has nine horizontal rows of points, which is enough to permit it to bend smoothly.

In using deformation techniques it is also important to carefully place the local origin, or pivot point, of the object. As you saw in the section on *Transformations,* the placement of the local origin affects the way an object transforms, since transformations are calculated with reference to that local origin. The same principle applies to the transformation of the points of an object; the placement of the local origin can radically affect the final result of a bend,

(a)   (b)

(c)   (d)

Figure 2-87. If a model has too few points defining its surface, it will not deform smoothly.

Figure 2-88. The placement of the object's local origin affects the way it will deform.

(a)   (b)   (c)   (d)

twist, or taper operation. An undeformed object is shown in Figure 2-88a. In Figure 2-88b, c, and d, the placement of the local origin is indicated by small crosshairs. Depending on the placement of the local origin, the cylinder bends in very different ways.

CHAPTER 3
Rendering Basics

3.1 Introduction

So far you have been reading about techniques for defining "geometry," or the data that describe the three-dimensional shape of an object. This process constitutes the modeling of an object and involves thinking and working spatially, in the round, in all three dimensions.

It is an irony of three-dimensional computer graphics, however, that when you sit at a computer graphics workstation and work three-dimensionally, you see on the screen a two-dimensional picture of your model. That is, the computer processes the three-dimensional data that define your model to produce flat, two-dimensional representations of the model. As you work, you react to these two-dimensional pictures.

The process of producing a two-dimensional picture from three-dimensional data is called **rendering**. The word is used here in the same way that an architect speaks of producing two-dimensional "renderings," or drawings, of an architectural design.

The simplest computer graphics rendering approach represents an object as if the object had no surfaces at all, but instead were composed only of wire-like edges (Figure 3-1a). **See-through wireframe** rendering, or simply **wireframe rendering**, is very easy and fast for a computer to calculate and therefore is part of all 3D computer animation systems. Because it is easy to calculate, wireframe rendering is fast enough to allow **real-time interaction** with the model, which means that at the same time that you manipulate a device, such as a mouse, a pen, or a joystick, the image on the screen changes.

The disadvantage of see-through wireframes, however, is precisely that they are transparent. Almost all of the objects you might be interested in modeling do, in fact, have surfaces, and the see-through wireframe cannot represent these surfaces. Moreover, wireframes of this sort can be ambiguous, in that sometimes it is difficult to tell which of the "wires" of an object are to the front of the object and which are to the rear.

A second rendering approach overcomes these limitations by taking into account the fact that an object has surfaces and that these surfaces hide, or occlude, the surfaces behind them (Figure 3-1b). In **hidden-line rendering**, the edges of the object are still represented as lines, but now some of these lines are hidden by the surfaces in front of them.

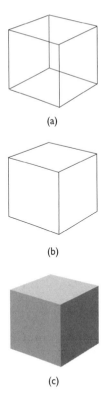

(a)

(b)

(c)

Figure 3-1. Three rendering approaches: see-through wireframe, hidden-line, and shaded rendering.

Hidden-line rendering is computationally more complicated than wire-frame rendering. In order to know which lines should be hidden, the system performs certain calculations to determine which surfaces are in front of other surfaces. As a result, hidden-line renderings take longer than see-through wireframe renderings, and may update more slowly on your screen. Another disadvantage is that while hidden-line renderings recognize the existence of surfaces, they tell you nothing about the character of those surfaces: the color of the surface, the shininess of the surface, and so on.

A third rendering approach overcomes even these limitations and is, predictably, still more complicated to compute and therefore slower to render. This approach provides information about various surface characteristics and about lighting and shading, and therefore is called **shaded-surface rendering**, **shaded rendering**, or—since it corresponds to the use of the word "rendering" outside of computer graphics—simply **rendering** (Figure 3-1c).

A number of hardware manufacturers have developed special-purpose **graphics cards** capable of producing simplified shaded-surface renderings in real time. When your workstation uses one of these cards, you can interactively rotate and move your model at the same time that you view it as a shaded rendering. You normally use this kind of equipment with high-end three-dimensional modeling and animation packages.

Very complex and higher-quality shaded renderings, however, may take a long time to compute. An extremely high-quality, very sophisticated rendering of a complicated model might take anywhere from a few minutes to more than an hour to calculate, depending on many factors, including the speed of your computer. The advantages of high-quality shaded rendering, however, clearly outweigh the disadvantages, and all 3D animation systems provide some means of producing such renderings.

In general terms, you can think of the process of producing a two-dimensional rendering of a three-dimensionally defined scene as involving six major components (Figure 3-2). The first of these, as you saw in chapter 1, is the geometry of the model, the three-dimensional shape of the model. The remaining components are the point of view from which you see the scene (also referred to as the "camera"); the lighting of the scene; the definition of the surface characteristics of the model; the specific approach, or algorithm, the system uses to calculate the shading on individual surfaces; and finally, the algorithm the system uses to render the whole picture, once the other information is complete.

Figure 3-2. Rendering can be thought of as consisting of six basic components.

Remember that even though for the sake of conceptual convenience we are considering modeling and rendering separately, in practice it is impossible to segregate these two tasks. Normally you develop the geometry to a certain point, then develop some of the rendering characteristics, then return to the geometry, then return to the rendering, and so on. The modeling and the rendering *together* produce the final model.

3.2 The Camera

When you look at a scene in the real world, what you see—that is, which portion of the scene and how much of that portion—is determined by your point of view. When you create a computer rendering of a three-dimensional scene, you first define the point of view from which the scene is to be observed.

A point of view consists of two factors: where you are standing, and where you are looking. Suppose the scene you want to render is your friend's house and the grounds around it. If you stand in front of the house and look at the dining room chandelier, you see one image (Figure 3-3a). If you stand behind the house and look at the same chandelier, you see a very different image (Figure 3-3b). This example is an illustration of changing the "where you are standing" factor, while keeping the "what you are looking at" factor the same.

Now reverse the situation and keep the "where you are standing" factor constant, but change the "what you are looking at" factor. In the first instance, you stand in front of the house and look at the dining room chandelier (Figure 3-4a). In the second instance, you stand in the same spot but look at the chimney (Figure 3-4b).

In computer graphics, the point of view is part of what is called the **camera**, or, to emphasize that it is not physical, the **virtual camera**. The definition of the camera incorporates both of the components of a point of view.

The first factor—where you are standing—usually is called the **camera location** or **eye location**. The location of the camera is a point in space and as such is specified as a triplet of XYZ coordinate values. You might say, for example, that your camera is located at (−10, 2.5, 17.6). Three-dimensional computer graphics systems allow you to specify this camera location either by typing in those number explicitly or, more commonly and more conveniently, by interactively positioning the eye/camera with some device, such as a mouse. As you move the location of the camera you view the scene as it appears from that vantage point, changing in real-time.

You can deal with the second factor—where you are looking—in either of two ways. The first way, used throughout this book, is to think of "where you are looking" as an actual point in space, as in "looking at the chandelier." This point in space is called the **center of interest** or **camera interest** and,

(a)

(b)

Figure 3-3. In these two views, the point at which you are looking remains the same, but the location of your eye changes.

(a)

(b)

Figure 3-4. Here, the location of your eye remains constant, but the point at which you are looking changes.

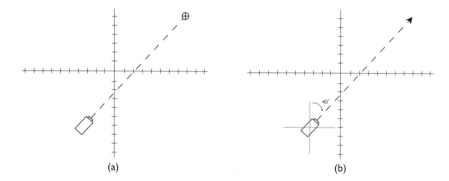

Figure 3-5. Two different methods of representing where the camera is looking: as a point in space, or as a rotation of the camera.

(a)   (b)

like the camera location, is specified as a triplet of XYZ coordinate values. You can change the center of interest in the same ways that you change the camera location: either by interactively repositioning the center, or by typing in numbers. (In Figure 3-5a, the rectangular icon represents the location of the camera—where you are standing. The circle with the cross hairs represents the camera's center of interest—where you are looking.)

A second, less common approach is to think of "where you are looking" in terms of rotation of the camera—in other words, pointing the camera in a certain direction. When you use this rotational approach, the system specifies the **camera direction** as a triplet of XYZ rotational values: *rotate (0,–40,0)*, for instance (Figure 3-5b).

If you stand in one spot and turn your head to the left or to the right or up or down, this is equivalent to keeping the camera location fixed and moving the center of interest. Such a **camera move** is called a **pan**, a term taken from the film industry. Figure 3-6a is a diagram of a camera pan as seen from above, while Figure 3-6b shows the two-dimensional renderings that might result from such a pan.

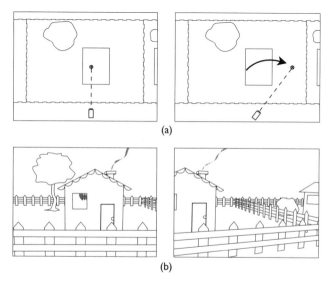

(a)

(b)

Figure 3-6. A camera pan.

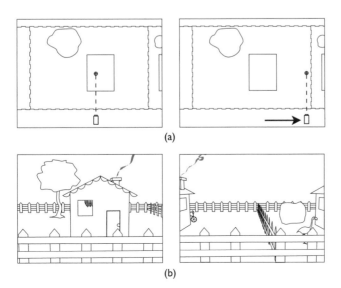

Figure 3-7. A camera tumble.

The opposite of a pan, called a **tumble** or **orbit**, keeps the center of interest stationary while moving the camera location. This corresponds to fixing your gaze on one point in space while walking around it. Figure 3-7a is a diagram of a tumble as seen from above, while Figure 3-7b shows the two-dimensional renderings that might result.

Another standard camera move, called a **track**, involves changing the camera location and the center of interest at the same time, as a unit (Figures 3-8a, 3-8b). Again the term comes from filmmaking, in which a "tracking shot" is often made by sliding a wheeled camera along a railroadlike track.

Figure 3-8. A camera track.

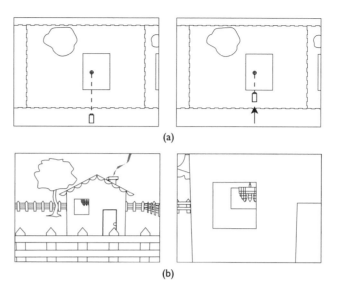

(a)

(b)

Figure 3-9. A camera dolly.

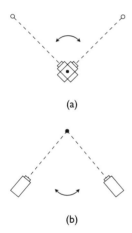

(a)

(b)

Figure 3-10. A pan and a tumble involve rotations of the camera around different pivot points.

If both the camera location and the center of interest are moved in or out—that is, along the Z axis—the movement is called a **dolly** (Figures 3-9a, 3-9b).

If a system uses the rotational approach rather than the center-of-interest approach to specify where the camera is looking, these same moves apply, but the moves are specified in terms of rotations of the camera. A pan is a rotation of the camera about an origin located at the camera location (Figure 3-10a). A tumble is a rotation of the camera about an origin located at the center of interest (Figure 3-10b).

Although the terminology used to describe these camera moves is largely taken from the film industry, occasionally a three-dimensional computer graphics system uses terminology taken from aviation. This is especially likely if the system was developed primarily for engineering applications. In such a system, **pitch** is a rotation of the camera around the X axis, **yaw** is a rotation of the camera around the Y axis, and **roll** is a rotation around the Z axis. The "rolling" of the camera around the Z axis is like what happens in aviation when a plane banks or, in extreme cases, turns upside down. In the more common center-of-interest approach, the same effect is called **tilt** and describes what happens when you tilt your head: the image you see changes. This is most noticeable when you tilt your head 180 degrees—that is, when you stand on your head. The image of the world you see is upside down. In Figure 3-11, all three renderings employ the same camera location and the same center of interest. Only the tilt of the camera varies.

If a system uses the rotational approach to defining the camera, tilt is specified automatically by the rotation around Z. If a system uses the center-of-interest approach, however, you need additional information to indicate how

(a)   (b)   (c)

Figure 3-11. A camera tilt.

the camera is tilted. One technique is simply to borrow from the rotational approach and specify the tilt as a separate rotational value. Another technique is to specify a point in space that indicates the **top** or **up direction** of the camera (corresponding to the top of your head). In Figure 3-12a the tip of the arrow icon, which is the "up" point for that camera, is directly above the camera and the camera is upright. In Figure 3-12b the up point has moved to the side, causing the camera to tilt correspondingly. Notice that the length of the arrow is not significant; the direction of the arrow controls the camera tilt. Placing the up point anywhere along the arrow has the same effect on the camera tilt.

All of these factors—the location of the camera, the point at which the camera is looking, and the tilt of the camera—constitute point of view, and as such become part of the definition of the virtual camera. Several additional factors, however, can be part of that definition.

One additional camera parameter, called simply **zoom**, simulates the effect of a zoom lens. In photography, changing the zoom on your camera has two effects. First, it makes objects appear closer or farther away. This effect is reflected in the terminology used, as in "zooming *in*" and "zooming *out*." It is important to understand, however, that a photographic zoom really does not involve any movement in or out of either the camera or the scene: zooming in only *magnifies* the image.

The second effect of a photographic zoom is to exaggerate the perspective with which you view a scene. Think of the classic example of converging railroad tracks as an example of perspective: you have "more perspective" where the convergence is greater and "less perspective" where the convergence is lesser. In this sense, a zoom-in creates more perspective and a zoom-out creates less perspective.

Both of these characteristics of the photographic zoom—the apparent increase in size of the objects, and the increase in perspective distortion—are replicated in computer graphics by the zoom parameter of the virtual camera. Figure 3-13a shows a scene as it would appear with a "normal" zoom, which approximates what your eyes see naturally. Figure 3-13b is the same scene zoomed in, as with a wide-angle photographic lens. Notice that the size and the perspective of the image have changed.

(0,3,0)

(a)

(1.75, 3, 0)

(b)

Figure 3-12. The tilt of a camera can be represented by an "up" point in space.

(a)   (b)

Figure 3-13. A camera zoom both magnifies and changes the perspective of an image.

(a)

(b)

(c)

Figure 3-14. Three renderings that illustrate the perspective distortions of zooming.

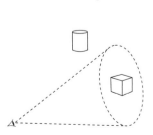

Figure 3-15. Objects that lie within the cone of vision are visible. Those that lie outside the cone of vision are not.

When working with the zoom parameter, however, you must remember what zoom really does and does not do. A zoom-in on a scene is not the same as a dolly into the scene. A dolly, as you saw above, involves translating the camera location into the scene along the Z direction. A zoom, on the other hand, involves no movement of the camera location. Because of this, the visual results of a zoom are quite different from the visual results of a dolly. These differences might be hard to detect when the changes in the zoom or dolly values are small. With larger changes, however, the differences become apparent. A zoom involves a change in perspective, while a dolly keeps the perspective the same at all times. A substantial zoom-in on a scene creates a noticeable distortion of perspective. Figure 3-14 shows a cube rendered three times, each time with a different zoom factor. (In order to isolate the effects on perspective, the magnification effect of the zoom has been counteracted with a simultaneous dolly-out.) In Figure 3-14a the camera has been zoomed out extremely far, producing a rendering with almost zero perspective—that is, an orthographic rendering. Figure 3-14b is a rendering with a normal zoom. Figure 3-14c is a rendering with an extreme zoom-in, which produces an extreme exaggeration of the perspective.

Whether a zoom or a dolly is the more appropriate camera move depends on the effect you want to achieve. If you intend to simulate a person walking through a scene, a dolly is appropriate, being an actual translation of the camera through the scene. If you intend to create the effect of someone focusing his or her attention on a detail of a scene, a zoom may be more appropriate.

As with other camera parameters, you can change the zoom either interactively with a mouse device, or by typing in numerical values. In order to understand the significance of the values used to define zoom, you must understand a bit about how a zoom is calculated in computer graphics.

When you look at the world around you, objects too far to the left or right or too far above or below you are not visible. They are outside the range of your peripheral vision, or your **field of view**. The human field of view (for each eye) can be thought of as a cone-shaped area, often called a **cone of vision** (Figure 3-15). Objects that lie within your cone of vision (such as the cube in this figure), are visible to you. Objects that lie outside your cone of vision (such as the cylinder) are not visible.

In computer graphics, the cone of vision becomes a **pyramid of vision**, in order to conform to the rectangular shape of computer monitor screens. One of the factors that determine the shape of this pyramid is the angle from top to bottom of the pyramid (Figure 3-16). Usually referred to in computer graphics as the **field-of-view angle** or simply the **field of view** or even more simply the **fov**, this angle is measured in degrees.

A change in the *fov* angle causes a change in zoom. A very large *fov* angle results in the same extreme perspective distortion as a wide-angle lens. A very narrow *fov* angle produces a "flattened" rendering with very little perspective distortion. The reasoning behind this relationship is that everything that the eye, or virtual camera, "sees" within the pyramid of vision must be distorted by perspective calculations so that it fits onto the rendered screen of the computer system. A large field of view produces a pyramid of vision that is very wide at the back. Since everything within the pyramid of vision, including those objects at the back of the pyramid, must fit onto the rendered screen, a more extreme perspective distortion is necessary for those pyramids that have wider backs.

When you view a scene, either through a photographic camera or with your eyes, some objects appear in focus and some appear out of focus. Rendering programs reproduce this effect through a parameter called **depth of field** (a term borrowed from photography). There are several methods for specifying depth of field. One method is to give two numbers: the first represents the nearest distance at which objects will be in focus, and the second represents the farthest distance at which they will be in focus. Another method is to specify the distance from the camera at which objects are in focus and to give an **f-stop** number. Here f-stop is used as it is in photography, with a smaller f-stop indicating a narrower range of in-focus area, and a larger f-stop indicating a broader range of in-focus area. An f-stop of 16, for example, would mean that objects relatively far from the perfect-focus point would still be in focus; an f-stop of 3 would mean that only objects quite close to that point would remain in focus.

Figure 3-17a is a schematic representation, as viewed from the top, of a camera and a scene. The dotted lines emanating from the camera icon represent the field of view of the camera. The parallel dotted lines within this field of view represent the near and far values of the depth of field. The shaded area between these two values is the area within which objects are in focus. In this example, the cylinder and cone are out of focus, since they lie outside of this area (Figure 3-17b). The cube, on the other hand, is in focus.

One last characteristic of the computer graphics camera has no direct parallel either in photography or human vision: when a program renders a scene, it must restrict that scene to a finite three-dimensional space. This is necessary because a program dealing with the infinite space of an endless Cartesian

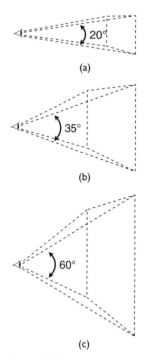

(a)

(b)

(c)

Figure 3-16. Increasing the field-of-view angle of the pyramid of vision produces a zoom-in.

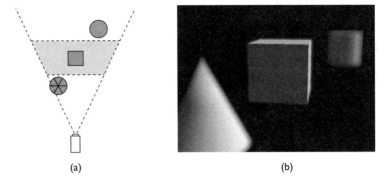

Figure 3-17. Depth of field can be specified, causing objects to be rendered in or out of focus.

(a)

(b)

coordinate system would continue rendering forever. That is, the program always would be looking at some new area of space to see if any objects within that space needed to be rendered. You can think of the limited world that a rendering program deals with as the "viewable" world.

The most basic restriction that a rendering program imposes in order to limit the viewable world is the restriction imposed by the four edges of the computer screen. The rendering program looks through this screen as if through a window, then deals with only that space viewable through the window.

Figure 3-18a is a diagram, as seen from above, of a modeled scene. The short dark line represents the screen on which this scene is rendered. Beyond the screen is the virtual camera. The dotted lines extending from the camera past the edges of the screen represent the field of view and demarcate the viewable world of the camera. Of the objects in the scene, only the cube lies within the viewable world of the camera, and so only the cube is rendered (Figure 3-18b). The sphere and the cone, which lie outside the viewable world, are not considered by the rendering program and are said to be **clipped**.

This example illustrates how the viewable world is clipped on the right, left, top, and bottom. But what about the space extending in the Z direction? If this space is not also limited in some way, the rendering program could, in

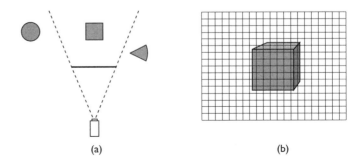

Figure 3-18. The viewable world of the virtual camera is clipped by the edges of the screen.

(a)

(b)

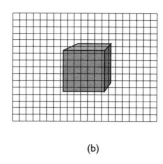

(a)   (b)

Figure 3-19. The viewable world is also clipped in the Z direction by the near and far clipping planes.

theory, look forever through this space to see if there were any other objects—a million miles away and beyond—that should be rendered.

To handle this situation, computer graphics programs include an invisible vertical plane, called the **far clipping plane**, beyond which nothing is renderable. Objects farther away than the far clipping plane, like objects that lie beyond the edges of the screen, are clipped. In the same way, a **near clipping plane** prevents objects closer than the near clipping plane from being considered by the rendering program.

In Figure 3-19a the screen is represented as a heavy horizontal line. The two thinner horizontal lines represent the near and far Z clipping planes. The shaded area between these lines is the space viewable by the camera. The cube is "seen" by the camera and is rendered (Figure 3-19b). The cylinder, however, lies beyond the far Z clipping plane and therefore is not viewed by the camera, even though the cylinder lies within the viewable pyramid created by the edges of the screen. The pyramidal volume of space created by the clipping from the edges of the screen has been truncated at both front and back by the Z clipping planes. Any object that lies outside this truncated pyramid is clipped, not rendered, by the rendering program.

This concept of a truncated pyramid is important. If you combine the clipping of the viewable world by the edges of the screen and the clipping of the same world by the near and far clipping planes, you end up with a viewable world in the shape of a pyramid with its top and bottom cut off (Figure 3-20). This volume is called the **viewing frustum**, and in any given scene only those objects that lie within the viewing frustum are renderable.

Notice also that the near clipping plane need not coincide with the placement of the screen. In Figure 3-19, for example, the near clipping plane is slightly farther away from the camera than is the screen itself. Most high-end software packages allow you to position the near and far clipping planes wherever you want, either interactively with a mouse device or by typing in numbers to indicate the depths of the planes.

A curious effect of Z clipping planes is that an object straddling one of the Z clipping planes appears to be sliced in half, because only the portion of the

Figure 3-20. The combination of all the clipping planes produces a viewing frustum. Only objects lying within the viewing frustum are visible.

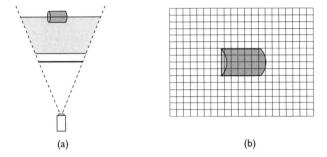

Figure 3-21. If an object straddles one of the clipping planes, part of it will be visible and part of it will be invisible.

(a)   (b)

object inside the viewable space is visible. In Figure 3-21a the solid parallel lines represent the near and far clipping planes, and the shaded area is the viewable volume between them. Notice that the cylinder sitting atop the far clipping plane is partially rendered, the front half lying within the viewable area and therefore visible, the rear portion lying beyond the far clipping plane and therefore invisible (Figure 3-21b).

3.3 Lights

In an environment where there is no light at all—for example, a windowless room, with the lights turned off—you can see nothing. The rendering of a three-dimensional computer graphics scene is similar. In order to "see"—that is, to render—a scene or any objects within that scene, you must define lights.

When defining lights with a 3D software package, you define many of the characteristics that lights possess in the real world. The first of these is **location**, which you usually specify either by positioning the light interactively with a mouse device or by typing in values (that is, a triplet of XYZ coordinates) with the keyboard. Placing a light at *(0,0,0)*, for example, locates the light at the center of the world. Placing it at *(9,4,0)* locates it to the right and up a bit.

Another parameter to be defined for all lights is **intensity**, which you usually specify as a range of numbers. The higher the number, the brighter the light. For example, if the range is 0.0 to 1.0, then an intensity value of 1.0 produces an extremely bright light, a value of 0.5 produces a moderately bright light, and a value of 0.0 turns the light off.

You usually specify a third parameter, the **color** of the light, as three numbers, one for each of the three primary colors of the standard computer graphics color system: red, green, and blue. These are referred to as **RGB**, for short. The most common method of defining RGB values is to use numbers ranging from 0 to 255, with 0 being no color and 255 being full color. Intermediate numbers produce colors that lie between these two extremes. For example, RGB = (0,0,0) describes pure black—no red, no green, and no blue.

RGB = (255,255,255) is pure white; RGB = (255,0,0) pure red; RGB = (0,255,0) pure green; and so on. RGB = (150,23,192) produces a purplish color composed primarily of red and blue.

Sometimes a software system combines the specifications for color and intensity into one parameter, asking you to indicate both color and intensity in one RGB triplet. In this case, the magnitude of the numbers indicates the intensity, while the ratio of these numbers to one another indicates the color. Thus, Light = (255,0,0) is a very bright, pure red light, while Light = (128,0,0), the red component of which has been decreased by half, is a pure red light of only half the intensity. Similarly, Light = (255,255,255) is a very bright white light, while Light = (70,70,70), also a white light (because all the color components are equal), is rather dim.

In addition to determining the location, the intensity, and the color of a light, you also must think about the type of light. In the real world, there are many different types of light, such as fluorescent light, incandescent light (the glow of standard light bulbs), daylight, and candlelight. Most 3D computer systems offer a range of light types that attempt to simulate the different types of real light.

The most common type of light in computer graphics systems, a **point light**, simulates the effect of a bare light bulb hanging from a wire. Located at a specific point in space, it radiates light equally in all directions: up, down, and to the sides (Figure 3-22a).

In addition to location, color, and intensity parameters, point lights often have another parameter associated with them. Intended to simulate the fact that the light from a light bulb does not travel forever, but fades with distance, this parameter often is called **decay** or **falloff**. A decay value of zero means that there is no decay—the light continues forever at the same intensity (a very unrealistic situation). The larger the decay value, the more quickly the light fades as it moves away from the point light.

Unlike a real light bulb, however, a point light does not have any size or any shape. In other words, it has no geometry. It is formless. In a computer graphics rendering you normally do not see a point light. You only see the effects the point light has on objects in the scene (Figure 3-22b).

Even though a point light has no geometry and does not render as an object, most 3D systems allow you to treat the point light as a **logical object**, also sometimes called a **node**. This means that you can select it, delete it, move it, and even, if you choose, group it hierarchically with other objects. In order to allow you to do this, most systems provide some iconic representation of the light (see Figure 3-22a).

Hierarchically grouping a light becomes especially important if you want to have an actual light-bulb model in your scene. In order to do this, you first model the geometry of the bulb, perhaps using a surface of revolution. Next,

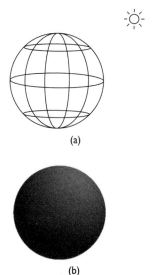

(a)

(b)

Figure 3-22. A point light emits light equally in all directions.

(a)

(b)

Figure 3-23. The spread of the cone of a spotlight can be adjusted.

you define a point light to be located at the center of this geometry—that is, inside the bulb. Finally, to make sure that the bulb geometry and the point light stay together, you hierarchically group them. In this way, if you move the bulb geometry, the light within the bulb moves with it.

Like the point light, a second common type of light is located at a specific point in space and has intensity, color, and decay parameters. You specify these parameters in the same ways that you specify them for a point light. In addition to these parameters, however, a **spotlight** has several additional parameters, which simulate the effect of a spotlight in the physical world. For instance, a spotlight throws light in a cone-shaped beam, and this cone of light can vary in width. In computer graphics a parameter, usually called **spread**, or **cone angle**, controls the width of the cone. The spread of a spotlight is the measure of the angle between the opposite sides of the cone. An angle of 30 degrees, for example, produces a rather narrow cone of light (Figure 3-23a). An angle of 80 degrees produces a much broader cone (Figure 3-23b). Objects that lie outside of the cone do not receive any of the light from the spotlight.

A spotlight also throws light in a certain **direction**, and in some systems a line or an arrow emanating from the spotlight icon indicates this direction. In most systems the same cone that indicates the spread indicates the direction. You change the direction by rotating the spotlight. As the spotlight rotates, the directional arrow or cone points this way or that way, clearly indicating which way the light will fall. Some systems allow you to control the spotlight's direction by positioning an **aim point**, a point at which the spotlight is aimed (Figure 3-24). For example, by moving the aim point left or right, you rotate the spotlight left or right.

Just as you do not see an actual point light in a scene, however (see Figure 3-22b), you do not see a spotlight nor its cone of light (Figure 3-25a). You see only the *effect* of that light on objects (Figure 3-25b). This makes sense within the artificial world of 3D computer graphics, in which the only things that are rendered, and therefore the only things that are visible, are surfaces. In the real world, you see a cone of light in the air because the light from the

Figure 3-24. You can aim a spotlight by moving its aim point.

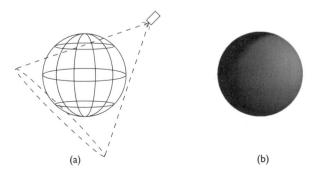

Figure 3-25. Anything outside the cone of the spot light is not illuminated.

(a)

(b)

spotlight hits the surfaces of thousands of tiny dust particles that float in the air. If you do not model any such surfaces in a computer scene, you typically cannot see the cone of light as it passes through the air. It is possible, however, to render this sort of effect by using special techniques that simulate the presence of the myriad tiny surfaces that constitute a real-world atmosphere. Several of these techniques are discussed in section 6.2.

Figure 3-26. The light from a spotlight fades in two directions and is controlled by two parameters.

You have seen that point lights fade with distance, and that decay parameters control this sort of fading. Spotlights also fade in this way and also normally have decay parameters. However, spotlights fade in another way as well. In the real world, the intensity of light fades not only with distance from the light source, but also with distance from the center of the light cone. That is, the intensity of the light decreases from the center of the light cone to the edges of the light cone. The parameter that controls this effect is often called **dropoff** (Figure 3-26). The larger the dropoff value, the more quickly the light fades toward the outer edges of the light cone. A dropoff value of zero produces no such fading. A dropoff value of zero would have produced a hard-edged demarcation between the dark and light portions of the sphere in Figure 3-25b, for instance. Instead, a dropoff value greater than zero produced a gradual change from dark to light and a certain fuzziness.

Yet another type of light provided by some 3D systems simulates the effect of an entire area, rather than a single point, emitting light. Two examples of this type of lighting are the banks of fluorescent lights in the ceilings of some offices, and the screens of television sets. Whereas the light from a spotlight begins at a point and emanates in a conical beam (Figure 3-27a), the light from an **area light** begins at a rectangular area and emanates in a rectangular beam (Figure 3-27b).

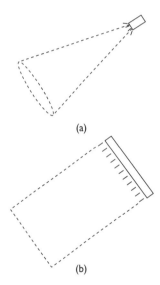

Figure 3-27. An area light emits a rectangular area of light.

The lights presented so far—point, spot, and area—are readily comprehensible to us, but calculating the effects of each light represents a different level of complexity for the computer. That is, it takes more time for a rendering program to calculate the effect of an area light than it takes to calculate the effect of a spotlight. And it takes more time to calculate the effect of a spotlight than to calculate the effect of a point light. Therefore, when you choose a light, consider the impact on rendering time of the different types of light. This becomes especially important when you render a large number of frames for animation, since any increase in rendering time is multiplied by the number of frames to be rendered. Often, a little experimentation with simpler light models can produce a result that looks as good as, but renders much faster than, a more computationally complex set of lights.

Another type of light, called **ambient light**, simulates the overall amount of daylight (or lack of daylight) in the world around you. An ambient light does not emanate from a specific location in space, nor does it flow in a specific direction. It is simply an overall level of light, present everywhere in the

(a)

(b)

(c)

Figure 3-28. Ambient light is the overall level of lighting in a scene. It comes from no specific direction or location.

environment. Consequently, when defining an ambient light, you specify only the intensity parameter and the color parameter. You might use a low-intensity purplish light, for example, to simulate twilight, or a high-intensity white light to simulate full daylight.

In reality, of course, no light, including daylight, behaves like this. The sun has a location, and sunlight arrives on Earth from a specific direction. The ambient light of computer graphics is a convenient abstraction, an easy way to alter the overall level of lighting in a scene.

The artificial, directionless quality of ambient light has a curious result. If the only light in a virtual 3D computer graphics environment is ambient light, all sides of all objects are lit equally, since the ambient light is present equally everywhere. A sphere, for example, rather than being darker on one side or the other, is lit equally on all sides and thus appears as a disk (Figure 3-28a). By itself, therefore, ambient light cannot provide a realistic rendering of a three-dimensional situation. Instead of using it in isolation, you must use ambient light in conjunction with other lights, of whatever different types you choose. Combining a point light and ambient light, for example, produces a very reasonable rendering (Figure 3-28b). Increasing the intensity of ambient light, while keeping a point light as is, increases the overall light and makes an object in the environment lighter (Figure 3-28c).

Infinite light, sometimes called **directional light**, is considered to be located infinitely far away (simulating, in effect, the great distance of the Sun). In this it resembles ambient light, which has no location. However, an infinite light, unlike an ambient light, has directionality, in that it moves from right to left, or from upper left to lower right, and so on. In this, it more accurately simulates sunlight, which comes from a certain direction. However, unlike other lights—such as spotlights and area lights—that also have directionality but that throw light within only circumscribed regions, an infinite light throws equal amounts of light everywhere. The light comes from a specific direction, but it comes from that direction equally throughout the scene.

On the computer screen an arrow icon often indicates an infinite light. The location of the arrow is insignificant. Only the direction of the arrow—that is, the angle of the arrow—matters. In Figure 3-29, the heavy arrow is the icon for the infinite light. In addition, a number of lighter arrows indicate that this infinite light projects down equally throughout the entire scene from the indicated direction. Thus, all objects within the scene—the sphere as well as the cylinder—receive equal amounts of light, and this light arrives at the same angle on all the objects.

One advantage of infinite lights is that it is very easy to get a reasonable (though not subtle) rendering with only a single infinite light. For this reason, many systems define an infinite light as the default lighting environment.

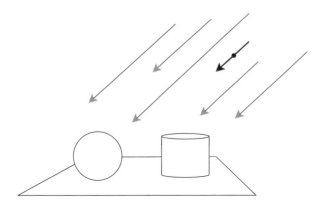

Figure 3-29. Directional light throws light equally throughout the scene from a given direction.

Another advantage is that it is very easy and not very time-consuming for the computer to calculate the effects of an infinite light.

Another type of light offered by some software packages is a **volume light**. The light cast by a volume light is restricted to a clearly defined volume of space, defined as one of several possible geometric forms. Figure 3-30 illustrates four of the most common volume shapes for volume lights. Illumination cast by the volume light illustrated in (a) is restricted to a spherical volume of space. The illumination of (b) is restricted to a cubic volume of space, that of (c) to a conical volume, and that of (d) to a cylindrical volume.

Volume lights are an extension of the basic concept of a three-dimensional light already discussed in this section. Since all lights in 3D computer graphics cast their light in a fully three-dimensional space, all lights effectively create volumes of lights. This is most obvious, perhaps, when we speak of the "cone of light" of a spotlight. What distinguishes volume lights, however, is that they make use of a very clearly and unequivocally delineated volume. A spotlight, for example, creates a cone of light, but its light might be cast infinitely far, creating an unending cone, if you will. Similarly, a point light emits its light equally in all directions and therefore can be thought of as emitting its light in a spherical pattern, but its light does not necessarily end abruptly at the edge of a specific sphere.

Figure 3-30. The light cast by a volume light is restricted to a clearly defined volume of space.

Figure 3-31. Only objects lying within the light's volume receive illumination from it.

Figure 3-32. Some software systems permit a light to be rendered with a glow effect. (Courtesy, Dongho Kim.)

Figure 3-33. The light in this scene has been given a very intense glow factor. In addition, the angle of the camera and the location of the light produce a lens flare.

The clear delineation of a volume light's volume is one reason for its usefulness. Any objects that lie outside the volume of the light's illumination will not receive any light at all from the volume light. This provides a convenient way to limit the effect of a light within a scene. In Figure 3-31, for example, the table and vase lie within the light's cubic volume and are therefore illuminated. The other objects in the scene, however, receive no light at all from the volume light. In section 6.2, you will see how some volume lights can also be used to render fog.

In the earlier discussion of spotlights, you saw that the cone of a spotlight is not visible. A similar problem arises when a light glows. A candle flame, for example, has a distinct glow around it. In order to address this situation, most software packages include a **glow** parameter. In Figure 3-32, for example, a point light has been placed at the tip of the wick. This light illuminates the models in the scene—that is, the candlestick and the wick. The glow parameter of this point light has been adjusted to create the luminous effect. How intense the glow is, how far the glow spreads, and even what shape the glow is can be controlled. These controls are separate from the intensity or decay of the point light itself. The light proper may have an intensity of 3.0, while the glow has an intensity of 2.5. If the glow intensity is turned down to 0.0, no glow is visible, but the point light of intensity 3.0 still illuminates objects in the scene.

Another specialized lighting effect, available in advanced systems, enables you to simulate the **lens flare** that sometimes occurs on the lens of a camera facing directly into a light. If the camera points toward a light whose lens flare parameter has been turned on, a "hot spot" of light will be rendered (Figure 3-33).

So far, you have considered lighting objects that are rendered in isolation, a deliberate simplification. In most scenes, however, there are many objects to be rendered, and this raises the distinction between "shading" and "cast shadows."

Shading is the effect of light on the surface of an object as the surface goes from lighter to darker. When one portion of a sphere is darker because the portion faces away from the light, this portion is shaded. If there are several objects in a scene, however, the situation can become more complex, in that each object not only is shaded but might also create **cast shadows** on other objects. All objects in a scene have shading, but not all objects necessarily have cast shadows.

The calculation of shading is fairly straightforward and is provided automatically by all 3D computer graphics systems. Cast shadows, however, are more time-consuming to calculate, and consequently most systems provide this capability as an option that you may turn on or off. The most common way to turn shadowcasting on or off is through a parameter associated with each light. When you define any type of light, you specify whether or not this particular light casts shadows. The reason you make this choice on a per-light basis, rather than globally for all lights, is that often the look you are after can be achieved by having only one or two lights casting shadows. This situation is much less complicated mathematically, and therefore faster for the rendering program to calculate, than if you were to turn on shadow casting for all the lights in the scene.

Most programs offer two methods of calculating cast shadows. One uses a **raytracing** algorithm (see section 3.6 for a more complete discussion of raytracing). This method calculates the movement of light beams as they bounce from object to object in the scene, or even as they pass through transparent objects. The raytracing approach to casting shadows produces very accurate shadows, but can be quite time-consuming and may slow down your renderings considerably.

(a)

An alternative method for calculating cast shadows is to use a **shadow depth map**. Here the software begins by calculating what the world looks like from the point of view of the shadow-casting light. Information about which objects are in front of which other objects is stored, pixel by pixel, in an internal image called a **depth map** (for a more detailed explanation of this technique, see the description of Z-buffering in section 3.5). Since most 3D software systems use the Z axis to represent the depth of a scene, this internal image is also called a Z **map**. Such an image is illustrated in Figure 3-34b. Figure 3-34a shows the scene as viewed normally from the camera. Notice the spotlight icon in the upper right. Figure 3-34b shows the depth information of the scene as it is viewed from the shadow-casting spotlight. In this depthmap image, objects that are farther away from the spotlight are represented as lighter, while objects which are closer to it are darker.

(b)

Figure 3-34. A shadow map uses a Z depth representation of the scene as viewed from the shadow-casting light.

Once the Z depth information has been calculated, the software then uses it to calculate how objects that are closer to the light project backwards onto objects that are more distant. The projection of each object backward becomes the shadow it casts onto those behind it.

The shadow depth map approach to shadow casting can be much faster than raytracing. However, it is also less accurate. In order to refine its accuracy, most software packages allow you to adjust the resolution of the preliminary Z map image that is produced. The higher the resolution, the more accurate the shadow calculations. Of course, the higher the resolution, the slower the rendering, as well.

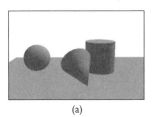
(a)

Cast shadows add a substantial degree of realism to a scene. They also can be crucial in conveying information about the three-dimensional placement of objects. Notice, for example, that in Figure 3-35a, with shadow casting turned off, you cannot tell that the sphere is hovering just above the large, flat surface. In Figure 3-35b, with shadow casting turned on, you can tell that the sphere is hovering by the way its shadow is cast onto that surface.

(b)

Figure 3-35. Cast shadows can lend an important degree of realism.

Figure 3-36. Lighting and shadows can be used to great emotional effect. (Courtesy, Seung Hye Choi)

In addition to adding realism to a scene, cast shadows can generate a powerful emotional effect when used carefully. In Figure 3-36 the exaggerated shadows cast on the floor and wall create an air of hyperreality that works to great effect with the dreamlike modeling of the scene.

An alternative technique that can nicely simulate cast shadows is **projector lights**. Projector lights function like a standard home slide projector—that is, they project light through an image. With a computer graphics projector light, however, the image is a picture file that you tell the software to use. The software then does its calculations as if that image were placed in front of the light, with the light shining through it. The result is that the image is cast, or projected, into the scene and onto any objects in its path (Figure 3-37).

The image that you project can be a full-color image, in which case the projection of that image onto the scene will also be full-color. However, one of the most useful applications of projector lights is the creation of cast shadows through the use of a black and white grayscale image rather than a color image (Figure 3-38). Figure 3-38a shows a black and white image of tree branches, the image to be projected. In Figure 3-38b this image has been projected by a spotlight through a rectangular window into a room, creating the illusion of a tree's shadow on the objects in the room. This technique is a much more economical way to create a complex shadowing effect than

Figure 3-37. A projector light shines light through a picture, projecting the picture onto the objects in its path.

modeling a tree and casting shadows from the tree model onto the floor. The projector-light technique not only allows you to avoid modeling the tree altogether; it also significantly reduces the rendering time for this scene, since projected images are much faster to calculate than true cast shadows. Notice, however, that it is only possible to employ the projector-light technique here because the tree itself is not visible in the scene. If the shadow casting objects are visible in the scene, as they were in the image in Figure 3-36, the use of a projector light would not be possible, or would be far less effective.

Color plate 8 shows another, very sophisticated example of a projector light. Here, rather than simulating cast shadows, the projector light projects an image proper—the film image shown playing on the movie screen. The image is, in fact, just one frame of a live-action film that was digitized and projected, frame by frame, through the projector light, giving the effect of a movie within the animation.

To give you additional control over the lighting of a scene, 3D computer systems provide the option to have a given light either affect or not affect a given surface. This, of course, does not correspond to what happens in the real world, in which a light that is turned on affects all surfaces that are close enough to it. In computer graphics, however, it is possible to create an artificial situation in which, for example, a spotlight over a table affects the table and the book on the table, but not the pencil lying on the book. This technique often is called **light linking** or **light association**. In the example just given, the spotlight is linked to the table and the book, but not to the pencil. Lights linked to specific objects are sometimes said to be **exclusive** or **selective** lights. Lights not linked to any specific objects are assumed to affect all objects.

(a)

(b)

Figure 3-38. A projector light can be used to easily simulate complex cast shadows.

The technique of linking lights to specific objects becomes especially useful when you have your lighting worked out for an entire scene, but one object (for example, the pencil) doesn't look quite right. If you did not have light linking, the addition or subtraction of a light to improve the lighting on the pencil would disrupt the otherwise perfect lighting on the rest of the scene. By making use of light linking, restricting the effect of the light to the objects that need it, you avoid having the new light affect the rest of the scene.

Like so much of three-dimensional computer graphics, lighting is very simple in concept but extremely subtle in practice. Most scenes require the placement and careful definition of anywhere from a few lights of various types to up to ten or twelve lights. That this work calls for a great deal of skill and, sometimes, patience should not surprise you. Think about the art forms of still photography and cinematography, in which setting up the lights for a shot is crucial, time-consuming, and highly demanding. In film making, it is common to have a specialist devoted to lighting, and to spend an hour setting up and fine-tuning the lights for a shot, which then may take only a few minutes, or even seconds, to shoot.

It is not difficult to explain to someone the basic techniques of applying paint to a canvas. It is another matter entirely for that person to paint a masterpiece. Lighting a virtual 3D computer scene can be similarly demanding. It can also be stunningly effective, and the time and patience you devote to it extremely rewarding.

3.4 Surface Characteristics

The next major element needed to produce a rendering of a scene is the definition of the surface characteristics, such as color and shininess, of the objects in the scene. These surface characteristics are treated as a conglomerate, with the grouping of characteristics of a particular surface called a **shader**, or sometimes a **material**. A shader for a given surface includes the definition of the color for that surface, the definition of the shininess of that surface, and so on.

One benefit of organizing a group of surface characteristics into a shader is that you then can save this shader independently of the surface for which you originally designed it. Later, when you work on another model, you can select the saved shader and assign it, with all of the defined characteristics, to a new surface. Both the original surface and the new surface will have exactly the same set of characteristics.

Doing this with a number of shaders, you can create an entire **shader library**. You can call up at any time any of the shaders saved into this library,

Figure 3-39. Slider bars can be used to define surface parameters.

and either assign that shader to a new model, or edit it to produce a variation on the original shader.

When you define the properties of a given surface, you normally think first of the **color** of that surface, and you normally do so in terms of the three primary colors of the RGB color system—that is, red, green, and blue, described earlier in section 3.3. Most systems allow you to use the RGB system to define the color of your surface in some convenient, interactive way, such as by manipulating a **slider bar** for each of the color components (Figure 3-39). As you drag (usually with a mouse device) the "button" of the slider bar for a particular color, you increase or decrease the amount of that color component in the final color. The final color is updated and displayed at the same time, so you can see at each moment what the current color is. This technique allows you very precisely and easily to define a color without having to think in numerical terms.

Sometimes, of course, it is more convenient to think in terms of the actual numerical values that compose an RGB color. Consequently, almost all systems allow you to type in those numbers, usually using a range of 0 to 255 for each color component.

You can also define the color of a surface according to a different color system. This color system, known as **HSL**, uses three different variables—hue, saturation, and luminance—to define a color. You specify hue, saturation, and luminance values in the same ways that you specify the red, green, and blue values of the RGB system—either interactively (for example, with a slider) or by typing in numerical values.

Hue is the "color" of the color, in the sense that one red may be a purer red than another. A pure red contains only one hue, while an off-red contains several hues. Related colors—for example, crimson and vermilion—are related because they are close in hue.

Saturation is the amount of the hue in a color. A very saturated red will be brilliant. A "desaturated" red will be dull. As saturation increases, colors tend to take on a kind of neon look. As saturation decreases, colors tend to approach gray. A fully desaturated color, in fact, *is* a tone of gray.

Luminance is the brightness of a color. A color of a given hue and a given saturation can be made lighter or darker by changing the luminance.

In addition to determining the color of a surface, you must define the way that light bounces, or reflects, off the surface. You usually define this phe-

(a)

(b)

Figure 3-40. The diffuse component of a surface controls how much light bounces off a surface—that is, the overall tendency to brightness of that surface.

(a)

(b)

Figure 3-41. Specularity controls how shiny an object is.

(a)

(b)

Figure 3-42. Highlight size can be used to fine-tune the surface definition of a shiny object.

nomenon through a combination of several parameters, the first of which is **diffuseness**, the measure of how much light reflects, overall, from a surface. A surface with a small diffuse component will be darker (Figure 3-40a), because it reflects less light, than a surface with a large diffuse component (Figure 3-40b), even if both surfaces are defined to have exactly the same color and are lit by exactly the same lighting. You usually specify diffuseness, often with a slider bar, as a number between zero and one. A value of zero means that no light reflects off the surface, and the surface renders as black. A higher value means that more light reflects off the surface.

Diffuseness controls the overall brightness of the surface, but does not produce highlights on the surface. The word *diffuse* here means equally, in all directions. A highlight is produced because a lot of light is reflecting in a specific direction. If you activate only the diffuseness parameter, the surfaces you generate will be perfectly matte—without any highlights—like a piece of cardboard.

To create highlights, you activate several other parameters. The first of these controls how shiny the surface is, and is called **specularity**. To say that a surface is very specular means that it has very bright highlights. For instance, metallic surfaces, shiny plastic surfaces, and soap bubbles have high specularity, while unfinished wood, paper, and cloth have low specularity. You define specularity in conjunction with diffuseness, first supplying a diffuse value to control the overall brightness of the surface, then supplying a specular value to control the brightness of the highlights. You specify the value for specularity in the same way that you specify the value for diffuseness.

The sphere in Figure 3-41a has a somewhat low specular component of 0.2, for example, while the sphere in Figure 3-41b has a higher specular component of 0.6. Both spheres have exactly the same diffuse component and are rendered with exactly the same lights, but the higher specular component of the sphere in Figure 3-40b produces the much brighter highlight on that sphere.

Many systems provide additional control over highlights with a second parameter, called **highlight size**. At first, it might not be obvious why you need this. It might seem that if you want to make a surface shiny, you just increase the brightness of the highlight with the specular component. However, different materials produce highlights of different sizes. A highlight on a very shiny chrome surface is not only very bright but also very condensed—that is, small and focused (Figure 3-42a). A highlight on extremely shiny plastic, on the other hand, while also very bright, is broader and less focused (Figure 3-42b). Using both the highlight size parameter and the specularity parameter, you can define surfaces that closely resemble specific materials.

Again, it might not be obvious why you need yet another parameter for defining highlights, but different materials actually have slightly different **highlight colors**. Plastic of any color, for example, tends to reflect a white highlight. Aluminum, on the other hand, tends to reflect a highlight of the same color as the color of the aluminum. To specify highlight color, you usually use the standard RGB slider.

These last three parameters—specularity, highlight size, and highlight color—all help to define the shininess of a surface. Shiny surfaces, in addition to having highlights, however, also tend to be reflective, that is, the environment around them may be visible on them. An extreme example of this effect is a mirror.

(a)

(b)

Not all shiny surfaces are equally reflective. For instance, an extremely shiny plastic is less reflective than an equally shiny stainless steel, which is largely why you perceive stainless steel as stainless steel and not as silver-colored plastic. Some systems provide a parameter called, appropriately enough, **reflectivity**, to control this condition. As with the other surface parameters, you usually specify reflectivity as a value ranging from zero to one, with zero being a surface that does not reflect the environment at all and one being a perfectly reflective mirror. Thus, in Figure 3-43a the tabletop on which the bowl sits has no reflectivity. In Figure 3-43b the tabletop is slightly reflective. In Figure 3-43c the tabletop has a very high reflectivity value.

A surface also can be either opaque or transparent, and a **transparency** parameter allows you to control this characteristic. In most software systems, you again use numbers from zero to one, with zero creating no transparency at all—that is, complete opacity. A shower curtain might have a low transparency value, for example, making it slightly (and discreetly) transparent, while a wine glass would have a high transparency value. When using transparency, beware of making an object 100 percent transparent—it will be totally invisible!

(c)

Figure 3-43. A surface can be defined as more or less reflective.

When you define a surface to be transparent, the color of that surface is rendered by combining the color of the transparent object with the color of whatever is behind the object (Figure 3-44). In some rendering situations, there is nothing behind the transparent object—only a black background. In this case, the effect of transparency is to combine the color of the transparent object with the black of the background, producing a rendering of the object that simply looks darker, not more transparent. Transparency is most effective, in other words, when there are other modeled objects or a background of various colors behind the transparent object. It is least effective when the background is of some uniform color.

Another unexpected result of transparency can be a decrease in the effect of any highlights you have defined. In fact, an object that displays a clearly visible highlight when opaque may have no highlight at all when rendered as

(a)

(b)

(c)

Figure 3-44. The refractive index controls how light bends as it passes through a transparent object.

transparent. This is because the highlight, as well as the normal surface color, blends with whatever color is behind the object. Often you can solve this problem by substantially increasing the specularity parameter for the transparent surfaces.

Another surface characteristic addresses how light bends as it passes from one material to another. A classic example of this phenomenon is the straw that appears to bend as it enters water in a glass. This phenomenon, **refractivity**, cannot be rendered with all rendering algorithms, as we will see in section 3.6, but raytracing programs (discussed in that section) provide a refractive index parameter.

Physicists have determined experimentally the refractive index values for materials in the real world, and rendering programs that make use of refractivity also use these values. Air, for example, has a refractive index of one. Refractive indices other than one cause light to bend and therefore create distortions as you look through the material in question. Indices larger than one bend the light one way, and indices less than one bend light the opposite way. If you model a transparent sphere and give it a refractive index of one, light will not bend as it enters that surface, because both the air and the sphere have the same refractive indices (Figure 3-44b). If the sphere has a refractive index slightly less than one (Figure 3-44a), or slightly more than one (Figure 3-44c), the light will bend.

Most surfaces in the world absorb and reflect light, but only a few surfaces emit light. A light bulb is one example. To better render light-emitting surfaces, some systems provide a parameter called **incandescence**. This parameter, usually specified with a number from zero to one, adds a certain amount of brightness to the original color of the surface. The larger the incandescence value, the more brightness is added and the more the surface appears to glow. Note that incandescence is a different quality than the "glow" effect discussed in the previous section, however. Incandescence applies to surfaces, while glow effects apply to lights, which are not surfaces.

The upcoming sections on texture mapping present many more techniques for defining the characteristics of a surface, but in this section you have seen the most essential surface characteristics. Understand, however, that in defining a given shader you do not necessarily define all of the parameters discussed here. Many shaders can be defined very effectively with only a handful of parameters. It is, in fact, to your advantage to keep your shader definitions as simple as possible while still achieving the desired look, because each additional parameter increases the time required by the rendering program to calculate the final picture.

Another reason for being conservative in your use of shader parameters is that people tend, simply because it is so easy to do and creates such stunning effects, to use lots (or all) of the shader parameters much (or all) of the time.

This results in trite computer graphics images. To paraphrase a remark Ernest Hemingway made about writing, "The difficult thing is not knowing what to render, but knowing what not to render."

3.5 Shading Algorithms

In our discussion of rendering so far, we have investigated how the camera, lighting, and surface characteristics affect the final rendered image (refer to Figure 3-2 for an overview of the rendering process). The next question is how this information is used by the software to produce the rendered darks and lights, or **shading**, of a given surface. There are several approaches to this task. In computer science, a well-thought-out, logical procedure for doing something is referred to as an **algorithm**; one devoted to the calculation of shading on a surface is a **shading algorithm**, or sometimes a **shading model**.

All shading algorithms represent simplifications of what happens in the real world, where the complexity of lighting and shading is enormous. In order to render these effects, any algorithm must make assumptions that allow it to manage the otherwise overwhelming complexity of the process. The closer the assumptions are to the real-world situation, the more natural the renderings look. However, the closer the assumptions are to the real-world situation, the longer the rendering process takes.

One such simplifying assumption is that any flat surface is the same color at every point on the surface. This is not normally true in the physical world, where a flat surface might be darker at one end than at another. Rendering each flat surface with only one color gives objects a faceted look (Figure 3-45), and therefore the approach that makes this assumption is known as **faceted shading**. Faceted shading results in very fast renderings and was one of the first shading algorithms to be implemented in 3D packages. It is still useful in certain situations, especially illustration-style renderings.

The concept of faceted shading introduces another concept important to all shading algorithms. In order to calculate the color of a given surface, any shading algorithm must know whether the surface it is about to render faces or does not face the light, because the surface will be darker or lighter depending on its orientation. If, for example, a surface faces in exactly the opposite direction from the light, it receives no light and appears a very dark shade of whatever color it is. If the surface faces slightly toward the light, it receives some light and appears a lighter shade. If it faces the light directly, the surface receives a great deal of light and appears an extremely light shade.

In order to measure the direction a surface faces, computer graphics programs employ a concept called **surface normals**. A surface normal is a line (or, more specifically, a **vector**—a line with both length and direction)

(a)

(b)

Figure 3-45. Examples of faceted shading. Each face of the cube (a) has been rendered with a single color. In the polygonal approximation of a sphere (b), each polygon has been rendered with a single color.

Figure 3-46. The surface normal indicates the orientation of each surface, which in turn affects the brightness of the surface.

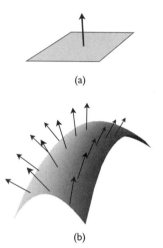

(a)

(b)

Figure 3-47. Representing the direction of a flat surface requires only one surface normal. Representing the directions of a curved surface requires many normals.

perpendicular to a surface at a given point on that surface. A surface normal is usually represented as an arrow coming off the surface. For a flat surface, a single surface normal suffices to indicate the orientation of the entire surface, since all points on a given flat surface face in the same direction.

With the information provided by surface normals, a rendering program can compute the exact angle at which a surface is oriented toward the light. In Figure 3-46, for example, several flat surfaces are connected, and a surface normal appears on each of them. Those surfaces that face most directly toward the light—that is, on which the normals point most toward the light—are brightest. Those surfaces that face farthest from the light, as indicated by the direction of the surface normals, are darkest.

Although all points on a flat surface face in the same direction (Figure 3-47a), a curved surface is more complicated (Figure 3-47b). Many normals are necessary in order to describe the orientation of a curved surface, because each point on the surface faces in a different direction. In fact, a curved surface has infinitely many different surface normals because it has infinitely many points on its variably curved surface. Because a flat surface can be accurately represented with far fewer surface normals than a curved surface, many 3D software packages that use truly curved, spline-based patch geometry actually convert curved surfaces into polygonal approximations just before rendering. By converting a curved surface into a polygonal approximation of a curved surface, the calculation is simplified.

Part of this process, called **triangulation**, subdivides curved surfaces into triangular polygons. Triangles are used because a triangular polygon is necessarily flat. Polygons of more than three vertices may or may not be flat.

Polygonal approximations, however, can present a problem. If the polygons are rendered with faceted shading, the actual shape of the polygons is apparent. This is not a problem if you want to see the shape of the polygons, as you do, for example, with a cube. But if the surface you are rendering is smoothly curved, you probably want it to *look* smoothly curved, not faceted.

Several shading algorithms have been developed for rendering polygonal surfaces so that they look smooth. As a group, these are referred to as **smooth-shading** algorithms. All of them make use of one critical observation, which is that the surface normals for a smoothly curved surface change gradually over the length of the surface (Figure 3-48a). By contrast, the normals of faceted surfaces change abruptly from one flat surface to the next (Figure 3-48b).

Figure 3-48. The normals of a truly curved surface change much more gradually than the normals of a polygonal approximation of that surface.

(a)   (b)

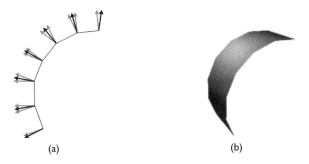

(a)   (b)

Figure 3-49. The Gouraud-shading technique artificially adjusts the normals of polygons to create the appearance of a curved surface.

One of the earliest smooth-shading algorithms to be developed is **Gouraud shading**, named after Henri Gouraud, who invented it. Gouraud shading creates a smooth look on a polygonally approximated surface by artificially adjusting the surface normals of the polygons. First, the algorithm positions a normal at each corner, or vertex, of each polygon. This normal is, as it should be, perpendicular to the surface of the polyon. Figure 3-49a, for example, shows a side view of the same polygonally approximated curved surface you saw in Figure 3-46. At each vertex where two polygons touch, two surface normals—one for each of the two polygons involved—are drawn as gray arrows. Each of these is perpendicular to the corresponding surface.

The Gouraud algorithm then calculates an average of the normals at a given vertex. This new, averaged normal is drawn as a black arrow in Figure 3-49a. Notice that the averaged normals look more like the gradually changing normals of a curved surface than like the abruptly changing normals of a faceted surface.

Finally, the Gouraud algorithm calculates the color at each vertex, based on the averaged surface normal at that vertex. Once all of these corner colors have been calculated, the colors between vertices are calculated by interpolating from one corner color to another.

Notice, in the rendered version of the polygonally approximated surface (Figure 3-49b), that the Gouraud technique produces a smooth progression of the color along the surface. Even though the surface is made up of flat polygons, you see it as being smoothly curved. Notice also, however, that the underlying polygonal structure of the surface is still apparent at the edges of the surface. If the polygons are large enough, you see flat edges from certain angles, even though the interior of the model looks smooth.

A critical issue for all shading algorithms is highlights. If light hitting a surface bounces off equally in all directions, as in Figure 3-50a, the surface is said to be **diffuse** because the light bounces diffusely—that is, spreads out. If a surface is 100 percent diffuse, it has no highlights at all, and is therefore sometimes also called **matte**. By contrast, if the material of a surface causes the light to bounce off only in one, concentrated direction (Figure 3-50), we see a highlight, and the surface is **specular**, meaning "mirror-like."

(a)

(b)

Figure 3-50. On a surface without highlights, light bounces off diffusely. On a surface with highlights, the light bounces off in a concentrated way.

(a)

(b)

Figure 3-51. A Lambert surface has no highlights.

Figure 3-52. Gouraud and Phong shading compared.

(a)

(b)

Figure 3-53. On some specular surfaces, the light bounces off in a very concentrated way; on others, it bounces with very slight diffusion.

Lambert shading, named after the physicist who developed the mathematics behind it, is the most commonly used algorithm for diffuse surfaces (Figure 3-51). Because it assumes there are no highlights, it is relatively fast. Be aware, however, that this assumption means it is 100 percent impossible to get highlights with Lambert shading.

The Gouraud shading algorithm we discussed earlier, on the other hand, does handle highlights. While not as simple as faceted shading or Lambert shading, it is still very fast, and is therefore usually implemented as one of the smooth-shading algorithms available on real-time graphics cards.

But Gouraud shading has its limitations. Most serious, the technique of interpolating one vertex color to another sometimes makes the seams between polygons visible (Figure 3-52a). A seam is most apparent when it is near a bright highlight.

In order to overcome this limitation, a technique called **Phong shading** was developed. Named after Bui Tuong Phong, who invented it, Phong shading averages surface normals at each polygon vertex, just as Gouraud shading does. However, instead of interpolating the colors between these vertices, Phong shading adds another step, calculating interpolated surface normals between vertices. From those interpolated surface normals it then calculates the colors of the surface. This approach yields a more accurate calculation of the colors, a more accurate rendering of the highlight, and invisible seams along the edges of the polygons (Figure 3-52b). Because it involves extra calculations, Phong shading is slower to render than Gouraud, but is still fast enough to be renderable in real time on today's graphics cards.

The Phong algorithm has its own limitations, however. Notice in Figure 3-52b that the brightness at the edges of the highlight drops off abruptly, creating a sharply delineated highlight. Phong shading makes the assumption that the surface at any given point is perfectly smooth. This results in the light bouncing off that point in a very concentrated way, as we see in Figure 3-53a. For many glossy plastics and metallic surfaces, this works well. However, some materials, such as aluminum, have softer, less concentrated highlights. This is because, at a microscopic level, their surfaces are *not* perfectly smooth, and light bounces off in a slightly diffused way (Figure 3-53b).

If an object's surface has sufficiently large microscopic irregularities, light hitting the surface bounces among them before leaving the surface, slightly

(a)   (b)   (c)

Figure 3-54. The slight microscopic irregularities of a surface can cause a very slight diffusion of light as it bounces off a surface.

diffused, toward our eye (Figure 3-54). The **Blinn shading** algorithm, named for its developer, Jim Blinn, handles this situation by performing extra calculations to account for the light's bouncing among the microscopic surface crags. The parameter allowing you to control the diffusion of the highlight is usually called **eccentricity**, meaning the degree of deviation from the center.

Figure 3-55 shows a comparison of Phong shading (a) and Blinn shading (b). By turning up the eccentricity on the Blinn surface, an extremely soft highlight was produced.

A surface with a pattern of grooves or shallow gouges presents another shading problem, for its highlights tend to follow the pattern of the grooves. Examples of such surfaces include a plastic CD, metals that have been brushed in noticeable patterns, and certain fabrics, such as satin. The patterned highlights created on these surfaces change depending on your point of view. Since an object that looks the same from every direction is called *isotropic*, these surfaces are called *anisotropic*, meaning not isotropic. An **anisotropic shading** algorithm performs special calculations to account for such grooved surfaces. Figure 3-56a shows a flat disk rendered with a Blinn shader, while the disk in (b) is rendered using exactly the same light but with an anisotropic shader, creating highlights in a noticeable pattern and making it look like a CD. An **angle** parameter allows you to adjust the orientation of the highlights. In our example, animating the angle parameter from 0 to 360 would cause the highlights to rotate around the disk.

Figure 3-55. Phong shading produces more sharply delineated highlights. Blinn shading can produce softer, more diffused highlights.

(a)

(b)

3.6 Rendering Algorithms

In the previous section, we discussed several approaches, or algorithms, for rendering the light and dark shading on individual objects. We now turn our attention to algorithms that handle the rendering of entire scenes. These **rendering algorithms** make use of the shading algorithms discussed in the previous section, but each rendering algorithm does so in a different manner.

The goal of any rendering algorithm is to calculate the color of every pixel of the digital image, and so the first task of any algorithm is to decide the **pixel order**, the sequence in which the pixels will be considered. There are two common approaches to this: the first is **scan-line rendering**. Each row

(a)

(b)

Figure 3-56. The anisotropic surface in (b) has highlights that follow the patterns of grooves on the surface. Anisotropic highlights change depending on your point of view.

Figure 3-57. Scan-line rendering steps through the pixels of an image pixel-by-pixel and scan-line-by-scan-line.

Figure 3-58. The quadtree approach recursively breaks the image down into smaller and smaller quadrants.

Figure 3-59. The raycasting algorithm casts a single ray through each pixel. If the ray strikes a surface, the color of the surface is calculated and assigned to the pixel.

of a picture's pixels is a **scan line**. Scan-line rendering means that the program looks at each pixel, one after the other, scan line by scan line, and calculates the color that pixel should be rendered.

One telltale sign of this methodical, scan-line-by-scan-line approach is that a partially completed picture consists of some lines that have been rendered (usually from the top down), and some that remain unrendered (Figure 3-57).

Other rendering programs determine pixel order by repeatedly subdividing the image space into four quadrants. This second approach, **quadtree rendering**, decides whether or not to subdivide the image depending on the amount of detail in that section of the image. If the software concludes, based on internal settings, that a given quadrant has too much detail, it subdivides that quadrant into four smaller quadrants. This process repeats **recursively** (see section 6-3 for a discussion of recursion) until the software decides it can render that area. Each rectangular segment of the image is then rendered in turn (Figure 3-58).

Once it has decided the pixel order, the rendering algorithm must now determine what color each pixel should be. One common approach to answering this question is a process called called **raycasting**. From the point of view of the camera, which is also referred to as the "eye," a ray is cast through the first pixel of the screen, as if the eye were looking through a tiny, pixel-sized window into the three-dimensional world on the other side of the screen. The eye then follows the ray until the ray either hits the surface of an object or exits from the viewable world. (Exactly what constitutes the viewable world was discussed in section 3.2.) If the ray hits an object, the program calculates the color of the object at the point where it has been hit. This color becomes the color of the pixel through which the ray had been cast. Having completed the calculation for the first pixel, the raycasting algorithm then moves on to the second pixel and goes through the same steps. The algorithm steps through all of the pixels of the image in the same fashion, casting a ray through each one and calculating the color of the pixel.

In Figure 3-59 each pixel has one ray cast through it. (The illustration shows only four of those rays, for the sake of simplicity.) The topmost and

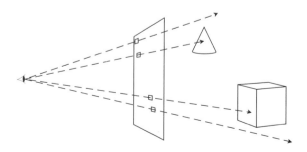

bottom-most rays hit nothing when cast, so the pixels through which those rays were cast have no color. The two middle rays hit surfaces, so the pixels are colored, each with the color of the surface at the point hit by the ray. Exactly what color the surface should be at that point is determined by the combination of all those factors we discussed in earlier sections of this chapter—the camera, the lighting, the surface characteristics, and the shading algorithm.

What happens if several objects, one behind the other, are in the path of the ray? How does the rendering program know which of these objects is the one to be rendered? How does it know which objects are in front of, and which are obscured by, other objects?

One approach to this problem is to sort all the objects by depth before rendering begins, so that the rendering program then can start rendering those objects that are farthest away. Once rendered, each new object covers up distant objects that already have been rendered. This procedure resembles the way a painter might complete the background of a scene before painting the apple in front of it. In fact, the technique of presorting objects by depth so that the objects rendered last are the objects closest to the eye is often called the **painter's algorithm**.

To presort by depth can be very time-consuming, though, particularly when a scene involves a large number of objects. Not only does each of these objects have to be sorted by depth, but each polygon of each object has to be sorted by depth! An alternative, and very common, solution to this problem is known as the **Z-buffer algorithm**.

When a computer graphics picture is rendered, the digital information for the picture is stored in a large block of memory called a **frame buffer**, which organizes the color information for the picture on a pixel-by-pixel basis. The Z-buffer algorithm makes use of a similar block of memory, called a **Z-buffer**. Like the frame buffer, this area organizes information on a pixel-by-pixel basis. Here, however, the information being stored is not the color of a surface but rather the distance of the surface from the eye. If a point on the surface is far away, the Z-buffer stores a large number. If a point on the surface is close, the Z-buffer stores a small number.

The Z-buffer algorithm renders objects in any order, without presorting them according to depth. When a ray is cast through a pixel, that ray might hit any one of several objects that lie in its path. Since the objects are not presorted by depth, the ray could hit an object in the back of the scene before hitting an object in the front of the scene. No matter the order of the encounters, as the ray hits each object, the depth in Z of that object is calculated and stored in the Z-buffer, at the Z-buffer pixel corresponding to the pixel through which the ray was cast. For example, if a ray cast through pixel one of scan line one hits some object, the depth value of that object is stored in pixel one, scan line one of the Z-buffer.

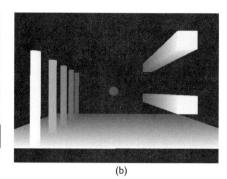

Figure 3-60. A Z-buffer stores depth information for a scene by storing a number at each pixel. The brightness of the pixel corresponds to the depth of the surface.

(a)   (b)

When the same ray encounters a second object, the depth in Z of that object is calculated and compared to what is already in the Z-buffer. If the new value is less than (that is, closer than) the old value, it overwrites the older, more distant value in that pixel. By comparing the Z values of the different objects at each Z-buffer pixel in this way, the rendering program can determine at every pixel which objects are in front of which other objects.

The depth information written into a Z-buffer normally is not viewed as a picture, but it can, in fact, be displayed as such. Figure 3-60a shows the normal rendering of a scene. Figure 3-60b shows the Z-buffer image of that same scene. Notice that the numbers assigned to distant objects became dark pixels in the Z-buffer image, and the numbers assigned to closer objects became bright pixels. The result of displaying such a Z-buffer image is a gray-scale image in which near objects appear brighter and distant objects appear darker.

The Z-buffer algorithm is very powerful and very commonly used in 3D rendering programs. Graphic accelerator cards often incorporate Z-buffering into their hardware so that depth sorting can be done in real time. But the approach is also very flexible, in that Z-buffer information can be used in a number of ways besides depth sorting for standard rendering. It can also be used to calculate cast shadows, as discussed in in section 3.3, to produce mattes for compositing (see section 8.2), and to produce maps for such techniques as bump mapping (see section 3.8).

All the algorithms you have seen so far, even though they address different aspects of the rendering process (depth sorting, shading, etc.), fall within the general category of raycasting algorithms. Raycasting can produce very sophisticated renderings, as you can see, for example, in color plates 10 and 2, both of which were rendered with raycasting. A great many of the illustrations in this book were rendered with raycasting.

All raycasting algorithms, however, have one fundamental limitation: they deal with the shading of each object in the scene as if it existed in isolation, as if there were no other objects in the scene. Even in the case of depth sorting, once it has been determined which object is closest to the eye, the more distant objects do not have an effect on the object being rendered.

As a result, creating reflections becomes a problem, since reflections involve the reflection of *other* objects onto one object. Another problem is cast shadows. In order to take into account a shadow being cast on an object, you must know of the existence of another object in a position to cast a shadow. And a third problematic issue is transparency, which involves looking through one object and seeing some other object or objects behind it.

You can address these problems through various raycasting "tricks": simulating reflections through environmental reflection mapping (see *Solid Texture Mapping* later in this chapter), generating shadows through a clever use of the information stored in Z-buffers, simulating transparency by rendering several objects into one pixel and combining the colors of the different objects. Researchers have developed all of these techniques to the point that they are quite effective and usually very easy to use. But the fundamental problem remains that the raycasting technique does not in and of itself produce these visual effects in a physically accurate way, because it concerns itself with only one object at a time.

A different category of rendering algorithm, called **raytracing**, addresses this fundamental weakness by dealing with all of the objects in a scene simultaneously. When you look at a specific point on a surface, the color at that point is being affected not only by the light falling from the light source onto that particular surface, but also by the light bouncing onto it from nearby surfaces—or perhaps even, if the object is transparent, by the light traveling through other objects in the scene. In other words, every point on a surface is affected not merely by one light ray, but by many light rays hitting it from many different parts of the scene. If you are to get an accurate rendering of that surface point, you need to trace these different rays back to their sources to see what contributions they are making to the final color of the surface.

Figure 3-61 shows the tracing of a ray that might be needed to render a single pixel. As with the raycasting technique, a ray is projected from the eye through the pixel and into the scene. The ray hits a first surface, the cylinder. Because the cylinder has been defined as somewhat reflective, the ray

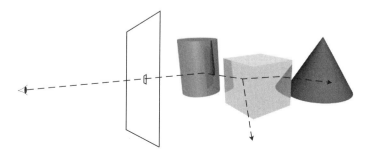

Figure 3-61. The raytracing algorithm traces a light ray back as it bounces off objects in the scene.

bounces off the cylinder and hits the cube, which has been defined as partially reflective and partially transparent. This contact generates two ray paths. Because the cube is partially reflective, one ray bounces off the cube and travels toward the bottom of the picture. In this simple example, the ray travels without hitting anything until it disappears off the edge of the world. Meanwhile, because the cube is partially transparent, a portion of the light coming from the cylinder passes through the cube and changes direction slightly, as light does when it passes through objects. When this ray emerges from the cube, it changes direction again and continues until it hits the cone. Since the cone has been defined as 100 percent matte, with no reflection, the ray stops traveling when it hits the cone.

In order to calculate the color of the cylinder at the point where the ray first hit it, you begin by calculating the color of the cube at the point indicated, since light bounces from the cube to the cylinder. But in order to calculate the color of the cube at the point indicated, you need to know the color of the cone, since light from the cone passes through the transparent cube and contributes to the color of the cube. You also need to know the color of the space around the cube, since one of the rays hitting the cube has come from the empty space around the scene. In short, in order to calculate the one point on the surface of the cylinder that you are interested in, you first must calculate the color of the cone, then the color of the background space, then the color of the cube.

The examples given here, though very simplified, illustrate both the complexity and the power of raytracing. A much more complex rendering technique than raycasting, raytracing requires the calculation of many surfaces in order to arrive at the final calculation for a single surface point. For each pixel, you have to trace many rays, and consider many contributing surfaces. As you might expect, all these extra calculations take time, and raytracing can be much slower than raycasting.

Consider the result, however. Because the calculation of each surface point takes into consideration all the different surfaces in the scene, the effects of all those surfaces show up in the final rendering. Cast shadows, reflections, and transparency are all automatically calculated by the raytracing technique. Notice the reflections throughout the scene in color plate 2, for example, especially on the salt and pepper shaker. Notice also the shadows cast by the different objects onto the table. Finally, notice the bending, or refraction, of light as it passes through the transparent water in the glass, causing the flower stems to distort.

Another striking example of raytracing can be seen in color plate 20 in which virtually every surface is somewhat reflective.

In a complex scene with a great many objects, raytracing can become immensely complex. If you continue tracing the path of a ray in such a scene, the ray can go on bouncing off and through hundreds of objects, creating a tree of ray paths so complex as to be impractical to render. In fact, a ray in this situation could, in principle, continue bouncing forever, in which case your rendering would never finish! Consequently, most raytracing programs ask you to define the maximum number of bounces that each ray should be followed. This is called the **depth** of the raytracing. The larger the depth number, the more accurate, but also the more time-consuming the rendering. If the depth is zero—that is, if no bounces are followed—the ray tracer becomes effectively the same as a ray caster.

Some software systems expand on this concept of tracing depth by providing several depth parameters to control different aspects of the rendering. For example, there might be a parameter to control how many rays should be followed when calculating shadows. Another parameter might be provided to control the number of rays followed when calculating reflections.

In many scenes, however, most of your models are neither transparent nor reflective, and using raytracing on them would accomplish nothing, other than to increase your rendering time. Because of this, many programs offer the ability to do **selective raytracing**, allowing you to render only specific models with the raytracing algorithm while using the less computationally expensive raycasting for the rest. We see a subtle example of this in color plate 9. Most of the objects in this scene do not require raytracing. An exception is the old man's glasses in which the transparent lens has been rendered not only as transparent, but as refractive—that is, the light bends as it passes through the lens, distorting the flowers behind him. A similar approach is frequently beneficial with cast shadows. Since cast shadows are defined on a per-light basis, you can decide whether each light's cast shadows should be calculated with raytracing or with the faster Z-buffer approach (see section 3.3).

In addition to the rendering algorithms discussed in this section, there are several algorithms designed for specific lighting situations. We discuss these in section 6.10.

3.7 Background Images

By default, 3D software packages render objects against a black background. We saw in section 3.6 that rendering algorithms calculate the color of an image pixel-by-pixel. If no object occupies any portion of a given pixel, that pixel receives an absence of color—that is, R,G,B = 0,0,0 —yielding the default black background we see in Figure 3-62.

It is very common, however, to want to place an image of some sort behind your scene models. We will see in section 8.2 that one way of doing

Figure 3-62. CG pictures are rendered with a black background by default.

this is to composite your three-dimensionally rendered image with another image or sequence of images.

It is also possible for your three-dimensional rendering software to render your scene directly with an image behind it. In some packages, this is accomplished by a menu selection designated specifically for defining a **background image**. Other packages offer a more generalized approach whereby you define a plane attached to your camera, and then assign a texture image to that plane. This sort of plane is referred to as an **image plane**.

(a)

(b)

Figure 3-63. A scanned or painted image can serve as a background.

Regardless of how it is done, once a background image has been defined, the image to be assigned to the background can be specified in one of two ways. The first is to assign a **picture file** to the background. This picture file can be generated with a myriad of imaging techniques, including scanning preexisting photographs or drawings, as in Figure 3-63a and b, or generating images directly within digital imaging or illustration programs.

Alternatively, you can use a **procedurally-generated image**. In this case, you use a set of menu selections to call upon a software-programmed **procedure** to generate your image. In Figure 3-64a, a fractal procedure (see section 6.3 for a discussion of fractals) has generated an irregularly patterned image which is then applied to the background. In Figure 3-64b a ramp procedure has been used to define a graduated color pattern progressing from black at the bottom to light gray at the top.

It is important to understand that background images created in these ways are two-dimensional, and that the models of your scene cannot interact with them in any way. That is, scene models do not cast shadows on the background images, and vice versa; models that are reflective do not reflect the imagery of a background image; if you move your camera, the background image does not shift with it.

(a)

(b)

Figure 3-64. Procedures can be used to generate a background image.

A background image is, in short, like a screen backdrop in a theatrical presentation. In theater, the people and props on the stage are three-dimensional, moving around among themselves and interacting with each other. The screen backdrop, however, is a two-dimensional image hung behind the three-dimensional scene. The background image in computer graphics is similarly, and strictly, two-dimensional.

We will see in section 6.6 that there is a special technique for using background images such that they *do* interact with a three-dimensional scene, receiving shadows and reflections. However, even in the simpler, strictly two-dimensional case described in this section, background images broaden the visual vocabulary of the artist considerably, and can produce striking results.

In a scene with many models, a background image shows through wherever there are no models. It may also be visible through transparent objects, provided there are no other opaque models behind them. In color plate 8, the sunrise visible through the sliding glass doors is a two-dimensional back-ground image. Notice that we see it through both the open door and the glass of the closed door. Everything else in this scene is modeled three-dimension-ally, with lighting carefully defined to simulate the light that would come from the sunrise in the background.

3.8 Surface Texture Mapping

A set of techniques, known collectively as **texture mapping**, permits you to enhance the definition of the surface characteristics of a model with great subtlety. Earlier, in the discussion of surface characteristics, each surface was defined as having only one color; it might be blue or red or green, but not dif-ferent colors simultaneously. In real life, of course, many surfaces are multi-colored. Part of what makes wood look wooden is color variations caused by the grain. Clothing, to take another example, is as often multicolored as not, frequently with patterns and images printed on it. Perhaps a bit more subtly, a plain gray concrete wall is almost certainly not the same shade of gray at every point on the surface, but is more likely to range from a very light gray to a very dark gray, depending on the wear and tear of the wall.

The most basic kind of texture mapping is **surface texture mapping** in which a two-dimensional picture is applied to the surface of a three-dimen-sional model. The two-dimensional picture is the "texture." Texture in this context means something like "pattern," rather than the minuscule bumps you might associate with the term.

A texture image can be generated in any number of ways, as we will dis-cuss in more detail at the end of this section. It can be scanned into the com-puter from a photograph or other hardcopy image. It can be painted directly within the computer using a digital paint program. Or it can be generated procedurally (that is, generated by a small subprogram) within the 3D soft-ware package by choosing a menu selection—a selection to create a grid pat-tern, for example.

The process of applying a texture to a surface is known as "mapping." Mapping may be implemented in two ways: by projecting the texture image or by stretching it onto the surface.

PROJECTION MAPPING

In **projection mapping** the texture image is projected through space. Wher-ever the texture image "hits" the surface of the model, the surface takes on the colors of that section of the texture image. Think of an image projected by a slide projector: if you place an object in the path of the projected image, the

(a)

(b)

(c)

(d)

Figure 3-65. Planar projection mapping.

object takes on the colors of the slide image wherever those colors hit the object.

In Figure 3-65a the grid pattern image is the texture image to be projected. In Figure 3-65b the projection has come from the left; in Figure 3-65c the projection has come from above, and in Figure 3-65d the projection has come from the right. In these examples of **planar projection mapping**, the texture image, in this case the grid pattern, has been projected along each of the three axes—X, Y, and Z.

This sort of projection mapping is very simple conceptually, and so it is a very commonly found mapping technique. Notice, however, a severe limitation of the projection-mapping technique just described. Since the texture image is projected in only one direction, it streaks along the sides of the mapped object. In each case in Figure 3-65, only one side of the cube receives a reasonable mapping. All of the other sides are streaked. The streaking on these sides is so extreme, in fact, that it results simply in straight lines, and a complete loss of the grid pattern, because each of these other sides is parallel to the direction of the projection. Only if the surface of a model is perpendicular to the direction of projection does that surface receive a completely accurate mapping of the texture image.

You can alleviate the streaking problem somewhat by rotating the model relative to the direction of projection. However, the price of doing this is that now *no* side receives a completely accurate mapping, since no side is exactly perpendicular to the projection.

In an effort to solve this problem, most systems offer several other ways of projecting a texture image simultaneously in several directions. The first of these multidirectional projection techniques is **cylindrical projection mapping**. Here, the two-dimensional texture image is bent into an imaginary cylinder before any projection takes place. The object to be mapped resides within this imaginary cylinder, and the image is projected inward from the surface of the cylinder to the axis of the cylinder.

In Figure 3-66a the model being mapped is a cylinder, the cylinder has been mapped using planar projection, and the grid pattern has been projected from the left. This process produces a reasonable mapping on the left side of the cylinder. (The far right side, if you could see it, also would look reasonable.) However, the grid pattern on the side of the cylinder closest to you is quite noticeably stretched. On the top of the cylinder the stretching is even worse.

In figure 3-66b the grid pattern has been mapped onto the cylinder using cylindrical projection. Notice that the grid pattern looks correct all the way around the cylinder, but on the top of the cylinder the pattern is still badly deformed, although in a different way. This streaking happens on the top and bottom of any model because the cylindrical technique projects the texture

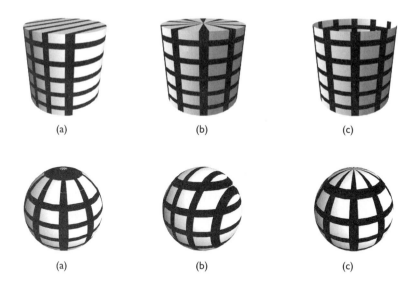

(a)　　　　　　　(b)　　　　　　　(c)

Figure 3-66. Cylindrical projection mapping is more effective for approximately cylindrical objects.

(a)　　　　　　　(b)　　　　　　　(c)

Figure 3-67. Spherical projection mapping is more effective for approximately spherical objects.

image in from the sides of the imaginary cylinder. If the model has no top, as in Figure 3-66c, the cylindrical technique can work very successfully.

Another technique offered by most systems, **spherical projection mapping**, sometimes can eliminate difficult streaking problems. Here, the two-dimensional texture image is bent into an imaginary sphere before being projected, and the image is projected inward from the sides of the imaginary sphere to the center. The projected pattern is mapped onto the surface of an object placed within this imaginary sphere

In Figure 3-67a, a sphere has been mapped using planar projection. Projected from the left, the grid pattern appears streaked on the side and the top of the sphere. Figure 3-67b, in which the grid pattern has been mapped onto the sphere using the cylindrical technique, shows a marked improvement, as you might expect, since a sphere is symmetrical along the Y axis just as a cylinder is. However, cylindrical mapping fails to do an adequate job at the top of the sphere. Mapping the sphere with spherical projection, as in Figure 3-67c, improves on this considerably. Now both the sides and the top of the sphere receive a reasonable mapping of the grid pattern.

Another variety of projection is **cubic projection**, in which the texture image is projected inward from each of the six sides of an imaginary cube. In Figure 3-68 we see the same grid pattern projected onto a cube with cubic projection. This is the same as performing six different planar projections, one from each side. Cubic projection simplifies this process for you by doing all six projections automatically.

Each of these projection techniques—planar, cylindrical, spherical, and cubic—has particular uses, with each being most suited to objects similar in

Figure 3-68. Cubic projection projects the texture from the direction of each of six faces of an imaginary cube.

shape to the projection method. Planar projection is most effective when the object to be mapped is relatively flat, such as a rug; cylindrical projection works best when the object to be mapped is itself roughly cylindrical in shape, such as a vase, and so on.

PARAMETERIZED MAPPING

All projection-mapping techniques are limited by the tendency to streak, but in spite of that fact they appear in many systems, because they are relatively easy for the computer to calculate. This is especially true of planar projection. Because of the limitations of projection-mapping techniques, the second technique of mapping, called **parameterized texture mapping**, or **UV mapping**, also commonly appears in 3D software packages.

Parameterized texture mapping is most readily understood through an analogy. Imagine that you wish some three-dimensional surface to be multicolored. Imagine also that you have a flat sheet of flexible latex onto which you print a multicolored image—that is, a texture. If you stretch this flat sheet of latex tautly over the three-dimensional surface, covering it entirely, the three-dimensional surface will look as if it were colored with the two-dimensional image. This stretching of the texture image onto a three-dimensional surface is the basic concept of parameterized texture mapping.

The picture of a face in Figure 3-69a is a two-dimensional pattern, or texture. In terms of the analogy, this image would be on the flat sheet of latex. Figure 3-69b shows a three-dimensional surface, a curved patch, onto which the two-dimensional texture has been "stretched." The process of stretching the two-dimensional texture onto the three-dimensional surface corresponds to the mapping of the texture onto the surface.

Figures 3-69c and 3-69d show two other three-dimensional surfaces—a sphere and a revolved surface—with the same two-dimensional texture image mapped onto them using the same parameterized-mapping technique. Notice first that there is no streaking of the sort you saw with projection mapping, since the image is stretched rather than projected onto the surface. Notice too, however, that the more the shape of the three-dimensional surface differs from the shape of the original two-dimensional texture image, the more the image may be distorted as it is stretched to cover the three-dimensional surface. The two-dimensional texture image is normally rectangular, so any three-dimensional, nonrectangular surface causes some distortion in the mapping process. (Later in this section you will learn about ways to avoid this distortion.)

You have just seen the simplest case of 2D parameterized texture mapping. In practice, many subtleties are possible with this sort of mapping. In order to understand how these variations work, you need to understand in more detail what happens during the mapping process.

(a)

(b)

(c)

(d)

Figure 3-69. Parameterized texture mapping.

x,y = 511,511

x,y = 213,189

x,y = 0,0

x,y = 511,0

Figure 3-70. The texture image is organized into an XY grid of pixels.

(a)

(b)

Figure 3-71. Each pixel in the XY space of the texture image maps to a rectangular area in the UV space of the surface.

A two-dimensional computer graphics image is, by its nature, divided up into a discrete number of tiny rectangular areas, called **pixels**. These pixels exist in a two-dimensional Cartesian coordinate system, with the pixel in the lower left of the image normally said to be located at XY = (0,0). If the image is 512 pixels wide by 512 pixels high (a standard image size for texture maps), then the pixel in the upper right corner of the image is located at XY = (511,511) (Figure 3-70).

The basic idea of parameterized texture mapping is that each area, or pixel, of the two-dimensional image is applied to (mapped to) a corresponding area of the three-dimensional surface. This requires that the three-dimensional surface be divided into the same number of rectangular areas as there are pixels in the texture image. In order to divide the three-dimensional surface into the correct number of discrete rectangular areas, you step along the surface in two different directions in the same way that you step along the two-dimensional picture in the X and Y directions (Figure 3-71a). Since a surface patch is defined in terms of two directions, or parameters, called U and V, you step along the surface of a patch in the U direction and in the V direction (Figure 3-71b).

The color in the rectangular area located at XY = (0,0) on the two-dimensional texture image maps to, or is applied to, the rectangular area located at UV = (0,0) on the three-dimensional surface. The color of the texture area located immediately to the right of XY = (0,0) maps to the area on the three-

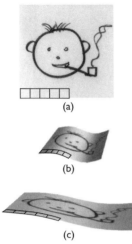

(a)

(b)

(c)

Figure 3-72. A texture image may stretch as it maps to a surface.

dimensional surface immediately to the right of UV = (0,0), and so on. This mapping continues area by area, stepping simultaneously across both the two-dimensional texture image (Figure 3-72a) and the three-dimensional surface (Figure 3-72b).

Thinking of the mapping process in this way explains image distortion on many three-dimensional surfaces. When a surface is very differently shaped (say, longer and narrower) than the original rectangular configuration of the two-dimensional texture image, the subdivision of the three-dimensional surface into rectangular areas can result in each of those areas being stretched, since there must be the same number of areas on the surface as there are on the texture image (Figure 3-72c). (For the sake of clarity, both the texture image and three-dimensional surface in the figure are subdivided into only a handful of rectangles.)

MAPPING CONTROLS

In all the mapping examples so far, both parameterized and projected, the texture image was mapped exactly once to the three-dimensional surface. In practice, however, you have considerable control, both with parameterized mapping and with projection mapping, over where and how large the two-dimensional image maps onto the three-dimensional surface.

The first form of control that most computer graphics systems permits is the ability to specify the **scale**, or size, of the final mapped image. The default (seen in the examples so far) is a scale of 1.0—that is, the two-dimensional texture image covers 100 percent of the three-dimensional surface (Figure 3-73a). If the scale were 0.5, the image would cover only 50 percent of the surface, in both the U and V directions (Figure 3-73b). A scale factor of 0.25 would cause the image to cover only 25 percent of the surface in each of the directions (Figure 3-73c).

When the mapped image covers less than 100 percent of the three-dimensional surface, the area of the surface not covered by the texture image retains whatever color was originally assigned to the surface before any mapping took place. For example, if the original color of the three-dimensional surface in Figure 3-73 was orange, then all but the lower left quadrant of the surface would be orange in Figure 3-73b.

In addition to controlling the scale of the final mapping, most systems allow you to control the **placement** of the mapped image. For UV-mapped images, placement controls make use of the U and V coordinates of the parameterized mapping. For projection-mapped images, most programs provide slider bars that simulate the UV space of true parameterized mapping. In either case, you usually begin by specifying where on the surface the mapping process should begin. By default, the process begins at UV = (0,0). By choos-

(a)

(b)

(c)

Figure 3-73. The texture image can be scaled as it maps onto a surface.

(a)   (b)   (c)

Figure 3-74. A texture image may also be positioned on a surface.

ing some other point in the UV space of the surface, however, you offset the mapping. Most systems consider the UV space of a surface to range from 0.0 to 1.0. Using this system, if you keep the scaling of your map at 0.25 (Figure 3-74a), you can change the starting, or offset, point of your mapping from the default UV = (0,0) to UV = (0.5,0) (Figure 3-74b). If you change the offset to UV = (0.75,0.75), you place the image toward the upper right corner of the surface (Figure 3-74c).

(a)

(b)

(c)

Figure 3-75. A texture image may wrap around a surface.

In the previous examples, the scale was very small, so the image never went over the edge of the surface. Imagine, however, changing the scale back to 1.0 and using a nondefault offset. When UV offset = (0.0,0.0), the image covers the surface exactly once, starting in the lower left corner (Figure 3-75a). When UV offset = (0.5,0.0), the image starts halfway across the surface in the U direction, but then, because it is so large, wraps around, so that the right half of the texture image appears on the left half of the surface (Figure 3-75b). Further, when UV offset = (0.5,0.5), the image wraps around in both the U and V directions (Figure 3-75c)

Many systems provide a variable, often called either "wrap" or "repeat," that allows you to turn on or off this **wrapping** effect. If wrap is turned off, depending on the offset values you get one of the results in Figure 3-76.

If the two-dimensional texture image is a representational image, like the face in these examples, you probably do not want the image to wrap around to the other end of the surface. On the other hand, if the texture image is some repeating pattern, such as the design on a rug or some wallpaper or a piece of cloth, the wrapping of the pattern may be precisely what you want.

In addition to controlling the scaling, placement, and wrapping of a texture image onto a three-dimensional surface, you can control the **effect** of the mapping. In the case of color texture mapping, the effect of the color mapping is the saturation of the colors. Many systems allow you to scale this effect—that is, to increase it or decrease it—by multiplying it by some factor, usually in the range 0.0 to 1.0. When you scale up the effect of color texture mapping, you increase the saturation of the colors. If, for example, the color of a particular pixel in the two-dimensional texture image is RGB = (100,0,40), scaling the effect of the color mapping by a factor of 2.0 produces

(a)

(b)

(c)

Figure 3-76. The wrapping of the texture image can be turned off.

(a)

(b)

Figure 3-77. Transparency mapping.

color values of RGB = (200,0,80). Scaling the color by a factor of 0.5 desaturates the color of the pixel by half, producing a color of RGB = (50,0,20) on the surface. Many systems allow you to scale each of the three components of an RGB color individually, in order to make the mapped color "redder," or "greener," for example.

Since a scaling operation is a multiplicative one, a curious thing happens when you scale the color effect by 0.0. No matter what the RGB values of the original colors on the texture image, all of the pixels—and all the area on the three-dimensional surface—become a pure black, RGB = (0,0,0).

All of these controls—scaling, placement, wrapping, and effect—can usually be specified either by typing in numbers directly or by adjusting slider bars. In addition, higher-end programs allow you to make adjustments visually and in real time by using the mouse. As you drag the mouse, you see the texture slide across the surface of the model, change size, and so on.

MAPPING APPLICATIONS

However you create your map and whatever process you use to manipulate it, the pixel values in the two-dimensional texture image can be interpreted in any number of ways, to produce any number of effects. In **color texture mapping** the pixel values are interpreted as color and consequently change the color of the three-dimensional surface onto which they are mapped. In the other applications of texture mapping, the pixel values are interpreted as, and therefore change, some other characteristic of the three-dimensional surface.

In **transparency texture mapping**, or simply **transparency mapping**, the brightness of each pixel in the two-dimensional texture image is interpreted as the amount of transparency of the three-dimensional surface. The brighter the pixel, the more transparent the corresponding area of the three-dimensional surface; the darker the pixel, the more opaque the area of the surface. When the circular pattern in Figure 3-77a is mapped onto a three-dimensional patch, for instance, with the pixel values of the texture image interpreted as degrees of transparency, the result is the surface you see in Figure 3-77b. The "hole" in this surface is not an actual geometric hole, but the result of the white circular area from the texture image, interpreted as transparency, creating a corresponding circular area of transparency on the patch.

When a pixel of the texture image is neither completely black nor completely white, but has a brightness of some intermediate value, the transparency of the corresponding area on the three-dimensional surface, such as around the rim of the circular hole in the patch, is of an equally intermediate level.

Another interesting example of this effect is shown in Figure 3-78, in which the flame of the candle was rendered using transparency mapping. The original surface of the flame is an approximately ellipsoidal shape. The texture pattern was a fractally generated pattern of irregular blacks and whites (see section 6.3 for a discussion of fractals). Because of the irregularity of the texture pattern and because of the subtlety of the tonal gradations in the texture image, a flamelike pattern of transparency is produced.

Notice that for the purposes of transparency mapping, you do not need to have a full-color, twenty-four-bit RGB image as your texture image. A simple, eight-bit black-and-white image serves just as well, since the information the mapping procedure needs is simply brightness, which can as easily—in fact, more easily—be represented through a gray-scale as through a full-color image.

Bump texture mapping, or simply **bump mapping**, simulates the small bumps and irregularities of some surfaces. Examples of such surfaces—the individual bumps of which may be so small that you cannot perceive each one of them separately—include fabrics with a noticeable weave, dirt, coarse sand, the surface of a concrete wall. To try to model the myriad tiny bumps of these surfaces geometrically, by pulling control points or polygon vertices, would be both extremely tedious and wasteful.

To understand bump mapping, recall that how dark or how light a color is at a certain point on a surface depends largely on the orientation of the surface relative to the light sources. If it faces a light source, the surface is brighter. If it faces away from a light source, the surface is darker. The orientation of a given point on the surface is determined by the surface normal at that point. A perfectly flat surface has surface normals that point straight up, all across the surface (Figure 3-79a). A bumpy surface, however, has surface normals that point in all different directions (Figure 3-79b). Bump mapping works by "fooling" the rendering program. That is, it artificially tilts the surface normals (Figure 3-79c), so that the rendering program "thinks" the surface is bumpy when really it is not. This artificial tilting of the surface normals is called, amusingly, **perturbing** the normals. The bump-mapping technique interprets the brightness of each pixel of the texture image as more or less perturbation of the surface normal at the corresponding area of the three dimensional surface. If a texture pixel is very bright, the surface normal is perturbed a lot in one direction. If the texture pixel is very dark, the normal is perturbed a lot in the other direction. And if the texture pixel is some intermediate value of brightness, the normal is perturbed some intermediate amount.

When a rendering program encounters perturbed normals, it renders the darkness of the surface exactly as it would if that surface were bumpy and had those same normals. The bumpiness you see on the surface in Figure 3-80a, for example, is entirely a result of bump mapping. The geometry of the surface is totally flat. A fractally generated texture pattern was used to create a black-and-white texture image, which was then interpreted as a bump map for this surface. One odd but important fact about this bump-mapping process is that if you tilt the surface a bit (Figure 3-80b), you see that the edges of the rendered surface are straight: the bumpy rendering of the surface has no effect on the underlying geometry.

Figure 3-78. The flame of the candle was modeled using transparency mapping. (Courtesy, Jia-Ming Day.)

(a)

(b)

(c)

Figure 3-79. Bump mapping simulates the irregularity of surface normals by perturbing the normals.

(a)

(b)

Figure 3-80. Bump mapping does not change the underlying geometry, as the straight edges of the surface show.

Figure 3-81. Photographs of chameleon skin and tree bark were scanned in as maps in this sophisticated example of bump mapping. (Courtesy, Tim Cheung.)

(a)

(b)

(c)

Figure 3-82. Displacement mapping alters the geometry of the mapped surface.

Figure 3-81 illustrates the effectiveness of bump-mapping. The bumpy textures on both the chameleon and the branch were created by scanning in photographs and using them as bump maps. Color plate 10 shows another effective use of bump mapping. Here, the tiny grains of sand are rendered with bump mapping.

Yet another application of texture mapping, called **displacement mapping**, deals with situations in which you want to model a lot of irregularities into a surface and you want the irregularities large enough to be individually noticeable. Examples of this type of model are a hilly terrain and the surface of an ocean.

Like transparency and bump mapping, displacement mapping uses the brightness of the pixels of a two-dimensional texture image as a source of information. In the case of displacement mapping, however, the brightness is interpreted as an actual geometric displacement of the height of the surface at that particular location. The brighter the texture pixel, the more the three-dimensional surface is displaced upward. A black texture pixel means no displacement of the surface at all. A white texture pixel means very great displacement.

In Figure 3-82a, the texture image is an irregular pattern created by a fractal procedure. The original, unmodified three-dimensional surface is the patch in Figure 3-82b. After the displacement mapping, the geometry of the three-dimensional surface is modified, producing the craggy, terrainlike structure in Figure 3-82c. Notice that, unlike bump mapping, displacement mapping does change the geometry of the surface, as is apparent if you look at the edges of the displaced patch. In fact, of all the mapping techniques discussed, displacement mapping is the only one that actually modifies the geometry of the surface. All of the others are only rendering enhancements. In this sense, displacement mapping might be more properly considered a modeling technique than a rendering technique, and we discuss it in more detail in that context in section 5.7.

All of these mapping techniques—color, transparency, bump, and displacement—are implemented in such a way that you can manipulate all of the same control parameters discussed earlier in this section. That is, you can adjust the scaling, or size, of the mapping. You can control the offset placement of the mapping. You can make any of these maps wrap or not wrap. And you can alter the effect factor of any of them. Changing the scale, placement, or wrap for any of these varieties of texture mapping is easy to understand, but a few words are in order about changing the effect factor of a mapping.

In a transparency map, scaling the effect increases or decreases the overall range of transparency values for the surface. If the effect factor is set to two, then the transparency values at the various locations of the surface are twice as transparent as normal. If the effect factor is set to zero, the transparency mapping is effectively turned off, since transparency will be zero, or opaque, at every location of the surface. If the effect factor is made negative, all transparency values are reversed. That which was transparent becomes opaque, and that which was opaque becomes transparent.

Similar things happen with bump mapping. If the effect factor is zero, the bump mapping is effectively turned off and the surface appears without bump mapping. If the effect is scaled negatively, bumps that went up now go down (becoming hollows), and vice versa. Analogous sorts of things happen to a displacement map when the effect factor is changed.

There are a number of other, less common types of surface texture mapping in addition to those discussed in this section. Basically, any useful way of interpreting the pixel values of a texture image can be developed into a mapping procedure. For example, some systems provide **incandescence mapping**, in which the pixel values are interpreted as more or less incandescence—that is, a glowing brightness added to the color of the pixel. Sometimes you find **specularity mapping** and **reflectivity mapping**, in which the amount of specularity or the amount of reflectivity are made to vary across the three-dimensional surface. In effect, the numbers and types of surface texture mapping are theoretically unlimited.

TEXTURE CREATION

Regardless of whether the mapping is done through the projection technique or through the parameterized technique, and whether the map is interpreted as color information, transparency information, bump information, or any

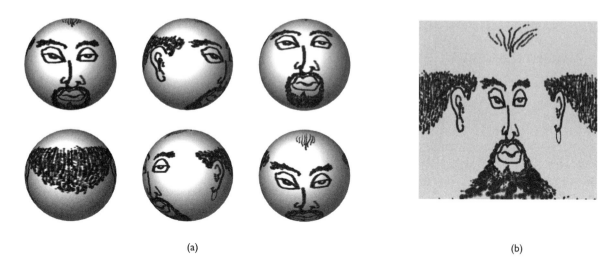

(a)   (b)

Figure 3-83. A 3D paint program allows you to paint directly onto the surface of a three-dimensional model, automatically creating the necessary distortion in the two-dimensional texture image.

other variety of texturing, in all cases the mapping begins with a two-dimensional image. How that two-dimensional image is generated, however, can vary. Very commonly it is scanned from a photograph or an actual object. It also can be painted in a two-dimensional digital paint program. Another extremely powerful approach to creating two-dimensional texture images is **3D paint programs**. These programs allow you to paint directly onto the surface of your three-dimensional model. As you do so, the 3D paint program automatically creates for you the predistorted two-dimensional texture image that would produce your three-dimensionally painted results (Figure 3-83).

However they may be implemented, 3D paint programs function similarly. You begin by creating your model and defining its mapping (parameterized, spherical projection, etc.) in your 3D modeling program. Next, you read this model into your 3D paint program. Inside the 3D paint program, you can turn your model around interactively, usually with the mouse, just as you can inside a normal 3D program. At this point, the 3D paint program resembles a two-dimensional painting: it offers a selection of brushes, colors, and application techniques. Selecting these, you paint directly onto the surface of your three-dimensional model. In Figure 3-83a, for example, the model is a simple sphere. The animator has turned the model around and painted a human head on it. Notice that the painting has taken place all around the surface of the sphere. In this example, you might begin by painting the facial features on the front of the sphere. As you work on the beard, you would tilt the sphere up so that its underside is visible. To work on the hair, you would rotate the sphere to reveal the sides, back, and top as necessary.

At the same time that you are painting three-dimensionally in this way, the program is automatically and simultaneously producing a flattened, stretched two-dimensional texture image (Figure 3-83b). Recall that all surface texture

(a)   (b)   (c)

Figure 3-84. 3D painting allows you to very intuitively place color on specific areas of your surface.

mapping techniques, whether parameterized or projected, involve some amount of stretching, streaking, or distortion. In this example, which employs spherical projection, the distortion would be most noticeable at the top and bottom of the sphere, where the texture image will tend to pinch together. The advantage of a 3D paint program is that it predistorts the texture image automatically, allowing you to think only in terms of your final visual result.

You can see this effect most clearly in the beard and forehead hair. Notice how much these need to flare outwards in the 2D texture image of Figure 3-83b in order to produce the desired result in Figure 3-83a.

Lacking a 3D paint program, if you want to create this texture on a sphere-man, you would have to paint the 2D texture directly in a 2D paint program, render it onto the sphere to see how it looks, then repaint the texture and rerender it, repeating this process many times until you finally achieved the desired mapping. With a 3D paint program, you paint the end result, and the program calculates the distorted 2D image necessary to give you that result.

The example used here is a simple color texture mapping: the colors of the texture become the colors of the model. But 3D paint programs allow you also to create any of the different varieties of texture maps—color, bump, transparency, displacement, and so on. Each different map is usually painted on a separate **layer**, in the same way that you compile your image layer by layer in two-dimensional drawing and painting programs. If you wanted your sphere-man to have a mole on his cheek, you might go into bump-texture mode and create a separate bump painting on a separate layer. Just as a predistorted 2D texture image was generated for your color mapping, the program would generate another predistorted texture image for your bump mapping.

We see another example of 3D texture painting on more developed geometry in Figure 3-84. In (a) you see the geometry without any texture; in (b) you see the texture created with the 3D painting technique; and in (c) you see the texture-mapped model. The visually intuitive nature of 3D texture painting allowed the artist to create this texture in a matter of several minutes.

(a)   (b)   (c)

Figure 3-85. Procedures, or miniature subprograms within the software, can be used to generate a texture image.

A completely different approach to the problem of creating two-dimensional texture images is **procedural mapping**, in which the software system itself creates the image by means of a collection of procedures, or subprograms (Figure 3-85). When generating a texture procedurally, you normally begin by specifying which procedure you wish to use. Your choices may range from a relatively simple procedure that calculates a grid pattern to a very sophisticated procedure that calculates a fractally based pattern of cloudlike elements. Some procedures are quite specific. A procedure might be designed, for example, to create an image that then creates the effect of water ripples when used as a bump map.

In selecting a procedure, you normally indicate values for a number of different variables, or parameters, that control the look of the procedurally generated two-dimensional image. For a grid-generating procedure, for example, you might be asked to indicate the number of horizontal bars, the number of vertical bars, the color of the bars, and the color of the background. For more complicated procedures, the number of parameters can increase dramatically. The aforementioned water-ripple procedure might have twenty or more variables that allow you to control various characteristics of the water image.

Surface texture mapping is an extremely powerful technique, as you can see by studying any of the color plates in this book, all of which make extensive use of it. In this section we have presented the fundamentals of this technique. Sections 6.5, 6.6, and 6.7 present more advanced details on this same rich topic.

3.9 Solid Texture Mapping

All of the mapping techniques discussed in the previous section involve the mapping of a flat two-dimensional pattern onto a surface. A great many interesting effects can be created with the different varieties of this kind of texture mapping. Some rendering effects, however, do not lend themselves to this two-dimensionally oriented mapping approach, but require instead a more fully three-dimensional method. A good example of this is wood, which has

(a)　　　　　　　(b)　　　　　　　(c)

Figure 3-86. Wood-grain patterns are difficult to render effectively with two-dimensional mapping techniques.

a grain. When you cut or carve something out of wood, the grain of the wood is visible on all the exterior surfaces of the object. The wood-grain patterns vary, however, depending on the angle of each surface relative to the direction of the grain (Figure 3-86).

Surface mapping techniques (see the previous section), which either project a pattern onto a surface or wrap a pattern across the surface of an object, do not handle this kind of effect very successfully. To continue with the example of wood, the result of parameterized mapping would look more like a block wrapped in wood-grain-patterned paper than like a block made of wood. Nor would projection mapping work any better, since it would produce a streaking effect along some of the surfaces. Neither of these approaches produces the effect of an object made *of* the material. Surface mapping techniques, whether projected or parameterized, tend to produce the effect of a pattern placed *on* the object.

The technique developed to solve this problem is known as **solid texture mapping**. The idea behind this technique is that you create a virtual *volume* of texture and then immerse your object in that volume. Depending on how the object "floats" in the volume, it picks up different colors of the volumetric texture.

The simplified volumetric texture in Figure 3-87a consists of a few wavy lines projected back (with some irregularity) through space. In Figure 3-87b a block-shaped object has been dropped into this texture volume. Figure 3-87c shows the patterns on the surface of the object that result from this "immersion." Wherever one of the wavy lines went through the block, a pattern is left on the block.

(a)　　　　　　　(b)　　　　　　　(c)

Figure 3-87. In solid texture mapping, the model is immersed in a volume of texture.

Figure 3-88. Transforming the model within the texture volume changes the patterns which appear on the surface of the model.

(a)

(b)

Figure 3-89. The texture volume itself can be transformed to produce a different pattern on the model.

(a)

(b)

Since the pattern of texture is a three-dimensional volume, the color patterns that end up on the surface of the mapped object can be altered simply by transforming the object within this volume in some way. In Figure 3-88a the block of the previous illustration has been given a rotation, which causes it to pick up a different pattern of lines. In Figure 3-88b, the block has been translated downward slightly, which produces yet another pattern of lines.

Just as the object can be transformed within the texture volume to produce a different pattern of marks, the texture volume itself can be transformed to produce different marks on the object. Thus, in Figure 3-89b the block has not moved from the position it occupies in Figure 3-89a, but the entire texture volume has been rotated. This rotation causes a different pattern of lines to cross the block immersed in that volume. The different patterns on the rendered blocks are the result solely of this rotation of the texture volume.

Software packages that permit this kind of transformation of the texture volume also make it possible (usually through a menu selection) to link the transformations of the texture volume to the transformations of the object being textured. This is done by making the texture volume a hierarchical child of the object being textured (see section 2.9). Thus, if the object moves to the right, the texture volume moves exactly the same amount to the right. If the object rotates, the texture volume rotates exactly the same amount and in the same direction. This linking of transformations is done to prevent the texture pattern from moving about on the surface of the mapped object whenever the mapped object moves. If the two sets of transformations are not linked, the pattern on the object shifts, as you saw in Figures 3-88 and 3-89. In an animation, this kind of shifting causes the patterns on the surface of an object to swirl and slide across the object as it moves about in space.

With solid texturing as with surface texturing, you can adjust parameters to control the result of the procedure. A "wood" procedure, for example, includes a number of parameters for controlling the density of the wood grain, the color of the grain, the color of the wood pulp, and so on. A procedure that simulates the effect of marble includes various parameters for controlling the veining of the marble, the colors of the marble patterns, and so on. Notice how the vein patterns seem to run "through" the urn in Figure 3-90. This effect is especially apparent around the rim of the urn.

Figure 3-90. A procedurally generated solid texture that simulates marble. Notice how the texture passes through the form at the lip of the urn.

Along with using solid texturing to generate patterns of color on the surfaces of objects, you can use solid texturing in numerous ways similar to the different interpretations of surface texture mapping. For example, the volume of texture might be interpreted as a pattern of transparency rather than of color. The result of this interpretation would be to make transparent holes in the surface of the rendered object (Figure 3-91). This technique can be especially useful, for example, when trying to create a smoke effect with either volumetric fog lights (section 3.3) or particles (section 7.8). Bump mapping is another common application of solid texturing.

So far you have looked at the general principle of the solid-texturing process and the general effects of the process on an object, but you have not seen how you actually go about generating the volume of texture at the heart of the whole process. There are several ways that you normally can do this.

One simple way to create a volume of texture is to create a flat two-dimensional image and to extrude that image straight back through space along the Z axis. In Figure 3-92a the original image is a pattern of three wavy lines. In Figure 3-92b you see this two-dimensional image pushed straight back through space to produce a cubic volume of three-dimensional pattern.

Figure 3-91. Solid texturing can also be used for transparency mapping.

Notice that this is the same process used by the planar-projection-mapping technique discussed in the previous section. In fact, planar projection mapping, as well as all the other projection mapping techniques, create simplified volumes of texture, and are therefore in a certain sense "solid." The simplified volumes created by projection mapping, however, are so regular that there is no sense of solidity or true volume when they map to objects. What you see with these techniques has very much the feel of an *image* on a *surface*.

To make the patterns of texture volume more interesting and more useful, a **noise** parameter is added to the process in order to generate randomness as the image extrudes back through space. This parameter permits you to control how regularly or irregularly the extrusion takes place. As the noise is increased, the extruding pattern fluctuates more and more as it

(a)

(a)

(b)

(c)

(d)

Figure 3-92. The volume of texture is generated by pushing a two-dimensional pattern through space. Randomness is added to create irregularity in the texture volume.

moves back through space. In Figure 3-92c the noise parameter has been given a low value, resulting in a slight wobbling of the image as it extrudes back along Z. In Figure 3-92d the noise parameter has been increased to produce a more pronounced wobbling and a much more irregular volume of texture.

It is this irregularity of the volume texture that gives it the appearance of solidity. Because the texture is everywhere different within the volume, no part of a textured object receives the same texture. This avoids the streaking problem of projection mapping. At the same time, because the texture maps to the object according to the object's immersion in the volume, the stretching problems of parameterized mapping are also avoided.

So far, we have been discussing solid textures created by projecting and distorting a two-dimensional image. In practice, it is more common to create your solid texture without explicitly providing a two-dimensional image. To do this, the software generates the texture volume procedurally, in much the same way that two-dimensional textures are generated procedurally. Systems that offer this kind of solid texturing usually offer within menus several specific procedures to achieve specific effects. For example, a "marble" procedure might procedurally generate a volume of marblelike texture; a "cloud" procedure might procedurally generate a volume of wispy cloudlike texture. Many of these three-dimensional solid-texturing procedures make use of noise and randomness to achieve the desired irregularity in the texture. Many of them also make use of fractal mathematics (see section 6.3) so that the irregularity and randomness of the solid texture is maintained no matter how much detail is seen in the final rendering. Figures 3-86 and 3-90 are examples of procedurally generated solid textures.

The immersion approach of solid texture mapping, discussed above, solves another problem encountered with surface mapping techniques, both parameterized and projected. With surface mapping, it can be extremely difficult to get a single texture pattern to map smoothly across the adjacent surfaces of two objects without a visible seam between the surfaces. In Figure 3-93a there is a noticeable discontinuity in the texture pattern where the top cylinder touches the bottom cylinder.

Figure 3-93. Solid texture mapping can produce continuous texture patterns across the seam between two objects.

(a)

(b)

It is possible, however, to apply a single solid texture to an entire hierarchy of objects. Since the entire hierarchical object is immersed within one texture volume, the solid-texture-mapping technique now creates a smooth, continuous texture pattern across the seam between the two cylinders (Figure 3-93b).

3.10 Final Rendering

RESOLUTION

When it comes time to render the final frames of an animation, you must think about several factors that affect the look and quality of the final images. One of the most basic of these factors is **resolution**. As you have seen, any digital picture is composed of a grid of tiny rectangular picture elements, or pixels. The density of this grid is called the "resolution" and is measured as the number of pixels in the horizontal, or X, direction by the number of pixels in the vertical, or Y, direction. Thus, an image with a resolution of 300 × 200 has 300 pixels in the X direction and 200 pixels in the Y direction. In terms of columns and rows, this image has 300 columns in the X direction and 200 rows in the Y direction.

Generally, higher resolutions result in better-quality renderings. An image rendered at 300 × 200 (Figure 3-94a) looks considerably cruder than the same image rendered at 600 × 400 (Figure 3-94b), and that image looks smoother yet if rendered at 1,200 × 800. The cruder, more "pixelized" look of the lower-resolution image is especially apparent around the edges of the objects.

In some cases, however, you accomplish nothing by increasing the resolution of a rendering. If the final image is displayed very small, a low-resolution rendering may do perfectly well. An animation produced for a four-inch screen at a bank automated teller machine, for example, gains nothing by being rendered at a very high resolution. The additional detail gained by a higher resolution rendering would be imperceptible to the human eye. The same is frequently true in the game industry, where because of both screen size and the need to play the animations in real-time, rendering resolution is often deliberately kept low. On the other hand, if the image is displayed very large—for example, as a large-screen projection in a movie theater—then a very high-resolution rendering is critical. In this case, if the resolution is too low, the individual pixels become visible when the image is blown up to full size. A typical resolution for this sort of application might be a few thousand pixels in each direction.

Unfortunately, as in life, nothing in computer graphics comes free. The higher the resolution of an image, the longer the rendering takes. Remember

(a)

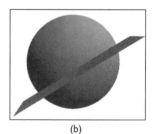

(b)

Figure 3-94. The resolution at which an image is rendered affects the final image quality. (For the sake of comparison, the lower-resolution image has been enlarged so that it is the same size as the higher-resolution image.)

that when a picture is rendered, a beam is projected from the eye through each pixel, and the system calculates what color that pixel should be. If twice as many pixels must be colored, twice as many calculations must be done, requiring twice as much time. In fact, increasing resolution increases rendering time even faster than you might think. If you double the resolution of a picture, you do not merely double the rendering time—you quadruple it!—because when you double resolution, you double it in both directions. For example, an image with a resolution of 300 × 200 has a total of 60,000 pixels to be colored (300 × 200 = 60,000). If you double this resolution to 600 × 400, you have a total of 240,000 pixels to be colored (600 × 400 = 240,000). The rendering for this second image thus takes four times as long as the rendering for the first image.

For this reason, it is important to be careful when you select a resolution. If a higher resolution gains you nothing, you save a lot of time and aggravation by working at a lower resolution. In fact, it is common practice to work at low resolution while performing rendering tests. Only when you know that everything is working to your satisfaction do you increase the resolution to produce the final frames.

The actual final resolution you use, however, is not arbitrary. Certain standard resolutions are used for specific purposes. Most 3D packages provide you with a menu that allows you to select any one of these standard resolutions.

When recording to video, for example, you must use one of several standard resolutions. Images with a resolution larger than the standard video resolution contain more information than can be recorded onto a frame of video and so are cropped when recorded to video. Images with a resolution that is too small, by contrast, do not fill the entire video screen.

The standard resolution for the **NTSC** (National Television Systems Committee) video format, used in the United States and many other countries, is 640 x 480. The ratio between the X and Y resolution, called the **picture aspect ratio**, of an NTSC frame is 1.333:1—that is, one and one-third times as long as it is high (640/480 = 1.333).

Remember that any digital image is made up of pixels. On many hardware devices, pixels are square—that is, they have a **pixel aspect ratio** of 1:1. In this case, the aspect ratio of the entire picture is calculated simply with the arithmetic we saw above: X resolution divided by Y resolution.

However, many hardware devices use non-square pixels, and this affects the total number of pixels needed to achieve a given picture aspect ratio. If each pixel is narrower in one direction, a greater number of pixels is required to make the picture as wide as it would otherwise be if the pixels had been square. Many **digital video devices**, for example, use **non-square pixels**. One common pixel aspect ratio for digital video is 0.888:1—that is, each rectangular pixel is 0.888 as wide as it is high. With such pixels, you need 720 pixels in the X direction to achieve a normal 1:333:1 NTSC picture aspect ratio (720 * 0.888 = 640). Thus, the correct resolution for such a digital video device is 720 x 480, with a pixel aspect ratio of 0.888.

While NTSC is the standard video resolution used in the United States, the **PAL** (Phase Alternation Line) video format, is used throughout most of Europe. A standard PAL resolution is 768 x 576.

It is important when rendering your final frames to be aware of both the picture aspect ratio and the pixel aspect ratio required by your recording device. Most software packages provide a selection of predefined settings for the correct combination of X resolution, Y resolution, and pixel aspect ratio for a given format and device.

The concept of screen aspect ratio has an additional implication. When changing the resolution of an image for testing purposes, be sure to retain the same aspect ratio in the smaller, test resolution that you plan to use in the final renderings. If you fail to do this, the smaller test rendering will not frame the scene in the same way that it will be framed within the final, full resolution. For example, if the final frame is to be at an NTSC resolution of 645 × 485, make sure that your test renderings retain the same 1.33 aspect ratio as the original—for example, by halving both the X and the Y resolutions to 323 × 243 (and rounding off to whole numbers).

If you are recording to film, a different aspect ratio is involved. The aspect ratio of 35mm film is 1.5:1—that is, one and a half times as wide as it is high. When rendering a frame to be shot to 35mm slide film, therefore, choose a resolution that maintains this ratio. A typical resolution used for 35mm color slide film might be 2,048 × 1,365, which is high enough to produce a good-quality still-frame rendering and retain the correct 1.5:1 aspect ratio.

In the rendering of frames for 35mm motion-picture film, the issue is a bit more complicated, because there are two different standards in the film industry. One standard, called the **Academy aspect ratio**, leaves room in each frame for soundtrack information. The other standard, called the **Full Cine aspect ratio**, does not. Consequently the aspect ratios of the two different film standards are slightly different. A typical resolution for Academy frames might be 1,254 × 911, while a typical resolution for Full Cine frames might be 1,416 × 1,062.

PICTURE AND MOVIE FILES

When rendering your animation for viewing, you can render in one of several formats. A **movie file** is a single file containing your entire rendered animation. Once rendered, you can open this file and play your animation on your computer screen. If your hardware is fast enough, the animation will play smoothly in real time.

Since they contain all the rendered images of the animation in one file, movie files can become extremely large. To keep them smaller and more manageable, you usually render your movie with **compression**. Compressing a movie file makes it smaller, but at the cost of image quality. In section 6.11 we will discuss the various compression techniques and their advantages, as well as the standard movie file formats.

Because compression degrades image quality, movie files are usually not used for final, best-quality rendering. For this, you usually render a sequence of **still frames** in an uncompressed format. In addition to your software's proprietary, **native** picture-file format, there are a number of industry-standard picture file formats which we will discuss in detail in section 8.5. Once the frames are rendered, you bring them into your recording or editing software to produce files that can be put onto videotape.

TESSELATING PATCHES

You may recall (see section 3.5) that many 3D software packages convert spline-based curved surfaces into polygonal approximations before rendering, and that polygonal approximation grows more accurate as more polygons are used. A cylinder approximated by forty polygons around the sides, for instance, looks much more truly cylindrical than one approximated by eight polygons.

The process of converting curved surfaces to polygonal approximations prior to rendering is known as **rendering tessellation** (a *tessella* in Latin was a little square mosaic stone), or sometimes **rendering subdivision**. Most systems allow you to control the number of polygons used to approximate the patches. For testing, you might keep the subdivision level low in order to speed up the rendering. If each surface is approximated by fewer polygons, fewer polygons have to be rendered and the rendering takes less time. Later, when the final frames are about to be rendered, you can increase the subdivision level to improve the accuracy of the polygonal approximation.

(a)

(b)

Figure 3-95. When patches are subdivided into polygons before rendering, the number of subdivisions affects the accuracy of the rendering.

Figure 3-95a shows a NURBS sphere rendered with a very crude level of rendering tesselation. The flat sides of the polygons are clearly visible at the edges of the sphere. In Figure 3-95b the same sphere is rendered with a much higher level of rendering tesselation. The polygon edges are no longer visible and the sphere looks truly curved. Note that the original patch geometry of both spheres is the same; only the level of rendering subdivision has changed.

The issue of rendering tesselation, however, is not so simple as "more is better." "More," as always, costs more, and the more polygons you use to subdivide a surface, the longer your rendering takes. Consequently, you should increase the level of polygon subdivision only where such an increase is necessary. If your sphere is being viewed from a great distance, you can get away with a very low level of polygon subdivision, since the sphere will be very small and the polygons will be too small to see. If, on the other hand, you move your camera very close to the sphere, even the number of polygons used in Figure 3-95b might no longer be sufficient, and you might have to increase the level of subdivision.

The first and conceptually simplest method of determining the level of polygon subdivision is to specify the total number of polygons along each direction of the patch. For example, you might specify that along the U direction of a given patch the number of polygons is twenty, while along the V direction of the patch the number of polygons is thirty-five. Sometimes you specify these numbers more indirectly, in terms of the number of polygons inserted between each pair of control points on the patch. In either case, you specify the number of polygons as a fixed number in the U direction and a fixed number in the V direction.

Some systems also offer another, more sophisticated way of determining the number of polygons. This approach takes advantage of the fact that some sections of a patch need far fewer polygons than do other sections. In relatively flat areas of a patch, only a few polygons are necessary to produce a good approximation. However, where the curvature of a patch changes abruptly, a lot of polygons are required to make the rendering look smoothly curved. Specifying the minimum and maximum number of polygons to be used in any given region addresses this problem. If the region is relatively flat, the minimum will be used; if the region is relatively curved, the maximum will be used. Because the number of polygons adapts to the curvature of the surface, this technique is called **adaptive subdivision**.

Figure 3-96a shows a patch subdivided into polygons with the nonadaptive method. Notice that the lower portion of the patch, where the curvature is relatively small, is very nicely approximated by only a few large polygons. In the area of greatest curvature, however, at the "crook" of the patch, polygons of the same size—that is, the same level of subdivision—prove insufficient. Because the approximation of the curvature is crude, you can clearly see the flat edges of the polygons in the area of the crook. When the same patch is subdivided with the adaptive method, the flatter areas again are represented by a just a few polygons (Figure 3-96b). At the crook of the patch, however, the number of polygons greatly increases, making the curve look smooth.

(a)

(b)

Figure 3-96. Rendering subdivision can be either fixed or adaptive.

ANTI-ALIASING AND MOTION BLUR

When rendering final frames, you also must consider the staircasing effect inherent to computer images. Because any digital image is composed of a grid of tiny rectangular pixels, a curved or slanted edge of an object tends to

(a)

(b)

Figure 3-97. Aliasing, or the "jaggies," can be overcome by activating anti-aliasing calculations in the final rendering.

appear as a stepped pattern (Figure 3-97a). Often called the "jaggies," this effect technically is called **aliasing**, meaning that something appears to be other than it really is. For example, a truly curved line may appear to be a jagged line. Aliasing occurs when the system has too little information available for the phenomenon you want to represent. In this case, the phenomenon is a curved line and the information available is the rectangular grid of the pixels. Because the grid is too coarse, aliasing results.

The technique developed to handle this problem, **anti-aliasing**, consists of selectively blurring certain pixels along the aliased edge of a rendered surface. This blurring technique succeeds, even though the image is still composed of discrete pixels, because the color patterns of the pixels change very gradually, rather than abruptly, and the eye perceives the edges as smooth (Figure 3-97b).

Calculating the blurred pixels of an anti-aliased image requires additional time on the part of a rendering program. Because of this, you usually can turn anti-aliasing on or off. It is common practice, for example, when doing test renderings, to turn anti-aliasing off until you are ready to do the final renderings. In addition, most systems provide you with parameters for controlling the quality of the anti-aliasing. Some systems also permit you to select from among a variety of different anti-aliasing algorithms of differing qualities. As expected, the higher the quality, the more time required for the rendering.

The aliasing we have been discussing is caused by the nature of the two-dimensional space of your image, and is therefore sometimes called **spatial aliasing**. **Temporal aliasing** is a problem related to the spatial aliasing just described. It occurs when objects are moving very quickly. Sometimes the placement of an object within the frame changes drastically from frame to frame, and this produces a jerky effect when you play the animation back. In extreme cases, you see a strobelike effect. This variety of aliasing results from trying to represent the fast movement of an object with frames that are too coarse—for example, the frames rendered at the standard NTSC interval of one-thirtieth of a second.

One of the two ways of handling temporal aliasing takes place at the recording stage and involves a technique for creating and recording frames at smaller time intervals. (This technique and frame rates in general are discussed in section 6.11.) The other approach, **motion blur**, is similar to the spatial anti-aliasing of a picture and involves rendering fast-moving objects with a slight blurring or repetition at each frame (Figure 3-98). Like the blurring of spatial anti-aliasing, this causes the eye to fuse the frames so that they appear smooth.

It is interesting to note that motion blur occurs automatically, as a by-product of the process, when shooting live-action film. Since each frame of film is exposed for a specific amount of time, an object moving very quickly during that time appears blurred in the developed frame. In computer graphics, by contrast, objects are frozen in time by default, producing images without any blur. Because of this, you must take specific steps to turn on motion blur.

RAYTRACE DEPTHS

Another factor you need to consider when setting up the rendering process is related specifically to the raytracing algorithm. Recall that the process of raytracing involves following a light ray as it bounces from one object to another. The more the light ray bounces, the more physically accurate the shading calculations are. However, as usual, more calculations require more time, so you are in a position of having to balance precision against time. Most systems provide a parameter, often called **ray depth**, that controls how many bounces the rendering program will trace before performing the final color calculations for a given point on the surface. Setting the ray-depth parameter to zero causes the ray tracer to behave like a ray caster, tracing no reflective rays at all. In the interest of time, try to keep the ray-depth number as low as possible while still achieving acceptable visual results.

Most raytracing programs break down the ray-depth parameter into several component parameters, to give you more control. For example, one number may be used to limit the number of bounces a reflective ray may take, another number to limit the number of bounces a refractive ray may take, and a third number to limit the number of bounces a shadow-generating ray may take. As in all of these final-frame issues, you must make decisions which balance considerations of quality with considerations of rendering time.

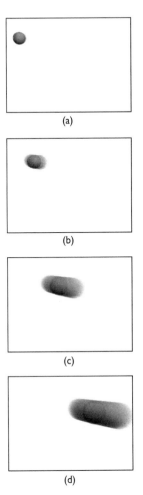

(a)

(b)

(c)

(d)

Figure 3-98. Very quickly-moving objects may need to be rendered with motion blur to avoid jerkiness. Here the ball begins, in (a), at a standstill. Motion blur increases, from (b) to (c), as the ball begins to move more quickly, then increases further, in (d), when the ball is moving very fast.

CHAPTER 4
Animation Basics

4.1 Introduction

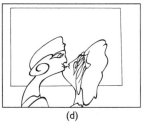

Figure 4-1. Some keyframes and in-between frames from a hand-drawn animation. Notice how the action changes gradually from one frame to the next. (*Dissipative Dialogues,* © 1982 David Ehrlich.)

Animation involves the production of a series of still images that, when played back in quick succession, appear as continuously moving. This illusion is produced by a physiological characteristic of our eyes known as **persistence of vision**. That is, when human eyes are stimulated—for example, by a still image—a slight afterimage is left on the retina of each eye after the stimulus is taken away. As a sequence of still images, or frames, plays back, each eye retains an afterimage of each frame for a brief moment, and this afterimage fills in the minuscule gap between the frame just past and the frame yet to come. As a result, adjacent frames seem to flow together smoothly.

If the time between frames is too long, the afterimage does not persist long enough to fill in the gap between frames, and you see a staccato playback of individual images instead. In film, for example, a playback rate of twenty-four frames per second works well. In video, the standard rate of playback is thirty frames per second. In either case, you must produce a lot of frames. A one-minute animation requires $24 \times 60 = 1,440$ frames on film and $30 \times 60 = 1,800$ frames on video. A one-hour animation requires 86,400 frames of film or 108,000 frames of video! This quantity is not difficult to produce using a live-action video or film camera: the actors walk around for one minute while the camera rolls, and frames are recorded in real time. If, on the other hand, an animator or team of animators must produce these frames one by one, an enormous amount of work and time can be involved.

In the early days of animation, and in particular at the pioneering Walt Disney Studios, a technique was developed to produce animation frames more efficiently. First a master animator would draw the most important, or "key," frames (called **keyframes**) of an animation sequence (Figure 4-1a and 4-1d). Then a number of less experienced animators would draw the **in-betweens**, or frames that fell between the master animator's keyframes (Figure 4-1b and 4-1c).

Much of 3D computer graphics animation, or **3D CG**, is based on this **keyframing** approach. In a computer keyframe animation system, the animator is the equivalent of the master animator. The animator sets up the keyframes, using any one of a number of techniques we will discuss later in this book, then instructs the computer to calculate the in-between frames. The computer, in other words, serves as an assistant to the human (master) animator.

4.2 Keyframing

You have already seen (in section 2.7) that when a three-dimensional object is modeled digitally, a set of transformations, called a transformation matrix, is associated with it. Each transformation matrix consists of values for the nine basic transformations—*translation* (x,y,z), *rotation* (x,y,z), and *scale* (x,y,z). The nine values of the transformation matrix control the overall placement, rotation, and size of the object. The simplest kind of keyframed animation involves changing the values of this transformation matrix over a period of time.

Imagine that you have modeled a cube, then positioned this cube by translating, rotating, and scaling it in some fashion (Figure 4-2a). With the cube transformed in some way that you like, you save this information as your first keyframe, keyframe 1. Saving the keyframe means that you save the values of the nine transformation parameters that define the configuration of the cube.

Having defined keyframe 1, you then reposition the cube—that is, translate, rotate, and scale it—as you want it to be for your next keyframe. Assume that you are making a two-second animation in video and that you want your next keyframe to be the final frame of the animation, frame 60. With the cube in that final position you save the transformations, and this becomes keyframe 60 (Figure 4-2e).

Once you have defined the keyframes for the sequence, you instruct the computer to calculate the in-between frames that should come between keyframe 1 and keyframe 60. The computer then calculates, for frames 2 through 59, the intermediate values for each of the nine transformation parameters. Calculating intermediate values is also called **interpolating** the values. These interpolated transformation values determine the intermediate placement, rotation, and size of the object at each in-between frame. For example, if the *translation* x of the cube is 6.0 at keyframe 1 and 0.0 at keyframe 60, then the interpolated value for the *translation* x of the cube at frame 30 (that is, halfway between frame 1 and frame 60) is 3.0.

In short, to say that the computer calculates an in-between frame means that it calculates the in-between, or interpolated, values of the nine transformation parameters for the object at that frame. When it does this for all of the in-between frames, you end up with a new set of nine transformation values in the transformation matrix of the object at each frame. With these transformation values the computer displays what the object looks like in each frame (Figures 4-2b, c, and d, for example).

Once keyframes have been defined and in-betweens calculated, you normally want to view the animation to evaluate it. In order to do this, you need to see more than just isolated still frames. That is, you need to play back the

(a)   f1

(b)   f15

(c)   f30

(d)   f45

(e)   **f60**

Figure 4-2. A sequence of computer-generated frames. Frames 1 and 60, outlined in bold, are keyframes explicitly defined by the animator. The other, in-between frames were automatically calculated by the computer.

frames as continuous motion. All computer animation systems provide this capability, called a **motion preview**, in one way or another. More sophisticated systems display higher-quality images as the motion plays back and offer more controls over the playback than do less sophisticated systems.

Upon seeing the motion preview, you may decide to change the animation. For example, you might decide that at frame 60 the cube should be flatter. You then retransform the cube, scaling it flatter, and save this as a new keyframe 60, overwriting the old keyframe 60. Having redefined keyframe 60, you instruct the computer to calculate new in-betweens and to play back the newly calculated animation. By setting and resetting keyframes, recalculating the in-betweens, and looking at motion previews, you can refine an animation until you are satisfied with the movement.

In actual practice, of course, most animations are much more complex than the simple example used here. It is very common for an animation sequence to be several hundred frames long and to involve dozens of keyframes for each of many objects. The basic principles remain the same, however, regardless of complexity.

We will see in subsequent chapters of this book that the same keyframing principles described here for the transformations of an object also apply to the animation of cameras, lights, surface points, and any other parameters you may define for your scene.

4.3 Interpolations

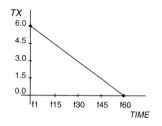

Figure 4-3. A linear interpolation of values between two keyframes.

A keyframe-based software system creates the in-between frames of an animation by interpolating the values from one keyframe to the next. The simplest kind of interpolation, **linear interpolation** (Figure 4-3), gets its name from the fact that if you draw a graph of the relationship between the two parameters (in this case, between frame numbers and transformation values), you get a straight line. In interpolating, say, from frame 1 to frame 60, frame 30, which is halfway between frames 1 and 60, receives transformation values that are half of the difference between the values at frame 1 and the values at frame 60. At frame 15, which is one-fourth of the way between frame 1 and frame 60, the transformation values are one-fourth of the difference between the values at frame 1 and the values at frame 60. The rate at which the value is changing stays the same over the length of the entire interpolation. Thus, if the *translation x*, or *TX*, value changes by −1.0—from 6.0 to 5.0—in the first ten frames of an animation, then *TX* also changes by −1.0 between frames 10 and 20, as it does between every set of ten frames.

If you imagine, however, having more than two keyframes in an animation, you can see the need for other kinds of interpolation. Suppose you want to extend your animation. The cube translates in X from 6.0 to 0.0 over the first sixty frames, but you need to create a third keyframe at frame 90, where the *translation x* value will be –6.0.

A linear interpolation on the *translate x* parameter for this new animation shows that a potential problem lies in what happens at frame 60 (Figure 4-4). The graph shows that at frame 60, the rate at which the cube is translating abruptly changes. The rate of change is represented by the **slope**—that is, the steepness—of the line. The steeper the slope, the faster the change; the flatter the slope, the slower the change. In this animation the cube moves smoothly and rather slowly from frame 0 to frame 60, but then at frame 60 it suddenly begins to move much faster. This may, in fact, be the movement you want to depict, but more likely, given the way things move in the real world, you want the cube to move smoothly through various positions, without any abrupt change in speed.

If you remember the discussions on curves and splines (see section 2.3), you can imagine the answer to this problem. The points on these interpolation graphs are effectively control points that determine the shape of a curve: in this example the "curve" consists of two straight lines connecting three control points. If you ask the computer to calculate a curve through these control points as a **spline interpolation** (in this case, an interpolating spline) rather than as a linear interpolation, you get the smooth curvature—the smooth change in *TX*—that you are looking for (Figure 4-5). Notice that there is no longer a sharp angle, or discontinuity, in the curve at frame 60. This means that there is no abrupt, or discontinuous, change in the rate at which *TX* is changing, so the cube translates smoothly from one point to another over the entire length of the ninety-frame animation.

Although it is the most common, the interpolating spline is not the only way to get a smooth interpolation through a series of values. Figure 4-6 shows another set of keyframe control points—here, for the translation in Y of some object—and the different interpolations that result when four different types of spline—linear, Cardinal, B-spline, and Bézier—are applied to those control points. Each of these interpolations produces a slightly different animation, even though all four have as initial data the same three keyfame values. Of the spline interpolations, the most commonly used is the **Bezier**. Not only does

Figure 4-4. If there are more than two keyframes, a linear interpolation can result in an abrupt rate of change between keyframes.

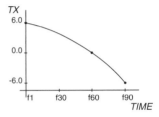

Figure 4-5. A spline interpolation through the keyframe values results in a smooth, continuous curve.

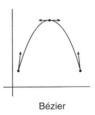

Linear   Cardinal   B-Spline   Bézier

Figure 4-6. For the same set of keyframe values, different types of interpolation yield different animations.

(a)

(b)

Figure 4-7. Spline interpolations can result in overshooting the intended values of a keyframe.

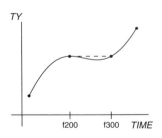

Figure 4-8. Spline interpolations by default produce a smooth curve, even if you intend a flat line.

this interpolating spline pass directly through control points, it also offers the convenience of tangent-handle editing, as we will discuss in section 4.4.

Now suppose that you modify the interpolation curve by moving the third keyframe closer in time to the second (Figure 4-7a). A problem occurs in the frames just before frame 200, the second keyframe. The spline interpolation must bend the curve upward above the value of the second keyframe so that when the curve comes down through the second control point (frame 200), the slope allows the curve to pass smoothly through the third control point (frame 220).

In a situation like this, you normally want the value at frame 200 to be the largest TY value that the object attains. The spline interpolation, however, forces the TY value to go higher, in the frames just before frame 200, than you probably intend. Suppose, for example, that the TY value represents the height of the ceiling in a room and your intention is to make the object rise until it touches the ceiling. The spline interpolation here unfortunately would cause the object to go through the ceiling in the frames preceding frame 200.

Notice also that this unexpected result is made even more extreme the closer the third keyframe is moved in time toward the second. If the last keyframe is advanced to frame 210 (Figure 4-7b), the curve has to bend up even more in order to come down smoothly through both frame 200 and frame 210.

This **overshooting** of keyframe values is a result of the requirement, built into the definition of a spline curve, that the curve always remain smooth, or **continuous**. Although the requirement of continuity is one of the great strengths of splines, in this instance it creates an unwanted side-effect, which you can adjust for by using a number of techniques discussed in the next section.

Now suppose that you want an object to remain motionless across a certain range of frames. The normal way to do this is to give the object the same transformation value at the beginning of the range and at the end of the range. In Figure 4-8, for example, four keyframes have been defined. Two of these keyframes, frame 200 and frame 300, have the same TY value. If this TY value remains unchanged between these keyframes, the curve should be flat in that section, as indicated by the dotted line. Notice, however, that instead of the curve remaining flat, it bends. This, again, is because the obligatory continuity of the spline causes the curve to bend up above the TY value at frame 200, then come down below it and curve gently upwards toward frame 300 again. Techniques for handling this situation appear in the next section.

Whatever the mathematics of your system's spline interpolation—for example, Bezier or some other—there are several common slope configurations, called **eases**, that appear as separate menu selections in many packages.

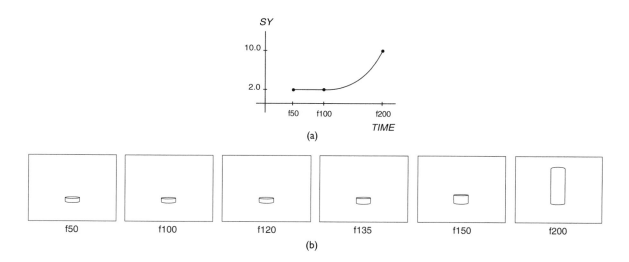

(a)

(b)

In animation you often want some change to begin slowly and then increase in speed. Suppose, for example, that you want a cylinder, at first not changing at all, to increase in height (scale in Y). Usually you want the transition from no movement to some movement—that is, the curve—to be gradual and smooth, rather than abrupt (Figure 4-9).

Between frame 50 and frame 100, the flat line indicates no change in the *SY* value. That is, the height of the cylinder remains the same. At frame 100, the curve very, very gradually begins to slope upward, and in the animation you see an almost imperceptible change in the height of the cylinder in the first few frames after frame 100 (Figure 4-9b). Farther from frame 100 the curve begins to rise more sharply, meaning that the height of the cylinder is increasing more rapidly. By frame 200, the *SY* value of the cylinder is increasing, and the cylinder growing taller, quite rapidly.

The interpolation between frames 100 and 200 is called an **ease-out**, or a **slow-out**, because the value changes slowly as it comes out of frame 100 and then more and more quickly as it approaches frame 200 (Figure 4-10). The opposite of an ease-out is an **ease-in**, or a **slow-in**, in which the value changes more and more slowly as it comes into the second keyframe.

Figure 4-9. In some animations, you want an interpolation to yield a very gradual change in the interpolated value.

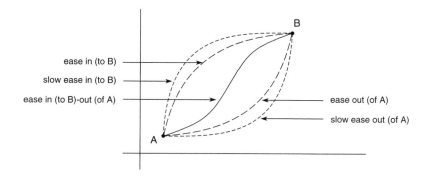

Figure 4-10. Different types of "ease" interpolations.

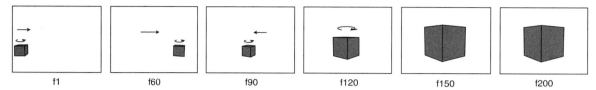

f1   f60   f90   f120   f150   f200

Figure 4-11. The animation of the cube as indicated by this storyboard requires several different types of interpolation.

Combining an ease-in and an ease-out produces an interpolation called an **ease-in-out**, in which the value changes slowly at first, then more quickly, and then slowly again.

Some systems, in addition to these three basic eases, also provide what might be called a **very slow-in**, sometimes called a **slow ease-in.** The opposite is a **very slow-out**, or a **slow ease-out.** These interpolations are just exaggerated versions of the normal ease-in and ease-out. If not explicitly provided as menu selections, you can make your own ease interpolations with the parameter-curve editing techniques described in section 4.4.

A simple animation can illustrate all of the different types of interpolations discussed in this section (Figure 4-11). As you see in the storyboard, the animation begins with a cube sliding in from screen left to screen right. The cube is rotating all the while. This action continues for sixty frames, until the cube reaches the right side of the screen. The cube then slides back, over the course of thirty more frames, to the center of the screen, where it stops but continues to rotate. After it stops at center screen, the cube increases in size, slowly at first, then a little faster, and then slowly again, until it reaches full size at frame 150. All this while, it is still rotating around a vertical axis. At frame 150, when it reaches full height, however, all movement, including the rotation, stops and the cube just sits there for a few seconds until frame 200.

In a graphical illustration of the way each of the nine transformation values for the cube animates over time, each transformation parameter is illustrated as a separate graph (Figure 4-12). Notice first that curves representing the translation in Y, TY, the translation in Z, TZ, the rotation in X, RX, and the rotation in Z, RZ, are simply flat lines. This means that the transformation values of those parameters do not change at all throughout the entire animation.

The TX curve, on the other hand, has a spline interpolation going through keyframes 1, 60, and 90, causing the cube to start at a low TX value (that is, at screen left), increase the TX value (move to the right) up to frame 60, and then come back again until $TX = 0.0$, placing the cube at the center of the screen. After frame 90, the cube doesn't translate in X at all, so the curve is flat.

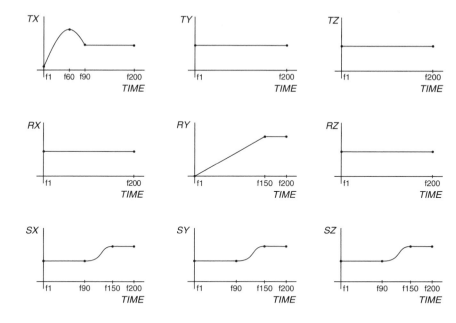

Figure 4-12. The different types of interpolation represented in these nine graphs bring about the animation in Figure 4-11.

Now notice that the *RY*, rotation in Y, value has a linear interpolation from frame 1 through frame 150, meaning that the cube is rotating at a constant speed all that time. At frame 150, which is where the cube reaches full size, the rotation abruptly stops, so the *RY* curve becomes a flat line.

The scale curves for this animation are all identical, since the cube increases in size equally in all three axes. From frame 1 to frame 90, the cube doesn't change size at all, so all three curves are flat. From frame 90 to frame 150, all three scale parameters have an ease-in-out interpolation, which is what causes the cube to grow in size—first slowly, then more rapidly, and then slowly again. From frame 150 to frame 200, the size of the cube does not change, so all three scale curves become flat lines again.

4.4 Parameter-curve Editing

Remember that in a keyframe-based animation system the most fundamental way to define the movement and timing of an object is to transform the object until it looks right visually, and then to save each set of transformations as a keyframe. There is, however, another very common and very powerful approach to defining the movement and timing of an animation. You saw in the previous section that it is possible to represent the changes in a given transformation parameter as a graph, with the changes in the value of a para-

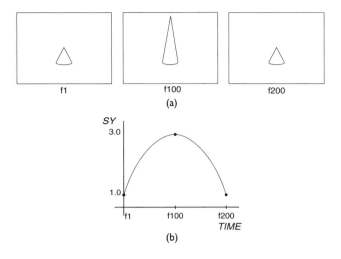

Figure 4-13. The graph of the animation of an object directly corresponds to the actual animation of the object.

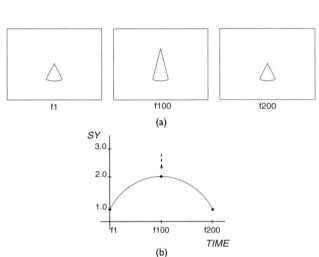

Figure 4-14. By pulling a keyframe control point down along the vertical axis, you change the value of the parameter—in this case, the height of the cone.

meter plotted against time. The alternate approach to defining animation takes advantage of this sort of graphical representation.

The underlying concept of this graphical approach is that any change made to the graph of some parameter causes a corresponding change in the animation. The graph, in other words, is a direct and immediate representation of the animation. If you change the graph, then you change the animation. Three-dimensional software packages allow you to modify, or edit, these parameter graphs and thereby to directly redefine, or edit, the animation itself.

Imagine that the height (that is, the scale in Y) of a cone increases and then decreases (Figure 4-13a; Figure 4-13b is the corresponding graph of the SY parameter). Using a system that allows parameter-graph editing, you can select the control point that represents keyframe 100 and pull it up or down to change the value of the *SY* parameter. Doing so immediately changes the height of the cone at frame 100. Pulling the control point at frame 100 down (Figure 4-14b), for example, lowers the height of the cone (Figure 4-14a).

It is also possible to push or pull a control point horizontally in the direction of time. For example, if you select and drag the control point at frame 100 to the left, leaving the point at frame 50, the height that the cone attains does not change (Figure 4-15). However, the timing of the animation changes, so that the cone achieves maximum height in only 50 frames, instead of the 100 frames it originally took—in other words, twice as fast as in the original animation. Moreover, the cone reverts to the lower height more slowly, in 150 frames instead of 100 frames.

In parameter-curve editing systems of this sort, it normally is possible to edit a curve in all the same ways that you might edit a curve for modeling purposes. For example, you might insert new control points into the curve, thereby changing the shape of the curve—as well as the animation controlled by the graph. To continue with the example of the cone, adding a new control point at frame 170 radically changes the animation, causing the cone to collapse almost to a flat circle at frame 170, where its *SY* value has been set to 0.1, before it returns to the original size at frame 200 (Figure 4-16).

In section 2.3 you saw that some curve representations allow you to manipulate the tangent vectors of each control point in order to edit the shape of the curve. This technique usually is possible in parameter-curve editing systems as well. Editing the tangent vectors in this way changes the curvature, or slope, of the curve in the area of each control point.

For example, editing the tangent vectors of the control point at frame 50 of the previous example yields a new curve (Figure 4-17). The tangent vector of the control point at frame 50 has been adjusted so that the curve is flat in the frames immediately following frame 50. This change causes the cone to linger near the maximum height for a longer time after frame 50 before beginning to shrink.

You can also select the type of interpolation used between any two control points. Any combination of interpolation types may be used between frames. For example, between one pair of control points the interpolation might be a **spline**. Between another pair of control points the interpolation might be **linear**. This technique is particularly useful when you want an element of your animation to change for a certain amount of time, but then to remain unchanging for another period of time.

For example, suppose you want to modify the previous animation so that the cone returns to its lower height (with an *SY* value of 1.0) at frame 170, then remains unchanging until frame 200. First, you move the control point at frame 170 up to give it a value of 1.0 (Figure 4-18a). Notice, however, that the *SY* value does not remain absolutely constant between frames 170 and

Figure 4-15. Moving a keyframe control point horizontally alters the timing of an action.

Figure 4-16. Additional control points can be inserted into a parameter curve to alter the shape of that curve and the animation it represents.

Figure 4-17. Adjusting the tangent vector of a control point changes the slope of the curve near that point. A change in the slope of the curve causes the changes in the action of the animation to happen more or less quickly.

Figure 4-18. In order to cause an object to remain stationary between two control points, you can apply a linear interpolation to that portion of the curve.

Figure 4-19. A stepped, or on/off, interpolation abruptly changes a parameter's value at the keyframed moment.

200. As you saw in the previous section, the mathematics of spline interpolation always produces a smooth curvature from control point to control point. As a consequence, the curve is forced to dip below the value of 1.0 between frames 170 and 200 before returning smoothly to exactly 1.0 again at frame 200. In the animation corresponding to this curve, the cone returns to the lower height at frame 170, but then continues to decrease in height for a few frames, before finally growing to the original size at frame 200.

In order to correct this dip, you can change the interpolation between frames 170 and 200 to a linear interpolation (Figure 4-18b). This change produces the flat line—and constant *SY* value—that you need in order to keep the size of the cone constant during these frames.

Another common type of interpolation, **stepped interpolation**, keeps a parameter value constant through a range of frames, then abruptly changes it to the next value at a given frame. In Figure 4-19, the value of TZ is 95.0 from frame 1 through frame 99. At frame 100, the value suddenly changes to 38.0. It remains at this value through frame 199, then abruptly changes to 61.0 at frame 200. The staircase-like appearance of the graph gives this interpolation type its name. Since the values pop from one to another instantaneously, it is also sometimes referred to as an **on/off interpolation**.

The effect of a stepped interpolation is that changes happen immediately, rather than gradually; this makes it a perfect interpolation type for turning a light on or off. You can also use stepped interpolation to animate the visibility of an object, another parameter offered by most software packages. Additionally, as we will see in section 4.10, it can be used for a camera cut, in which all the parameters of the camera abruptly change between one frame and the next.

Whatever interpolation type you use, it is very common to discover, during playback, that an animation or section of animation is too fast or too slow. To correct this you need to lengthen or shorten your sequence of animation, effectively changing the timing to make an action slower or faster. This editing capability usually is called **scaling the animation**.

One way to scale the animation is through a menu window, into which you type information such as the starting frame number of the sequence you want to scale, the ending frame number, and a scale factor. If the scale factor is two, for example, the sequence becomes twice as long—that is, twice as slow. This method allows you easily to scale an entire animation sequence, no matter how complex the sequence is or how many objects are in it.

Another way to scale animation is with dope sheet editing, as we will discuss in the next section.

A third approach entails using the parameter-curve editor to select a range of control points and stretch them out relative to some fixed control point. The fixed control point in this case effectively serves as the local origin about which the scaling operation is performed. In Figure 4-20a, for example, you see the original parameter curve. In Figure 4-20b the section of the curve defined by the last three control points has been scaled by 50 percent along the *TIME* axis. The fixed control point is the first of these—that is, the third from the right end.

This method of scaling an animation allows you great control over the scaling operation. Rather than performing a global scale on all the parameters of an object, you can scale specific parameters. If, for example, the whole animation sequence is fine, but the rotation of the cone around Y is too slow, you can scale just the *RY* parameter curve, without affecting the timing of any of the other parameters or any of the other objects. You also can control the scaling over a specific range of keyframes.

In addition to the operations described here, many systems allow you to cut and paste sections of parameter curves, to copy the curves of one object to another, to shift an entire curve up or down or left or right, and so on. Although the correspondence between the action of an animation and the graphic representation of that animation as a parameter curve may not be apparent to you in the beginning, with practice the correspondence becomes intuitive. Since any parameter in 3D CG can be animated and represented as a graph, the ability to interactively edit parameter graphs as described in this section becomes especially important. In addition to the standard transformation parameters of an object (translate, rotate, scale), you can edit the parameter graphs for the x,y,z locations of surface points, for lighting parameters such as color, intensity, or direction, for shading and texture parameters, for particle properties, and for many others.

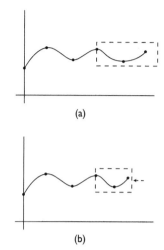

Figure 4-20. Curves, or sections of curves, can be scaled in time to slow down or speed up an action.

4.5 Dope Sheet Editing

We saw in section 4.4 that parameter-curve editing allows you to adjust both the timing and the values of animation parameters. Because so much of animation depends on timing, however, it is quite common to want to adjust only the timing of an action, leaving the parameters' values unchanged. To facilitate this, another editing technique is offered by many software packages.

In traditional animation, a chart, called either an **exposure sheet** or a **dope sheet**, is frequently used to organize animation information (Figure 4-21). This chart lists frames running vertically, with a number of columns running across the page horizontally. Each column contains information of different sorts for that particular frame—for example, notations about dialogue, or a camera change, or a special effect.

Adapted for three-dimensional computer animation systems, the dope sheet usually lists frames along the horizontal direction, consistent with the

Figure 4-21. In a traditional dope sheet, frames are listed by rows, with information about each frame listed in columns running across the page. (Metropolis Graphics.)

Figure 4-22. A CG dope sheet is used to modify timing. It lists frames horizontally, with a movable marker indicating each keyframe.

standard horizontal timeline of CG animation (Figure 4-22). Each vertically arranged row represents either an animated object or one parameter of an animated object. Keyframes are indicated by markers at the appropriate frames. Figure 4-22 shows a simplified dope sheet for an object called *car*, with keyframes at frames 1, 100, 120 and 200.

A basic dope-sheet function is to **offset** keyframes. Moving a keyframe left or right along the timeline changes the moment at which it occurs in time, and therefore changes the timing of that portion of the animation. We see this illustrated in Figure 4-23, where (a) shows the same dope sheet we saw in our previous illustration. In Figure 4-23b the keyframe that had been at frame 100 is offset to frame 80, making it occur twenty frames earlier than it had. This causes the first action (fl–f80) to happen more quickly than it had previously, and the second action (f80–f120) to happen more slowly.

In Figure 4-23c we see a second timing variation on the original animation. Here the last three keyframes have been offset 60 frames to the right. The original frames 100, 120, 200 have now become frames 160, 180, 260. The result is that the first action (fl–f160) happens much more slowly than it had in the original, but all the remaining actions happen at the same speed.

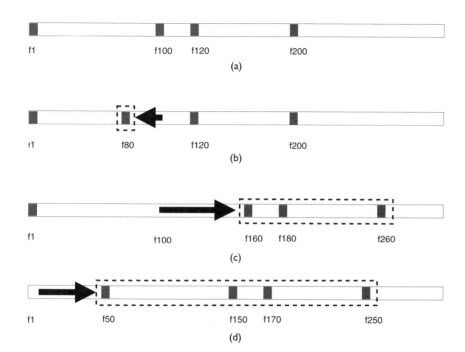

f1   f100   f120   f200

(a)

f1   f80   f120   f200

(b)

f1   f100   f160   f180   f260

(c)

f1   f50   f150   f170   f250

(d)

Figure 4-23. By offsetting individual keyframes or groups of keyframes, you make them happen earlier or later in your animation.

The last example, Figure 4-23d, shows the entire animation being offset to the right by fifty frames. This retains the original timing of all the actions, but starts them fifty frames later.

Another important dope sheet function is **scaling**. Here, you select a range of keyframes, indicate which end of that range will serve as the origin of the scale operation, and then drag the movable end of the range left or right. Stretching the range of frames causes all the action in that range to happen more slowly; squashing the range causes the action to happen more quickly.

In Figure 4-24a, we again see our original animation. In Figure 4-24b, its last three keyframes have been selected and scaled, using frame 100 as the origin of the scale. Since frame 100 was the origin keyframe, it remains unchanged. The other keyframes expand to the right, with the original keyframes at 120 and 200 becoming frames 140 and 300 after scaling. The result of this operation is that the timing of the animation remains unchanged from frame 1 to frame 100, but becomes 150 percent slower in the remainder of the animation.

Figure 4-24c shows another example. Here, all four keyframes of the original animation have been selected. Using frame 1 as the origin, they have

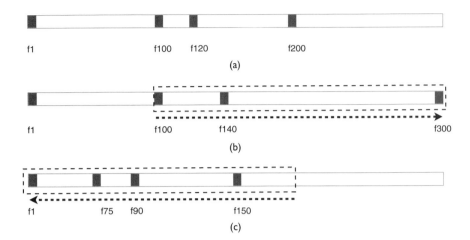

Figure 4-24. Scaling a group of keyframes makes that section of the animation run faster or slower.

Figure 4-25. Each animated parameter of an object has its own line in a dope sheet, allowing you to control the timing of either individual parameters or of the entire object.

been scaled to the left. The original frames 100, 120 and 200 have become frames 75, 90, and 150. That is, the entire animation will now run faster—specifically, in 75 percent the amount of time it used to take.

Our examples so far have been simplified to consist of a single timeline for a single object. It is also possible to use the dope sheet to change the timing of specific **parameters** of an object. In Figure 4-25, we see four timelines indicated in the dope sheet. The top line is for the entire object, *All*. Below that, we see timelines for each of three animated parameters for that object—the translation X and Z parameters, and the rotation Y parameter. Notice that the *All* row has keyframe markers at all frames having keyframes for any parameter. The individual parameter's rows, by contrast, have keyframe markers for only their own keyframes. Operating on the keyframes in a given parameter's timeline changes the timing only for that parameter. Moving keyframes in the *All* row changes the timing for all parameters of the object.

The parameters of models consisting of many moving parts can be similarly manipulated. As we will see in section 4.6, models can be organized into a **hierarchical structure**. In this case, each element, or node, of the hierarchical model has a separate row in the dope sheet. This allows you to adjust the timing separately for any of the individual nodes, or for the entire model

Figure 4-26. A hierarchical model has individual dope sheet lines for each hierarchical node, allowing you to control the timing of either each node individually, or of the whole object.

as a whole. Figure 4-26 illustrates this. If we want to change the timing only for the scoop of the shovel, we could select and operate only on the keyframes in the *scoop* row. Selecting only the keyframes in the *cab* row permits us to adjust its timing—for example, to make the cab rotate more slowly. By dragging a selection window around keyframes in all of the rows, we could adjust the timing of those keyframes for the entire model.

4.6 Forward Kinematics

So far, you have seen examples of the animation of simple objects, such as a cube, a cone, or a cylinder. You have seen how each of the nine parameters in the transformation matrix of an object can be set and interpolated, and how the interpolation of the transformation values over time produces the animation of the object.

As you saw in section 2.9, however, many models are more complex than a simple one-piece object. Many models consist of several parts, which you need to organize into a hierarchical structure in order to gain more control over the transformations you apply to different elements of the model.

Animating a hierarchically organized model is conceptually just an extension of the technique of animating a simple one-piece model, and is called **hierarchical animation**. It is also called **forward kinematics**. The word

f1

f20

f40

f90

f150

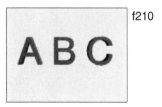

f210

Figure 4-27. A storyboard of a simple animation that requires the use of hierarchical animation.

kinematics means the study or calculation of motion. Forward kinematics calculates the animated transformations for each node of your hierarchy in the normal way—that is, in a forward direction down the tree of the hierarchy, from parent to child (we will see in the next section that this is in contrast to the technique of inverse kinematics).

Forward kinematics is simply an extension of what you do when keyframing a simple object like a sphere. What you do for the simple model in order to set keyframes and interpolate transformations you now do for *each node* of the hierarchical model. That is, for each node you position the model and set a keyframe, then reposition the model and set a new keyframe. You then tell the system to create interpolated in-between frames for that node.

For example, imagine an animation of a simple logo (illustrated in storyboard form in Figure 4-27). The animation begins with the letters coming from behind the viewer and tumbling forward, as you see in panels 1 through 3. When the letters reach center frame, they stop (panel 4, frame 90) and then, as a unit, spin quickly around the horizontal X axis (panel 5), coming to a stop again in panel 6, frame 210.

In order to create this animation, you must structure the elements of the model (Figure 4-28a) in an effective hierarchy (Figure 4-28b). Notice that the hierarchy is structured in such a way that you can either transform the entire logo by selecting the *Logo* node or individually transform any of the letters by selecting one of the lower-level nodes.

For the purposes of this animation you also must think carefully about the placement of the **local origin** of each node in the hierarchy. In order to get the tumbling effect of the individual letters, the local origin of each letter (one of the small crosses in Figure 4-28a) should be placed in the center of that letter. You also must place the local origin (the large cross) of the upper-level node, *Logo*. The local origin of this node controls the spinning rotation of the entire logo at the end of the animation. The most effective placement of this local origin is at the center-bottom of the whole structure.

Once you have structured your model properly, you define the animation. You probably begin by translating the entire logo—that is, the *Logo* node—to the initial position behind the viewer. You then save a keyframe for this node at frame 1. After that you translate the entire *Logo* node forward to the final position, panel 4, and save that transformation as frame 90. This series of steps defines the initial translation of the whole logo.

So far, however, the letters have not tumbled. You can go back to frame 1, rotate each of the three individual letters to the appropriate starting rotation value, and save this transformation as keyframe 1 for that individual node. You then view frame 90, which is where the tumbling of the letters ceases, and define—again, individually for each of the letter nodes—the appropriate final rotation value.

At this point, you have defined animation both for the *Logo* node and, separately, for each of the letter nodes, from frame 1 through frame 90. If you play back the animation now, you see the logo come forward, the letters tumbling as it does. This action continues for 90 frames, at which point both the forward movement of the logo and the tumbling of the individual letters stop.

Remember that *each* of the nodes must be positioned individually and that the position of each node must be saved as a keyframe. Most software systems provide a function that allows you with a single menu selection to save a given keyframe for all the nodes of a hierarchy.

The remainder of the animation entails a spinning movement of the entire logo so no additional keyframes need be set for the individual letters. You can create the spinning of the logo—the quick rotation about X called for by the storyboard—by selecting the *Logo* node and saving keyframes at the appropriate frame numbers. This is easy to accomplish, since you defined the pivot point of *Logo* at the bottom-center of the logo structure. Notice also that, because any transformation on a parent node propagates downward to the children nodes, the rotation you apply to *Logo* causes all of the individual letters to rotate with it as a unit.

In order to understand clearly what is happening when a hierarchical model is animated as described above, remember the concept of a local coordinate system (see sections 2.7 and 2.9). Remember that each node in a hierarchy represents a distinct transformation matrix, which functions relative to an individual local coordinate system. In other words, each node of a hierarchy has a local coordinate system, and the transformations applied to that node are calculated relative to the local coordinate system.

Think of the local coordinate system of a child node as being contained within the local coordinate system of the parent node, like a box within a box. Figure 4-29 shows how, in the logo model discussed above, the local coordinate system of the *B* model fits within the local coordinate system of the *Logo* model. Each local coordinate system here is represented as a cube drawn with dotted lines. The larger dotted-line cube represents the local coordinate system of the whole *Logo* node.

In Figure 4-29a the *B* and *Logo* models are untransformed. In Figure 4-29b the *B* has been rotated within its own local coordinate system. This rotation has no effect on the *Logo* coordinate system, since *B* is a child of *Logo*, not a parent, and transformations are transmitted only from parent to child. For a real-world analogy to this situation, think of rotating a shoebox within the larger box of your house. The rotation of the shoebox does not cause any other objects in the room to rotate, nor does it cause the house to rotate.

In Figure 4-29c the *Logo* node of the hierarchy has rotated, as represented by the rotation of the large dotted-line cube. Since this node is a parent of the *B* node, the *Logo* rotation causes the *B* to rotate along with it. To resume

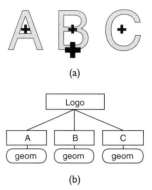

(a)

(b)

Figure 4-28. The hierarchy of the model is structured to allow the movements called for by the storyboard.

(a)

(b)

(c)

Figure 4-29. Each node of a hierarchy functions within an individual local coordinate system.

(a)

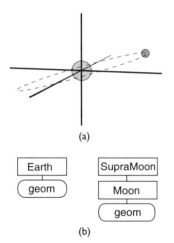

Earth   Moon

geom   geom

(b)

Figure 4-30. Animating the moon in a path that lies in the XZ plane does not require any hierarchical structure.

(a)

Earth   SupraMoon

geom   Moon

geom

(b)

Figure 4-31. To achieve a rotation around an arbitrary axis, a dummy node can be created above the original node.

Figure 4-32. In hierarchical animation, a transformation in one local coordinate system is embedded within the transformation of another local coordinate system.

the shoebox analogy: rotating the house (the house movers have arrived?) causes all of the objects within the house, including the shoebox, to rotate. This concept of the transformations of local coordinate systems and the embedding of local coordinate systems within one another allows us to deal very easily with an animation problem that otherwise would be very difficult to resolve.

Suppose you want to animate a moon rotating in a circular path around the Earth (Figure 4-30a). Notice that the path of the moon lies conveniently in the XZ plane. This allows you to place the local origin of *Moon* at the center of the earth model and then rotate *Moon* around Y. A rotation around Y of 360 degrees causes *Moon* to rotate one complete orbit around the Earth. Notice, in the diagram of the structure of this scene, that you do not have to build a hierarchy in order to create this animation (Figure 4-30b). You can operate directly on the sphere object that is the moon.

Imagine now, however, that you want the moon to rotate around the Earth at an angle (Figure 4-31a). This presents a problem. Since the orbiting path of the moon no longer lies flat in the XZ plane, you cannot do a simple rotation around Y, or any of the three axes, to produce the desired animation.

By making use of hierarchical animation, however, creating an additional hierarchical node directly above the *Moon* node, you can solve this problem (Figure 4-31b). A node such as this, which has no geometry connected directly to it, is sometimes called a **dummy node** or a **null node**, and in this example the dummy node is called *SupraMoon*.

Even though the *SupraMoon* dummy node has no geometry, it does have a local coordinate system. Initially, the local coordinate system of *SupraMoon* and the local coordinate system of *Moon* are in perfect alignment (Figure 4-32a). The local coordinate system of *Moon* is represented by the smaller of the two dotted-line cubes. The local coordinate system of *SupraMoon* is the larger cube, which encompasses the smaller.

Rotating *Moon* around Y still creates a simple rotation of the moon in the XZ plane. However, if you also rotate the local coordinate system of *SupraMoon* around Z (Figure 4-32b), you produce the tilted rotation of the moon that you

(a)

(b)

want. In short, you produce a rotation around no particular global axis by creating a hierarchy of several embedded local coordinate systems.

From a conceptual point of view, hierarchical animation is not complicated. That is, you animate each node of the hierarchy, positioning and saving keyframes. By carefully placing the pivot point of each node before you begin, you control the way the transformations affect that node. Also, by creating dummy nodes in the hierarchy, you divide one seemingly impossible transformation into several very simple transformations.

Hierarchical animation, however, can become more complicated when you have an elaborate hierarchical model. This can happen, for example, when using forward kinematics to animate a complex machine, an application for which this technique is particularly well suited. The more movable

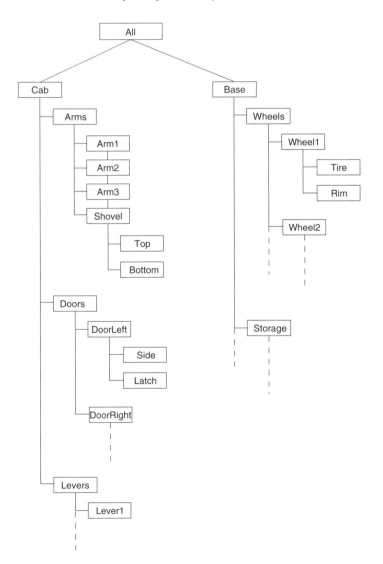

Figure 4-33. Regardless of the complexity of the hierarchical structure of a model, forward kinematic animation remains conceptually simple.

parts your model has, the more nodes in the hierarchy, with each node being individually animated. Recall the example of the shovel model from section 2.9. This simplified model already has twelve nodes in its hierarchy (Figure 2-77). If we added doors, windows, latches, levers, and other objects, we might easily have a hierarchy with thirty or forty nodes, each of which might have to be animated (Figure 4-33).

Fortunately, there are techniques for simplifying this process, one of the more important being pose-based animation, as discussed in section 4.12. Other techniques include hiding or compressing the display of your hierarchical nodes, and functions that save keyframes automatically every time you move a node.

4.7 Inverse Kinematics

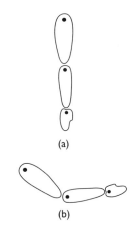

(a)

(b)

Figure 4-34. An arm model lends itself to the inverse kinematic technique.

In animating some hierarchical models, the procedure described in the previous section—that is, selecting each node of the hierarchy, transforming that node, and saving the transformation—makes perfect sense. In other situations, however, the structure and intent of your model make the process of selecting and transforming each node cumbersome. If you look at a simple arm model in one position (Figure 4-34a) and think about moving that model to another position (Figure 4-34b), for example, you probably want to do what you do in real life. That is, you probably want to move the "hand" end of the arm and have the rest of the arm follow. This is the way you intuitively think of this kind of movement: "I moved my hand from here to there," you think, not "I rotated my upper arm, then I rotated my lower arm, then I rotated my hand—with the result that my hand ended up there."

The forward-kinematic approach of hierarchical animation, however, does force you to think this way. You can think in terms of transformations on specific joints, and you can animate this way, but it is not well suited to the sort of limbed model you usually find in figure animation.

In the real world, the position of the hand determines the position of the arm joints, because all the parts of the arm are connected and remain so as the arm moves. If the hand moves, the lower arm must follow. If the lower arm moves, the upper arm must follow. You know this intuitively, and that is why intuitively you want to place the hand and let the joints follow, rather than individually rotating each joint in order to get the hand to a specific location. This is a **goal-oriented** approach to movement: you move the hand toward its goal, and the position of the arm's joints follow the hand's movement.

The technique that implements this approach is **inverse kinematics**, or **IK**, for short. As we saw in the previous section, kinematics refers to the study of motion. Inverse here refers to the fact that the flow of transformations within the hierarchical model is calculated in the opposite direction to the normal, forward, calculation. Normally (as you saw section 2.9), you think of the transformations of a hierarchy as propagating *downward* through the hierarchy (Figure 4-35a). The transformations of *LowerArm* affect *Hand*, but those of *Hand* have no affect on *LowerArm*. The transformations of *WholeArm* effect both *LowerArm* and *Hand*, because the transformations for *WholeArm* travel downward through the hierarchy.

In an inverse kinematic model, however, the transformations applied to the lowest level, *Hand*, determine the transformations of *LowerArm*. The calculation of the transformations travels *upward* through the hierarchy, rather than down through it (Figure 4-35b). The standard downward propagation of transformations, recall, is referred to as *forward kinematics* to emphasize the difference.

Fortunately, 3D computer animation systems that provide inverse kinematic capabilities make all this mathematical calculation of transformations transparent to the animator. The animator can think simply in terms of "placing the hand at X" and let the system calculate as it will.

Because the animator does think in a different way when working with a forward kinematic model than when working with a standard hierarchical model, a number of specialized terms are commonly used.

Since inverse kinematic models are frequently used for human and animal figures, the hierarchical structure of an inverse kinematic model is usually called a **skeleton**, with the end point of each segment being a **joint**, and the space between the joints a **bone**. The end point of the final bone in an inverse kinematic skeleton—the point that you move—is called the **effector**, because moving this point effects the rotations of the various joints. The starting point of the first bone in the skeleton—the one point of the whole skeleton that is fixed—is called the **root** of the skeleton.

Figure 4-36a shows these elements and their relationships to one another. Each of the bones of the inverse kinematic skeleton is drawn as a straight line, and the joint of each bone is marked with a dot. This dot also represents the pivot point of that joint. Remember that an inverse kinematic skeleton is actually a hierarchical model, and that each joint of the skeleton is a node in that hierarchy. Each node of a hierarchy has an individual pivot point, or local origin, about which all the transformations on that node take place. Here, the starting point, or dot, of each joint is also the local origin of that bone.

The local origin of the first bone, the root of the entire skeleton, is represented here as a square, which means that it is also the pivot point of the entire skeleton. The end point of the final bone in the skeleton is the effector, and is marked by an arrowhead. It is this effector point that you select and move in order to reconfigure the skeleton.

Figure 4-36b shows a standard hierarchical diagram for this same skeleton. Note that *joint1* here is the root joint, and is the parent node of the entire

(a)

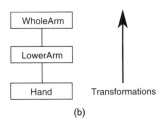

(b)

Figure 4-35. In standard hierarchical animation, transformations are calculated down the hierarchical tree. In inverse kinematics, the transformations are calculated upward from the bottom-most joint.

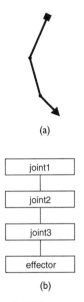

(a)

(b)

Figure 4-36. Two ways of diagraming the structure of an inverse kinematic chain.

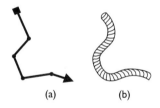

Figure 4-37. Unrestricted rotations of the joints of an inverse kinematic chain can be useful for certain types of models.

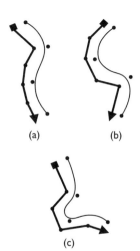

Figure 4-38. Moving the CVs of a spline-curve controller changes the configuration of its IK skeleton. This is especially useful when the skeleton must bend in many different directions.

Figure 4-39. Some systems constrain the rotation of a joint in order to simulate the movements of the joints of our own bodies.

hierarchy. Both diagrams illustrated in Figure 4-36a and b are accurate; they simply illustrate different aspects of the same model.

In principle, you can rotate the joints of a skeleton in any direction, and at a variety of very irregular angles (Figure 4-37a). Unrestricted rotations of this sort are appropriate if, for example, you model a rope (Figure 4-37b). For this sort of model, a single effector at the end of the skeleton is not an effective way to control the rotations of the joints, since moving the effector could produce any number of possible joint rotations. Instead, you usually define a spline-curve to control the skeleton. This **IK spline controller** is associated with the joints of the skeleton so that any changes to the shape of the curve produce corresponding changes in the shape of the skeleton (Figure 4-38).

Inverse kinematics, however, is most frequently applied to human and other animal models. In the real world of animal flesh and bone, joints are not, in fact, capable of moving in unrestricted directions, as are the "joints" of a rope. Human and animal joints have limits—points beyond which they cannot bend. The human elbow, for example, does not bend beyond approximately 180 degrees—that is, into a position where the upper and lower arms form a straight line. The same is true of the knee joint and most of the finger joints, and you find similar limits in the joints of other animals.

Because of this, it is common for a 3D animation system to impose a default 180-degree-rotation limit on the joints of an inverse kinematic model. Moreover, as we will see in section 7.3, you can also define the number of degrees at which to limit the rotation of a given joint. In practice, this means that most joints of a skeleton are able to bend in only one direction, like an elbow or a knee. In the simple two-joint model in Figure 4-39, the lower joint can bend only to the right. It is constrained from bending at all to the left, beyond an imaginary center line.

This 180-degree restriction might pose a problem when you want the bend of a limb model to change direction. In Figure 4-40a, for instance, the figure bends its lower arm joint up and down on the left side of the 180-degree dividing line, while in Figure 4-40b it bends the same joint on the right side of this dividing line. Both bends are reasonable human movements.

The solution to this seeming difficulty is the same solution you use in real life. In order to accomplish these movements, since your elbow joint really is limited to approximately 180 degrees of rotation, you rotate your whole arm about the shoulder joint, in addition to rotating your elbow joint. In inverse kinematics, if you rotate the entire limb about the root pivot point, you produce the "reversed" rotation you want.

Another constraint that some systems impose on the movements of inverse kinematic chains has nothing to do with physical bodies. It happens to be much more complicated mathematically to calculate rotations about all three axes than it is to calculate rotations restricted to two axes. In other

Figure 4-40. In order to overcome a 180-degree-rotation constraint, the entire skeleton can be rotated at the root.

words, the rotations of a ball-and-socket joint that can move freely in all three axes are much more time-consuming to calculate than are the rotations of a hinge joint that moves in only the two axes of a plane. Since complex calculations translate into slower graphic displays, some systems provide the option to restrict the movements of inverse kinematic skeletons to two-dimensional movements in a plane.

You can overcome this restriction, however, by rotating the entire skeleton, as you saw above. If, for example, you want to bend an arm in the XY plane and then later bend it in the XZ plane (Figure 4-41a), you can rotate the entire inverse kinematic skeleton 90 degrees about X (Figure 4-41b).

The plane you rotate is sometimes called the **rotation plane** of the skeleton. In addition to using it to deliberately rotate a skeleton, as described above, the rotation plane also becomes important as a way to correct a common problem in inverse kinematics. Recall that the rotations of a skeleton's joints are determined by the location of the effector. When you move the effector, the software calculates—inversely, from the effector joint upwards—the rotation values for each joint. However, any single location of the effector can yield an infinite number of possible joint rotations. In Figure 4-42, the effector for each skeleton is in exactly the same location—a certain distance directly below the root. Yet, the rotations of the joints of the two skeletons are very different—one is bent to the left, the other is bent to the right. Both configurations (and all the configurations in between) are mathematically valid.

The result of this mathematical ambiguity is that, as you move the effector, your skeleton may suddenly **flip** to another configuration. This is especially common as the effector gets closer to the root (Figure 4-43). If the joints flip, you can use the skeleton's rotation plane to rotate the skeleton back to the orientation you prefer. By keyframing both the effector's location and the

Figure 4-41. Some systems limit the rotations of a joint to rotations in a plane. In this case, the entire plane can be rotated to achieve a fully three-dimensional rotation.

Figure 4-42. Any position of a skeleton's effector can produce more than one possible orientation of the skeleton.

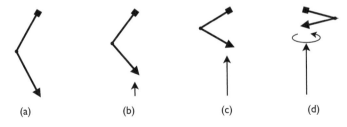

Figure 4-43. As you move the effector closer to the skeleton's root, the chances increase that the joints will flip 180 degrees.

rotation plane's orientation, you can control exactly how your skeleton bends at all times.

The discussion so far has centered on isolated inverse kinematic skeletons—one arm, one leg, and so on. In practice, of course, you need to combine these isolated skeletons if you want to model complete figures and other more complicated models. You do this with the normal hierarchical grouping techniques that all 3D computer animation systems provide. For example, a simple inverse kinematic human model might consist of one skeleton for each of the legs, one skeleton for each of the arms, a separate skeleton for a flexible backbone, and a final skeleton for the head/neck combination. Each of these skeletons is itself a hierarchy, and each skeleton can be grouped within the larger hierarchy that defines the entire figure. The result can be illustrated either as an inverse kinematic diagram or as a standard hierarchical diagram.

In Figure 4-44a we see a diagram of a simplified human skeleton, showing the joints and bones, and their connections. Figure 4-44b is a hierarchical diagram of the same skeleton, with the icons for each joint arranged to correspond to the positions of the skeleton's joints: the spine joints rise from bottom to top, the arm sections descend from the *neckbottom* joint, and so on. The *pelvis* joint is highlighted to indicate that it is the parent node of the entire

Figure 4-44. There are several ways to represent the structure of an inverse kinematic skeleton. Each approach emphasizes a different aspect of the structure.

(a)

(b)

(c)

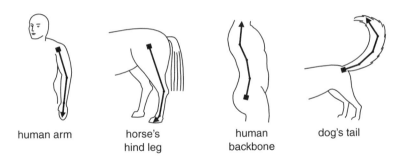

human arm   horse's   human   dog's tail
                   hind leg   backbone

Figure 4-45. The structure of an inverse kinematic skeleton must take into consideration the form and the functionality of the model it will be animating.

hierarchy. Figure 4-44c is the exact same structure, now organized to emphasize the parent-child relationships, with each child node place under its parent node. All three of the diagrams in Figure 4-44 illustrate the same structure and all are correct. Each emphasizes a different aspect of the structure.

Whatever constraints a system imposes and whatever the complexity of the model, it is important that you define the structure/skeleton of your model in a way that allows you to make the kind of movements you want to make with your model. In order to do this, of course, you must first know what those movements are. How, for example, does a horse's foreleg move? And how is that different from the way a horse's hind leg moves? You also must be aware of the technical constraints of the system you are using. Are angles limited to 180 degrees? Are rotations in all three axes possible? You must also think about which techniques will best control the movements of your skeleton—for example, effectors, spline-curve controllers, or any of the other techniques to be discussed in section 7.12. With a combination of technical and visual acuity, you then can build a suitable inverse kinematic structure (Figure 4-45), one that reflects the thought you have given to the number of joints, the length of each joint, the relative angles of each joint, and the direction in which the joints bend.

The discussion so far has dealt with the structure of an inverse kinematic model, but what about the **geometry** that goes into the skeleton? In working with inverse kinematics, the development of the internal structure, or skeleton, of a model can proceed independently of any consideration of the geometry of the model. This is quite different from what happens with a standard hierarchical model, where you must define the geometry before structuring it into a hierarchy.

Once you have defined an inverse kinematic skeleton, you can associate either deformable or non-deformable geometry with it. We will discuss techniques for putting deformable geometry on a skeleton in sections 4.9 and 7.13. Here we discuss the simpler case of **non-deformable geometry**, also sometimes called **rigid geometry**.

The standard technique for attaching rigid geometry to an IK skeleton is to make each geometry model a child of the appropriate joint. When this

Figure 4-46. Individual models can be grouped under each joint of an inverse kinematic skeleton. When the skeleton moves, the models move with it.

(a)   (b)

Figure 4-47. The initial placement of the models associated with each joint is critical.

is done, the parent joints' rotations are transmitted down the hierarchy to the child geometry, causing it to rotate along with the joint. In Figure 4-46a we see a hierarchical diagram of the skeleton plus its attached geometry. The joint nodes have been highlighted to make the structure clearer. In (b) we see the skeleton and its geometry in one position, and in (c) the skeleton's joints have been rotated by moving the effector, causing the two cylinders and sphere to follow along.

When creating an IK skeleton with geometry, you can either define the skeleton first and position the geometry on it afterward, or vice versa. Many animators prefer to create the geometry of their model first to get the exact form of their model, adding in the skeleton afterwards. However you do it, you must align geometry and joints exactly. A misaligned model will indeed rotate with its parent joint, since a child node inherits the transformations of the parent node. But a misaligned model will remain offset during its rotation by any transformation discrepancies it may have had initially, as we see in Figure 4-47.

In Figure 4-48, we see a more complex example of this technique. Here, the animator first modeled the robot character. She then drew an IK skeleton within it, lining up the skeleton exactly with the model parts, and defining effectors as needed. Finally, each component model was made a child of the appropriate IK joint. With this structure, she was able to animate the entire character by operating on the IK skeleton; as she moved the skeleton, the model parts moved with it.

Techniques for attaching deformable geometry to an inverse kinematic skeleton are introduced in section 4.9 and elaborated on in section 7.13.

Figure 4-48. Making your model's geometry into children of the appropriate IK joints allows you to easily animate a complex nondeformable model. (Hye Won Han.)

4.8 Motion Paths

So far you have seen two broad approaches to animating an object moving through space. The first approach involved visually positioning the object and saving a keyframe for each position. The second approach, a variation on the first, involved editing the parameter curves for the object in order to change either the keyframe values or the interpolation between them. In some situations, however, it is easiest to define the motion of an object through space in terms of a path that the object follows (Figure 4-49).

The basic idea is very simple. First you draw a curve in space, using the standard curve-drawing techniques that most systems offer. This curve, usually referred to as the **motion path** of the object, represents the path along which the object will move. You then select the object to be animated and tell the system, through some menu selection, that the motion of this object will be along this motion path and will take place over a certain number of frames. The computer then interpolates the in-between location of the object along that path for each in-between frame of the sequence.

For example, suppose you draw a motion path and assign it to a cube, beginning at frame 1 and ending at frame 400 (Figure 4-50). If you use a standard linear interpolation, then at frame 200, which represents half of the total time, the cube will be located halfway along the path. At frame 100, which is one-fourth of the time, the cube will be located at one-fourth of the distance along the path. And so on.

Even after you have assigned a motion path to an object, you can change the path, using any of the standard curve-editing tools. As soon as the path has been changed, a new interpolation of in-between positions is automatically calculated, resulting in a new animation along the new path.

The basic linear interpolation described above moves the cube along the path at a constant rate of speed throughout the length of the animation. Of course, you may not want such a perfectly constant rate of movement along the path, and so most systems provide a technique for controlling the rate of

Figure 4-49. The movement of some objects is most easily described in terms of a path that the object follows.

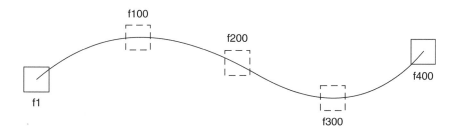

Figure 4-50. The position of an object in space may be interpolated along the length of a motion path.

Figure 4-51. A timing curve represents the position of an object along the path for each moment of time. If the interpolation of the timing curve is linear, as here, the object moves at a constant rate along the path.

Figure 4-52. If the interpolation of the timing curve is changed, the rate of movement of the object along the path is changed.

Figure 4-53. A flat section of timing curve means that the object is not moving during that section. A downward-sloping section of curve means that the object is moving backwards.

movement by adjusting the interpolation of a second curve, called a **timing curve**, which represents the rate of movement along the path. The timing curve plots time on one axis and the percentage of distance on the path along the other axis (Figure 4-51).

The timing curve is very useful, because you can edit it as you would any other parameter curve. Using the curve-editing tools provided by the software, that is, you can modify the interpolation applied to the position of the cube along the path. This modification might involve changing the type of interpolation, adding a control point, moving a control point, and so on. By changing the timing curve, you change the rate of movement along the path. For example, say you change the linear interpolation of the curve to an ease-in interpolation (Figure 4-52b). The cube still follows exactly the same motion path, but it does so now at a different rate of speed (Figure 4-52a). The cube moves very slowly along the path in the beginning of the animation, covering only a short distance in the first frames, then picks up speed along the path, until it moves very rapidly and covers a great distance in the final frames of the animation.

A few interesting, and perhaps surprising, effects can result from the editing of a timing curve. For example, if the timing curve is flattened and made horizontal over a certain range of frames, the object remains at the same location on the path for that range (Figure 4-53a). In other words, the object stops, remaining fixed at a point that is, say, 60 percent of the way along the path, from frame 200 through frame 300. In another situation, if the timing curve slopes downward, the object moves backward: it is located 60 percent of the way along the path at frame 200, but later, at frame 300, it is located only 40 percent of the way along the path (Figure 4-53b).

Another issue that you must consider when animating an object along a motion path is the orientation of the object relative to the path. Suppose you are animating a paper airplane along a motion path (see Figure 4-49). Undoubtedly you want the nose of the airplane to stay on the path (Figure 4-54a). In more technical terms, you want the airplane to remain **tangent** to the curve. Some systems do this by default. Other systems, however, do not adjust

(a)

(b)

the tangency of the object automatically, but by default always keep the object in the original orientation as it moves along the path (Figure 4-54b). In this situation, you must adjust the orientation of the object in a separate operation. One common way of doing this is to tell the software which axis of your object is to remain tangent to the curve.

Figure 4-55 shows a good example of motion-path animation. The animator first drew a spline curve, and then used it to model the curved tracks of the roller coaster. Next, she animated the cars of the roller coaster along that same path. This approach allowed her not only to keep the cars on the track, but also to use a motion-path timing curve to adjust their speed, slowing the cars as they climb up an incline, and increasing their speed as they shoot down the steep slope of the track.

Because architectural presentations so frequently benefit from fly-throughs or walk-throughs of the planned architectural space, motion-path control of the camera is particularly common in that field (Figure 4-56). In section 4.10 we discuss camera animation, including camera paths, in more detail.

(a)

(b)

Figure 4-54. In most situations, it is important to keep the object moving tangent to the direction of the path.

Figure 4-55. Motion path animation lends itself to moving objects along a complex three-dimensional path. (Kate Chapman, "Roller Coaster" 2002.)

Figure 4-56. Architectural applications frequently use path animation to create a camera fly-through. (Courtesy, Stacey Mariash.)

4.9 Shape Deformations

All of the techniques discussed so far have involved the animation of rigid objects. You have transformed objects by translating, rotating, and scaling them, but you have made no attempt to change an actual shape: to reform or deform the shape of the surface of an object. Although you might think that a change of scale is a change of shape, a change of scale does not constitute a change of shape in the sense meant here. Scaling an object makes it uniformly longer or shorter in one or more directions, but it does not alter the *configurations* of the surface. It does not alter the "bumps and hollows" (to use Auguste Rodin's phrase) of the surface.

In the real world changes of shape are very common. When a flower is brushed by a breath of air, the stem bends and the petals and leaves may also bend and change shape subtly. When a dog curls up and lies down on a rug, its body bends into a semicircular arc. The expressions of the human face are almost exclusively a matter of the face changing shape. In order to achieve any kind of successful animation of these or similar events, you have to be able to animate changes of an object's shape, or its **shape deformations**.

Shape deformations are referred to by a number of phrases, including **flexible surfaces**, **shape metamorphosis**, and **shape changes**. The basic idea is quite simple. Remember that in animating a rigid object, you define the transformations for the object, save these transformations as a keyframe, and then ask the computer to interpolate the transformation values between the two keyframes. The interpolated transformation values yield the in-between positions of the object.

Similarly, in animating a flexible, or deforming, surface, you determine the positions of the surface points (the control points or polygon vertices), save the positions of these points as a keyframe, reposition the surface points, save a new keyframe, and then ask the computer to interpolate the values between the two key positions. The interpolated positions of the surface points yield the in-between shapes of the object.

Figure 4-57, for example, shows a shape-deformation animation for a simple spline-based sphere. The sphere in an undeformed state, at the top, serves as keyframe 1. Notice that the coordinates of the control point on the far right of this sphere are (10,0,0). The third or bottom image in the illustration is a second keyframe, keyframe 100. In this keyframe, the same control point, pulled to the right, is now at a location of (20,0,0). Between these two key positions is one of the interpolated in-between frames, frame 50. Notice that the coordinate values of the control point—which has been moved and interpolated in a linear interpolation—are now (15,0,0); that is,

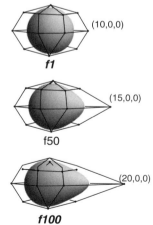

f1

(10,0,0)

f50

(15,0,0)

f100

(20,0,0)

Figure 4-57. Animating a shape change involves animating the positions of the points that define the surface of the object.

the control point is located halfway between the location of that point at the two keyframes. It is the interpolation of the location of the control point in space that has changed the shape of the sphere over time.

Animating the surface of a polygonal model (see section 2.2) is similar to animating the surface of a spline model, except that you have to move more points in order to create a smooth shape change. If you move only a single surface vertex on a polygonally defined sphere (Figure 4-58a), you produce an angular shape change (Figure 4-58b).

Repositioning many surface points individually can quickly become tedious. In the case of a polygonally defined sphere, you have to move quite a large number of points in order to make even a relatively simple change. With a spline-based model, simple animations are not difficult, but complex animations might require a great deal of very careful selecting and moving of control points.

For some effects, there is no way around this problem. If you want to create a very specific metamorphosis, you may have to go to the trouble of meticulously selecting and moving many control points or surface vertices. Fortunately, however, a number of techniques, collectively known as **deformers**, have been developed to simplify the process of animating the surface-defining points of a model. All of these techniques are based on the concept of associating the many surface-defining points of your original model with a very limited number of controlling points on some other object. By moving the few points of the controlling object, you move the many points of the original model.

One such technique helps you organize surface points into a collection. As you work on a model's deformations, you may find that you repeatedly want to operate on a particular collection of surface points—for example, the points in the area of a character's jaw. Defining these surface points into a **point cluster**, sometimes also called a **point set**, creates an entity consisting of those points. You can optionally name the cluster—for example, *jaw points*. Once you have defined a cluster of points, you can easily select all the points within the cluster either by clicking on the icon for the cluster, or by typing in its name. You then operate on these points as a group with any of the three standard transformations—move, rotate, or scale. Since the cluster is defined as an entity, it has its own pivot point, or local origin, which you can reposition as necessary to achieve the effect you want.

Figure 4-59 shows a simple model of a human head. Three clusters were defined: one in the area of the mouth, another in the jaw area, and a third in the area of the brows. Positioning the local origin for each cluster and then moving and rotating the clusters allows you to quickly create the two facial expressions seen here. By then keyframing the clusters' transformations, you create animation of the character opening his mouth.

(a)   (b)

Figure 4-58. In a polygonal model, animating only one point may be insufficient. You may need to animate many points to achieve the desired shape change.

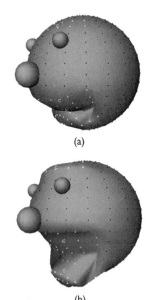

(a)

(b)

Figure 4-59. Defining a set of surface points as a point cluster allows you to easily manipulate those points as a group.

By default, all the points in a point cluster move equally when you transform the cluster. For example, if you translate the cluster +4.0 in the X direction, all of the cluster's points move exactly +4.0 in that direction. In some situations, this creates undesirable creases or edges at the borders of the cluster. To address this problem, you can adjust the **cluster weight** of each point. A weight of 100 percent means the point moves 100 percent of the amount the cluster itself is moved; a lesser weight moves the point proportionately less. Giving points progressively smaller weights as they approach the border of a cluster's area can produce a smoother deformation of the surface.

We saw in section 4.7 that it is possible to attach rigid, non-deforming geometry to an inverse kinematic skeleton. Frequently, however, you want the geometry of your IK model to deform. For example, the surface of a human arm, unlike a mechanical robot's arm, is flexible and deforms as the elbow bends. The sleeve of your jacket deforms as well. To achieve this sort of deformation, attach your model's geometry to your IK skeleton as a deformable **IK skin**, sometimes also called an **IK envelope**. We will discuss the subtleties of this process in more detail in section 7.13, but the basic idea is simple.

Recall that when you translate an inverse kinematic skeleton's effector, the software calculates the appropriate rotations of the skeleton's joints. When geometry is attached to this skeleton as an IK skin, the surface points of the geometry are translated as a function of the joints' rotations—the more the joints rotate, the more the points translate. As the surface points translate, the geometry deforms. We see this illustrated in Figure 4-60.

When you attach, or **bind**, a deformable IK skin to a skeleton, the software organizes the surface points of your model into clusters and associates each cluster with a specific joint. Thus, when *joint1* rotates, the points in the associated *cluster1* translate. The software also calculates an appropriate cluster weight for each point in each cluster to assure smooth deformations. All this is done by default, as part of the simple process of binding a skin to an IK skeleton, without any further user intervention. We will see in section 7.13 that in order to achieve certain effects you may need to reassign surface points to different clusters or adjust the cluster weights of individual surface points. One benefit of the skinning technique, however, is that a default assignment is automatically calculated for you as soon as you bind your geometry to your skeleton, producing immediate, reasonable deformations of even a complex model.

A deformable skin can be assigned either to a single skeleton, as it was in Figure 4-60, or to a hierarchy consisting of several skeletons. In this case it is sometimes referred to as a **global skin**, or **global envelope**. A character model, for example, might be bound to a hierarchy consisting of a skeleton for each leg, each arm, the spine, and the neck (Figure 4-61).

(a)   (b)

Figure 4-60. As the inverse kinematic skeleton deforms, the envelope associated with it also automatically deforms.

Figure 4-61. A model can be bound as a skin to a complex IK skeleton, allowing you to control the deformations of the entire model by manipulating the IK skeleton.

(a)   (b)

Figure 4-62. A skinned model can consist of multiple pieces of geometry. Here, the body, shirt, and shorts of the character are skinned to the skeleton.

In a complex character model, your character will probably consist of numerous surfaces. Any combination of these surfaces can be selected simultaneously and bound globally to either the entire skeleton or portions of it. Figure 4-62 shows an example of this approach. Here, three surfaces—the character's body, his shirt, and his shorts—are all bound simultaneously to the entire skeleton. When the skeleton joints are rotated into a new pose, the body, shirt, and shorts all deform with the joint rotations. As with any IK skinning, you may want to fine-tune the cluster definitions and cluster eights (section 7.13) to make your whole character model deform more smoothly as you manipulate its IK skeleton.

We see more complex examples of this same technique in section 4.12, as well as in color plate 2.

In another deformation technique technique, called **lattice animation**, you define a rectangular box, or lattice, of points to exist around the object you want to animate (Figure 4-63a). Each point of the box/lattice is associated with a cluster of surface-defining points—that is, with a cluster of control points if the model is spline-based, or with a cluster of surface vertices if it is a polygonal model. For example, the upper right, front vertex of the box might be associated with a cluster of control points in the area of the upper right forehead, eyebrow, and eye. Moving a few points on the lattice moves many associated points on the surface of the model and deforms the model (Figure 4-63b and c). Another way of thinking of this deformation process is that the rectangular lattice defines a space inside of which the head model

(a)   (b)   (c)

Figure 4-63. Lattice animation allows you to animate the shape of a complex model by operating on the points of a far simpler rectangular lattice structure.

exists. If the "space" of the head is deformed (quite an Einsteinian thing to do!), the head within that space is also deformed.

In order to produce an actual animation with the lattice-animation technique, you animate the points on the lattice structure by positioning them and saving keyframes. When these lattice points animate, the surface points they control also animate; when the surface points animate, the shape of the surface animates.

The great advantage of lattice animation, as with all surface deformation techniques, is that the number of points you must deal with in order to produce a complex shape deformation is drastically reduced. In the previous example, only a handful of points on the lattice had to be manipulated in order to make the two very radical, and complex, shape changes. If you had to select and move the individual control points that define the shape of the head, making these same changes would require a great deal more work—even more, of course, if the model were polygonally defined.

In the previous example, we defined a lattice around the entire head model. It is also possible to define a lattice to affect only certain portions of a model—for example, around only the jaw of our head model. You do this by selecting the points in the area of the jaw, then defining a lattice to control those points. When you deform this more restricted lattice, it deforms only the jaw area of the model. Separate lattices could be defined for other portions of the model.

Another deformation technique, called **spline deformation** or **curve deformation**, allows you to draw a curve through an object. The CVs of this curve are then associated with clusters of the model's surface points. As you change the shape of the deforming curve by moving its CVs, the clustered surface points of your model move as well, deforming its shape. In Figure 4-64, the deforming curve is drawn along the Y axis of the object. As this curve deforms, the head model deforms.

As with a lattice, a spline deformer need not deform the entire object. Rather than applying it to the whole object, you can apply a spline deformer to only specific points of an object, in which case, it is sometimes called a

Figure 4-64. The axis-deformation technique defines an axis of the local coordinate system to be curved. Since the space of an object is curved, the surface of that object curves.

(a)   (b)

(a)   (b)   (c)

Figure 4-65. The patch-deformation technique also deforms the space in which an object resides. A curved patch is substituted for one of the normally flat planes of the coordinate system of an object.

wire deformer. For example, you might draw a short curve horizontally across the mouth area of a character's head and tell the software that this curve controls only the surface points in that mouth area. Changing the shape of the wire deformer curve now changes the shape of the mouth.

In yet another technique, **patch deformation**, you substitute a curved patch for one of the normally flat planes of the Cartesian space of an object. The curved patch (Figure 4-65b) bends the space in which the model exists (Figure 4-65a), bending the model in the process (Figure 4-65c). This technique is especially useful for relatively flat objects that lie approximately in a plane.

Yet another shape-deformation technique, **path deformation**, is conceptually very similar to the spline-deformation technique. Remember that it is possible to animate an object along a path. A variation on that technique is to also deform the object as it moves along the path. The surfaces of the object (Figure 4-66a) are deformed according to the curvature of the section of path they are on at the moment (Figure 4-66b).

You can use any of the deformer techniques we have presented here either as a modeling tool to create a static deformation of an object, or as an animation tool to create animation of an object's deformation over time. When used for animation, there are two broad approaches to defining your keyframes. The first, as discussed so far in this section, entails directly keyframing the points of the deformer—for example, the points of your lattice, spline, or cluster. Since the deformer controls the shape of your model, animating the shape of the deformer in this way animates the shape of your final model.

(a)

(b)

Figure 4-66. In path deformation, the shape of an object deforms as that object moves along a motion path.

Figure 4-67. The keyshape technique applied to a sphere. Each of the keyshapes is outlined; between these three shapes are the in-between shapes generated by the computer.

For a complex shape-deformation animation, however, this approach can become cumbersome. For example, creating facial animation for a character might easily require many different facial expressions and deformations. To facilitate the process of making a great many shape deformations, you can use the **keyshape** technique (Figure 4-67). Using this approach, you begin by making several duplicates of the model to be animated. You then move control points or polygon vertices on the first copy of the model until you produce the right shape for frame 1. After saving this model as keyshape 1, you manipulate the points of the second copy of the model until you produce the right shape to save as another keyshape, perhaps keyshape 60. Then you alter the next model, save it as a keyshape, and so on. When you have defined all the keyshapes, you instruct the computer to produce the interpolated shapes that come between them.

A more powerful and useful variation on the simplified keyshape approach just described is the **blended keyshape** approach. As before, you begin by modeling several duplicates of your model, deforming each to create a set of keyshapes. Next, however, you use a menu selection to create a slider which permits you to blend these keyshapes together, producing new shapes. By keyframing the values of your blending slider, you create animation of the changing shapes.

Figure 4-68 illustrates the modeling stage this process. Figure 4-68a is the original model—in our case, a simple sphere. Each of the three models to its right was created by duplicating the original sphere and then moving some surface points. These four models—the original plus its three variations—are the keyshapes that define our blended keyshape deformer.

Figure 4-69 shows how this blended keyshape deformer creates animation. Each slider gives you a percentage of its associated shape. Moving the slider all the way up gives you 100 percent of that shape. With all the sliders set to 0.0, your result is the original, undeformed sphere. By moving the several slider bars up or down, you mix the shapes together. Your few original keyshapes, in other words, have become building blocks from which you can

Figure 4-68. The first step in the blended keyshape approach is to make several duplicate models all derived from your original.

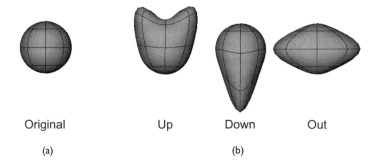

Original   Up   Down   Out

(a)   (b)

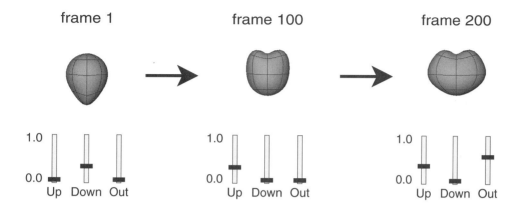

produce an infinite number of new keyshapes. In our illustration, the three keyshapes at frames 1, 100, and 200 were produced by moving the slider bars as indicated below each shape. Once you have adjusted the sliders to produce a shape you like, you keyframe that combination of slider bar values. The software interpolates between these key values to produce animation of your object changing shape over time.

Facial animation, because of the complexity of deformations involved, is one of the primary applications of keyshape animation (see section 7.14 for a much more detailed discussion of facial animation). In Figure 4-70, we see three keyshape variations on the girl's face model. By adjusting a mix of his blended keyshape sliders, the artist produced this very expressive animation.

It is important to realize that at the same time that you deform an object's shape using any of the shape-deformation techniques discussed in this section, you can simultaneously move, rotate, or scale the object. For example, at the same time that you animate the deformations of Figure 4-70, you can also rotate and move her head. By combining shape deformations with normal object transformations, your animation possibilities are vastly extended.

Figure 4-69. Using slider controls, blend different amounts of each keyshape, keyframing your results at the appropriate frames.

Figure 4-70. The blended keyshape approach is frequently and effectively used for the complexities of facial animation. (Courtesy, Yukito Kurita.)

(a)   (b)   (c)

Bear in mind, however, that animating a shape change is much more computationally expensive than animating a simple transformation of a rigid object. In the animation of a rigid object, at most nine values (three translations, three rotations, and three scales) must be interpolated and recalculated for each frame. In a shape-change animation, on the other hand, the number of values that need to be recalculated for each frame depends on the number of control points or polygon vertices being moved with each frame. If sixteen control points define the surface of a spline-based sphere, and each of these points has an X, Y, and Z value, then 48 values (16×3) must be calculated for each frame. If the sphere is polygonally modeled, it easily could have a ten by ten mesh of polygons, with each polygon having four vertices and each vertex three coordinate values. This operation requires the recalculation of 1,200 values ($10 \times 10 \times 4 \times 3$) per frame! As a result of all this calculation, the interaction time of many computers may be slowed down considerably.

This computational overhead, however, goes with the territory, and, as always, the quality of the results can outweigh the inconveniences of the process. Animating the changes in the shape of an object is usually critical for the success of an animation. Also keep in mind that computational issues of this sort become less problematic with each new wave of more powerful and less expensive hardware releases.

4.10 Camera Animation

Most of the animation examples so far have involved objects, whether we transformed them or changed their shape. It is also possible, however, to animate rendering parameters, such as the point of view from which a scene is observed, over time.

One of the most critical aspects of an animation may be just such camera animation. In fact, there is no animation in which the movement or lack of movement of the camera is not significant. As examples, think of these scenes from well-known films, both live action and animated. In the famous shower scene in Alfred Hitchcock's *Psycho*, the camera is positioned initially so that the viewer sees someone enter the bathroom well before the victim in the shower is aware of his presence. Once the attacker strikes, the camera cuts repeatedly and rapidly (there are about fifty camera moves in the scene overall) between the attacker, his victim, the shower head, the attacker's knife, the victim, and so on. Almost all of the tension and emotional impact of this powerful scene derives directly from the use of the camera.

By way of contrast, an animated film well known to students of computer animation, *Luxo, Jr.,* employs an absolutely stationary camera throughout the entire animation. In this case, *not* moving the camera becomes extremely effective, as the viewer must try to anticipate what little Luxo is doing each time he moves off screen, out of the range of the camera.

Given the importance of the camera, it is not surprising that 3D computer animation systems provide a number of approaches to animating the camera. The simplest of these approaches is to use a basic keyframing approach for the camera just as for individual objects. In fact, most systems treat the camera as an object, almost (but not quite) as if it were a cube or a sphere, and allow you to manipulate it very much as you would any other object, translating it and rotating it. You select the camera, manipulate it to produce the desired point of view, and then save the settings of the camera as a keyframe. Once you have saved a series of keyframes, the computer interpolates the in-between camera positions for each frame that lies between the keyframes.

Any of the parameters that define a camera in three-dimensional computer graphics—location, direction, field of view, and focal length (see section 3.2)—normally can be animated with this basic keyframe approach. Usually you do this by selecting any of the standard camera moves (pan, track, dolly, zoom, etc.) from a menu.

The top row of Figure 4-71, for example, is a storyboard representing an animation. In the first three panels of this storyboard (from left to right), both the camera location and the camera center of interest change. Between the first and second panels, the camera pans right—that is, as it moves to the right, the camera continues to look straight ahead. Between the second and third panels, the camera tumbles, or rotates, though the center of interest, or "gaze," remains fixed on the house. From the third panel to the fourth panel, the camera zooms in—that is, the field of view changes. In the final panel, a change in the focal length of the camera forces the objects in the distance, behind the house, to go out of focus.

In the bottom row of Figure 4-71 is a diagrammatic illustration of this same sequence. From the first panel to the second panel of this diagram, the

Figure 4-71. All of the standard camera manipulations that might be used when setting up a still image also can be animated with the keyframing approach.

Figure 4-72. A camera cut is an abrupt change from one point of view to another.

(a)   (b)

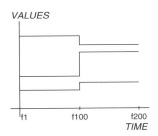

Figure 4-73. One way to affect a camera cut is to apply a stepped interpolation to the camera's parameter curves.

location of the eye and the center of interest move as a unit—that is, pan—to the right. In the third panel, the center of interest remains stationary, but the eye rotates about it. In the fourth panel, the field of view, represented by the dotted-line triangle emanating from the eye, narrows, indicating a zoom-in. And in the last panel, the farther of the two parallel dotted lines within the field-of-view triangle moves closer, indicating that the maximum distance at which things remain in focus has gotten closer. This last movement represents the shortening of focal length that results in the defocusing of the more distant objects in the last panel of the storyboard.

When you keyframe a CG camera, the software creates a default interpolation between the keyframes, just as it does for a keyframed object. This default is usually a **spline interpolation**, and tends to impart a soft, floating motion to the camera. If the differences between one camera keyframe and another are great enough, this floating motion becomes more extreme, resembling a roller-coaster point of view. This style of camera motion, because it is so easy to generate and so visually flamboyant, tends to be very overused by beginners, and should be avoided unless serving a specific purpose.

Frequently, the best use of your camera is a **camera cut**, in which the camera abruptly changes between one frame and another. A camera cut can be created by applying a **stepped interpolation** (section 4.4) to the camera's parameter curves. We see an example of this in Figures 4-72 and 4-73. The cut from the medium shot in Figure 4-72a to the close shot in (b) is accomplished by the sudden change in parameter values at frame 100. As we see in Figure 4-73, the parameters are constant from frame 1 through 99; at frame 100 they abruptly change, and then remain constant again.

Many of the parameters of a CG camera correspond to what actually happens in the physical world with cameras and with our eyes. Animating these camera parameters tends, consequently, to be intuitive for most people. Remember, however, that the camera of computer graphics also includes invisible walls, called clipping planes, that define the near and far limits of the visible world (see section 3.2). Most systems permit you to animate the locations of these near and far clipping planes. Animation of clipping planes, however, may be less intuitive than that of other parameters, since clipping planes do not correspond to any part of the way either real eyes or real cameras function.

The most common application of this technique is to improve the Z-buffer rendering resolution of a scene. Recall that one approach rendering programs use to calculate which objects in a scene are in front of which other objects is to store information about the Z location of each pixel in a separate buffer, called a **Z-buffer** (see section 3.6). The larger the amount of space to be dealt with, however, the less accurate this Z-location information will be, because the algorithm divides the space into a fixed number of subdivisions. (The specific number of subdivisions used is determined by the number of bits of memory devoted to each pixel. For example, eight bits of memory produce 256 subdivisions.) Moreover, the amount of space to be dealt with is determined by the location of the near and far clipping planes.

If the distances represented within an animated sequence vary significantly over the course of the sequence, it may be worthwhile to animate the near and far clipping planes in order to optimize the Z-buffer resolution during rendering. For example, in Figure 4-74a the viewer (that is, the camera) is watching a bird fly up from the far distance towards it. There are some trees (here drawn simply as circles) in the foreground. At the beginning of the sequence, the clipping planes (the solid parallel lines) must be set very far apart, behind the bird and in front of the trees, to include both the bird in the far distance and the trees in the foreground. In Figure 4-74b, as the bird flies closer to the camera, animating the back clipping plane to stay close to the bird improves the Z-buffer rendering resolution and results in a more accurate rendering.

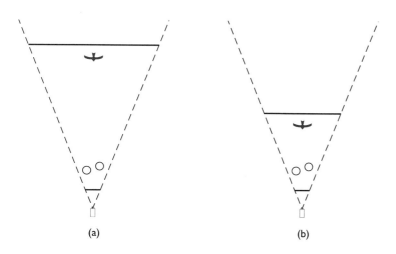

(a)   (b)

Figure 4-74. The location of the clipping planes can be animated to improve the accuracy of Z-buffer rendering.

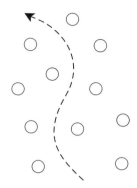

Figure 4-75. Some camera movements are best represented as movement along a path.

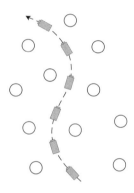

Figure 4-76. If the center of interest stays on the path, the camera always looks down the path.

Figure 4-77. The direction in which the camera is looking can be animated along a separate path.

Although the discussion of camera animation so far has been in terms of the basic keyframe approach to animation, the same alternate techniques discussed in conjunction with the animation of geometric objects can be applied here. For instance, just as you can edit the animation of the transformations of an object by graphically editing parameter curves, so you can edit the graphs of the camera parameters to change the camera animation. You can also apply motion-path animation to a camera just as you would to an object. If you were animating the frantic air-bike chase scene from George Lucas's film *Return of the Jedi*, for example, it would be a prime candidate for **camera path animation**. Much of the effectiveness of this scene is the result of the camerawork simulating the hero's ride through a forest at breakneck speed.

A diagram of this scene might look something like Figure 4-75. Here the circles represent tree trunks, and the curving line moving through the forest of circles/trees represents the path of the hero's air-bike. Since the camera is intended to represent the hero's point of view, it should follow this same path.

Clearly, thinking of the movement of the camera in this scene as a path is much more intuitive than thinking of it as a sequence of keyframes. You already have the path of the air-bike, so it makes sense to apply it to your camera. In fact, one way of doing this is to make your camera a hierarchical child of the air-bike, or, better yet, of the character riding on the air-bike. In this way, wherever your models go along the path, the camera will go with them.

However, some complexities arise when you think of camera animation in terms of motion paths. The camera, remember, is not a simple unary object like a sphere. A camera actually consists of both location and center of interest of the camera, and in setting up a motion path for the camera, you somehow must deal with both components.

To return to the example, imagine that you have assigned the motion path to the camera-location component of the camera. You still must determine the direction the camera is looking in as it moves down the path. You probably want the camera—that is, the hero's point of view—to look down the path as the air-bike speeds along through the forest (Figure 4-76.) This is the same issue that you encounter when moving an object along a path. That is, just as you want the paper airplane in Figure 4-54 to remain tangent to the curve, you want the camera—to think of it for the moment as an actual thing—to remain tangent to the curve.)

This choice may, however, produce a look that is too mechanical—too perfect. A person sitting on that air-bike would not always be looking exactly down the center of the motion path. Instead, the rider's gaze would slide from one side of the path to the other, now a little to the left, now a little to the right. Some systems allow you to get this effect by specifying a separate path for the center of interest (Figure 4-77). Notice that the path for the center of interest (drawn here as a dotted line) tends to slide away from the location path (the solid line) whenever there is a sharp turn in that path. This tendency simulates a bit more naturally what the (all too human) eye would do as the air-bike speeds around sharp turns.

One last aspect to consider with respect to motion paths is the issue (introduced in section 3.2, and illustrated here in Figure 4-78) of the tilt, or roll, of the camera around the Z axis. In systems that represent the direction of the camera as a set of rotational values, this tilting of the camera can be created automatically through a menu selection controlling a **bank** or **tilt** parameter. In systems that represent the direction of the camera in terms of center of interest, the tilt factor can be represented as a point in space that defines the "top" of the camera, and a separate motion path can be defined for that parameter to create the effect of banking around a turn. This method is similar to drawing the extra camera path, as you saw above, for the center of interest of the camera.

One of the common uses for camera path animation, alluded to in section 4.8, is architectural fly-throughs (Figure 4-79). Because of the complexity of the spaces defined and the importance of showing them clearly, frequently the best approach is to draw a path through the space and move your camera along that path.

Figure 4-78. The tilt of the camera can also be animated to produce a banking effect.

Figure 4-79. Moving the camera along a motion path is useful for architectural fly-throughs. (Courtesy, Stacey Mariash.)

Both camera path animation and keyframed camera animation can be very effective tools when used properly. Because it is so easy in most 3D computer animation systems to produce very dramatic camera movements, however, animators often overuse the camera. Keep in mind that camera animation should be used for a purpose. Sometimes the most effective use of the camera may be to keep it perfectly still, or to use a simple camera cut. As you set up your camera animation, ask yourself the question, "How does this camera benefit the animation?" If you don't have a clear answer, then you probably should not use that camera.

4.11 Animating Lights and Surface Properties

Any of the factors that influence the rendering of a scene—lighting, shading, coloring, and so on—can be animated over time. In principle, these animations are no different than the animation of modeling parameters. When you move an object from one place to another over the course of 100 frames, you really are creating an interpolated set of values for the *translation x*, *translation y*, and *translation z* parameters of that object. It is as easy for a computer to create an interpolated set of values for some rendering parameter—for example, the *shininess* parameter—as to create values for the *translation x* parameter.

One of the most significant factors in the rendering of any scene is the lighting. You have seen in section 3.3 that lights can be defined and placed in the virtual scene just as if they were normal objects. Lights can be transformed in space in all the same ways that, for example, a cube can. It is possible to position a light, save that position as a keyframe, reposition it, save a new keyframe, and then create the interpolated animation of the light moving from the first position to the second. This is how a moving highlight, or gleam, is created. As the light moves through space, the highlight it creates on the shiny logo moves about as well, creating a moving "gleam" on the surface of the object.

In addition, you might rotate a spotlight, to create the sort of roving-spotlight effect seen in an "Opening Night at the Movies" animation. Or you might scale some specialized light such as an area light, the definition of which includes a specified size.

It is also possible to place a light within a model's hierarchy. For example, a spotlight might be placed within the shade of an adjustable desk lamp, or on a miner's helmet, or within the headlight model of a vehicle. Wherever the model moves or rotates, the light, as its hierarchical child, will follow.

In addition to transforming a light, it is also possible in many systems to animate the other parameters that make up the definition of a light. That is,

(a)   (b)   (c)   (d)

you might animate the brightness of the light over time, or the color of the light, or the spread of the light cone of a spotlight, and so on. You most often animate these parameters by adjusting the parameter as desired, then by making a menu selection to save a keyframe for that parameter, with that value, at that moment in time. You can then use the full range of interpolation types as well as parameter-curve editing capabilities for the animation of these lighting parameters.

Figure 4-80. Both the position and characteristics of a light can be animated.

Figure 4-80 consists of four panels, *a* through *d*, from an animation. A simple point light provides all the illumination in the scene. Over the course of this animation, the location of the light animates, moving from the lower right of the frame to the upper left. This movement was accomplished by placing the local origin of the light in the center of the large sphere and rotating the light around that origin over time. At the same time that the light moves, several properties of that light also animate. The intensity, or brightness, of the light increases over time. At the same time, the intensity of the glow parameter also increases: the software package used to produce these frames includes an additional parameter associated with the glow parameter that permitted the animator to make the ring effect more pronounced as the glow increased. Finally, notice that in panel *c*, a lens-flare effect results from turning on the lens-flare parameter for this light.

Just as you can animate various properties of lights over time, you can animate the surface characteristics of objects, such as color, shininess, diffuseness, highlight size, and highlight color (see section 3.4 for a discussion of these parameters).

As you also saw in the sections *Solid Texture Mapping* and *Atmospheric Effects* in chapter 2, a number of mapping techniques are commonly used to create certain surface effects. In applying any of these mapping techniques, you must set certain parameters to define how the mapping will take place—for example, to locate the map on the surface, to scale the effect (that is, the color saturation, the amount of bumpiness, etc.) of the map, and so on. You can animate these mapping parameters, again usually by typing values into a menu window.

Figure 4-81. Animating the rotation parameter of a two-dimensional texture map.

(a)   (b)

You might, for example, rotate a color texture map on a surface over time (Figure 4-81). Here, the surface geometry and all other properties of the surface remain static. Only the rotation parameter of the texture map is animated.

Or you might scale the effect factor of a displacement map over a sequence of frames (Figure 4-82). Here, all parameters are constant except for the scaling parameter on the displacement map. Or you might animate the "noise" parameter in a fractal-based transparency map, producing cloud patterns that swirl about over time (Figure 4-83). This latter technique can be especially useful when used with volumetric fog lights or particle systems to create a drifting, shifting fog, or smoke effect.

You can animate the same sorts of parameters—color, placement, and so on—in a solid texture as you can in a flat texture. However, it is also possible, because of the nature of solid textures, to produce an unusual sort of mapping animation.

You have seen that the volume of a solid texture is treated like a three-dimensional object and has a transformation matrix associated with it. In

Figure 4-82. Animating the effect parameter of a displacement map in order to increase the cragginess of the surface.

(a)   (b)

Figure 4-83. Animating the noise parameter of a fractal-based map causes the patterns to swirl about.

(a)   (b)

Plate 1. This example of hyper-realism in facial modeling and animation required meticulously developed geometry and texture maps. Below the final rendering, two of those maps are reproduced (a color texture on the left, and a bump texture on the right. (© 2001 Alceu Baptistão/Vetor Zero Brazil.)

Plate 2. The character's natural pose we see here, combined with his vivid facial expressions, show the importance of these two elements in effective character animation. The animator developed a library of poses for this character. (Courtesy Bill Burg.)

Plate 3. In this stunning model, several particle systems were used to create the hairs of the tarantula. The parameters of the particles were carefully adjusted to control the length, thickness, density, and color of the hairs. (Courtesy, Gevel Marrero.)

Plate 4. To create the intricate swirling forms behind the buddhas, the artist applied scanned versions of hand drawings as transparency maps on simple surfaces. The visual density of the scene belies its geometric simplicity. (Courtesy Mika Matsuura.)

Plate 5. The two CG characters in this frame are composited with the live-action scene using a background shader. The computer-generated lighting replicates the live-action lighting and shadows. (© Michael O'Rourke, 2002.)

Plate 6. This image uses global illumination techniques to achieve realistic indirect lighting in the interior spaces of the house. Here, physically-accurate lighting simulation replicates late afternoon light, around six o'clock p.m. (Courtesy, Henrik Wann Jensen.)

Plate 7. This sequence of frames illustrates the beauty and complexity possible with cloth dynamics. The dancer is performing a traditional Korean dance, wearing the customary long-sleeved dress. (Courtesy, Yi-sul Yoon.)

Plate 8. Several sophisticated lighting techniques create a densely composed frame in this powerful animation. A projector light with volumetric fog projects an animated sequence of digitized video frames onto the movie screen. The streaks of rain and the mist in the background are also created through volumetric fog lights. (*The Seventh Day,* Courtesy, Hamid Rahmanian.)

Plate 9. In this animation, the artist used cloth dynamics for the old man's sweater and vest, and paint-based modeling for the trees and flowers. The plants and branches gently sway in a motion-dynamics-generated breeze, as the old man talks lovingly to his plants. (© 2000 Matt Vitalone.)

Plate 10. This peaceful image uses particles and motion dynamics to create the sand kicked up by the crab. The beach surface is a series of attached NURBS patches, with subtle bump and color texturing. The crabs are animated with keyframing. (© 2001 J. Adam Burke.)

Plate 11. The artist effectively combined realistic and cartoon-style imagery in this animation. The grass was modeled with a paint-based technique, and animated with motion dynamics. The fox was modeled by hand, and keyframed. (Copyright 2001 Unju Lee.)

Plate 12. The animator used ray tracing to create the stunning reflections and refraction of light as it passes through the glass that holds the flower. (© Kyeng-Im Chung.)

Plate 13. Motion-path animation allows the camera to follow the lines of this abstract form as it swirls and twists through space. This same form also was built as a physical piece of sculpture. (© Frank Stella.)

Plate 14. Shape deformation techniques accomplished the naturalistic modeling and animation of the body of the dolphin. The rendering used a blue "atmosphere" to simulate the effect of water on the color of the dolphin. (Courtesy, RGA/LA. Joseph Francis, creative director.)

:03   Total:03

Fade up from black to close shot of figure in dark, cave-like room. Silence

:04   Total:07

Fade up of distant sound of people marching. Figure turns his head at sound.

:07   Total:14

Cut to exterior long shot of building. Louder sound of same footsteps. Overcast skies, sound of blowing wind. A column of dark figures is marching toward building.

:04   Total:18

Cut back to interior shot. Figure reaches for candle extinguisher. Distant, faint sounds of marching footsteps.

:06   Total:23

Cross-dissolve to column of marching souls, now entering building. Sound of footsteps and low moaning.

:07   Total:30

Cut back to figure. Shadows of marching souls pass by on wall. "Death" figure extinguishes candles one by one. As each candle goes out, one shadow disappears.

Plate 15. This storyboard segment illustrates the clear visuals, verbal descriptions, and timing and soundtrack notations that are key to good storyboarding. The 3D animation that resulted from this storyboard was very close in visual style to these watercolor panels. (© Ayako Hayashi.)

Plate 16. Radiosity realistically captures the soft lighting in the well of this stairway structure. Most of the light in the lower sections of the structure results from daylight bouncing indirectly off the diffuse stone and concrete surfaces. (Copyright © Chen QingFeng, cqfcqfcqf@sina.com.)

Plate 17. Modeling and rendering for real-time applications can achieve subtlety and complexity in spite of limitations inherent to the medium. This character consists of less than 1,000 polygons. Carefully developed textures applied to individual polygons provide visual detail. (© Cyber Warrior Inc.)

Plate 18. An architectural application of 3D computer animation. The dome structure opens and closes to form a roof. The design for this structure was created as a three-dimensional computer model to demonstrate how the final structure would look and behave. (*Iris Dome*. Invention and design by Chuck Hoberman. Rendering by Andrew Holdun. © 1994 Chuck Hoberman and Andrew Holdun.)

Plate 19. The transformation of the dinosaur skeleton in this animation was accomplished through a digital wipe between a skeleton model and a chrome model of the dinosaur. (Courtesy, R/Greenberg Associates, Inc. Commercial for Philips, created by Backer, Spielvogel and Bates, New York. Directed by David Ashwell of BGCS, with visual effects by R/Greenberg Associates. Computer animation directed by Joe Francis.)

Plate 20. The artist used raytracing to achieve the subtle reflections on the table and metallic surfaces. The light tubes were rendered with a glow function. (© 2000 Justin Pieroni.)

most cases, since you want the solid texture to "stick" to the surface, the transformation matrix of the texture volume and the transformation matrix of the surface are linked together so that they both have exactly the same transformation (see section 3.9).

It is possible, however, to create certain unusual effects by animating the transformation matrix of the texture volume independently of what is happening to the transformation matrix of the surface. For example, if you animate a separate rotation on the texture volume, the texture patterns swirl over the surface: Figure 4-84a shows the object as it receives the solid texture pattern before any transformation of the texture volume. Figure 4-84b and c show the effects on the same object of rotating the texture volume over time.

Another very interesting possibility in the animation of texture maps is that, rather than using a single, static image as the texture for the mapping procedure, you can use an animated sequence of pictures as the source texture images. For example, suppose that you already have produced—either through animation or live-action footage—a sequence of frames, such as the sequence of images from the work of the photographer Eadweard Muybridge (Figure 4-85a). Suppose further that you want to map this sequence of texture images onto the screen of a computer monitor that you have modeled. By specifying that at frame 1 you will use texture image number 1, and at frame 2 you will use texture image number 2, and so on, you can map the animated sequence of images onto the surface (Figure 4-85b).

(a)   (b)   (c)

Figure 4-84. The texture volume of a solid texture can be animated independently of the object being textured. Here, the texture volume has been rotated over time.

Figure 4-85. A sequence of images can be mapped onto a surface to create an animated image on the rendered surface. (Images from *The Human Figure in Motion* by Eadweard Muybridge, New York: Dover, 1955.)

f1   f7   f14   f20

(a)

f1   f7   f14   f20

(b)

In most systems, a technique very similar to this also can be applied to the use of background pictures. By specifying that a sequence of background pictures is to be used throughout the animation sequence, you can create an animated background in front of which models complete some series of actions.

Most systems allow you to create moving textures by defining your source texture to be either a sequence of still frames or a movie file.

4.12 Pose-based Animation

Many 3D software packages offer the ability to define and store key poses for a model. This is frequently referred to as a **pose-based approach** to animation. Once poses have been created, you or anyone on your team can retrieve these poses at a later time, applying them to your model as an important first step in creating an animation sequence.

The process begins with defining the set of parameters that will be stored in your pose definitions. This set is sometimes called a **pose set**. It may also be called a **character set**, although this latter name can be misleading, since the models need not be character models. (In some software packages offering nonlinear animation (section 7.14), this set may be identical to the **clip set** used for that technique.) To define a pose set, you select all those parts of your model that will be animated, and tell the software to store the parameters for those parts into the pose set. For example, if you select all the joints and all the effectors for an IK skeleton, you could save the translation x,y,z and rotation x,y,z parameters for each of those elements into the pose set (Figure 4-86).

With the pose set defined, you then use normal animation techniques to position the model and its parts into a desired pose. Next, you use a menu selection to save that pose. Saving a pose saves the current values for each of the parameters in the pose set. You repeat this process for as many poses you wish, saving them into a **pose library** (Figure 4-87). By working in this way, you gradually build up a very useful vocabulary of poses.

With poses stored in your pose library, you can retrieve a pose, apply it to your model at a given frame, and save a keyframe for your model at that frame. Moving to your next keyframe, you repeat the process, retrieving a pose from your library, applying it to your model, and saving a keyframe for your model at that frame. In this way, you build up your animation.

One potential problem that can arise with the pose-based approach is the quantity of data that may become involved. When you save a pose, you are saving information for all the parameters you defined to be in your pose set. If you are not careful, this can become an unwieldy amount of data. For example, the simplified character skeleton we saw in Figure 4-86 consists of nineteen joints and four effectors. If you carelessly define your pose set to include

Figure 4-86. The first step in pose-based animation is to define which parameters of your model will be posable. These are stored as a pose set.

the standard translation, rotation and scale transformations for each of those joints and effectors, you will have 207 parameter values saved for every pose (nine transformation values * (19+4) = 207). When you then keyframe your model, you will be saving 207 values at every keyframe! The situation could become even more cumbersome with a more detailed skeleton model, which might have thirty or forty joints and effectors, rather than nineteen.

The solution to this problem is to be selective about which parameters you define as part of your pose set. For example, you do not need to save scale values for any of your joints or effectors in our example, since inverse kinematics does not take scaling information into account for them. Moreover, many of your joints will have their rotations calculated automatically based on the translation of the effector, so you do not need to include those joints at all in your pose set; by including the effectors' translation values, you assure the rotations of the joints. Exceptions to this would be any joints not controlled by an effector—for example, joints controlled by an IK spline deformer, or joints you intend to animate with forward kinematics. For such joints, you would include the appropriate values—the translation values of an IK spline's CVs, or the rotation values of the forward kinematic joints. By thinking in this way, you can drastically reduce the number of parameters in your pose set. From the original 207 values in our example, you would probably be able to reduce the number of pose set values to between twenty and fifty. This will make a dramatic difference in the speed with which your software can calculate frames.

There is another implication of the data stored in a pose set. Since different models will normally have very different pose sets, poses generated for one model cannot usually be applied to another model. The exception to this rule is when two models share exactly the same structure and parameters. In some cases, models are developed with this restriction in mind. For example, you could build a boy model and a girl model. If the IK skeleton for each is structured identically, and if the naming of the joints and effectors is identical, then a pose developed for the boy could be applied to the girl.

Figure 4-87. The poses you save into your pose library can be retrieved by anyone on your production team. These poses then become the starting point for your keyframe animation. (Courtesy, Bill Burg.)

The pose-based approach can be extremely useful either for an individual animator building his own library of poses, or for a team of animators. In a team setting, a senior, lead animator may develop the key poses. Less experienced, junior animators can then retrieve those poses, applying them to the model at the appropriate point in the animation's timeline. With the key poses thus defined at the key moments, the junior animators fine-tune the timing and the in-between interpolations using the standard parameter-graph and dope-sheet techniques we saw in sections 4.4 and 4.5. This quite effectively mimics the production methods first developed by the Walt Disney Studios in which senior animators did the most crucial drawings (the keyframes), and junior animators did the intermediate drawings (the in-betweens).

Figure 4-87 shows a sequence of poses developed using the techniques discussed here. Notice the sense of **gesture** and **weight** in each of these poses. In character animation, capturing the gesture is critical to the success of your animation. If you freeze-frame on a good character animation, you will see that, no matter where in the animation you freeze-frame, the gestures of the character in those still poses will look natural. If they do not, it will be impossible for the animation itself to look natural. In Figure 4-87, the boy's body language is extremely expressive in every pose. If we add to that the character's expressive facial animation (see section 7.13 for a discussion of this topic), we get an extremely effective set of character poses.

CHAPTER 5
Advanced Modeling

5.1 Introduction

In Chapter 2 we examined many of the basic modeling techniques found in most off-the-shelf 3D software packages. In this chapter we turn our attention to some of the more advanced techniques you are likely to need as you create your models. All of the techniques presented here build on the concepts and principles of the more fundamental techniques. If you have not already done so, you should familiarize yourself with the material in Chapter 2 before proceeding.

5.2 Virtual Sculpting

Many high-end 3D software packages offer a flexible and powerful modeling technique based on the paradigm of clay modeling. This approach, called **virtual sculpting** or **virtual clay**, allows you to push, pull, and deform a surface in a visually intuitive way, similar to modeling a lump of clay.

Corresponding to your finger or wooden clay-modeling tool, virtual sculpting software defines a **sculpting brush**, with several adjustable parameters. The first parameter is the brush **size**, corresponding to a larger or smaller clay-modeling tool. A second parameter is the brush **action**, or functionality. Typical actions include **pull**, **push**, and **smooth**. A third parameter is the **strength** or **force** of the brush, usually controlled by a slider bar. A final brush parameter is the directionality of the brush. If a brush's direction is **normal** to the surface, the force is applied perpendicular to the surface—that is, either directly into or directly away from the surface. Alternatively, you could elect to apply the force in the direction of any of the x, y or z axes. The combination of these parameters determines how your sculpting brush behaves. For example, a strong, narrow *push* brush normal to the surface might correspond to pushing hard with the tip of your little finger directly into the lump of clay.

The virtual sculpting software represents all of these parameters in real-time as icons on your screen. In Figure 5-1, the size of the brush is represented by a circle—the larger the circle, the larger the brush. We see two brushes represented in our illustration, both of the same size. The strength and directionality of the brushes are represented by a **vector**, a line possessing both length

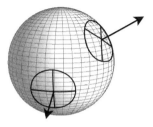

Figure 5-1. With the virtual sculpting technique you define the size and direction of a sculpting "brush." The direction is usually normal to the surface.

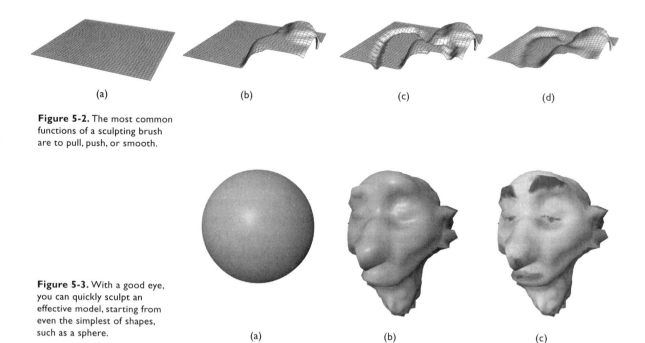

(a)   (b)   (c)   (d)

Figure 5-2. The most common functions of a sculpting brush are to pull, push, or smooth.

(a)   (b)   (c)

Figure 5-3. With a good eye, you can quickly sculpt an effective model, starting from even the simplest of shapes, such as a sphere.

and direction. In our illustration, each brush circle has a vector arrow coming out of its center. The brush in the upper right is a stronger brush (longer vector) pulling toward the upper right; the brush on the lower portion of the sphere is weaker (shorter vector), and is pulling toward the lower left. The action of both brushes is *pull*, and was determined by a menu selection.

By adjusting the parameters of your sculpting brush and making repeated **sculpting strokes**, you can intuitively and quickly deform a surface. Figure 5-2a shows an undeformed, flat surface. Notice that the surface has a dense array of surface points to permit detailed surface deformations. In Figure 5-2b, the surface has been deformed with a broad, strong *pull* brush. In Figure 5-2c, another deformation has been created on the left side of the surface, this time with a narrow and weaker *push* brush. In Figure 5-2d, a broad *smooth* brush has been applied to the entire surface, softening the bumps and hollows of the surface.

A more developed example is shown in Figure 5-3. From the polygonal sphere seen in Figure 5-3a, the artist used the virtual sculpting technique to produce the head model seen in (b). Figure 5-3c shows this same model with a texture map applied.

Because virtual sculpting is so visually and tactilely oriented, it is usually not appropriate for models requiring an industrial or mechanical level of precision. As we see in the illustrations above, however, it can be extremely useful in modeling more free-form shapes.

5.3 Digitizing Techniques

All the modeling techniques described so far in this book have pertained to models being designed and constructed entirely within the computer. In some situations, however, a physical model or some other real-world data already exist, and you want to develop a digital model from that given model or data. Say, for example, that you want to include a very realistically modeled human head, perhaps even a portrait of a specific person, in an animation. The best way to do this is to take measurements from the person and bring that information into the 3D modeling software package. Or if you are developing an architectural model or animation for which detailed data, perhaps in the form of architectural drawings, already exist, you undoubtedly want the digital model to accurately reflect these data.

The **special-effects** branch of the film industry also frequently makes use of real-world data. The design phase of many films entails the fabrication of physical sculptures of the characters, creatures, vehicles, and other objects that will become part of the film's special-effects scenes. This approach is so common that large production companies frequently have full-time sculptors on their staffs. Once a design has been settled on, the next step is to develop a digital model corresponding as exactly as possible to the physical sculpture.

Such applications require some method of getting information from the physical world into the computer modeling program. This process is known as **digitizing**, since it involves the conversion of real-world information into the digital form required by computer programs. A variety of digitizing techniques exists. Most of these techniques work directly from three-dimensional models, while some work from two-dimensional representations of three-dimensional data.

One common technique that works directly from physical models is a **3D digitizing pen**. Touching the tip of this pen to the surface of the object to be digitized produces a set of three-dimensional XYZ coordinate values, which the computer records. Each time the tip touches the surface, the location of another point is recorded. In this way, you compile a list of three-dimensional coordinates representing all the critical points on the surface of the object. The modeling software then uses these coordinates to build a surface, most commonly a polygonal model, that corresponds to the surface of the original object.

In order to produce data that have some regularity and are not randomly placed over the surface of the object, when using a 3D digitizing pen you should plan out exactly which points you want to record, and in what order. You can do this by either drawing or taping lines onto the surface of the object. Using this pattern, you then guide the pen to precise locations. Drawing the pattern of lines in a grid permits points to be recorded in an orderly fashion.

Figure 5-4. A 3D digitizing pen can be used to produce a list of polygon vertices.

On the left in Figure 5-4 is a physical object to be digitized—in this case, a sculpted head. The head has been marked all over with a pattern of lines, and the pen is about to touch one of the intersections of this pattern. Notice that the pattern of points does not have the same spacing throughout. It is denser where the curvature of the object changes abruptly in significant ways. For example, the areas around the eyes, nose, and mouth have a relatively dense pattern of lines applied to them. This density allows the digitizing process to capture the detail of those areas. By contrast, the top of the head is marked with a less dense pattern. This area has fewer significant changes of surface curvature, and consequently fewer points are needed to replicate it satisfactorily.

Notice also that the head is sitting in a shallow box. Most 3D digitizing pens make use of inaudible sonic waves as a means of keeping track of the location of the pen. A boxlike device emits sonic waves simultaneously from different directions. The digitizing device, like a bat locating an insect by sonar, locates the pen within this sonic field by measuring the amount of time it takes each sonic wave to reach the tip of the pen.

Finally, on the right in this figure, some of the individual digitized points are displayed on the computer screen. After all the points have been digitized, the digitizing software generates a polygonal surface, converting each digitized point into a polygon vertex.

A very different type of three-dimensional digitizing technique works on the principle of building up a surface from contour curves. This makes use of the lofting process (see section 2.8). First, a sequence of contour curves is developed, with each curve at a progressively higher Y location. Once these curves are in place, a lofted surface can be generated from them, either as a polygonal mesh or as a parametric surface.

The central issue of such a digitizing process, of course, is how to generate the contour curves. The most common approach, often referred to as

Figure 5-5. A succession of laser scans along the surface of an object produces a sequence of contours, which can be lofted to form a surface.

laser contour scanning, is to use a laser beam to scan around the surface and generate a list of points as it goes (Figure 5-5). The object to be digitized is placed on a turntable that slowly rotates. A laser beam is projected onto the surface of the object, and the distance the beam travels to the object is recorded. This continues for one complete 360-degree rotation of the object, producing one contour curve, which is displayed on the computer screen. Then the beam is lowered a bit, the object completes another 360-degree rotation, and another contour curve is recorded. When all the curves have been completed, a lofted surface is built from them.

In order to make the illustration clearer, the distance between each contour curve in Figure 5-5 is greatly exaggerated. In actual practice, the laser beam is capable of producing extremely fine readings, with only a fraction of an inch between contour curves and with many, many points on each curve. For this reason, laser contour scanning can produce extremely accurate and detailed digitized models. A disadvantage of this refinement, however, is that the technique can also produce extremely large and unwieldy sets of data. The more refined the resolution of the laser scanning, the more data generated. Consequently you may use a process, called **thinning**, or **culling**, that selectively throws away some data in order to make the remaining data more manageable. This process requires that you specify a maximum number of points allowable on each curve. Some of the original digitized points are then discarded, and a new curve is recalculated. Of course, there is a trade-off between accuracy and quantity of data. The more points discarded, the more manageable the data, but also the less accurately the recalculated curve represents the original surface.

Notice also that the laser-scanning process is a relatively dumb, brute-force technique, in that it produces an admirable amount of detail but makes no attempt to decide where that detail is needed and where it is not. For example, the same density of points appears on the top of the skull, where you do not need it, as appears around the eyes.

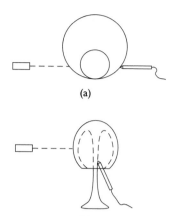

(a)

(b)

Figure 5-6. Both 3D digitizing pens and laser scanners have limitations. Certain surface configurations are inaccessible to both techniques.

Both the 3D digitizing pen and laser contour scanning can be extremely useful, depending on the nature of the original model and what you want to do with the digitized result. Both of them, however, suffer from one notable limitation: they digitize only the *exterior* surfaces of objects. If the object you want to digitize consists, for example, of a steel ball within a semitransparent plastic ball, with either a pen or a laser beam you can reach (and therefore digitize) only the exterior plastic ball (Figure 5-6a).

In some situations even exterior surfaces are inaccessible to either technique. A mushroom-shaped object, for example, presents difficulties, because neither a laser beam nor a digitizing pen is able to reach the top of the stem of the mushroom (Figure 5-6b).

This limitation can be significant for some applications. Many sculptural objects, for example, involve inward-curving forms similar in principle to the mushroom shape. And in many scientific applications it is crucial to be able to see and model surfaces within surfaces.

In fact, a number of digitizing techniques have been developed to handle such situations in science and, especially, medicine. These techniques are based on the idea of creating a series of **cross-sectional slices** and building a model by stacking the slices. The effect is the same as when you slice Swiss cheese. That is, viewing the cheese from the outside, neither you nor a 3D digitizing pen, nor a laser beam can see the holes inside the cheese. But when you cut the cheese into slices, these holes become apparent on each slice.

Several medical technologies implement this technique, including **X rays**, **Magnetic Resonance Imaging (MRI)**, and **Computerized Axial Tomography (CAT)** scans. Each of these technologies involves the emission of a signal capable of passing through certain materials of our bodies. When the signal reaches an interior material of a different character, it sends back information to the computer about the location in depth of this material.

A variation on this digitizing technique is possible even for those computer modelers and animators who do not have such extremely elaborate and expensive medical equipment at their disposal. A sort of poor person's CAT scan, this technique works with very simple objects. If the object to be digitized is cut into slices, both the interior and exterior contours are revealed on each slice. Tracing around these contours with a digital pen device digitizes the shape of each contour. By stacking these digitized curves, offsetting them by the thickness of each slice, you can generate a three-dimensional lofted surface.

On the left in Figure 5-7 is the mushroom-shaped object from Figure 5-6b. Here the object has been sliced into several slabs. The first three of these have already been digitized, and the digitized shapes of these slabs appear on the computer screen. The fourth slab is lying on the 2D digitizing tablet, in the process of being traced. Notice that this cross-sectional technique

Figure 5-7. Cutting an object into slices produces contour data. Any surface of any complexity can be digitized with this approach if the slices are fine enough.

captures the contours defining the space between the stem and the inner surface of the bell. A significant disadvantage to this technique, however, is that at several stages of the process it is subject to human error. If the slabs are not cut uniformly or if the tracing is not done with extreme care, accumulated error can distort the final digitized version of the model.

When you digitize cross-sectional contours by hand in this way, you also must properly align each slab with the slabs above and below it, and you do this by putting **registration marks** on all of the slabs. By aligning registration mark number 1 of slice A with registration mark number 1 of slice B, and so on, you can position all the digitized contours relative to one another.

Two-dimensional tracing plays a key part in another digitization process, provided by some 3D modeling systems, called **orthographic reconstruction**. This technique is related to the production, notably in architecture and industrial design, of scale drawings. These drawings are done orthographically—that is, without perspective foreshortening—and from three different right-angle views: front, side, and top.

The process begins with the digitization of each of the two-dimensional drawings. That is, you place each drawing on the 2D digitizing tablet and trace or scan over the key elements with a digitizing pen. As with the hand-drawn cross-sectional contours, you must properly register the drawings to one another. In the case of three orthographic drawings (Figure 5-8a), this usually is done by defining **fiducial points**, which are located within the drawing space of the paper and which remain constant through each of the three drawings. (The word "fiducial" means "something you can trust.") Once the data from the three orthographic drawings have been entered into the computer, the software then reconstructs an object consistent with the three sets of data (Figure 5-8b).

It is important to understand that any orthographic reconstruction process makes significant assumptions about the nature of the shapes involved. The silhouette information in the orthographic drawings in and of

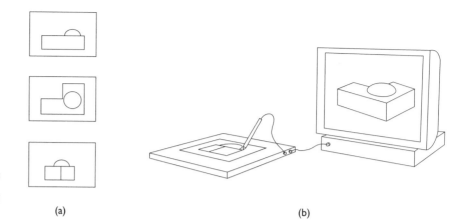

Figure 5-8. Three orthographic drawings can be used to reconstruct a three-dimensional object.

itself does not indicate whether the front wall of the previous example is flat (Figure 5-9a) or whether it is has a slight bow in it (Figure 5-9b). The orthographic drawings cannot resolve this ambiguity because the critical information—the bowing of the concavity as it would be seen from the side and top—is hidden by the other walls of the structure.

The orthographic reconstruction on the screen in Figure 5-8b, in other words, is based on the assumption that all walls are flat unless a silhouette suggests otherwise. For some designs in the architectural and industrial worlds this assumption is perfectly reasonable and the orthographic reconstruction technique works well. For some applications, however, the assumptions of the orthographic reconstruction process are too limiting and the process is ineffectual.

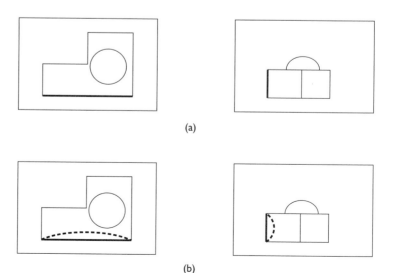

(a)

(b)

Figure 5-9. In order to deal with ambiguous forms, the orthographic reconstruction technique must make assumptions about the nature of the forms.

5.4 Procedural Modeling

Another technique offered by many systems involves a very different kind of approach to modeling. In these systems, there is an intermediate step between your interactive modeling of a scene and the software's final rendering of this scene. When you are ready to render, the software produces a text file, called either a **script file** or sometimes a **scene file**, consisting of a complete verbal and numerical description of everything in the scene—the models, the lights, the surface characteristics, the camera, as well as any animation that these elements might have.

A 3D software system might use a proprietary language for this scene file, or it might use a standardized language. In either case, the scene file is written in a programmable language. (Since professional graphics programmers very commonly use the C programming language, many scene-file languages are adapted from that language.) By editing the text file with a word processor or text editor, you can generate or modify any aspect of your scene. Since a program is often referred to as a procedure, this technique is called **procedural modeling** (if animation is involved, it is called **procedural animation**).

Effectively, anything that can be defined in terms of some variable or set of variables can be programmed in a script file. In doing so, you have access to the same programming elements, functions, and subroutines that you have available in a normal programming language. Variables, arrays, loop statements, conditional statements, sine and cosine functions, the absolute-value function, remainder functions, various types of ease functions, and so on, are standard tools in most programmable scene languages.

A simple example of procedural modeling is use of the programmable scene language to create **instances** of an existing model (see section 2.7 for a discussion of instances). Suppose you use the standard functions of a software package to interactively model a tree. You then write out a scene file. This text file contains a description of the geometry and the surface characteristics of the tree, and these descriptions constitute the definition of the tree. You then edit the scene file, adding a loop statement that generates a number of instances of the original tree model. Each time the tree is instanced within this loop, the transformations on the tree (location, rotation, and scale) are recalculated, so that each new tree is in a different location and is of a slightly different size and orientation. Using this procedural approach, you can easily model a simplified forest of trees.

Figure 5-10 shows example of the sort of procedural modeling that might accomplish such a task. This program is written in **pseudocode**, which is an informal, Englishlike version of the logic of a program. In actual practice, you write this code in the specific scene language of the software package you use. Notice that in this pseudocode objects and variables can be defined, just as in

```
/* define all elements of the scene */

define variables

define image size
define camera for scene
define surface characteristics
define lights

define tree model geometry

/* model a forest by instancing the tree model with
appropriate transformations */

for each tree
    {
    calculate the transformations on the tree
    instance the tree model
    }
```

Figure 5-10. A pseudocode version of a procedure to generate a forest model. The actual code would be written in the scene-file language of the software package.

Figure 5-11. The components of this plant were modeled interactively. They were then composed procedurally within a scene file. (© 1992 Sylvain Moreau.)

a normal programming language, and that looping is one of the programming tools available.

Procedural-modeling applications often make use of **randomness**. The forest model described above, for example, will not be very convincing if all the trees are positioned at very regular intervals, are all of exactly the same height, and so on. A certain amount of irregularity and unpredictability makes the model feel realistic.

Total randomness, however, is rarely useful. If, for example, the size of the trees is totally random, some of them might be only an inch high and some might be miles high! Clearly, this will not work. More commonly, the randomness programmed into a procedural model is constrained by certain probabilities, such as a relationship between the number of trees in the forest and the height of the forest above sea level. You also probably want the height of the trees to fall within a certain range of reasonable heights, with trees of "average" height being more likely than trees that are very tall or very short. This sort of controlled randomness in a procedure is called **stochastic modeling** and is a very powerful branch of procedural modeling.

The forest example as described so far is a very elementary use of procedural modeling, in that each tree is a copy of every other tree, and only the number of trees and the transformations on the trees are produced procedurally. To make the application more interesting, the tree model itself might be produced procedurally.

One way of doing this is to model interactively the components of the tree (trunk, branches, leaves, etc.), and then use the scene-file language to write a program that procedurally constructs a tree from these components. The plant model in Figure 5-11, for instance, was generated in this way. The thickness, density, and spacing of the branches and leaves were controlled by a stochastic procedure. Though this application of procedural modeling is

```
/* define all elements of the scene */

        .
        .
        .

define trunk model geometry
define branch model geometry
define leaf model geometry

        .
        .
        .

/* model a tree by instancing its components with
appropriate transformations */

push /* push trunk transformations */
calculate transformatons for trunk
instance trunk

calculate number of branches
for each branch of the tree
    { /* start branch loop */

    push  /* push branch transformations */
    calculate transformations for branch
    instance branch

    calculate number of leaves
    for each leaf of the branch
        { /* start leaf loop */
        push  /* push leaf transformations */
        calculate transformations for leaf
        instance leaf
        pop  /* pop leaf transformations */
        } /* end leaf loop */

    pop  /* pop branch transformations */
    } /* end branch loop */

pop  /* pop trunk transformations */
```

Figure 5-12. Pseudocode for the plant modeled procedurally in Figure 5-11.

clearly more complex than the simple instancing of predefined trees to make a forest, the procedurally modeled trees are conceptually the same as the forest example. That is, a few model elements were modeled interactively using standard modeling techniques, then instanced procedurally within a program loop. Transformations were calculated for each instance of each element within the appropriate loop.

Figure 5-12 shows an example of what the pseudocode for such a procedural model might look like. Notice that the pattern is the same as in the pseudocode for the forest: define model geometry, loop, calculate transformations, and instance. In the more complicated procedure, however, special care must be taken with the placement of the transformations relative to one another. The model being generated by this procedure should be organized hierarchically if it is to function properly. That is, the transformations effected on the whole tree should propagate downward to all the branches of the tree; the transformations on each branch of the tree should propagate downward to all the leaves of that branch; and so on. In order to accomplish this, you use one of the standard textual representations for the hierarchical structuring of transformations (see chapter 2, *Hierarchies*). For example, curly brackets can be used to push and pop the transformations of the hierarchy.

Both of the examples discussed so far involved using procedural modeling to instance and transform preexisting geometry. However, you also can use procedural modeling to generate the geometry of a model. With this approach, you write a section of program code in the scene file to generate actual geometric data. These data might consist of a list of polygon vertices and corresponding coordinates, or perhaps, if the system is a spline modeler, a list of control points and corresponding coordinates. Using this approach you could write code to generate the geometry of any model you wish. The mathematics involved in doing so, however, will normally be much more complex than simply applying randomness to the placement of instances, as we discussed earlier.

Just as a model can be defined procedurally, so too can the motion of a model be defined procedurally through the process known as **procedural animation**. Anyone familiar with basic trigonometry can program simple geometric patterns, such as circles and parabolas and sine curves. Using a few simple trigonometric functions, you can develop a scene-file program in which objects move about in these patterns. On a somewhat more complex level, you can program the growth of plants procedurally, by controlling the number and size of the branches and leaves over time, or the density of leaf development. You also can define and animate surface characteristics and lighting for any model procedurally.

Some of the most impressive examples of procedural modeling and animation involve very sophisticated uses of the programming techniques discussed here in conjunction with complex mathematics and physics. When scientists develop animations to simulate the orbit of a satellite around a planet, or the growth of a storm front, they use procedural modeling and animation, usually employing data from real-world measurements to produce their simulations.

The film industry produces some of its most stunning special effects through three-dimensional procedural modeling and animation as well. Large special-effects houses normally have both artists and programmers on staff, and when a job comes in that requires a new special effect, the artists and programmers collaborate. Based on what the artists and art directors are looking for, the staff programmers develop code to procedurally generate and animate the models involved. The artists then work with these proce-

Figure 5-13. Techniques that originally required procedural modeling by the user have now become standard features in most software packages. Here, the balls' motion dynamics, originally hand-programmed by the author, is now standard in 3D packages. (*Iggy's Dream #819*, © Michael O'Rourke.)

dures and make suggestions for changes. This process goes back and forth until the desired effect is achieved.

But what about those animators who do not have a staff of professional programmers to help develop procedural techniques? Sophisticated procedural modeling and animation can require programming skills that many artists and animators do not possess. In addition to the programming skills, these techniques require (depending on the task) a knowledge of physics, biology, meteorology, or other sciences. Clearly, not everyone possesses the scientific skills to develop sophisticated simulations or special effects. However, any animator willing to devote a little time to learning the grammar of a programmable scene language can gain access to some of the power of procedural modeling and animation.

Also bear in mind that all of the techniques discussed in this book began as procedural techniques available only to programmers. It is the nature of the research-and-development process in 3D computer graphics that a technique initially can be accomplished only by those who know how to write the program code that makes it happen. If the technique has wide appeal, however, it will be developed by professional programmers into a commercially-available product. Initially, this product may be a **third-party plug-in**—that is, a set of code produced by an outside company to run within the existing code of a major software package. Eventually, the technique will be written into the interactive portion of all major software packages. In both cases, the new technique becomes available to a wider range of users, including artists and animators, who may have no particular programming skills.

For example, the flying and bouncing bowling balls in Figure 5-13 were animated with motion-dynamics techniques. At the time this animation was

Figure 5-14. The water in this scene was modeled and animated with plug-in software—that is, a set of procedures developed by third-party vendors, but not yet standard in off-the-shelf packages. (Courtesy, Phoenix Tools SRL [Italy].)

produced, these techniques were not available in any interactive software package on the market, and the artist had to write program code in a scene file to produce the motion dynamics of the balls. The motion-dynamics calculations he had to write himself are now a standard part of all 3D software packages, and can be accomplished completely interactively using standard menu interfaces, without any programming (see section 7.7).

Another example is seen in Figure 5-14. The water in this image was modeled and animated with plug-in software running on one of the major 3D packages. A few years ago, this sort of sophisticated modeling and animation of water, based on fluid dynamics, was possible only in research laboratories. Today, it is available as third-party plug-ins. Tomorrow it will be a standard feature in all 3D animation programs.

5.5 Stitched Patches

Recall from section 2.3 that the primary advantage of patches as a modeling technique is that patch surfaces, unlike polygonal surfaces, are mathematically truly curved. No matter how closely you zoom in on a patch surface, its curvature can always be displayed smoothly.

The disadvantage of patches, on the other hand, is that their **topological structure** must always be a grid—that is, a network of rows (the U direction) and columns (the V direction). When you want to add a control point to a patch surface, therefore, you must add an entire row or column of control points. This can be limiting in certain modeling situations. For example, when modeling a human face, you will need more points in the areas of the eyes and mouth than you will in the chin or forehead areas. With a patch model, if you want more points in the eye area, you will need to add several rows and columns of points going all the way around the head.

The **patch stitching** technique is a solution to this problem. With this technique, several patches are joined together to form what appears to be one seamless surface. The patches do not actually become one patch—they remain separately defined from each other. Since they remain separate patches, each can have its own individual topology of control points. For example, one patch might have four rows and seven columns; another might have sixteen rows and eleven columns. Even though they are separate surfaces, the mathematics of the stitching technique forces the edges of each patch to remain connected to the edges of adjacent patches. It also forces the surfaces of the patches to remain **tangent** where they touch at the seams—that is, to retain a smooth curvature across the seam between the two patches. The result is that the several stitched patches appear to be one seamless patch, even though they are not.

(a)

(b)

An example can be seen in Figure 5-15. In Figure 5-15a, we see three patches stitched together. The edges of each patch are indicated as a darker line. Notice that the three patches each have very different topological structures—that is, different numbers of rows and columns. Figure 5-15b shows this same set of stitched patches deformed to give it some curvature. Notice that the curvature of each patch is the same at their shared edges, making it appear that the three patches are one smoothly curved surface. In Figure 5-15c, we see a shaded rendering of these same stitched patches, showing the seamlessness of their rendering.

(c)

Figure 5-15. Stitching patches together allows you to keep different UV structures for each patch, but still create a seamless appearance.

The advantage of this approach is that you retain the mathematical smoothness of the patch approach, without being limited by the normal topological constraints of patches. Each of the stitched patches can have its own topology, or structure.

A more complex example of this approach is seen in Figure 5-16. Notice in Figures 5-16a and b that individual patches are created for separate areas of the face. Notice also that each patch has its own UV grid structure, suitable to the needs of that area of the head—more points around the eye, fewer on the forehead, etc. And notice in Figure 5-16c that the final rendering appears to be one smooth surface.

In building a stitched-patch model like this, you frequently begin with a single patch surface—a sphere, for example—and move its CVs to get an approximate, low-detail version of your model. The next step is to split this single patch into several patches. Most software packages provide a function that allows you to split a patch into two patches along either a row or a

(a)   (b)   (c)

Figure 5-16. The topological UV structure of each stitched patch can vary, depending on how many points you need in that area of your model. (Courtesy, Bill Burg.)

column. Using this function, you split your original, low-detail patch into several patches. This assures that the patches you now have share edges with each other. Once you have these individual patches, you modify each patch by adding or subtracting UV rows and columns, and by then moving the control points of the patch to get the shape you want. When you've done this to all the patches, they are all stitched back together with a menu selection. This is the approach that was used to build the head model in Figure 5-16.

The mathematical precision demanded by the stitched-patches technique can be demanding, and not all software packages perform the calculations flawlessly in all situations. In some software packages, if the stitched patches are deformed a great deal, you may detect a slight seam. This, of course, defeats one of the main goals of the technique. If the software performs the calculations correctly, however, the stitched-patch technique can be extremely effective.

5.6 Subdivision Surfaces

Throughout our discussion of modeling techniques, we have seen that one of the challenges of computer modeling is to achieve a surface which is both smooth and topologically unlimited. Patches meet the first requirement because they are mathematically truly curved. However, they must be built with grid-like topology, a structure of UV rows and columns (see section 2.3).

Polygonal models meet the second requirement in that they do not have topological restrictions. Polygons can be attached to each other in any order, and in any structure. However, polygonal surfaces are not mathematically smooth, and the faceting of the polygons can present a problem when rendering (see section 2.2).

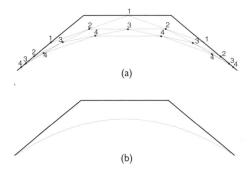

Figure 5-17. Infinitely subdividing a polyline eventually produces its limit line, which is mathematically truly curved.

In the preceding section, we discussed the stitched-patch approach to solving this problem.

Another approach is **subdivision surfaces**. In this technique, each polygon of a relatively simple polygonal model is repeatedly subdivided into smaller polygons, until the resulting polygons take on the appearance of a truly curved surface.

Imagine a simple, two-dimensional sequence of straight lines connected end-to-end (Figure 5-17). We saw in section 2.3 that this is referred to as a linear approximation of a curve. Now imagine that we subdivide each of these straight-line segments by placing a point halfway down its length. In Figure 5-17a, these points are labeled with the number *1*. We then connect each of these points, producing new straight-line segments. Next, we subdivide each of these new line segments at their halfway point. In the illustration, these points are labeled with the number *2*. As before, these points are connected with a straight-line segment. Each time we subdivide the line segments and connect the halfway points with new line segments, we produce a new linear-approximation curve that looks progressively more curved. The more we subdivide, the more closely the result approaches true curvature. Our illustration shows just four levels of subdivision. Mathematically, however, if we were to subdivide infinitely, the result would be truly curved, and the resulting curve is called the **limit curve**.

This subdivision approach can be extended to flat polygons as well. We see an example of this in Figure 5-18, where the original polygonal object, consisting of three polygons, is on the outside. Within that, we see the truly curved **limit surface** that results if each polygon is subdivided infinitely, to achieve true curvature.

Figure 5-18. A polygonal surface can also be subdivided to produce its limit surface.

There are a variety of algorithms for subdividing polygons in this way, but they all yield a limit surface. Of course, in actual practice, no software can perform an infinite number of subdivisions (if it tried to, it would never finish). Because the mathematical possibility is there, however, the software can perform as many calculations as it or you, deem advisable.

With the subdivision-surface technique, therefore, the user begins by making a relatively simple polygonal model. Since the starting-point model is polygonal, there are no topological restrictions. You can add or delete polygons at will, cut holes through your object, extrude polygons to form arm-like appendages, and so on. As you work, the software calculates the subdivided surface for you. In most software packages, you can elect to view only the subdivision model, or only the original polygon model, or both simultaneously. Figure 5-19 illustrates this. Here we see a simple polygonal model, rendered in wireframe, with its corresponding subdivision surface rendered inside it in shaded mode. Notice the irregularity of the polygonal object's topology: the extended arm, and the hole cut in the top.

Figure 5-19. Subdivision surfaces offer the advantage of both topological irregularity (the hole and the protrusion) and mathematical smoothness.

One of the important features of the subdivision technique is that you can operate on either the original polygon model, or directly on the subdivision model. If you operate on the original polygon model—for example, by adding, deleting, or moving some points or edges—you also alter the resulting subdivision model, since the subdivision model is generated by the polygon model. Alternatively, you can operate directly on the subdivision model by moving its points, edges, or faces. Changes you make to the subdivision model directly in this way do not cause changes in the original polygon model.

The combination of these approaches is very powerful. You can operate on the original polygon model to create the overall, general form of your model. You can then operate directly on the subdivision model to create the details of your model. This is the technique that was used to create the character we see in Figure 5-20. Notice that the topology of this model is very irregular, with arms, legs, feet, and beak protruding in all directions. And yet, because of the subdivision technique, the character is generated as a single, smooth surface. This will have great advantages when it comes to animate and deform the character—for example, by flapping his arms. Since the model is a single surface, there will be no seams as it deforms.

Figure 5-20. The subdivision approach easily handles the appendages of a character model.

Some software packages offer an enhancement to this technique by allowing you to add points directly to the subdivision model in a **hierarchical** fashion. With this technique, you can add points to a certain area of the subdivision model. The software considers these points to be at a specific level in the hierarchy of subdivision points—for example, level 1. By selecting a level 1 point, or set of points, and further subdividing that part of the surface, you can create additional points in that area, these being at level 2. This process is sometimes called **refinement**. If level 2 points are refined, the new points

(a)   (b)

Figure 5-21. Facial modeling is a good candidate for subdivision surfaces because of the topological irregularities of human faces—holes for the eyes and mouth, and ear and nose protrusions. (Courtesy, Bill Burg.)

will be created at a level 3. With your subdivision-surface points organized in this hierarchical fashion, it is easier to select them and operate on them.

A more complex example of a model built with the subdivision surface technique is seen in Figure 5-21. Notice the original polygon model, indicated in wireframe, surrounding the head in Figure 5-21a. Within that original polygon model we see the much more refined subdivision surface model. In the rendered version of the final head in Figure 5-21b, we see that the subdivision surface technique has produced a very smoothly curved surface, while still allowing you to work with the irregular topologies of polygonal modeling.

5.7 Displacement Mapping

In sections 3.8 and 3.9 we examined several approaches to texture mapping as part of our discussion of rendering. All the techniques discussed in those sections affected only the rendering of your models—that is, the visual characteristics of the surfaces, but not the geometry of the surfaces. Even bump mapping, which appears to add bumps and hollows to a surface, does not actually alter the geometry of the surface. Rather, it achieves the appearance of bumps and hollows by perturbing the normals of a surface, thereby causing the rendering program to render dark and light tones that give the appearance of bumps and hollows. The limitations of this approach are most noticeable at the edges of the surface (Figure 5-22), or when you zoom in very close to your model.

Figure 5-22. Bump mapping does not alter the geometry of the model.

The **displacement texture-mapping** technique, however, does alter the geometry of surfaces. It can be used for a wide variety of modeling tasks, but is most useful for situations in which you want to create a great many irregularities on a surface, and you want these irregularities to be true surface deformations of the geometry.

(a)

(b)

Figure 5-23. This model uses the same texture as Figure 5-22, but now applied as a displacement map, dramatically altering the geometry of the surface.

Figure 5-24. As with any modeling technique, the number of surface points determines the amount of detail you can achieve.

Like the transparency and bump mapping techniques discussed in section 3.8, displacement mapping starts with a two-dimensional texture image and uses the pixels of that image as a source of information. In the case of displacement mapping, however, the brightness is interpreted as an actual geometric displacement of the height of the surface at that particular location. The brighter the texture pixel, the more the three-dimensional surface is displaced upward. A black texture pixel means no displacement of the surface at all. A white texture pixel means very great displacement.

In Figure 5-23 a flat surface is modified with displacement mapping to produce the craggy surface on the right. The texture image used is the same fractally-generated texture used to produce the bump-mapped image in Figure 5-22. Here, however, the darks and lights of this texture actually displace the geometry of the original surface.

In order to displace geometry, of course, there must be sufficient geometry available. As with all modeling techniques, the number of surface points on your model—either CVs for a patch, or polygon vertices for a polygonal surface—limits the amount of detail you can achieve. In Figure 5-24 we see two models created with the same displacement mapping applied to our previous example. In Figure 5-24a, however, the mapping was applied to a flat polygonal surface with relatively few vertices. In Figure 5-24b, the same mapping was applied to a flat polygonal surface with many more vertices, resulting in much more precisely detailed surface deformations.

The two-dimensional texture image you begin with can be any 2D image, whether procedurally generated, hand-drawn, or scanned. Figure 5-25 shows a variety of approaches. The grid texture in Figure 5-25a was scanned and applied to a flat plane to produce a tray form. The porcupine-like form in (b) results from applying a fractal texture to a scaled hemisphere. A hand-drawn, squiggly-line texture applied to a flat plane produced the maze of walls in 5-25c.

One of the most common applications of displacement mapping is the modeling of **landscapes**, which frequently requires a great deal of geometric irregularity to be convincing. Creating that three-dimensional irregularity by individually pushing and pulling surface points is possible but tedious. By contrast, creating irregularity in a two-dimensional image, even if you do it

Figure 5-25. Displacement mapping can be used for a wide variety of applications.

by hand, is relatively easy. Moreover, **fractal procedures** (section 6.3) automatically generate just such irregularity in great detail. Using a fractal image to displace a flat or nearly flat surface can therefore quickly produce a landscape-like surface. You can even combine fractal techniques and hand-drawn techniques, as was done in Figure 5-26. Here, the texture image was originally generated with a fractal procedure, then imported into a painting program and selectively erased. The resulting displacement-mapped surface has plains, hills, and a ridge of mountains.

Figure 5-26. Terrain modeling is a common application of displacement mapping, with fractal procedures being especially useful for texture generation.

5.8 Hair and Fur

The modeling and rendering of hair and fur have historically been extremely challenging for three-dimensional computer graphics because of the very large quantities of data involved. A human head may have thousands upon thousands of individual hairs growing from its scalp. The hairs that make up the fur of an animal are even more numerous. For the first few decades of computer graphics, therefore, realistic hair and fur were not possible. The best one could do was texture map a hair-like image onto a surface.

Recently, increases in hardware speeds and the development of more robust rendering algorithms have made it possible to create imagery with these effects. There are now several approaches to producing fur and hair, all of which take steps to avoid the problem of dealing with huge quantities of three-dimensional data.

One approach is to treat hair and fur as rendering issues. Without creating any geometry, a **two-dimensional post-process** creates the hair or fur at render time, adding it to your rendered frame after all the three-dimensional surfaces have finished rendering. In spite of the fact that no geometry is created for it, the hair behaves fully three-dimensionally; it occludes other objects, can be occluded by them, reacts to light, and so on. This is because the location and direction of each rendered hair is determined by three-dimensional data—for example, the normals of the surface to which the hair is attached, and the camera angle. Figure 5-27 was created with this technique.

A second approach is to create hair and fur with **particle-system** software. Recall that one of the parameters of a particle system is its trail life, the amount of time a particle's trail remains visible. If the trail life is set to a sufficiently large number, the trail of the particle will never disappear, effectively creating a solid wirelike column behind it as it "grows" through space. Combining this technique with careful use of transparency, color, self-shadowing, and other parameters, you can effectively model different types of hair. Figure 5-28 shows three examples, all emitted from a spherical source. A more developed example of this technique can be seen in color plate 3. The geometry of the tarantula is quite simple, consisting mostly of ellipsoids. Each of these is a particle-emitting source, from which hair particles grow.

Figure 5-27. One approach to the modeling of hair is paint-based. A hair stroke is painted onto a surface, generating painted hairs at render time. (© GeeJae Lee.)

Figure 5-28. Hair and fur can be modeled with particles by making each particle leave an opaque trail behind it. (Courtesy, Gevel Marrero.)

A variation on the particle system approach is a **paint-based approach** (discussed in more detail in section 5.9). As applied to hair, this approach allows you to interactively draw lines on your surface. From these lines grow hairs in the form of your selected hair brush stroke. The wig in Figure 5-27 was created in this way.

Yet another approach to modeling fur and hair creates actual **three-dimensional geometric surfaces** for each hair, but postpones any full display of the myriad hair surfaces until render time.

When working interactively on your workstation with any of these approaches, you view only a rough wireframe representation of the hairs, with one wireframe line representing many of the final hairs (Figure 5-29).

Whichever approach it uses, any hair software offers you a number of controls for the appearance of the hair or fur. One is the **density** of the hairs. The fur on a lion's foreleg is denser than the hair on a man's arms. You can also vary the density over the surface of your model, for example, to mimic the baldness of a man's head. You typically do this either with an interactive paintbrush approach or by applying a texture map to control the density. You can also adjust the **thickness** of individual hairs—to capture the difference between a child's and an adult's hair, for example. Most software packages allow you to define thickness both at the base and at the tip of the hairs.

Another important parameter is hair **direction**. In Figure 5-30 the hair has been parted in the middle, pushing the hairs on each side of the head in opposite directions. Many software packages offer interactive tools that permit you to comb the hair of your model with paintbrush strokes, making it very easy to interactively create complex patterns of hair direction.

It is also possible to apply **motion dynamic forces** to hair and fur (see section 7.7 for a discussion of motion dynamics). In Figure 5-31a, the hairs of this character's head and beard receive their direction solely as a result of gravity pulling them downward. Being subject to motion dynamics forces, the hairs can also react to other forces such as wind or the movements of their parent surface. When the character in Figure 5-31b shakes his head, his hair and beard fling left and right in reaction to his movements.

Figure 5-29. Because of the large amounts of data involved, hair and fur software initially display a rough wireframe of your model during the interactive stages. Only at render time do you see your final result.

Figure 5-30. The direction of hairs can be controlled. Some packages offer brushes that allow you to interactively comb the hair.

(a)   (b)

Figure 5-31. Most hair software can apply motion dynamics forces to the hair. Here, the hair falls under gravity, and shakes with the turn of his head. A parameter controlling irregularity has simultaneously made the character's hair and beard quite scraggly.

Figure 5-32. Adjusting the parameters carefully allows you to create the effect of a dense animal fur. (Courtesy, Phoenix Tools SRL [Italy].)

Figure 5-33. A texture map can control the color of the hair.

Another important characteristic is the **irregularity**, sometimes also called the **scraggliness**, of the hairs. Adjusting this parameter introduces randomness into the shape of each hair. The mop of hair in Figure 5-30 has almost zero irregularity, whereas in Figure 5-31 the hair and beard have considerable irregularity, contributing to the character's rather wild, unkempt look. In Figure 5-32 the teddy bear's fur has been given just enough irregularity to give it the furry, cuddly look important for this model.

For any model, hair **color** is also critical, and there are several ways to control this parameter. One way is to specify, for all the hairs as a group, the colors at the **base** and **tip** of each hair. This becomes especially important for animal hair, where the base and tip colors are frequently different. Another approach is to use a **texture map** to determine hair color, as was done in Figure 5-33. Most effectively, you can combine all these techniques, using one texture for the base colors and another for the tip colors. This approach allowed the artist of Figure 5-34 to create an extremely realistic Siamese cat model, with the coloration distinctive of that breed. Notice also that the cat's fur has been combed to accurately capture the patterns of fur growth, most noticeably in the area between her front legs.

Most packages allow you to also define the **tip transparency** of each hair. Although real hairs are not transparent at the tip, their extreme thinness can cause individual hairs to effectively disappear at the tip, where they are not clumped with other hairs. Consequently, making each hair fade into transparency as it approaches the tip can add a level of realism to your rendered image.

Figure 5-34. Realistic fur and hair is quite complex. Here, the color of the fur is determined by a texture map. The direction of the fur has been combed to resemble a real cat. (Copyright © 2000 Jerome Chia-Horng Lin.)

We saw in section 3.3 that **cast shadow** calculations can be quite time-consuming, even for simple objects. Cast shadows become an even larger problem, of course, when you have thousands of objects, as you do with hairs. Consequently, when working with hair and fur, you can usually elect one of several shadow-casting options. The most physically accurate is to do three-dimensional calculations for all shadows, including **self-shadows**—that is, shadows cast by the hairs onto themselves. Another option is to calculate shadows only from the hairs onto objects other than the hairs. A third option offered by some software packages is to calculate **pseudo self-shading**. This technique takes advantage of the fact that the bases of most hairs are in shadow, and so renders them darker without actually calculating three-dimensional shadows. Figure 5-35 is an example of effective fur shading. Notice especially the accuracy of the irregular perimeter of the shadow cast onto the floor.

Figure 5-35. Shadow casting can be computationally expensive, and consequently a variety of options controlling the quality of shadow casting are possible. (Courtesy, Phoenix Tools SRL [Italy].)

5.9 Paint-based Modeling

Many natural phenomena present special modeling challenges because of the amount and complexity of the data required for a convincing result. Examples of such phenomena include a grove of trees, a field of grass, and a garden of flowers. While it is possible to model a single plant, such as a tree, with standard modeling techniques, modeling an entire grove of trees would be both time-consuming and data-intensive.

One approach which can minimize the amount of time involved is procedural modeling (section 5.5) in which a special-purpose software program is written to generate the geometry of the trees. This approach has two potential drawbacks, however: first, it requires programming skills that may be beyond the abilities of an individual artist; and second, it can result in large quantities of geometric data.

Another approach to this problem is **paint-based modeling**. With this technique, the artist selects a "brush"—for example, a maple-tree brush—from a library of brushes provided by the software, and then draws a three-dimensional curve in the scene. As the curve is drawn, the software generates instances of the selected brush, thus creating, in our example, a line of maple trees.

Paint-based modeling does not create geometric surfaces for the objects it generates; rather, it creates **brush strokes** in three-dimensional space. The definition of the brush stroke includes its shape as well as how it will render. Figure 5-36 shows a tree created in this way. Notice that in figure 5-36a, where the tree is seen at a distance, we cannot distinguish the details of the brush stroke. In the closer view of Figure 5-36b, however, the paint stroke is

(a)

(b)

Figure 5-36. Paint-based modeling creates no geometry. Only at render time does the technique "paint" its models. In some circumstances, the painted quality of your object may be evident.

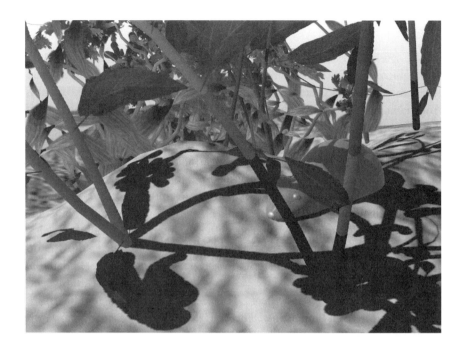

Figure 5-37. Although no geometry is created, paint-based models are fully three-dimensional, occluding other objects, and casting shadows.

(a)

(b)

Figure 5-38. Paint-based models are enhanced by texture mapping, using either the software's default textures or your own individualized textures.

apparent. We will discuss in a moment how the rendering of these strokes can be improved.

Even though the strokes do not create any surfaces, they are positioned in three-dimensional space, making them more than merely a painting technique. Each object generated by the brush strokes exists in the same **three-dimensional space** as the other objects of your scene. **Occlusions** are calculated with paint-based models just as with standard surface models. In Figure 5-37, we see a close-up of some flower stems. Within the same scene are a ground surface and a mouse model. All of these—the ground, the mouse, and the plants—interact with each other in space, with the paint-based plants occluding each other and the ground plane, and being occluded by it in return. Notice also that **shadows** are cast from the plants onto both the ground and the mouse.

Brushes may generate their objects by simply painting color in space. This was the case with the example we saw in Figure 5-36. More usefully, however, a brush definition may include **textures**, as we see in Figure 5-38. In this case, each texture image is accompanied by an alpha channel, allowing the texture to cut out a particular shape from the brush stroke at the same time that it determines its color, using the same color mapping and transparency mapping techniques we saw in section 3.8.

Figure 5-38a shows the tree generated with the software's default textures. Figure 5-38b shows the same tree with different textures for both the bark and leaves. By creating and controlling your own textures, you can individualize the standard library brushes to suit your own artistic purposes.

In addition to textures, each brush has a large number of **parameters**, all of which can be changed by the user to alter the configuration of the plant created. The overall size of the plant, the thickness of branches, the number of branches, the length of branches, the size and density of leaves—all can be modified. In Figure 5-39, the same tree has been rendered twice, once with a dense leaf growth, and once with a sparse leaf growth.

Not only can you change each of the brush's parameters, but, like any parameter in a sophisticated animation program, you can also animate them. This allows you to create animations of plants changing shape and color, growing, and moving.

Paint-based modeling software is usually derived from **particle-system** software. We will see in section 7.8 that particles can be rendered in a great variety of ways to obtain different effects. In paint-based modeling, the trace left by moving particles is rendered as a single brush stroke.

Since they are based on particle systems, paint-based models can be animated with many of the same **motion dynamics** capabilities of particle systems. The plants generated with a paint-based approach can be influenced by gravity and other forces, such as wind and turbulence. In fact, the default definition of many plant brushes includes such effects. By modifying the dynamics parameters, you can create very convincing animations of your paint-based plants blowing in the breeze. Figure 5-40 shows a sequence of frames illustrating this. Here, the grasses are simultaneously blown in different directions by a wind force and pulled down by a gravitational force. Notice the different positions of the grass blades in each frame.

While paint-based modeling is most frequently used for vegetation, it can also be used to generate other forms, depending on what your software provides in its library of brush strokes. Some other possible forms include feathers, fire, and flowing water. In section 5.8 we saw that it can also be used effectively to create hair and fur.

Several interesting examples of paint-based modeling are included elsewhere in this book. Colorplate 11 shows a sequence of three frames from an animation in which a cartoon fox moves through a naturalistically-rendered

(a)

(b)

Figure 5-39. With paint-based plants, you can adjust a great many parameters, ranging from the density of leaves, to the age of the plant, to the genus of the plant.

(a)

(b)

(c)

Figure 5-40. Most paint-based modeling techniques allow you to apply motion dynamics to your models. Here, the grasses are simultaneously blown by wind and pulled down by gravity.

field of waving grass. Color plate 9 shows an old man tending to his paint-based garden. Paint-based modeling was also used extensively to generate the lush flowers in the cover image of this book.

5.10 Higher-level Primitives

As you saw earlier in section 2.6, almost all 3D software packages provide functions that generate certain simple forms—such as the cube, the cylinder, and the cone—called "geometric primitives." To use these functions, you do not explicitly define each surface of the form to be modeled. You do not, for example, draw a curve and revolve it to form the side of a cone. Rather, you simply indicate that you want a cone and specify certain parameters to control size and location. Employing an internal definition of what a cone is, the "cone" function then automatically generates the appropriate form.

In principle, a computer programmer could apply this approach to any one of an infinite variety of forms. A function to generate hats, for example, would include an internal definition of what a hat is (a brim, a circular interior, a band around the rim, etc.). The function could be set up so that certain parameters would be specified by the user to control the style, size, and shape of the hat. A *style* parameter might contain such possibilities as: *Panama*, *Baseball Cap*, *Navy Watch Cap*, and so on, and these settings would be equivalent to the *Cube*, *Cone*, and *Cylinder* settings in a "geometric primitive" function.

Reflecting the fact that you create them with a single set of menu selections, but also that they are much more complex than merely a cone or other simple geometric form, models created in this way are called **higher-level primitives**. Any form you conceive can in principle be made into a higher-

Figure Figure 5-41. Human-figure primitives are useful because of the complexity of modeling involved. You can usually select gender, and frequently adjust other parameters as well. (Courtesy, Sherrie Johnson.)

(a)

(b)

level primitive. In practice, however, there is more demand for certain forms, and so these are programmed into many off-the-shelf packages.

One such form is the human figure (Figure 5-41). Many software packages offer **human-figure primitives**, allowing you to generate with a single menu selection a complete human-figure model. In some simpler approaches, the software calls up a predefined model from its database, allowing you to select only the **gender** of the model—male or female. Some more powerful functions allow you to also specify a variety of **parameters** to control the configuration of your model—age, height, proportions, weight, muscularity, and so on. In addition to creating the geometry of your model, some packages offer fully rigged inverse kinematic skeleton primitives (Figure 5-42). See sections 7.12 and 7.13 for a discussion of character rigging.

Figure 5-42. Some packages offer completely rigged inverse kinematic skeleton primitives. (Courtesy, Phill Avanzato.)

Another important primitive offered by some packages is a human face primitive. Once again, you can select male or female models, and once again, in the more powerful software packages, you can adjust a variety of parameters, in this case to fine-tune the specific facial features (Figure 5-43).

Since both the modeling and rigging of human figure and face models can be very time-consuming, primitives for these are extremely useful. A danger, however, is that your character model will look generic—that is, identical to all the other character models made by the same software package. This is especially problematic if the software doesn't offer the option to modify the proportions or features of the primitive model. A solution to this is to use the package's human primitive as your starting point, but then adjust the model with any of the standard modeling techniques—for example, by making the ears larger, the belly fatter, or the arms longer.

Another common higher-level primitive involves plants. We saw in section 5.9 that one way to generate plants is with a paint-based approach. However, since this approach does not generate any three-dimensional surfaces, it

(a)   (b)

Figure Figure 5-43. Face model primitives include parameters to individualize specific facial features. (Courtesy, Phill Avanzato.)

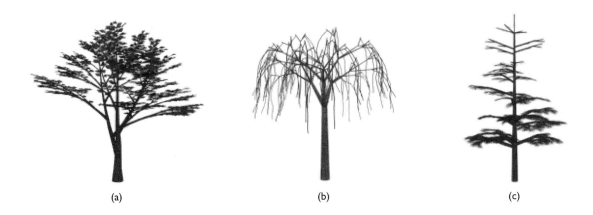

(a)   (b)   (c)

Figure 5-44. Trees modeled three-dimensionally by a plant-generator function. The artist specified the species of tree.

may not be effective for close-up views. Higher-level **plant primitives** address this need.

To use plant generator functions, you first specify a **plant-type** parameter. Having narrowed the category to a specific plant type, say a tree, you then specify the **plant species**. From among the category of trees, for example, you might choose a maple, a willow, or a spruce (Figure 5-44a, b, c). Bear in mind that these illustrations look deceptively flat because the intended scale of the trees is so large. The trees modeled here are, indeed, *models*. That is, they are not merely pictures of trees, but have been defined as fully three-dimensional objects. When part of a 3D computer graphics scene, these models exist in all three dimensions, and you can move around them visually in the same way that you can move around a cube or a cone.

Having selected a species of plant, you next specify various parameters that control the size and shape of the plant. Usually, one of these parameters is **age**, and you normally specify this value in years. A relatively young maple tree (Figure 5-45a) looks substantially different from a maple tree that is many years older (Figure 5-45b), despite the fact that all the other parameters defining these trees are identical.

As you will see in chapters 3 and 4, good 3D animation systems handle any parameter as a variable whose value can be changed over time. Changing the value of a variable over time effectively animates the model. When the age parameter of a plant model is animated, the plant will appear to grow. Because of this, some sophisticated plant-generator functions are often referred to as **growth models**.

Randomness plays a role in all natural phenomena, and therefore is important in making plant models look convincing. Part of what makes the two maple tree models in Figure 5-45 look like real trees is the fact that their branches and leaves are not all of the same length or size and are not placed at regular intervals along the trunk. Because of the importance of this

(a)   (b)

Figure 5-45. Often an age parameter can be applied to a plant model. Here are a young maple tree and an older maple tree.

randomness factor, many plant-generator systems also offer a **randomness** or **noise** parameter to give you greater control over just how the final plant looks. When generating grass with a "grass" function, for instance, by employing a randomness factor you can control both the length of the blades of grass and how irregularly they splay out from the center (Figure 5-46).

As we discussed at the beginning of this section, any higher-level primitive makes use of **procedures** written into the program by the software developers. In section 5.4 we saw that most 3D software packages offer **scripting languages** that permit you to write your own procedures. With the same scripting language you can also add your own menu selections to your program's interface. By first writing your own procedure to generate a model and then creating your own menu window to call this procedure, you can create your own **user-defined primitives**. With this approach you can create a primitive for any form you wish, programming into your script whatever parameters you wish. For example, you could create a user-defined primitive to generate hats, as discussed at the beginning of this section. Or, you could define a primitive to create automobiles, with parameters to control the make, model, year, and color. Moreover, by using the software's scripting capabilities to also create menu selections that call your primitive, your user-defined primitive (no matter how idiosyncratic) becomes accessible to other users, for example, members of your production team. It is also common for individual artists to make the scripts for their user-defined primitives available for free on the **World Wide Web**. A number of websites exist specifically for this purpose.

Although not incorporated into software packages upon purchase, **database models** are related to the concept of higher-level primitives. Many companies collect and sell libraries of predefined models. You can purchase models for different types of animals, vehicles, airplanes, human characters, fish, and any number of other objects or creatures. The human figure model seen

Figure 5-46. This grass model was generated by a "grass" function. A degree of randomness is critical to producing convincing models of this sort.

in Figure 2-17 is such a database model. Many of these are generated with 3D digitizing techniques (section 5.3) and are quite accurate physically. All are available in standard file formats, such as **DXF** and **IGES**, and are therefore compatible with a wide variety of software packages. In addition, just as many individuals make their modeling scripts available for free on the World Wide Web, many also make their completed model data available. In these cases, the models are most frequently in the proprietary model file format of a specific software package.

However acquired, the danger of using database models is the same as with any higher-level primitive. The lack of originality in the model may work very much to your disadvantage. For some commercial applications where originality is not valued, this may not be significant. But the more creative and artistic your project is intended to be, the more serious this problem becomes. As with primitives, however, you can always treat your database model not as a final model, but as a starting point, modifying it as necessary to suit your needs and tastes. In this way you can adjust your model to make it serve your specific project.

CHAPTER 6

Advanced Rendering

6.1 Introduction

Chapter 3 of this book introduced the basic concepts and techniques of computer graphic rendering. Here in Chapter 6 we focus on some of the more advanced rendering techniques offered by most packages. All of the techniques presented here build on the concepts and principles presented in Chapter 3. If you have not already done so, you should familiarize yourself with that material before proceeding here.

6.2 Atmospheric Effects

3D computer graphics images sometimes have a distinctive crystal-clear quality. Sometimes this clarity is intended by the artist and proves a very useful effect. But sometimes the hyperclarity of 3D computer imagery is not desirable and creates instead an appearance of unreality and falseness.

GLOBAL ATMOSPHERIC EFFECTS

The reason so many 3D computer images have this crystal clarity is that they do not, by default, take into account an important optical effect. In the real world, the perceived colors of objects change depending on the distance of the objects from the viewer. The colors of a distant mountain range are muted by the atmosphere. This effect is sometimes known as **atmospheric perspective**, which the painters of the Renaissance developed so effectively in their landscapes. In Leonardo da Vinci's famous painting known as the *Mona Lisa*, you can see the effect of the atmosphere on the colors of the countryside in the distance. The colors of distant rocks are much less vibrant than those of near-by rocks.

When light travels through the air, it loses some color as it travels. The farther the light travels, the more color it loses. This phenomenon causes the atmospheric perspective effect. The light rays coming to your eye from the mountains in the distance are scattered along the way by the tiny molecules that make up the atmosphere. By the time the light rays reach your eye, some of the original green of the mountains has been lost, and the remaining color has been modified, picking up some of the blue of the sky. This effect is even more pronounced if fog or haze (or smog, unfortunately) is in the

(a)

(b)

(c)

Figure 6-1. A simple, horizontal fog obscures objects in a scene depending on their distance from the camera. The density of the fog can be varied.

(a)

(b)

Figure 6-2. Fog can be adjusted vertically, with variable starting and ending locations of the fog along the Y axis.

atmosphere. The greater the density of molecules to deflect the light rays, the more severely affected the colors of objects. In a dust storm or underwater, the atmospheric effect on the color of the objects is even more pronounced.

Most 3D computer rendering programs do not render this sort of **global atmospheric effect** automatically. When you model a scene—for example, a cube in the foreground and a cone in the far distance—the computer considers only the surfaces explicitly modeled to exist. There are no tiny molecule-sized surfaces in between the cube and the cone to deflect the light, so the cone in the far distance is rendered with the same clarity as the cube in the foreground.

To address this, you can generate atmospheric effects such as fog and haze through a series of menu selections and parameter settings. The software incorporates these parameters into the color calculations when it renders the final frame, and the resulting frame displays the correct atmospheric adjustments.

The simplest and most common kind of atmospheric effect that you can define in these packages varies according to depth along the Z axis. With this sort of **Z-depth fog**, or **horizontal fog**, an object located at a Z depth of 100 meters is more obscured by the atmosphere than an object located at 50 meters. Frequently, the calculations done to determine how obscured an object is at a given distance are linear interpolations, which means that an object at 50 meters will be half as obscured as one at 100 meters and one-quarter as obscured as one at 200 meters. Many software packages permit you to specify a variety of other types of interpolations—for example, exponential—to control how quickly the density of the fog accumulates.

In addition to the type of interpolation, you also control the density of fog by specifying the color of the atmosphere and the distance at which that color completely overrides the colors of objects. For example, to render a scene with a reddish haze, you might specify that the RGB components of the color are (200,100,100) and that objects at a distance of 1,000 meters are completely obscured by this reddish haze. Assuming a linear interpolation, these specifications mean that an object at a distance from the eye of 100 meters, for example, is one-tenth obscured—that is, one-tenth of the final color comes from the red of the haze and nine-tenths of the color comes from the original color of the object itself.

In Figure 6-1 you see the effect of horizontal fog. Figure 6-1a is a simple scene with no fog at all. In Figure 6-1b, a white fog has been added, and in Figure 6-1c the same fog has been made denser.

It is also possible to define an atmospheric fog that obscures objects along the vertical, or Y, axis. This sort of **vertical fog**, or **layered fog**, can be useful, for example, in rendering mountains, the feet of which may lie in fog while the peaks rise above the fog. The procedure here is usually similar to the procedure for defining fog along the Z axis. First you specify the color of the fog/atmosphere. Next you specify the range along the Y axis where this vertical atmosphere will be in effect. This latter specification usually involves a maximum and a minimum Y value: the fog is densest at one end of this range and dissipated completely at the other end.

Figure 6-2a shows our sample scene now with a vertical fog added to the horizontal fog. Notice how the tops of the columns are less obscured than their bases. In Figure 6-2b the lower bound of this vertical fog has been raised, resulting in a band of fog that hovers in the middle sections of the columns. Figure 6-3 shows another example of vertical fog, restricted here to a very short range—from the ground to the character's mid-calf—creating the effect of a mist hovering just above ground level.

Figure 6-3. An example of vertical fog density in a rendering. (*Iggy's Dream #56,* © Michael O'Rourke.)

The discussion so far has involved atmospheres of constant density, whether along the Z axis or along the Y axis. In reality, however, atmospheric density is rarely perfectly constant. The fog enveloping a mountain, rather than dissipating in a linear fashion as it moves up the mountain, instead may not dissipate at all up to a certain height, then dissipate very quickly for a while, then more slowly, and so on. On a smaller scale, the fog that hovers above the surface of a lake on a damp morning will vary in density, floating and drifting in the morning breezes. Most programs allow you to achieve such variable fog density through a **noise** parameter in the fog procedure's menu. By adjusting this parameter, often with a slider bar, you can cause irregularities in the fog's density, creating patches of more or less dense fog, making the patches larger or smaller, and making the patches nearer or farther from each other (Figure 6-4). In most programs, noise can be added to both vertical fog, as in Figure 6-4, and to horizontal fog.

Figure 6-4. Introducing noise to fog creates variations in the density of the fog.

Applying this sort of global atmospheric haze or fog to a terrain model can greatly enhance the naturalism of your scene. In Figure 6-5, both vertical and horizontal fog have been added to the scene, with the vertical fog adjusted to be denser at the base of the hills than at the top.

Figure 6-5. A combination of horizontal and vertical fog is especially useful for landscapes.

Figure 6-6. The density of water atmospherically affects objects much more than does the density of air. With such water effects, light normally enters from above.

Some software packages offer a variant of this effect specially designed to render **underwater** scenes, which differ in several important respects from terrestrial scenes. First, the atmospheric effect is frequently much more pronounced underwater because light from distant objects is deflected much more by water than by air. The color of underwater scenes can also be very distinctive, ranging from bluish to greenish to brownish. Finally, light typically enters an underwater environment only from above—that is, from the surface of the water. Adjusting the appropriate parameters, you can effectively use global atmosphere to convey the submarine aspect of your scene, as we see in Figure 6-6. Notice in this image the density of the atmospheric coloration and how the columns are more obscured at their bases—that is, farther away from the water surface and the light. Notice also the shark's shadow cast from above onto the columns.

LOCALIZED ATMOSPHERIC EFFECTS

All of the techniques discussed so far for rendering atmospheric effects work very well for scenes that involve large distances. If the distance between your eye and some set of objects is very short, the light rays coming from those objects do not have a chance to become scattered and there is no visible atmospheric effect. In some situations, however, the effect of the atmosphere on light is important even at close distances—for example, when a spotlight is shined through the darkness. When this happens, the air in the path of the spotlight is illuminated, which is a critical visual cue for interpreting the scene. If you remove the illuminated air from the scene, leaving only the illumination of the spotlight on the objects it hits, the scene looks wrong, because your eyes expect to see that distinctive cone of spotlit air.

What makes this scene difficult to render is, once again, the lack of surfaces in the air. The reason the real-life spotlight creates a cone of light is that it is lighting thousands of tiny dust particles in the air. In the pristine world of computer graphics, there are (normally) no dust particles.

The most effective technique for rendering this sort of **localized atmospheric effect** is to use **volumetric fog lights**. In section 3.3 you saw that many software packages provide volume lights, in which the area lighted is restricted to a specific, geometrically shaped volume. Most packages offer volume lights that also produce fog, or atmosphere, within their volume. Figure 6-7 shows a spotlight whose conically shaped volume has been rendered with fog in it. Notice that the fog is fully three-dimensional and volumetric. It not only fills the conical volume of the light, but also has shadows cast on it by the cylinder and the platform.

As with the horizontal and vertical fog discussed at the beginning of this section, you can apply noise to the fog of volumetric lights to create irregularities in the density of the fog. You do this most frequently by applying a

Figure 6-7. Volumetric lights can be rendered with a three-dimensional fog within their volume.

(a)

(b)

Figure 6-8. Different sorts of noise can be applied to volumetric fog lights to create irregular patterns of density in the fog.

Figure 6-9. A volumetric point light with a spherical volume of fog, properly adjusted with noise, can simulate clouds.

fractal texture (section 6.3) to the fog density parameter. Figure 6-8a shows subtle random noise applied to the fog to give it a less uniform, more smoky look. In Figure 6-8b, noise applied in a radial pattern creates the streaked effect of light streaming through a window.

Volumetric fog lights are not limited to the conical volumes of spotlights. Any volume light could have fog in it. Figure 6-9 shows a volumetric point light placed behind the objects. The spherical volume of the point light has been filled with fog. Adjusting various noise parameters made the fog look cloudlike. Notice also that the pronounced noise, by making the fog patchy, has also made the spherical shape of the volume light less obvious.

(a)

(b)

Figure 6-10. Particle systems can create effective animated smoke effects.

Color plate 8 uses a volumetric fog light to project both fog and image through the upper-right corner of the composition.

Another situation in which a localized atmospheric effect may be necessary is when **smoke** is present. Because of the density of smoke, even a faint light passing through it will make the smoke visible. A common technique for rendering smoke is particle systems, which we discuss in much more detail in section 7.8. As with volumetric fog lights, the goal is to account for the tiny particles that float in the air and deflect the light. Like all the techniques discussed in this section, any parameters you set can be animated. In Figure 6-10, we see two moments in the life of a particle-system smoke effect. In (b) the smoke has expanded and risen relative to its original configuration in (a).

6.3 Fractals

In the 1970s, a French mathematician named Benoît Mandelbrot began refining an unusual new branch of mathematics, which has turned out to be extremely rich in possibilities for computer graphics. He termed this new mathematics **fractal** mathematics, because it involves the possibility of writing mathematical equations for geometries of fractional dimensionality. Normally, you think of dimensionality in terms of whole numbers: a point in space is 1-dimensional, a drawing on a piece of paper is 2-dimensional, a wooden box is 3-dimensional, and so on. In Mandelbrot's system, it is possible to think of something that is 1.76-dimensional, for instance, or 2.24-dimensional.

It is common for mathematicians to make visual representations, or graphs, of their mathematical formulas. To take a simple example, the visual representation of the equation $y = x^2$ is a parabola (Figure 6-11). This curve can be plotted by listing several x values, calculating the y value for each x value, and then drawing a mark at each (x,y) combination.

The images that result when fractal equations are plotted are much more complex than this simple example, and mathematicians working with fractal

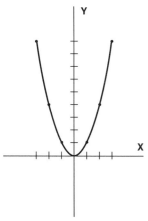

Figure 6-11. Any mathematical equation can be visually plotted. Here a simple equation is plotted as a parabola.

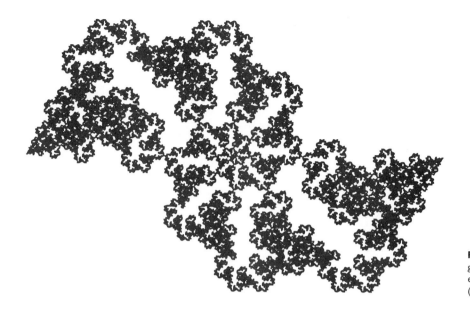

Figure 6-12. A pattern generated by plotting an equation of fractal mathematics. (Bathsheba L. Grossman, 1985)

mathematics soon discovered that visual representations of their fractal equations produced some very intricate, unexpected, and beautiful results. Most interestingly, they found that graphs of fractal equations produce imagery that captures some of the characteristics of natural phenomena. That is, fractal imagery often has an irregularity and an unpredictability, an intricacy of detail, and a similarity of detail to overall form reminiscent of forms found in nature (Figure 6-12).

As fractal mathematics developed, computer graphics researchers began to develop techniques that took advantage of these characteristics by producing both two-dimensional pictures and three-dimensional models. Today, these fractal techniques have become an integral part of all 3D CG systems, and are used for both modeling and rendering.

One of the most important characteristics of fractals is that at any level of detail you can see similarities in the forms. The forms at the most minute level bear a resemblance to the forms at grosser levels, and these in turn look similar to forms at even higher levels. This characteristic, called **self-similarity**, belongs to many phenomena in nature as well. The large-scale crags and peaks of a mountain are similar in shape to the smaller abutments that make up those crags. Individual rocks on the mountainside have a similar "cragginess" to them, but on a much smaller scale. The pebbles that break off from such rocks have similar forms, and if you examine one of these pebbles with a magnifying glass, you would find miniature "crags" similar to the cragginess of the mountain itself.

To see how self-similarity works in a fractal image, take a simple and common example, called the **Koch curve**. You start generating this fractal curve

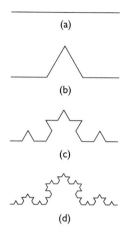

Figure 6-13. A Koch curve exemplifies the two fractal principles of self-similarity and recursion.

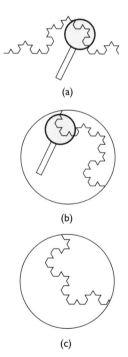

Figure 6-14. A fractal image has, as part of its definition, an infinite amount of detail. No matter how much you magnify an image, you will always see additional detail.

with a simple straight line (Figure 6-13a). Next you break this straight line into a pattern, which is called the **generator** (Figure 6-13b). Breaking each of the four straight lines that make up the generator into yet smaller versions of the generator pattern yields a new pattern consisting of four occurrences of the generator (Figure 6-13c). Subdividing each straight line of that pattern into the generator pattern yields the next **generation** of the curve (Figure 6-13d). You can repeat this process of subdivision indefinitely, creating ever more detailed and refined repetitions of the generator pattern.

Notice that each new generation of the Koch curve is defined in terms of a previous Koch curve. For example, Koch-curve generation number 22 consists of Koch-curve generation number 21 with a generator pattern substituted for each straight line of number 21. In other words, in order to create a Koch curve, you first must create a Koch curve: the definition is **self-referential.**

This process of defining something in terms of itself is called **recursion** and the process is said to be **recursive**. Because it is self-referential, a recursive process in principle can go on forever. A common example of recursion in the physical world is what happens when two mirrors are placed face to face. If you look in the first mirror, you see yourself reflected in the second, which in turns reflects an image of yourself looking in the first mirror and being reflected in the second, which in turn reflects an image of yourself in the second mirror looking at yourself in the first mirror and being reflected in the second, which is being reflected in the first—and so on.

In a fractal curve there can be an unlimited number of generations—that is, it contains an unlimited amount of detail, even if you cannot see it. Beyond a few additional generations, for example, you could not see any more detail in Figure 6-13d. The image on the page is simply too small for your eye to pick up such tiny detail. For this practical reason, therefore, you probably would not attempt to draw too many additional generations. It is important to understand, however, that by definition these additional generations of the curve are there, even if you choose not to draw them.

If you imagine magnifying a section of the curve, you can understand more clearly that no matter how much you magnify a section of a fractal curve, there will always be, if you choose to draw it, more detail to see. Imagine that you place a magnifying-glass over a section of a Koch curve (Figure 6-14a). Notice that even at a magnified level the same amount of detail is available (Figure 6-14b). If you zoom in yet again, as indicated by the magnifying-glass icon, the resultant image again has a full level of detail (Figure 6-14c). The definition of the original curve includes all of these levels of detail—that is, all of these generations.

Some software packages offer fractal procedures that allow you to directly model a surface. If you now imagine trying to model the mountain described at the beginning of this section by using the nonfractal modeling techniques discussed earlier in Chapter 2, you can see that none of those techniques allows you very successfully to simulate the infinitely craggy quality of the mountain. First, complexity and irregularity make the forms involved tremendously difficult to model by positioning vertices and control points. Second, trying to model these forms in enough detail to make them look convincing both from the altitude of an airplane and from the height of a person walking on the surface of the mountain is impractical.

Moreover, if, through some tremendous exercise of saintly patience, you manage to create such an exceedingly detailed model, you will produce a wasteful rendering situation. Since all of the details of this model have to be dealt with, the rendering process will spend a lot of time rendering detail that is not visible. From the height of the airplane, the renderer will render even the tiniest details, even those details too small to be seen in the final picture.

Fractal models solve both the theoretical problem of whether it is possible to create such a complex model, and the practical problem of how to render it once you have created it. On the theoretical side, fractals are by definition very irregularly shaped and contain an unlimited amount of detail, so a fractal technique can, in fact, solve the problem of how to model a mountain. On the practical side, fractal techniques offer control over how many generations of a pattern are going to be created. Depending on the level of magnification needed, the software creates more or fewer generations, in the same way that you increase or decrease the number of generations—that is, the level of detail—in the Koch curve. The most common technique for applying fractal mathematics to three-dimensional modeling is very similar to the approach illustrated by the Koch curve. This process is called **recursive subdivision.**

Imagine that you have a simple rectangular patch (Figure 6-15a). If you subdivide this patch into four smaller subpatches, and then displace the corners of each patch some irregular amount, you produce the model in Figure 6-15b. If you then subdivide each of these subpatches into four smaller patches, with the corners irregularly displaced, you produce a model with more displacement (Figure 6-15c). By repeating this process many times, you can model a very irregular, terrainlike surface (Figure 6-15d). Further, depending on how much detail you need to see on the surface from a given point of view, using this modeling procedure the modeling software can produce a higher or a lower generation of the fractal geometry. A lower generation is suitable for viewing the terrain from a distance. A higher generation is suitable for a close-up view.

More commonly, fractal mathematics is used in off-the-shelf software to generate **texture images** that are, in turn, used for a wide variety of rendering applications. Most software packages offer a range of fractal texture

(a)

(b)

(c)

(d)

Figure 6-15. A fractal terrain model can be developed by recursively subdividing and displacing a patch.

Figure 6-16. Fractal textures are especially useful, both in modeling and in rendering. (*Off the Map*, © 1991 Sylvain Moreau.)

procedures, each adjusted to accomplish a specific purpose. One might make a cloudlike pattern, another a stony-surface pattern, and so on.

A fractal texture might be used for color texture mapping to create an irregular pattern of color. It can also be used for bump texture mapping to create an irregular pattern of bumps on a surface. In color plate 10, the texture of the sand was created with a fractal bump map. Fractal bump mapping can also be useful in conjunction with a fractally-generated displacement map (section 5.7). With this approach, the displacement map creates the large-scale geometry changes, while the bump map (section 3.8) creates the appearance of small-scale bumps.

Applied as a transparency map, a fractal texture can introduce a random irregularity into an atmospheric fog (section 6.2), or can cause the rendering of particles to look smoky (section 7.8). When attempting these effects, you most commonly use fractal procedures to generate solid textures (section 3.9), thereby creating a three-dimensional volume of transparency that varies as you move through the space of the fog or smoke.

The image in Figure 6-16 uses fractal texture mapping in several ways. The material partially covering the woman's face is actually a flat surface with two fractal textures applied—one as a bump map and the other as a transparency map.

6.4 Lighting Subtleties

We have discussed lighting in several other sections of this book. Section 3.3 introduced the basic concepts and techniques of lighting, and in section 6.2 we discussed the use of volumetric fog lights to render smoke or haze within a light. In this section, we turn to more details of lighting a three-dimensional scene. If you have not read those earlier sections, particularly section 3.3, you should do so before proceeding.

Three-dimensional lighting is an art form. Deciding how many lights to use, what kinds of lights to use, where the lights should be placed, and how each light's parameters should be set—all requires a great deal of skill and attention. In many professional situations, in fact, there are specialists whose sole job is to set up lighting. This happens in CG animation companies, in professional photographic shoots, and in traditional filmmaking. The effort you put into lighting will be well rewarded, however. Good lighting can make a scene memorable; bad lighting can ruin it.

MULTIPLE LIGHTS

Most 3D scenes require several lights to get the effect you want. However, you do not want to use too many lights unnecessarily. When a rendering program renders a picture, the shading calculated for every surface takes into account the effect every light in the scene has on that surface. If you use too many lights, your rendering time may increase to the point of impracticality.

When lighting a three-dimensional scene, it is common to think in the same terms as lighting designers in other media. In photography, lights are frequently conceived as being one of three types. The first is a **key light**. This is the primary light in your scene, in terms of its position, its intensity, and its shadow-casting qualities. It can be a spot light, a point light, a directional light, or any type of light. For example, if you are lighting a close shot of a character's face, you might use a spot light as your key light, placing it in front of, above, and a bit to the right of your character (Figure 6-17a).

The location of your principal, or key, light can have a profound effect on the mood you create. Placing the key light below the character and close to his face would create very eerie, exaggerated lighting suitable for a horror film. Placing the light off to the side and perpendicular to his face would create extremely strong shadows, perhaps appropriate for a *film noir* look.

The second of the two main light types frequently used in film shoots is the **fill light**. In the real world, fill lighting usually happens automatically, because any lights you are using will also bounce off the surfaces in your scene and throw indirect light onto your subject from those other angles. Thus, while your subject receives its primary light from your key light, it also receives some from the bounced light. This effect softens the lighting, providing some light on the shaded areas so they become a less intense black, and muting cast shadows at the same time.

If you are using global illumination software (section 6.10), much of this fill lighting is calculated for you automatically. If you are not, or if your scene is such that the bounced light of global illumination is not sufficient, you can place your own fill lights. Since a fill light serves to reduce the contrast in

(a)   (b)   (c)

Figure 6-17. It is common to use several lights in your scene, with a standard configuration being a combination of key, fill, and back lights.

your lighting, you frequently place it opposite, or nearly opposite, your key light. With our character model, if we have our key light in front of, above, and to the right of the character's face, we might place a fill light in front of, at face level, and to the left of his face (Figure 6-17b). With this position, and if we keep the intensity of the fill light somewhat low, it will gently illuminate the left side of the character's face, which would otherwise be in deep shadow with only a key light.

The third major type of light is the **back light**. If you place a light behind your subject, you will illuminate the perimeter of the subject, as seen from the front. This effect can be useful to visually separate the subject from the background, for without the lit perimeter, the shaded areas of your subject may be too similar to the darks of the background. It is not always necessary to use a back light, but it is an option that can be very effective in some situations. In Figure 6-17a, four point lights were added as back lights to make our character stand out from the background.

The concepts of key, fill, and back lights are derived from the real-world lighting of photography and cinematography. There are many features of virtual CG lights, however, that have no correspondence to the real world. One such feature offered by some packages is **negative light intensity**. A light with negative intensity subtracts light from the scene. This can be a useful way of fine-tuning the amounts of light in different areas of your scene.

When lighting a scene, there are no rules about the exact numbers or kinds of lights you should use. You might use one or several key lights; you might use one fill light, several, or none at all, and so on. There is only one rule: If it looks good, it's working.

EXCLUSIVE LIGHTS

As we have seen, CG lights have some characteristics that don't correspond to anything in the real world. One of these is the ability to designate which object a light affects. By default, a light illuminates all objects in a scene, just

(a)   (b)   (c)

as in the real world. An **exclusive light**, however, is defined to affect only specific objects. Any object not in the list of those affected by this light will receive no light from it at all. The process of building a list of which lights affect which objects is often called **light linking**.

The linking of exclusive lights to specific objects allows you tremendous control over the lighting of your scene. Imagine your scene consists of a room, desk, computer, and pencils on the desk. Now imagine that your lighting looks very good, except that you want more light on the pencil in front of the computer. If you add a normal light to your scene to accomplish this, you will simultaneously increase the amount of light the surrounding objects receive, thereby undoing the finely adjusted lighting you achieved on those other objects. If you insert a light and make it exclusive to the pencil, however, it will affect the pencil only, leaving the lighting on the other objects unchanged.

Figure 6-18 shows this process. In Figure 6-18a, there are two lights: a point light and an ambient light. Both are lighting all the objects in the scene. In (b), the point light has been made exclusive, with the cone excluded from its list of illuminated objects. The cone is consequently now much darker, receiving light only from the faint ambient light. The cylinder and sphere remain unchanged. In Figure 6-18c, a new light—a spot light—has been added to the scene, and made exclusive. The spot light illuminates only the cone, leaving the sphere and cylinder as they were.

Figure 6-18. Exclusive lights affect only specific objects. You can combine a variety of exclusive and non-exclusive lights in your scene.

OUTDOOR AND INDOOR LIGHTING

Outdoor scenes and indoor scenes have very different looks, and therefore present very different challenges to the artist. Outdoor lighting comes either directly from the sun, or indirectly from sunlight reflected off surfaces. The most common way to simulate **direct sunlight** is with a directional light. Recall from section 3.3 that calculations on this sort of light assume it is infinitely far away. Because of this, all of its rays are parallel, simulating natural sunlight very nicely.

The color and brightness of the sun, however, vary during the course of the day. Early morning light tends to be less bright and more pinkish than mid-afternoon light, which is usually whiter and much brighter.

Indoor lighting is frequently the result of artificial lights, which are usually best simulated with **point** and **spot** lights. Certain light-emitting objects, such as a television screen or a bank of fluorescent lights, might best be simulated with an **area** light. In addition to any artificial lights in the scene, there may also be sunlight streaming through a window or door.

In both outdoor and indoor lighting, some of the light comes directly from the lights themselves, but some of it also comes from **indirect light** reflecting off other objects. To achieve a high degree of realism, you must take into account both of these phenomena. As we will discuss in section 6.10, **radiosity** and **global illumination** are required for the reflection of light off diffuse—that is, non-shiny—surfaces. We see examples of this approach in color plates 6 and 16.

SHADOW SUBTLETIES

In section 3.3 we discussed the perceptual and compositional importance of cast shadows. We also discussed the two major algorithms for calculating cast shadows—raytracing and depth-map shadow casting. Because it handles shadows in a more physically accurate way, the raytracing approach allows you to achieve certain subtle effects that are impossible with depth map shadows.

One of these is **transparent shadows**. When light hits an opaque object, it is blocked entirely, and creates an opaque shadow. A transparent object, however, blocks only some of the light, allowing a portion to pass through. The result is a shadow whose darkness varies depending on the thickness and transparency of the surface. This sort of shadow cannot be rendered with the faster depth map approach; you must use raytraced shadows to achieve it (Figure 6-19).

When you do use the faster depth-map approach to shadow casting, it is important to understand the significance of the **resolution** of the depth-map image. Recall from section 3.3 that this technique creates a map, or picture,

Figure 6-19. The calculation of transparent shadows requires the raytracing algorithm. Depth map shadows are always opaque.

(a)   (b)

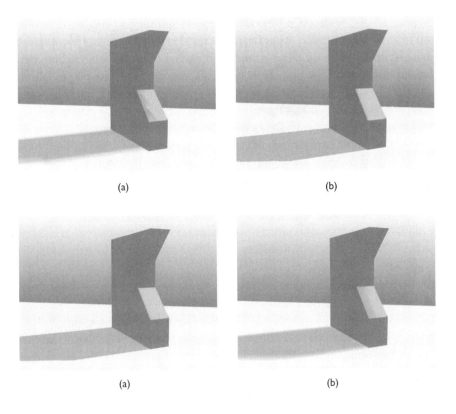

(a)   (b)

Figure 6-20. When using depth map shadows, the resolution of the depth map affects the quality of the shadow.

(a)   (b)

Figure 6-21. Most shadows have a more or less soft edge.

of the scene from the point of view of the shadow-casting light. This map image is used to calculate the final shadows. The higher the resolution of the map image, the more precise the shadow calculations. We see this in Figure 6-20, where (a) shows a shadow calculated with a very low-resolution depth map. Notice the inaccuracies and pixelation around the perimeter of the shadow. Figure 6-20b was rendered with a much higher resolution depth map, and the resulting shadow has more precise edges.

We do not always want a shadow's edges to be precise, however. In the real world, you only get crisp shadows from very concentrated lights. To mimic the **soft shadows** of the real world, you can adjust various parameters. For depth-mapped shadows, this is the size of the depth-map filter, a square area of pixels used in the calculations. The larger this area, the more blurry the shadow's edge will be (Figure 6-21).

Another phenomenon you see in the real world is multiple, overlapping shadows. In many situations, there is more than one shadow-casting light, and this causes several cast shadows, one from each light. Multiple shadows like this can quickly become visually confusing, and you will frequently want to simply your CG lighting to have only one or a few shadow-casting lights. But sometimes, creating **multiple cast shadows** is effective (Figure 6-22).

Figure 6-22. Multiple shadows can enhance an image, although overuse of them can clutter the image.

Figure 6-23. A glow effect is added to a light as a post-process. (© Mijeong Park.)

GLOWS

Unlike light sources in the real world, a computer graphic light source is not an object. It is an abstract entity that shines light on other surfaces, but itself has no surface. Because of this, we normally don't see the light source itself—we only see its effect on other objects. If we place a point light within a lamp model, for example, we will see the effect of that light on nearby objects, but the point light itself will not glow.

To correct this, 3D software packages offer a **glow** parameter. When this parameter is activated, the software initially renders your scene normally, and then, as a post-process after the normal scene has rendered, adds brightness to the picture in the area occupied by your light source. We see a simple example of this in Figure 6-23. Each fixture of the chandelier has a point light within its hierarchy, and each of these lights has its glow parameter turned on.

When working with light glows, you can specify how intense and how broad the glow will be. You can also elect whether the glow should be uniformly circular, as in our chandelier illustration, or whether it should have streaks in it, as might a glowing, twinkling star.

LIGHT MATCHING

There are some situations where you want to make the lighting of your CG scene match that of a real-world situation. In the simplest case, you might match your lighting to that of a **background image** (section 3.7). In Figure 6-24, the background image of a sunset is seen through the glass doors. The light sources of the 3D scene have been positioned to illuminate the interior of the room as if the light were coming from the direction of the setting sun. Notice the angle of light hitting the foot of the bed, and also coming through the skylights. In the color version of this image, we would see that the color of the lighting has a rosy-orange tint to match the color of the sunset.

Figure 6-24. Matching your CG lighting to that of your background image is necessary for visual consistency. (© Mijeong Park.)

Similarly, you may need to match your CG lighting to a background image when you use a **background shader** (section 6.7). An example of this approach is seen in color plate 5.

Special effects animation for **live-action** films also requires the same sort of light matching. When shooting your live-action scene, take note of the exact positions and angles of your lights. This information, combined with good visual skills on the part of the lighting artist, allows you to set up your virtual lights so that the lighting of any CG models or characters will be consistent with the lighting of the live-action scene. We see an example of this in Figure 7-100.

PHYSICALLY ACCURATE LIGHTING

Not only can you visually match your CG lighting to a real-world scene as described above, you can also use **real-world data** to do so. One application where such **physically accurate lighting** is especially important is the simulation of interior lighting for interior designers. Some software packages offer light entities called **luminaries**—lights with parameters simulating the physical properties of specific commercially available lighting products. A designer might want to know what his structure will look like using six fluorescent light fixtures of a given wattage and a given brand. Changing a luminary's parameters—for example, changing from fluorescent to incandescent, and altering the wattage—will produce a different lighting effect.

Another application where physically accurate lighting simulations are important is architecture. Consideration of how external lighting will affect your building is an essential aspect of its design. Will your building be in the cast shadow of some other structure during the winter months? Will the sunlight coming through the windows during the summer be too strong, causing the interiors of your space to overheat? To address questions like these, some software packages allow you to specify the **latitude**, and **longitude** of your

8 AM

10 AM

2 PM

6 PM

Figure 6-25. Accurate simulation of outdoor lighting makes use of geographical and chronological real-world data. (Courtesy, Henrik Wann Jensen.)

scene, as well as the **date** and **time of day**. From this information, the software calculates where the sun would be in the sky and how bright it would be. We see examples of this approach in Figure 6-25. The CG model here represents an actual building. The lighting in each frame is physically accurate, representing the true lighting for that building, in that location, at four different times of day. By keyframing these physical lighting parameters, you can create an animation simulating the movement of the sun across the sky at any time of the year, and how it affects your building.

6.5 Advanced Texturing

In sections 3.8 and 3.9 we discussed the basics of both 2D surface texturing and 3D solid texturing. In this section, we look further into these topics, discussing a number of techniques designed to address some of the more challenging aspects of texture mapping.

TILEABLE TEXTURES

In some situations, you want to cover a large area of surface geometry with a single, repeating pattern, such as the brick pattern on the side of a building,

(a)

(b)

Figure 6-26. If the opposing edges of a texture are not continuous, seams will be visible when it is repeated across a surface.

(a)

(b)

Figure 6-27. By adjusting the opposing edges of the texture, it becomes tileable.

the cracks of a long sidewalk, or wallpaper. Creating a single, large texture image to cover the entire surface is possible; however, since every texture image must be copied into RAM during rendering, very large texture images become impractical.

A solution is to use a smaller texture image that can be repeated across the surface of the model. We saw in section 3.8 that repeating an image in this way is a standard capability of texture mapping. Since the image in this case becomes a sort of repeating tile, this process is called **tiling**.

A typical rectangular image, however, may not tile successfully because its edges will appear as visible **seams** when it is repeated. We see an example of this in Figure 6-26. Figure 6-26a shows the texture image, and Figure 6-26b shows that image mapped to a surface. When repeated, the texture image maps to the surface with very noticeable breaks in the visual pattern at the texture's seams.

The solution to this problem is to modify your texture image so that the imagery at each edge flows continuously into the imagery of the opposing edge. That is, the top should flow into the bottom, and the left should flow into the right. This has been done to the modified texture image in Figure 6-27a. When mapped to the surface in Figure 6-27b, this new image repeats seamlessly, and is said to be **tileable**.

Most 2D imaging programs permit you to create a tileable image by **shifting** your image 50 percent either up/down or left/right. Doing so places the edges of the image in the center of your screen, where you can easily paint on them. Once painted, the image is shifted back to its original position.

Some imaging programs offer another technique—**wrapping**—whereby a brush stroke painted past one edge immediately and automatically continues onto the opposite edge.

STENCIL AND LABEL TEXTURES

Texture images, like all computer-generated images, are rectangular. In most cases, mapping the entire rectangle of the texture onto your surface gives you the result you want. In some cases, however, you want the mapped image to have a non-rectangular boundary, as would an irregularly shaped logo, for example. The technique that permits you to do this is **stencil mapping**, sometimes called **label mapping**, in which a portion of the texture image is rendered as invisible. To do this, you must specify which portion of the texture image is to be invisible. One technique is to create your image with an **alpha channel**, also called a **mask channel**—that is, a black and white image whose gray values define which portions of the image are visible. Figure 6-28a shows a texture image and Figure 6-28b shows its corresponding alpha channel image. Wherever the alpha image is black, the texture image renders as invisible, as we see in the rendered character in Figure 6-28c.

Another way of defining the invisible portion of a stencil texture is with **chroma keying**. Here, you define a particular color, or color range, to be invisible. For example, the color green plus or minus a certain amount of hue, saturation, or value might be the color range to be considered invisible.

CONVERTING SOLID TEXTURES TO SURFACE TEXTURES

We saw in section 3.9 that solid textures are advantageous in a number of situations. One situation in which they become problematic, however, is when the model deforms within the solid texture space. Remember that the solid texture is a volume of color within which the geometry of your model "floats." If your model changes shape, it will pick up different portions of the solid texture pattern as it does so. This results in the texture appearing to **crawl**, or **swim**, over the surface of the model as the surface deforms. We see this in Figure 6-29. In (a) we see the model with its solid texture applied. In (b), the model has been deformed. As the surface stretches to the right, it slides through the texture volume, revealing an entirely new set of texture lines as it does. The texture does not stretch with the surface, but rather appears out of nowhere as the surface extends to the right. This problem becomes even more noticeable in an animation than in a still image.

(a)

(b)

(c)

Figure 6-28. Stencil mapping allows you to put a nonrectangular texture onto a surface.

(a)

3D Solid Texture

(b)

Figure 6-29. If you deform a model that has a 3D solid texture applied, the texture will appear to animate as the model deforms through the texture's space.

(a)

2D Texture

(b)

Figure 6-30. By converting a 3D solid texture to a 2D surface texture, you assure that the texture will deform along with the model's deformations.

To solve this problem, the three-dimensional solid texture can be converted into a static two-dimensional texture image. When mapped correctly onto the model, this 2D image gives you exactly the same visual result as the original solid texture mapping, but deforms with the surface as the surface deforms. Figure 6-30 shows an example. In (a) we see the same model and solid texture we saw in Figure 6-29. When this solid texture is converted into a 2D texture and the 2D texture is then mapped onto the surface, it stretches with the surface as the surface deforms (Figure 6-30b).

This technique can be useful even in situations in which your model does not deform, since 2D texture mapping requires less computer processing than does solid texture mapping. Because of this, converting from solid to 2D textures is especially useful for real-time applications, such as interactive games.

A disadvantage of this conversion technique is that it requires one 2D image file for every object receiving the original solid texture. If a hierarchy of objects has received a single solid texture, converting this solid texture into 2D textures will produce one 2D texture for every surface in the hierarchical model. The bird in Figure 6-31 was originally mapped in this way, using a solid texture to produce a color pattern that flowed smoothly across the seams of each of the many feathers in the wings and tail. When converted to 2D textures, approximately forty individual textures resulted.

Figure 6-31. A solid texture applied to a hierarchical model flows smoothly across all the pieces of the model. When converted to 2D textures, the solid texture yields one 2D texture for each piece. (Image by Marcus Meyer and Michael O'Rourke.)

(a)   (b)

Figure 6-32. The 3D painting technique allows you to paint directly onto a three-dimensional surface, automatically producing for you the appropriate flattened 2D texture image.

(a)

(b)

Figure 6-33. Using a low-resolution painted texture as a guide, you can paint over in hi-resolution, retaining the precise placement of each part of the image.

TEXTURE PLACEMENT TECHNIQUES

Texture mapping frequently requires precise placement of the texture onto the model. A classic example is the human face, where even a slightly misplaced texture—for example, an eye—is very noticeable. A variety of techniques have been developed to permit the precision necessary for these situations.

One technique is simply the result of improvements in **real-time graphics hardware**. These special-purpose cards permit real-time texture mapping, allowing you to see the textures in your modeling window as you work. Frequently, you can control the level of visible detail in the textured image. More image detail implies slower screen updates and user interaction; less detail implies faster updates. For almost all computers, hardware texturing is not as precise as software texturing, and is used only to approximate your final texture placement.

An extremely useful technique for precise placement of textures is the **3D texture painting** technique mentioned in section 3.8 (Figure 6-32). Since this technique operates in real-time, however, it is subject to the same hardware limitations mentioned above. An effective way to circumvent these limitations is to create your texture image in two steps. First, use your 3D texture painting software to paint a **low-resolution** texture image. Then, bring that image into a standard 2D imaging package and, using the low-resolution image as a template, paint a higher resolution version on top of it. This allows you to precisely align the elements of your **high-resolution** image with the same elements of the low-resolution version. Once finished, map the high-resolution image onto your model, using all the same mapping parameter values as generated for the low-resolution version. In this way, the high-resolution texture maps onto the model with exactly the same placement as its low-resolution counterpart.

An example of this is seen in Figure 6-33, where (a) shows a detail of the eye area of the low-resolution texture seen in Figure 6-32. Figure 6-33b

1A	2A	3A	4A	5A	6A	7A	8A
1B	2B	3B	4B	5B	6B	7B	8B
1C	2C	3C	4C	5C	6C	7C	8C
1D	2D	3D	4D	5D	6D	7D	8D
1E	2E	3E	4E	5E	6E	7E	8E
1F	2F	3F	4F	5F	6F	7F	8F
1G	2G	3G	4G	5G	6G	7G	8G
1H	2H	3H	4H	5H	6H	7H	8H

(a)

(b)

Figure 6-34. Texturing a labeled grid onto your surface can serve as a guide, indicating where each portion of a texture will fall on the surface.

shows the high-resolution version of the same area of the image. When mapped back onto the head model with the same settings the low-resolution image used, this high-resolution version will produce a much higher quality texturing.

Another technique that can facilitate texture placement is to map a **labeled grid** image, similar to the one seen in Figure 6-34a, onto your model. When the model is rendered with this texture, note where each square of the grid lies on the model. In Figure 6-34b for example, square 6E lies on the character's left cheekbone. You then use the labeled-grid picture in a 2D imaging program as a template, and paint your texture image over it, noting which areas of the grid lay on which areas of the model. The finer your grid, the more precise you can be in the painting of your texture image.

COORDINATING MULTIPLE TEXTURES

We saw in section 3.8 that there are many varieties of texture mapping. A given surface might require a shader using color texture mapping, transparency mapping, and bump mapping—all simultaneously. When using multiple textures, there are certain situations that require special attention.

One such situation arises when using transparency mapping on a shiny surface. Recall from section 3.7 that transparency mapping makes portions of a surface appear invisible, but does not really remove these portions—that is, the geometry of the entire object remains. A consequence of this is that if a **transparency map** is used in this way, highlights might appear on the invisible portions of the model's surface. In Figure 6-35a we see such a surface. Notice the highlights in those areas that are supposed to be invisible.

To solve this problem, you can apply a **specularity map** to the same surface, making sure that the texture image and mapping parameters you use for your specularity map are identical to those you use for your transparency map. In this way, those portions of the surface rendered as transparent will also lack highlights, as we see in Figure 6-35b.

(a)

(b)

Figure 6-35. The mapping coordinates of multiple textures may need to be coordinated. Here, a transparency and a specular map align to remove unwanted highlights.

Another situation in which it can be important to coordinate several textures is when a **color map** needs to align with a **bump map**—to create texture maps for the bark of a tree, for example. To do this, you might use a photograph of actual tree bark as your color texture. You could then use that same photograph of the bark as a bump map. If you are careful to align the color and bump maps by using exactly the same mapping parameters, the dark areas of the bark in your color map will align with the hollows of your bump map, while the light color areas will align with its bumps. Many programs allow you to achieve this sort of precise alignment of textures by using a single texture, including all its mapping parameters, for several functions simultaneously—for example, for both transparency and specularity.

6.6 Texturing Polygons

In the previous section, we discussed a number of issues related to texture mapping in general. When working with polygons (section 2.2), there are special texturing issues, and we now turn our attention to those. In this discussion, we will also address the texturing of subdivision surfaces (section 5.7) because, recall, subdivision surfaces are generated from polygonal models. The texturing issues that apply to polygonal models apply as well to subdivision models.

An important issue when working with polygons and subdivision surfaces is that, unlike spline patch models, they do not have a default mapping system. Recall from section 2.3 that a patch surface has, by virtue of the way its geometry is generated, a UV parameterization. Each of the two spline curves, called U and V, that generate a patch is parameterized to extend from 0.0 at one end to 1.0 at the other. This same UV parameterization is used when a texture image is applied to that surface. The XY dimensions of the image map to the UV dimensions of the patch.

A polygonal model has no such inherent parameterization. Consequently, it is critical before applying a texture to it that you define how the texture should be mapped to the polygonal surface. Any of the mapping methods discussed in section 3.8 can be chosen—planar mapping, spherical mapping, etc.—but you must explicitly choose some mapping method.

A second important issue when working with polygonal models is that shaders and textures can be applied on a **per-polygon** basis. With many models, you may choose to apply a shader or texture to the entire object. With a patch surface, you have no other choice than to do so. With polygonal models, however, you also have the option of applying a shader or texture to a specific polygon. This becomes critical if your model is a single polygonal object but different portions of it need to be rendered differently. Figure 6-36 shows a construction machine whose cab is a single polygonal object. Those polygons that represent the windows of the cab have been assigned a transparent shader to simulate glass. The remainder of the cab's polygons has been assigned a different shader to give the appearance of metal.

Figure 6-36. Textures can be applied to individual polygons, allowing you to have several textures on one polygonal object.

Many software packages offer a polygon-mapping technique that is especially useful for the precise placement of a texture image. With this technique, the software produces an image showing the polygonal model **flattened**, or **unwrapped**, so that all its polygons lie in a flat plane. Over this, the software renders a similarly flattened version of your texture image. The space of the flattened texture image is referred to as the **UV texture space**—the U axis being in the horizontal direction, and the V axis in the vertical direction.

We see an example of this approach in Figure 6-37. The superimposition of the two flattened images allows you to see exactly which portions of which polygons receive which portions of the texture image. With this information, you can modify your texture image in a 2D imaging program as necessary, making specific portions of it align with specific polygons.

Special texturing issues arise when working with **real-time applications**, such as interactive games and CDs. These applications present unusual challenges to 3D computer graphics because frames must be calculated in real-time at least fifteen times per second. This has several very important implications for texturing.

The first implication is that textures take on a special visual importance in these applications. Since models intended for real-time applications require a

(a)

(b)

Figure 6-37. A polygonal object can be flattened, unwrapping its polygons into a plane and showing the alignment of each section of the texture with the individual polygons.

(a)   (b)

Figure 6-38. In the game industry, compacted textures convey much of the model's detail. Different sections of the texture are mapped to different sections of the model. ("Cale" © 2002 Junghwan Sung.)

simplified geometry, textures are frequently used to convey the **visual details** that might otherwise be in the geometry of a non–real-time model.

The **resolution** of real-time textures must also be kept small, since each texture image must reside in RAM. Frequently, texture images are as small as 256 × 256 pixels; rarely are they larger than 512 × 512 pixels.

A specialized technique for compacting texture images is also used in the game industry. With this technique, several images intended for different parts of the model are combined into a single, **compacted texture image**. Using special-purpose software, you then assign specific sections of that image to specific polygons of the model.

This technique permits you to use a single texture image for much, and sometimes all, of a complex model. We see an example of this in Figure 6-38. As seen in (b), the entire body is textured with only two texture images, each of which contains a number of smaller images. Portions of each texture—for example, the gloves in the lower texture—are assigned to specific portions of the model.

Another example of this technique can be seen in color plate 17.

A common way of assigning individual polygons to specific sections of the texture is with a variation of the flattened polygon approach discussed above, and which we illustrate again here in Figure 6-39. The model in Figure 6-39a is a subdivision-surface model, generated from a polygonal model. In Figure 6-39b we see the individual polygons of that model flattened into the UV space of the texture image. Notice the pattern of polygon outlines showing which polygons are assigned to which sections of the texture image. Specialized software then permits you to drag the outline of an individual polygon

(a)

(b)

Figure 6-39. Subdivision-surface models can take advantage of the flattened polygon approach, since they are derived from polygonal models.

and reposition it within the texture space, thereby reassigning a different portion of the texture image to that polygon. For example, you might position the polygons for the mouth area of the character in Figure 6-39a so that the mouth appears lower on the character's face.

6.7 Background Shaders

Sometimes it is desirable to combine 3D computer graphic imagery with live-action imagery, either still or moving. This happens frequently in films, where live-action footage is combined with computer animated dinosaurs, crashing vehicles, monsters, and sinking ships. It may also be required for more staid endeavors like architectural pre-visualizations, product design presentations, and accident simulations. Combining imagery in this way is known as **compositing** (see also section 8.2). We discuss one especially important rendering aspect of compositing here.

We saw in section 3.7 that it is possible to place an image—either a still image or a sequence of moving images—behind your computer-generated scene. The background image in this case acts like a backdrop on a theatrical stage; it is placed behind the action, but is not part of the action. A limitation of background images, therefore, is that the computer models of your scene cannot pass behind anything in the background image, nor can they cast shadows or reflections on it.

A solution to this limitation is the very powerful compositing technique known as **background shaders**. When a background shader is applied to a model, that model becomes invisible, revealing through it the background image you have defined for your scene. The software accomplishes this see-through effect by making use of the alpha-channel information of the rendered image. The power of background shaders lies in the fact that, although the model itself is invisible in this way, it can still receive and cast shadows or reflections. This has the visual effect of placing three-dimensional shadows and reflections directly onto the two-dimensional background image.

The procedure is as follows: First, you create or collect your **background image**. We see an example of this in Figure 6-40, a hand-drawn sketch of a street scene. This image is assigned normally as a background image for your scene, and displayed in the perspective window of your modeling system.

The second step is to create and position **stand-in models** for those elements of your scene that will receive this background image. These stand-in models must be positioned precisely so that they overlap and line up with those portions of the background image they are intended to represent. This requires not only positioning the stand-in models themselves, but also adjust-

Figure 6-40. A background image—either hand-drawn or photographed—is the first step in creating a background shader.

(a)   (b)

Figure 6-41. Simplified stand-in models are created for the scene, making sure they align with the background image. Your characters and other models are added later.

Figure 6-42. When the stand-in models receive the background shader, we see through them to the background image. Because of their geometry, however, they receive and cast shadows, and occlude other models.

ing your **camera perspective** so that your scene corresponds precisely to the perspective represented in the background image. This latter step is especially important because many 3D software packages default to a camera perspective much more exaggerated than that of most photographic or video cameras.

Figure 6-41a shows the stand-in models for our scene. These consist of a sidewalk, street, wall, window, and hydrant. Notice that the geometry of these models is somewhat simplified. This is possible because the details of the final rendering will come largely from the background-image drawing we saw in Figure 6-40. Notice also that the angle and perspective of the camera in our 3D scene match those of the drawing.

The third step is to define the **background shaders** themselves. Using the standard shader-definition menus of your software, you create a shader, defining its color to come from the background image. You also adjust **reflectivity** as necessary. In our example, two background shaders were defined. The first, with high reflectivity, was assigned to the window stand-in model. A second background shader, with zero reflectivity, was assigned to the street, wall, sidewalk, and hydrant stand-ins.

Finally, you place any other required models into the scene. These receive shaders and textures in the normal fashion. Figure 6-41b shows two human character models added to the scene.

Figure 6-42 shows the final rendering of this scene. Notice that the two human characters are casting **shadows** onto the background drawing. Note especially how the shadow of the plump man crawls up the curb of the sidewalk, following the geometry of the sidewalk stand-in model. The hydrant stand-in model also casts a shadow. Notice also the **occlusion** caused by the stand-in models: the hydrant obscures the lower legs of the thin man standing behind it. And finally, notice the reflection of the thin man cast into the window of the shop.

A background shader does not necessarily have to use a picture file as its background image. Any texture, including **procedurally-generated textures**, can serve as the background image. In Figure 6-43, a ramp procedure was used to generate the background image. This texture was applied as a background shader to a stand-in floor model, causing the dancer's shadow to be cast onto the ramp image.

The techniques just described can also be applied to a **sequence of moving images**. If the moving background footage involves a moving camera, you can use the techniques of **camera-motion mapping** (section 7.11) to replicate in your CG camera the motion of the live-action camera. In this way, you maintain the alignment of your stand-in models with their corresponding background-image elements as the camera moves.

One of the most powerful applications of the background shader technique involves the use of **live-action footage** as background imagery. This

Figure 6-43. A procedure can be used to generate the background image of a background shader. (Korean dancer, courtesy, Yi-sul Yoon.)

Figure 6-44. A live-action background shader can be combined with CG models.

Figure 6-45. Stand-in models that will be seen close-up require more precise geometry to assure accurate occlusions. The stand-in model for the man on the right has enough detail to correctly occlude the CG box.

and similar approaches (see section 8.2) underlie much of the **special effects** work produced for film in recent years, in which the goal is to make the computer animation and live action combine so seamlessly that we cannot distinguish the two. Alternatively, an artist may deliberately create a visual incongruity by using realistic background shaders with an obviously cartoon-style character. We see an example of this in Figure 6-44. This image is also reproduced in full color in color plate 5.

Regardless of the style, when working with live-action background imagery the artist must pay special attention to **light matching**, making sure that the lighting used in his CG scene is consistent with the lighting in the live-action scene. This includes the direction, intensity, color, and cast shadows of the lights. Notice in Figure 6-44 that the shadow cast by the penguin onto the sidewalk is consistent with the shadows cast by the live-action people in the scene. Moreover, the shadows cast by the trees onto the people are also replicated in those cast onto the body of the penguin. Light matching is discussed in more detail in section 6.4.

The amount of **geometric detail** needed in your stand-in models varies depending on several factors. Objects in the far distance require less detailed stand-ins than those in the near distance. Also, if your CG model passes behind a stand-in very quickly, that stand-in may need less detail since we will not have enough time to see how precisely the stand-in matches the background image.

Figure 6-45 shows the importance of this issue. The stand-in model for the man at screen-right was given substantial detail in the areas of his arms, legs, and satchel. As a result, the computer-generated box is convincingly occluded in those areas, while remaining visible in the spaces between his legs and satchel.

6.8 Non-Photorealistic Rendering

Historically, the goal of many CG artists and software developers has been to achieve imagery that is as realistic as possible. Applied specifically to rendering, the goal has been **photorealistic rendering**—that is, to render images as convincingly realistic as photographs. The efforts of both computer scientists and artists to achieve this level of realism are understandable: On the one hand, such realism is very difficult to accomplish and therefore a substantial challenge; on the other, we can judge relatively easily when our efforts have been successful. Consequently, for several decades the development of rendering software was largely driven by this goal of photorealism.

Recently, as photorealism has become more and more readily attainable, however, many software developers have directed their efforts differently, realizing what artists have known all along —that "realism" (if such a thing can even be defined) is not the only, and not necessarily the best, style. The result has been the development of **non-photorealistic rendering** techniques. These techniques produce renderings that are very definitely not "realistic," but are otherwise extremely effective for their purpose.

One area in which non-photorealistic CG rendering has become important is in **industrial design** applications. When presenting a design for a product, a designer's goal is to convey very specific information to the viewer. The industrial design field has developed a number of visual conventions to assist in this effort, ranging from "exploded" drawings that show the interior workings of a product, to color coding, to outlined drawings. Figure 6-46 shows an example of a computer-generated model rendered with an industrial-style, non-photorealistic approach. Notice the thin black outline around the perimeter of every form, helping the viewer to see where the edges of the forms are. Notice also the relatively simple interior shading on the forms.

Figure 6-46. One common application of non-photorealistic rendering is industrial design. (Courtesy, Amy Gooch and Bruce Gooch.)

(a)

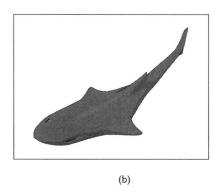

(b)

Figure 6-47. Cartoon shaders mimic the look of hand-drawn cartoons, outlining the form and using a simplified palette of tones on the object's interior. ("Moon" image © 2002 Jennifer Scheerer; "Shark" image, Geoff Smith © Cambridge Animation Systems 2002.)

Although no one would be fooled into thinking that this object is "real," the rendering makes its form extremely clear and easy to read.

We saw in section 3.4 that surface characteristics such as color, shininess, or transparency are stored in a **surface shader**. The characteristics of a non-photorealistic surface are stored in the same place, and by adjusting the shader's parameters, you control the look of your non-photorealistic surface.

A **cartoon shader**, also called a **toon shader**, is another commonly used non-photorealistic shader. Mimicking the look of hand-drawn cartoons, these shaders create a black outline around the perimeter of your model, and simultaneously limit the number of colors on the interior surface to a very few. The image in Figure 6-47a has such an outline, and only three tones of gray on the interior of the surface—a dark gray, a lighter gray, and a white. The result is a very cartoonish look indeed. Figure 6-47b is similar, now with only two tones of gray—dark gray, and very dark gray.

Creating a toon shader typically makes use of a **ramp procedure** to control the interior colors. In the standard use of a ramp procedure, you define a few colors and then instruct the software to create smooth interpolations from one color to another. For example, choosing red, yellow, and green as your three colors would produce a gradually ramped interpolation from red to yellow, and then from yellow to green. To achieve the limited palette of a toon shader, however, you instruct the ramp procedure to create an on/off interpolation between the colors. With this setting, the color of your surface will be red in one area, then, without any smooth transition, abruptly change to yellow in another. Then, equally abruptly, the surface color will change to green in another area (Figure 6-48).

To achieve the black outline of many toon shaders, you normally define a **conditional statement** within your shader. The condition examines the surface normal of the model and, if the direction of the normal changes appropriately, draws black at that location. By controlling the details of the conditional statement, you can make the outline thicker or thinner.

(a)

(b)

Figure 6-48. Cartoon shaders often make use of ramp procedures, setting the interpolation to on/off to give abrupt changes of color within the shaded surface of your model.

(a)

(b)

Figure 6-49. Non-photorealistic shaders can imitate other artistic media, such as watercolor or etching. ("Watercolor" image courtesy, Amy Gooch and Bruce Gooch; "Etching" image courtesy, Phoenix Tools Srl [Italy].)

The details of this sort of shader definition can become complex, and consequently many software packages and websites offer libraries of ready-made shaders, including a variety of non-photorealistic shaders. As with any ready-made, however, the danger of these shaders is that your work will look generic. If you understand how the shader works, however, you can select a pre-made shader and then modify it to create your own individualized shader for your application.

Although the styles achievable with a non-photorealistic approach are unlimited, it is very common to use them to mimic existing styles. Mimicking the look of other artistic media produces the so-called **artistic shaders** (something of a misnomer, since the artistic originality has been removed by the mimicry). We see two examples of such shaders in Figure 6-49, where (a) mimics the look of a watercolor painting, and (b) mimics the look of a pen and ink crosshatched drawing.

6.9 Reflection Maps and Environment Procedures

Reflections are an essential visual characteristic of certain objects and, unlike some surface characteristics, depend on the three-dimensional environment outside the object. A highly polished piece of steel, for example, looks like steel not only because it is shiny (that is, has very pronounced highlights), but also because you can see other objects reflected in the surface of the steel. If the shiny surface of a car does not reflect the environment as it drives by, you feel that "something is wrong with this picture"—that perhaps the car is made of plastic, rather than steel. Generating this kind of reflection requires a three-dimensional approach when rendering the car. Since the reflections on the surface of the car come from the three-dimensional environment around the car, you somehow must bring that three-dimensional environment into the rendering process.

REFLECTION MAPPING

The most common way of doing this, as you saw in section 3.6, is to use a raytracing program. Because ray tracers, by definition, trace each beam of light through the three-dimensional environment of the scene, accurate reflections are generated automatically, as part of the ray-tracing process.

But ray-tracing programs are computationally expensive, can be slow, and are therefore unsuitable for real-time applications. Games, instructional CDs, flight simulations, and other similar applications require some other, faster, way to achieve reflections.

The technique you use for this purpose is called **environmental reflection mapping**, or sometimes just **reflection mapping**. (Note that this technique is *not* the same as reflectivity mapping, which is discussed in section 3.8.) The basic idea behind reflection mapping is that you create one or several two-dimensional pictures to provide a simplified representation of the three-dimensional environment. You then map these two-dimensional pictures onto the surface to be rendered. The mapped pictures modulate the colors of the object, making it appear that the object is reflecting these pictures. The result can be quite convincing "reflections," even though there is no three-dimensional geometry being reflected. Since your object is reflecting only these two-dimensional texture images rather than true three-dimensional geometry, raytracing is not needed, and your rendering is computed much faster.

Since setting up reflection mapping can sometimes be complex and time-consuming, you typically avoid using this technique unless rendering time is critical, as it is in real-time applications.

The most common way of implementing environmental reflection mapping is through **cubic reflection mapping**. With this technique, six pictures, each on the interior face of an imaginary cube, represent the three-dimensional environment. This configuration simulates the effect you would see if you were standing inside a large cube and saw in each direction a picture of the environment as it looked in that direction (in Figure 6-50a the front face

Figure 6-50. Cubic reflection mapping maps six pictures of the environment onto the surface of a model.

(a)

(b)

of the cube has been left off so you can see into the cube). Notice how this technique simplifies the true three-dimensional environment, yet retains some of its three-dimensional character. It is not truly three-dimensional, because each wall of the imaginary cube is a flat picture, like a theatrical back-drop. Yet when you look in different direction, it feels somewhat three-dimensional because you see a different "scene."

Cubic reflection mapping uses this approach in the following way. The object to be rendered—and to receive the reflections—is positioned inside and at the center of the imaginary cube (Figure 6-50b). For each point on the surface of the object, an imaginary line, or vector, is drawn perpendicular to the surface at that point. (This vector, as you saw in section 3.5, is called the "surface normal" at that point.) Each of these vectors is then traced away from the surface until it intersects some point on one of the six cubic pictures. The color of the picture at that point is the color that needs to be reflected onto the surface at the base point of the vector.

Note that the imaginary cube of reflection pictures must be positioned in such a way that the object to be rendered resides at the center of the cube. Because of this requirement, each of the scene's reflective objects must have its own cube of reflection pictures. Imagine, for example, that a second object, say a cone, were to be positioned in Figure 6-50 to the left of the house. This cone would require a very different set of cubic reflection pictures than does the sphere. While the sphere would reflect the front of the house, the cone would need to reflect the back of the house. In short, each object to receive reflections through the cubic reflection technique requires that a unique set of six cubic reflection pictures be calculated for it.

This leaves you with the question of how to generate the six cubic pictures. One possibility, of course, is to draw them by hand, perhaps with a digital paint program. When doing so, you must be aware of how seamlessly each image fits against the neighboring images on all four sides. Any discontinuity between the images—for example, if the mountains in the background of Figure 6-50 don't connect seamlessly with the mountains of the right panel— shows up on the rendered surface of the object. The reflections will appear to have a line, or seam, running through them, destroying the sense of realism they were intended to convey.

A more useful technique for creating the six images needed for cubic reflection mapping is to render them from the three-dimensional data of your scene. The situation in Figure 6-50b—a sphere existing in isolation, onto which you map an imaginary environment—is rare. More often, such a sphere exists within a three-dimensionally modeled scene. For example, the tree in the right panel might be a three-dimensionally modeled tree posi-tioned to the right of the sphere. In order to produce convincing reflections, you must render the reflected tree in exactly the same style and with exactly

(a)

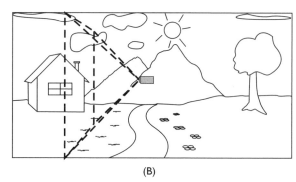

(B)

Figure 6-51. The six texture images of cubic reflection mapping can be generated by rendering the virtual three-dimensional environment from six points of view.

the same colors and lighting as the original tree is rendered. The best way to ensure such fidelity is to create six renderings of the three-dimensional scene, then use these six renderings as the six panels of your reflection cube.

In Figure 6-51a the entire environment—that is, the entire modeled scene—is represented as a panoramic line drawing. Hovering in the center of this environment is the virtual camera. The dotted lines emanating from the camera indicate the field of view of the camera and delineate the area of the environment that the camera sees as it faces to the right. Using this camera to render a picture produces the image on the right panel of the cube in Figure 6-50. Using the camera facing to the left produces the image on the left panel of the cube (Figure 6-51b).

Rotating the camera 90 degrees in each of the six directions produces the six cubic pictures you need for cubic reflection mapping. It is important to note that the field of view of the camera is a full 90 degrees (a very wide-angle lens). The field of view must be this full 90 degrees in order to ensure that the edge of each rendered panel matches up exactly with the corresponding edge of the adjacent panel.

Conveniently for the user, the process just described for creating the six cubic renderings necessary for cubic reflection mapping can be handled automatically by most software packages. Rather than positioning the camera and rendering each of the six views needed, you simply activate cubic reflection mapping through a menu selection, and the software does the rest, rendering the six cubic pictures for you automatically. There are some occasions, however, where you might want to exercise more control over this process, creating your own six cubic renderings by hand—either by rendering the three-dimensional scene as described above, or by drawing, painting, or photographing your own six pictures to generate a specific sort of reflection. For this reason, most 3D packages give you the option of either allowing the software to calculate the six pictures automatically for you, or having you specify them manually by typing in the names of the six picture files you wish to use.

Even automatic generation of the six cubic pictures can be cumbersome, however. A simpler variation of environmental reflection mapping, **spherical reflection mapping**, attempts to address this problem. This technique replaces the six pictures of cubic reflection mapping with a single picture. This one picture represents the whole world as if the world were on the inside surface of an imaginary sphere. Thus, the top of the picture matches up with the bottom of the picture, and the right side of the picture matches up with the left. The result is an image of the whole world seen in all directions, compressed into one rectangular picture (Figure 6-52). Notice that the edges of this hand-drawn picture have been left bare of imagery, so that each side matches up cleanly with the edge on the opposite side.

Figure 6-52. Spherical reflection mapping uses a single picture to represent the entire environment.

A disadvantage of spherical reflection mapping is that it is extremely difficult to generate a single picture that corresponds accurately to the three-dimensional environment of a particular animation. In many situations, however, reflections on a surface do not need to be precise in order to be convincing. Sometimes the reflection of general color patterns is convincing enough. The blade of a kitchen knife will reflect something when you pick it up. You almost certainly cannot tell *what* is being reflected. If it is sufficient to show that *something* is being reflected on a surface in your animation, without being too precise about exactly what is being reflected, spherical mapping can work very satisfactorily. If so, the advantage of producing only a single map picture, instead of the six pictures required for cubic mapping, can be significant.

All environmental reflection mapping, whether cubic or spherical, is based on the assumption that the objects in the surrounding three-dimensional environment—that is, the objects creating the reflections—are stationary. If the objects are moving, you have a problem, because as the environment changes the reflections should change. If, for example, a tree sways in the wind, you cannot use the same set of six static pictures for the whole animation.

In short, if any object in the three-dimensional environment moves, you must render new reflection-map pictures for each frame of the animation. In the case of cubic reflection mapping, this means that all six cubic-reflection pictures must be rerendered for each frame of the animation. These, plus the final animation frame itself, make a total of seven rendered pictures for each frame of animation. In such a situation, accurate reflection mapping becomes extremely time-consuming, and therefore impractical. In these circumstances, the solution for the designer of real-time applications is to design around the problem—that is, change your storyboard to avoid the problem in the first place.

In the sections 3.8 and 3.9 you saw that it is possible to generate a two-dimensional texture image procedurally. This is true of environmental reflection mapping as well. High-end software systems allow you procedurally to generate a three-dimensional environmental reflection map, which you then can apply to various models to produce convincing reflections.

ENVIRONMENT PROCEDURES

Some procedures, however, do much more than merely create environmental reflections. Called **environment procedures**, they actually create an entire three-dimensional environment. This means that when you render a scene, you can see, in addition to the refections generated by the procedure, the actual environment that created those reflections.

Figure 6-53 shows a simple example of this: a sky environment procedure has been used to create a three-dimensional environment of clouds. In the rendered image you see both the clouds themselves, behind the rings, and the reflections of the clouds on the rings. The clouds in the background are not merely a two-dimensional backdrop picture pasted in behind the rings. Rather, they are one rendering of a fully three-dimensional world of clouds. If you were to look (that is, point your virtual camera) in a different direction, you would see a different configuration of clouds. Even though you cannot see the clouds that are, for example, behind you or far above the rings, they are there, created by the environment procedure and therefore reflected on the rings' surfaces.

Notice also in Figure 6-53 that the details of the reflection are vague because of the curvature of the rings. You can see that the surfaces of the rings are reflecting something, and if you look closely you can make out cloudlike images on parts of the rings. But you do not need to be able to see specifically what is being reflected for the image to be effective. That the surfaces are reflecting something cloudlike tells you what you need to know about the nature of the surfaces.

Some environment procedures have more capabilities than merely making clouds. Advanced environment procedures can also generate other elements of an environment, such as a sun, atmospheric color, haze, terrain, and so on. Each of these elements is controlled by a number of parameters, to permit you to define exactly what the environment will look like. The color of

Figure 6-53. An effective example of reflection mapping. The environmental reflection map used in this image was generated procedurally. (*Art and Technology,* Courtesy of I.V. Kerlow, R. Castelblanco, V. Pinto, L. Ribolla, and the Computer Graphics Department at Pratt Institute.)

the sky, for example, could be defined by its Red, Green, and Blue component values, or by applying a two-dimensional texture pattern. The sun could be defined by specifying its size, color, and position in the sky. The amount and density of haze might be defined with slider bars.

Figure 6-31 shows a sophisticated example of such an environment procedure. The sky and clouds were generated entirely procedurally, just as described above. You can tell that they are truly three-dimensional because the overhead clouds, which are invisible from our point of view, are nonetheless reflected on the screen of the monitor. Notice also the rising sun and the effect its light has on the clouds and the atmosphere.

Some environment procedures also allow a **geographically accurate** definition of an environment by permitting you to specify the latitude and longitude of the location, as well as the month, date, and time of day. The procedure then simulates the position, color, and brightness of the sun accordingly—for example, a 5:20 A.M. sky on the 14th of January, 1999, in New Delhi, India. This can be especially useful for architectural or scientific visualization applications. We see an example of this in color plate 6. Also see section 6.4 for more discussion of geographically and physically accurate lighting simulations.

With advanced environment procedures, all the myriad parameters that you set to define your environment are also animatable, usually as a simple keyframing operation (see Chapter 4 for a discussion of keyframing). With this technique, you set the values for your parameters and make a menu selection to save those values at a particular moment in time. You then advance to another moment in time, set new values for the sky environment parameters, and save the new values. Using this approach, you might, for example, animate a sunrise, as in Figure 6-54, with the sun moving higher in the sky and changing color from a rosy-fingered pink dawn to a mustard-yellow early morning to a bright white midday sky. At the same time, you might animate a decrease in the amount and density of the early morning haze. If the software is sophisticated enough, it will also automatically change the

Figure 6-54. An environment procedure creates a fully three-dimensional sky environment, including animatable parameters for clouds, sun, and atmospheric haze.

(a)

(b)

apparent size of the sun as it rises, to simulate the magnification effect we experience when the sun is close to the horizon and seen through a great deal of atmospheric haze. The software may also diffuse the light of the sun according to how much and what sort of haze is present. Finally, you could animate the movement of the clouds. In Figure 6-54 this was done by animating the parameters of a solid fractal texture.

Recall, moreover, that all of this imagery that you render is being generated as a fully three-dimensional environment. You could, if you chose, move your camera through space as the sun rises, panning across the scene or looking around behind you to see the effect of the rising sun on the building you have just left.

6.10 More Rendering Algorithms

In section 3.6 we discussed several approaches, or algorithms, for calculating a final rendered image. In this section we expand on that discussion by addressing several additional, recently developed algorithms. This section assumes you are familiar with the concepts and techniques presented in section 3.6.

RADIOSITY

We saw in section 3.6 that the raytracing algorithm is very effective for calculating many effects, including reflections between shiny surfaces. Although the raytracing algorithm handles many optical effects very well, it does not handle well the **diffuse reflection** of light from one surface to another. This effect happens, for instance, when you hold a piece of red cardboard next to a white wall. Even though the wall is not specular (you see no highlights in it) and not reflective (you see no reflections in it), it nonetheless is affected by the color of the cardboard. The white of the wall takes on a pink hue because light bounces not in a concentrated way but in a very scattered way from the surface of the cardboard to the surface of the wall. The cardboard in turn picks up some of the color of the wall.

A **radiosity** algorithm handles this situation by breaking down every surface into a number of smaller surfaces. In Figure 6-55, where the large shape represents the wall and the small shape represents the piece of cardboard, each of these rectangular shapes has been subdivided into a number of smaller rectangles in such a way that, after all the radiosity calculations are done, the pieces fit together seamlessly.

The subdivision of each surface into smaller subsurfaces is necessary because the variations in color that result from diffuse reflection do not occur equally over the entire surface. Only a small portion of the white wall is

Figure 6-55. The radiosity technique subdivides each surface in order to calculate the diffuse reflections between these surfaces.

visibly affected by the red cardboard. Subdividing the surface enables the radiosity algorithm to deal with this uneven distribution of light. Once the surfaces have been broken down into sufficiently small subsurfaces, the algorithm determines how much any one subsurface affects any other subsurface; that is, how much of each subsurface is "visible" from the point of view of each of the other subsurfaces. The result of this calculation is called the **form-factor**. If two subsurfaces are close to each other and facing each other, approximately 100 percent of each surface is visible to the other: the number of the form-factor is approximately one. In Figure 6-55 the two subsurfaces highlighted with heavy lines have a very high form-factor. If two surfaces are at an extreme angle to each other or are far away from each other, a much lower percentage of surface area will be visible from one surface to the other, and the form-factor is a number closer to zero.

With this information, the radiosity algorithm calculates the color of each subsurface, taking into account the effect each of the other subsurfaces has on it; that is, taking into account the diffuse reflections between these subsurfaces. This calculation can be very time-consuming. However, unlike the calculation of specular highlights and reflections, which move about as you move your point of view, the calculation of diffuse reflections is unaffected by the position of your eye. Because form-factors are derived purely from the geometrical relationship of the surfaces to one another, the only time form-factors (and consequently diffuse reflections) change is when the surfaces themselves actually move. Because the calculation of diffuse reflections is independent of the camera, then, the radiosity algorithm can calculate the diffuse reflections for an entire scene just once, no matter how many frames of the scene are going to be rendered (again, assuming the surfaces themselves do not move). The rendering program can then store this information in memory. As it renders each new frame, the program retrieves the radiosity information and then performs the rest of the shading calculations (hidden surface removal, specularity, and so on).

In Figure 6-56 we see an example of radiosity rendering. Notice the softness of the lighting caused by the diffuse bouncing of light from one surface to another, especially in the far corners of the room. Color plates 6 and 16 also make extensive use of radiosity in their lighting calculations. We will see later in this section that radiosity can be combined, as it was in these color plates, with a variety of other rendering algorithms.

It is sometimes possible to mimic the effects of radiosity even if your software does not include that algorithm. You can do this by adding to your scene one or more carefully placed colored lights. Recall our original example of the red cardboard held close to a white wall and diffusely reflecting red light onto the wall. If you do not have a radiosity renderer, you could place a faint reddish light near the cardboard and direct it at the white wall. This will impart

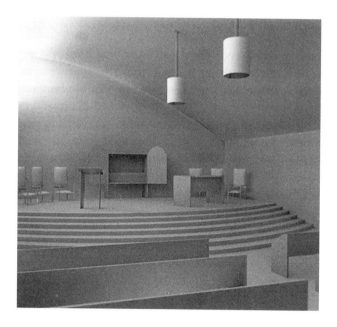

Figure 6-56. Radiosity calculates the reflection of light between diffuse surfaces. Here, the diffuse walls, ceiling, and floor bounce light off each other. (Copyright © 1992 Harold Zatz, Cornell Program of Computer Graphics.)

a reddish hue to the wall in that area. To make this work, you may have to make your colored light exclusive, as discussed in section 6.4, so that it affects only that white wall. You will also have to carefully fine-tune the intensity and direction of the light. If there are other objects in the scene that should also be diffusely bouncing light, you could create similar **fake radiosity** lights for each of them. This approach can sometimes work reasonably well for a simple scene, although it quickly becomes impractical as your scene increases in complexity.

CAUSTICS

Although raytracing is very effective at rendering most reflections, there are certain reflections, known as **caustics**, that it cannot handle. Caustics result when light is reflected many times onto a concentrated area. The word *caustic* originally means *burning*. A caustic surface is therefore one whose curvature, like a magnifying glass, collects light in a concentrated, potentially burning way. In computer graphics, the word *caustics* refers to this lighting effect itself.

One possible cause of a caustic lighting effect is the curvature of a reflective surface causing light to reflect back and forth on the surface many times, eventually producing a concentrated area of reflected light. An example of this is seen in the curved metal ring of Figure 6-57. As light reflects back and forth within the curved inner surface of the ring, it accumulates many reflections in the concentrated loop of light we see on the table inside the ring.

Another possible cause of caustics is the multiple refractions of the light passing through curved transparent materials. The cognac glass in Figure 6-58 is an example. Light hitting the transparent cognac and glass refracts, or

Figure 6-57. A caustic can be caused by light reflecting back and forth on a shiny curved surface. (Courtesy, Henrik Wann Jensen.)

Figure 6-58. Light passing through transparent materials or liquids can cause caustics. (Courtesy, Henrik Wann Jensen.)

bends, before passing out the other side of the glass. The refracted beams of light accumulate into patterns of overlapping light on the surface of the table.

The shimmering loops of light on the bottom of a swimming pool are another common example of caustics caused by light passing through liquid.

Raytracing cannot handle such reflections because of the unusual way it calculates reflections. Recall from section 3.6 that the raytracing algorithm traces a ray of light from the eye, or virtual camera, through a given pixel of the screen and into the three-dimensional virtual scene. When this ray of light hits a reflective surface, its path is traced backward to any surface it may have hit prior to this first surface. If the second surface is also reflective, the ray is traced backward again to any surface it may have hit prior to the second surface. This recursive process repeats many times, eventually yielding the color of the first surface. We see an illustration of the process in Figure 3-61.

In reality, of course, light does not travel from our eye to objects around us, but in the other direction—from the objects to our eye. In order to render caustic effects accurately, a rendering algorithm must trace the path of light in this forward direction. The most common algorithm used for this is **photon mapping**. Light is composed of billions of tiny photons. Photon mapping follows the path of these photons as they leave their light source, hit

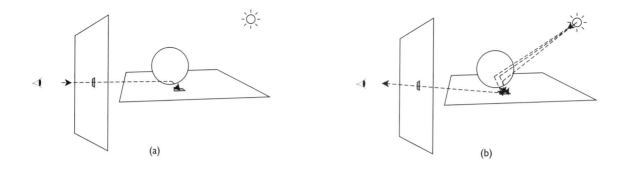

(a)   (b)

Figure 6-59. Raytracing cannot render caustic light effects because it traces each ray of light backwards from the eye. Photon mapping, on the other hand, traces the light forward from the light source to the eye.

objects, and continue on to our eyes. The algorithm develops a map of how the photons hit the various surfaces, hence the name.

Figure 6-59a illustrates a standard raytraced approach. A ray of light is traced from the virtual camera/eye backward through a pixel and into the virtual scene, a transparent sphere. It continues until it hits another surface—in this case, the unreflective surface of the tabletop. Since the tabletop surface is unreflective, the ray does not bounce off and the raytracing algorithm traces it no further. The color at that pixel, therefore, is calculated as simply the color of the tabletop—for example, brown.

Figure 6-59b illustrates the same scene calculated with a photon mapped approach. Starting from the light source, a number of photons are traced forward until they hit the transparent sphere. Each photon passes through the transparent surface, refracts, and passes out again, eventually hitting the tabletop. Since there are many photons and each one refracts slightly differently, a pattern of concentrated light—a caustic—accumulates on the tabletop. Instead of being its original brown color, that area of the tabletop is now colored with the color of the caustic light. This light is then traced forward through the pixel toward the eye, placing that color into the pixel.

Notice that the number of photons determines how accurately the caustic is calculated. Photon-mapping software allows you to control this number. As always, there is a trade-off between accuracy and rendering time.

GLOBAL ILLUMINATION

We have seen in this section and in section 3.6 that different rendering algorithms are able to account for different aspects of lighting. Radiosity handles the diffuse reflection of light from one object to another; raytracing handles the specular reflection of light from a shiny surface to other surfaces; and caustics handles the special case of concentrated reflections caused by certain curved surfaces. All of these, as well as the simpler raycasting approach, handle light emanating directly from a light source.

As rendering algorithms have become more sophisticated, it has become possible to combine all these capabilities into the **global illumination** rendering approach, which takes into account light from *all* sources—whether

Figure 6-60. Radiosity calculations contribute to the ability of the global illumination technique to account for indirect lighting, such as light entering from a distant window. (Copyright © Chen Qing Feng, cqfcqfcqf@sina.com.)

that light is coming from a direct light source, such as a light bulb or the sun, or whether it is bouncing off a surface, either diffuse or specular. This sort of rendering calculation, not surprisingly, can be computationally expensive, but the results can be stunningly realistic. Of course, not all 3D renderings strive for the photorealism possible with global illumination. We have seen throughout this book that many applications call precisely for styles other than realistic. But for those that do seek realism, the global illumination technique is important.

We see an example of global illumination in Figure 6-60. Notice how the light entering from windows at the far end of the room has permeated the entire room and is softly illuminating all the objects, as does real daylight. Even though the side table lamp and chandelier are not turned on, all the objects, even the armchair closest to us, are clearly lit because of the sunlight reflecting off the diffuse walls and other surfaces. As we discussed at the beginning of this section, this sort of diffuse reflection of light requires radiosity calculations.

We see another example of global illumination in Figure 6-61. In addition to the radiosity calculations that account for the sunlight bouncing off the walls and ceiling, there are very noticeable specular reflections of light on the polished floor and on some of the columns. There are also numerous light

Figure 6-61. Global illumination takes into account all sources of light. This includes the light sources proper, as well as light bouncing off surfaces, both diffuse and specular. (Copyright © Chen Qing Feng, cqfcqfcqf@sina.com.)

sources placed into the ceiling and above the painting on the back wall. All these sources of light—specular surfaces, diffuse surfaces, and light sources—combine to globally illuminate the scene in a very realistic way.

We saw in our discussion of caustics, that photon mapping can calculate these effects. Photon mapping is also very effective for radiosity calculations. Because it can handle both caustics and radiosity, photon mapping is quite commonly used for global illumination calculations.

Much of the effectiveness of global illumination comes from the radiosity calculations of reflected light from diffuse surfaces. This lighting effect occurs naturally in daylight situations such as in Figures 6-60 and 6-61. Photographers and lighting designers also deliberately mimic it in certain situations. It is very common in photo and film shoots to use **reflector screens** to bounce light from a light source onto the subject (Figure 6-62). This technique softens the light considerably, giving it a much more natural feel. In both photography and interior design, it is common to use **bounce lights** to illuminate an area with a soft light. By directing the light away from the subject and bouncing it off a diffuse wall or ceiling, you achieve the same effect as radiosity rendering calculates (Figure 6-63).

Figure 6-62. Reflector screens are commonly used in photo shoots to achieve indirect lighting.

Figure 6-63. A bounce light casts light against a surface, diffusing the light for a softer effect.

Color plates 6 and 16 are both worth studying carefully as sophisticated examples of global illumination. In color plate 6, the indirect, diffusely reflected light is seen most clearly on the left side of the room, while the right side is lit primarily with direct light and specular reflections. In color plate 16, there are no specular surfaces at all, and all the light is either direct sunlight or sunlight diffusely bounced off the stones and concrete.

6.11 Rendering for Output

In section 3.10 we discussed a number of issues that arise when doing your final renderings. In this section we build on those concepts, looking specifically at how your choice of output affects them. If you are not already familiar with the material in section 3.10, you should study it now before proceeding with this section.

As we consider different output media for animation, we will see that one recurring issue is **spatial resolution**, the number of pixels in an image. This has already been discussed in some detail in section 3.10.

A second issue that arises is **color resolution**, the amount of color information in an image. Images with greater color resolution have more computer **bits** of information devoted to each color. A full color image normally has twenty-four bits of color information—eight bits for each of the red, green, and blue color channels. (Images that also have an alpha, or mask, channel, have an additional eight bits devoted to that channel, giving them a total of thirty-two bits.) The mathematics of a computer's binary number system is such that eight bits of information yield 256 possible colors (2 to the eighth power = 256). A full twenty-four bits of color information yields over six million possible colors, which is more color subtlety than our eye can actually perceive, hence the designation *full color*. A black and white image typically has only eight bits of color information, yielding 256 possible tones of gray. An intermediate quality of color resolution could devote sixteen bits of information to color, dividing up those sixteen bits among the red, green, and blue channels, and yielding a total of about sixty-five thousand possible colors.

Throughout this book we have spoken many times of animation **frames**. The animation frame is the unit of **temporal resolution**—that is, how much information there is per unit of time. We will see in this section that different output media have different requirements for temporal resolution.

In section 3.10 we also introduced the concept of **file formats**. Looking more closely at this issue, we will see how these apply to the various output media. We will also examine other issues that arise specifically with certain output media.

VIDEO

In section 3.10 we saw that the **spatial resolution** of an image is quite important. As we saw in that earlier section, a typical resolution for NTSC might be might be 640 × 480. If the pixel aspect ratio of your device is 0.888, as it frequently is for **digital video**, your resolution would be 720 × 480. See section 3.10 for a more detailed discussion of these resolution numbers.

Final rendering of animation frames for video is normally done at **full color resolution**—that is, twenty-four bits per image. Frequently, an additional 8 bit alpha channel is rendered for use later in compositing (section 8.2).

Different video formats around the world have different **frame rates**. Standard NTSC video, as used in the United States, has a frame rate of thirty frames per second. Elsewhere in the world, other standards are used. Two of these standards that you might encounter are **PAL** (Phase Alternation Line) and **SECAM** (French for Sequential Color with Memory), both of which require a playback rate of twenty-five frames per second. Each of these standards is incompatible with the others, so video recorded in one format must be translated into the host format of the machine used to view it.

All of the numbers mentioned so far can be reduced when you produce a **compressed movie** file, as discussed in section 3.10. For example, an animation that you originally rendered at 640 × 480 resolution, with twenty-four bits of color, and at a thirty-frame-per-second rate might be compressed to a movie file that is only 320 × 240 resolution, sixteen bits of color, and fifteen frames per second. All of these reductions help compress the file size, but they also deteriorate the quality of your imagery. If you are producing a movie file for final recording, therefore, you normally produce an **uncompressed** file. Such a file is likely to be quite large, but will contain the maximum quality in spatial, color, and temporal resolution.

When rendering your animation frames, you typically render each and every frame of the animation–that is, all thirty frames of every second of an NTSC animation. This is called rendering **on ones**. Sometimes, however, it is possible to render and record fewer than the full thirty frames per second for each second of animation. For example, every other frame could be rendered and then held for twice as long when it is recorded. This process is known as recording **on twos**, and works as follows.

In the interest of saving rendering time, you render only every other frame: frame 1, frame 3, frame 5, and so on. That is, you render fifteen distinct frames for each second of animation, instead of the normal thirty frames. The video equipment onto which the animation is going to be recorded operates at a thirty-frame-per-second rate, however, so you must do something to stretch out the fifteen frames you have rendered to a full one second of time. When recording the animation, therefore, you hold each frame for twice as long as normal: each frame is recorded for one-fifteenth of a second instead of the normal thirtieth of a second. Another way of saying this is that each frame is held for a count of two frames. The frames of animation recorded onto the videotape effectively end up as frame 1, frame 1; frame 3, frame 3; frame 5, frame 5; and so forth.

In other words, using NTSC video, you need 600 frames in order to make an animation play back in twenty seconds. If you are going to animate on twos, however, you need to render only 300 of those frames (frame 1, frame 3, etc.). When you record them, you hold each of these frames for twice as long as normal, stretching 300 frames of animation into 600 frames of video.

The point of all this, as noted, is to save rendering time. Since only half as many frames are rendered, only half as much time is spent rendering. This can be significant. If each of three hundred frames takes five minutes to render, you save twenty-five hours of rendering time by rendering on twos (5 minutes × 300 frames = 1,500 minutes ÷ 60 minutes per hour = 25 hours). In a longer animation, the savings are even more dramatic.

There is a serious potential drawback, however, to animating on twos. For many kinds of motion, the animation may not look as smooth on twos as on ones. This lack of smoothness is most noticeable when there are very fast-moving objects in the animation sequence. Imagine, for example, a ball flying across the screen very quickly. Perhaps it takes only six frames for the ball to cover the distance from screen left to screen right (Figure 6-64a, in which each of the six frames is superimposed on one screen to show the relative placement of the ball from frame to frame). If you render and record this sequence on twos, you render only three frames: frame 1, frame 3, and frame 5 (Figure 6-64b). The distance covered by the ball between each two of these frames probably is large enough for the eye to notice when the animation plays back, and the result is that the motion of the ball appears jerky. Animating this sequence on twos, therefore, noticeably diminishes the quality of the animation.

In an animation in which the objects move very slowly, on the other hand, animating on twos may produce no visible deterioration of the image quality. Imagine the same ball drifting very slowly across the screen, over perhaps five seconds, or 150 frames. When rendered on ones, the distance covered by the ball between successive frames is almost imperceptible (Figure 6-65a). When rendered on twos, it still is barely perceptible (Figure 6-65b).

The two examples just given are extremes. In actual practice, most animations are neither so fast moving nor so slow moving, and a great many animations can be done on twos without any noticeable loss of quality. In order to find out whether recording on twos will cause an image to deteriorate, you must make a test recording.

Even when animating a sequence on twos will detract from the quality of the final animation, an animator often will produce test recordings on twos—or even on threes (rendering only every third frame) or fours (rendering every fourth frame). Only after the sequence has been developed and refined to the point that the final frames are ready to be rendered does the animator switch to working on ones.

In some situations an object moves so fast that even animating on ones does not produce a smooth look. A useful rendering technique in this situation

(a)

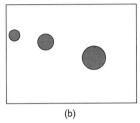

(b)

Figure 6-64. Rendering on ones, as in (a), produces smaller spatial increments between frames. Rendering on twos, as in (b), produces larger increments. For a quickly moving object, rendering on twos can result in jerky animation.

(a)

(b)

Figure 6-65. For a very slow-moving object, the spatial increment is very small whether the scene is rendered on ones or on twos.

is motion blur (see section 3.10). Another approach to solving this problem is offered by some high-end systems, which allow you to render and record animation frames at twice the temporal resolution of the standard video rate—that is, at one-sixtieth of a second instead of the normal thirtieth of a second. This approach is possible because of a peculiarity in the way a frame of video is generated.

You have seen that every frame of animation is composed of pixels and that these pixels are arranged into horizontal rows and vertical columns. A video image is also composed of rows and columns (as you can see if you examine a television monitor through a magnifying glass). When a frame of video is displayed, an electronic beam passes, or scans, over each row of the image, turning on the video equivalent of pixels—actually a tight cluster of three tiny vertical bars: one red, one green, and one blue—as it does so. This scanning across the rows is done in two passes, each of which is called a **field**. In the first pass, the beam displays the information of the odd-numbered lines of the frame, starting at the top of the image and progressing to the bottom. This information constitutes the **odd field**. As soon as the odd field has been displayed, the beam turns on the information for the even-numbered lines of the frame, again from top to bottom. This information constitutes the **even field**. Each of these fields takes one-sixtieth of a second to record. The two fields are said to be **interlaced** together—the odd field for one-sixtieth of a second, then the even field for one-sixtieth of a second, then the odd field again, and so on. The interlacing of an odd field and an even field, each taking one-sixtieth of a second, produces the thirtieth of a second that is the duration of the standard video frame.

Some systems take advantage of this fact and allow you to render and record by fields, rather than by frames. Doing this produces twice as many images as the normal rendering on ones produces. For each frame, an odd field is rendered and then, for a moment one-sixtieth of a second later, an even field is rendered. Effectively, this produces two "half-images" for each thirtieth of a second.

Figure 6-66a shows the odd-field rendering of a fast-moving ball at some moment in time. Notice that the ball appears in slices, because only the odd lines of the image have been rendered. (The slicing of the ball in this illustration is very exaggerated; it consists of only about 15 slices. It actually would consist of many more than that.) Figure 6-66b shows the even-field rendering of the same ball, rendered one-sixtieth of a second later than the first version. Again only alternate slices of the ball have been rendered—in this case, only the even-numbered lines of the image.

Since the two field renderings illustrated here are recorded only one-sixtieth of a second apart, the eye fuses the two images together seamlessly and sees them as one (Figure 6-66c). Notice, though, that because the two images

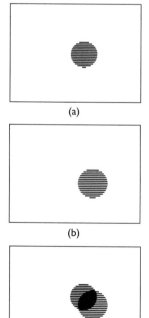

(a)

(b)

(c)

Figure 6-66. Rendering on fields renders only half the lines of each image, but does so twice as frequently.

represent the ball at slightly different moments, the two renderings are displaced horizontally from one another.

To see more clearly how rendering on fields can produce a smoother-looking animation than can rendering on ones, compare the six superimposed frames of a fast-moving ball rendered on ones (Figure 6-67a) with the twelve superimposed renderings of the same animation rendered on fields (Figure 6-67b). Notice how much shorter the distance between each ball is when the image is rendered on fields: it is this reduction of the distance between objects from frame to frame that makes a recording done on fields appear smoother than a recording done on ones.

Another issue you must concern yourself with when recording to video derives from the standards of the television broadcast industry—again, in the United States, the NTSC standards. Certain very saturated colors exceed the capabilities of video reproduction as defined by the NTSC, and because they cannot be properly represented by the NTSC color system these colors tend to spill over, or **bleed**, into neighboring areas of color. A very saturated red, for example, often does this, creating a blurry look around the edges of the red areas of the image. In extreme cases, very saturated colors produce a black area in the video image. These colors may look wonderful on a digital RGB monitor, but they are considered "illegal" video colors and cannot be broadcast as televised video. If you intend to have your work shown on television, then, you must desaturate certain colors before recording them to video, so that they will be within the legal range of colors.

Another issue when rendering for video has to do with the final viewing of the recorded video on television screens and monitors. That is, when the rectangular image of an animation frame is displayed on a television screen, the outer edges of the image are obscured both by the plastic housing of the screen and by the slightly rounded shape of the screen itself. This effect, called **TV cutoff**, is always present but varies from one television set to another, depending on the shape of the plastic housing.

In the case of a digital image in which a character standing at the far left of the frame watches a bird flying at the very top of the frame (Figure 6-68a), the edges of the image on all four sides will be cut off on a typical television screen (Figure 6-68b). In this frame of animation, the TV cutoff is disastrous. Since part of the main character and all of what he is looking at are concealed, a viewer cannot understand the action of the animation at all.

Thus, you must be aware of the effects of TV cutoff and plan the composition of your frames accordingly. Many software systems facilitate doing this by the inclusion of a **field guide**, which can be displayed temporarily on top of the animation frame (Figure 6-69). The guide consists of a rectangular grid of lines, called "fields." (These fields have nothing to do with the odd and even fields of a video frame.) Animators speak of placing their imagery within

(a)

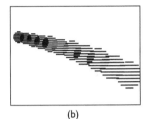

(b)

Figure 6-67. Animating on fields reduces the spatial increment between frames, which can result in smoother movement for quickly moving objects.

(a)

(b)

Figure 6-68. When a computer-generated frame is played on a television monitor, some portion of the image is cut off.

Figure 6-69. A field guide is used to determine whether the action of the animation frame is "TV safe."

certain fields of the guide—that is, within certain grid lines. For example, an image might be kept "within ten field."

With the field guide in place, you can see which parts of the image are likely to be obscured by TV cutoff, and adjust your composition accordingly. The area of the frame that will not be affected by TV cutoff is called **TV safe**. Sometimes, the TV safe area is further subdivided into two areas. The inner area, represented by an oval in the shape of a television screen, is known as **title safe**, meaning that titles and text should be kept within this area. A larger area, represented by a second, larger oval, is known as **action safe**.

Whenever you are rendering still frames of animation you must also be aware of the **naming conventions** for your files. We introduced this concept in section 3.10 and saw that most picture files consist of a name, and file-format extension, and a frame number. A rendered frame might be called *test.17.tiff*, indicating that it is from the sequence called *test*, it is frame number 17, and it is in the TIFF picture format. When naming your files, an additional convention applies to frame numbering. Some recording systems require that you use **frame padding**, the addition of leading zeros to frame numbers so that all frame numbers have the same number of digits. If you are using four-digit frame padding, for example, you might have file names called *test.0001.tiff*, *test.0017.tiff*, *test.0248.tiff*, *test.2739.tiff*, and so on. Frame padding is necessary on some computer systems because they can only list files alphabetically. Without the leading zeros of frame padding, an alphabetical listing of your frames would place *test.100.tiff* prior to *test.5.tiff*. Using the leading zeros, the alphabetical listing and the numerical listing are identical.

DIGITAL MEDIA

Not all animation is produced for output to video. Much contemporary animation is viewed in its final format on a variety of digital media, most prominently **CD-ROM**s (the acronym stands for *compact disk read-only memory*), and the **Internet**. Among the applications using these media are interactive games, instructional CDs, and millions of websites (Figure 6-70). All these digital media share one critical feature—the need for **real-time playback**. It is this need that underlies the special output requirements of these media.

When rendering animation for any of these media, you usually do not render at the full video resolution we described above. If you did, your files would be so large that no one would be able to play them back reasonably. Remember the arithmetic of spatial resolution. The total number of pixels in your image equals the number horizontally multiplied by the number vertically. To use simple numbers, imagine you have a 100-pixel-by-100-pixel image. This means there are ten thousand pixels in the image ($100 \times 100 = 10{,}000$). If you double the image resolution to 200 pixels by 200 pixels, you do not double the total number of pixels—you quadruple it! (200 × 200 = 40,000). Thus, halving your resolution reduces the total number of pixels by 25 percent—a huge savings in file size. For this reason, most animation for real-time digital media is rendered at **half resolution**, or sometimes even smaller.

For similar reasons, most animation for digital media is not rendered on ones. In the interest of reducing file size, the rate of **frames per second**, or **fps**, is reduced. If you halve the number of frames, you halve your file size. A common frame rate for digital media is **15 fps**. This yields a less smooth flow of motion than a normal video or film rate, but it is usually satisfactory for the purpose and helps keep the file size smaller. For interactive games in which the interaction speed has much greater precedence than smooth playback, animation is sometimes rendered at **8 fps**, to reduce file size still further.

Whatever playback rate you elect to render at, it is important to set up your compositing or editing software appropriately (sections 8.2 and 8.3). Suppose you have rendered a ten-second animation sequence at fifteen frames per second. This produces 150 individual still frames (10 seconds × 15 fps = 150 frames). If your editing software is expecting frames at the normal video rate of 30 fps, and you read in your 150 frames, the editing software will treat your sequence as being only five seconds long (150/30 = 5)—that is, it will play it back twice as fast as you intended. Editing and compositing packages usually have a *Preferences* menu selection where you can indicate the frame rate for the sequence you are about to read in.

Compression plays a large role in producing animation for digital media. Most **compression** software allows you to reduce not only the spatial resolution and the frame rate of your animation, issues we've just discussed, but also the color resolution. Reducing your color resolution from twenty-four bits to eight bits can produce a dramatic reduction in file size. It can, of course, also produce a dramatic reduction in image quality. To give yourself the most options, you typically render your frames at or near the maximum quality you think your medium can allow. For example, you might render at 320 × 240, twenty-four bits, and 15 fps. You then read your files into compression software and write out several tests, varying the compression settings until you get the balance you need between file size and image quality. Most often, you output a **movie file** in one of the standard movie-file formats, such as **QuickTime**, **AVI**, or **MPEG**.

FILM

Before the advent of video, all animation was recorded to film. For big-budget commercial films, this is still the case. Film, though much less convenient and much more expensive, can yield a much higher quality image because of the resolution and chemistry of film stock. For commercial films intended for large-screen viewing, this improved image quality is critical.

Figure 6-70. 3D modeling, rendering, and animation can be used effectively for the World Wide Web. (Copyright © 2002, Flora H. Y. Chen. All rights reserved.)

In the United States, the NTSC standard for video requires an image resolution of approximately 64 × 480 pixels. The resolution of film, by contrast, tends to be several thousand by several thousand. This does not mean that your animation frames must be rendered at such an extremely high resolution, but it means that they can be. Rendering animation frames for film at approximately twice the normal video resolution, for example, can result in a very noticeable improvement in the sharpness of the image.

Another advantage of using film as your recording medium is the accuracy of the color transferral. As you saw in the previous section, the range of colors that video can accommodate is not as great as the range of colors that digital imagery can accommodate. Consequently, there usually is some loss of color—especially among the more vibrant, saturated colors—when digital imagery is recorded to video. With film, this loss does not occur.

Rendering and recording to film is more time-consuming than rendering and recording to video, however. In order to take advantage of the very high image resolution of film, you must render frames at a higher resolution, and higher resolutions mean longer rendering times. Moreover, the actual process of recording frames to film is slower than the process of recording the same frames to video.

A second disadvantage of recording to film is cost. The cost of purchasing film stock and processing (that is, developing and printing) the film far exceeds the cost of a videotape. Film is inconvenient, too, because developing and printing a reel of film is normally an overnight process. Video, on the other hand, requires no processing at all. As soon as video footage is recorded, it is viewable.

A final disadvantage of film recording is simply that, for all of the reasons cited above, video recording of computer animation is much more common than film recording. While almost all 3D computer animation packages come equipped with software to permit video recording, it is much rarer to find film-recording capabilities in the same software.

Still, because of the dramatic advantages in image quality, rendering, and recording computer animation to film is the standard in the commercial film industry, where the large projection size of the final image demands the highest possible image quality, and where the substantial funding behind big-budget films permits the expenditure. This has become true especially in recent years as more and more live-action films incorporate computer animation and special effects, all of which must eventually be composited with and recorded onto the same film stock used for the live-action footage.

As with any output, you must pay attention to the **playback rate** of the equipment you work with. In film, the standard playback rate for both 16mm film and 35mm film is **24 fps**. As with all animation, it is possible to render and record frames either on ones (in this case, twenty-four distinct images per

Figure 6-71. Some digital film recorders use a laser beam to expose the film negative pixel by pixel. (*Iggy's Dream* #123, © Michael O'Rourke.)

Figure 6-72. Some digital film recorders shoot each frame, displayed on the screen of a high-quality black-and-white monitor, through color filters. Each frame is exposed three times: once for each of the red, green, and blue components of an image. (*Iggy's Dream* #123, © Michael O'Rourke.)

second) or on twos (twelve images, each of which is held for two frames). Note, however, that it is not possible to record to film on fields, which are unique to video technology and do not occur in film.

Since the frame rates of video and film differ, animation developed for one medium must undergo special processing before in can be recorded on the other. Thirty frames of video, if recorded directly to film, will yield more than the intended one second of animation. Because of this, animation houses that record to film use special software to alter video animation frames before recording them to film.

The actual process of recording a digital image to film involves either of two types of a **digital film recorder**. The first, used for animation and moving imagery, uses a **laser** beam to expose the film stock (Figure 6-71). In this case the recording device consists of a laser generator capable of emitting laser beams of varying intensities and colors, and a film-advance device that holds and advances the negative film stock. Digital RGB information for each frame of animation is sent to the recording device, where it is used to modulate, pixel by pixel, both the color and intensity of the laser beam. With each modulation, the beam exposes one pixel-sized area of the film negative. Scanning across the film negative pixel by pixel and line by line, the beam exposes the negative for that frame with the correct amount and color of light. The entire process takes place relatively quickly; sophisticated recorders require only a few seconds to expose and advance each frame.

An older and less expensive film-recorder technology is still used for recording still images onto film, and is based on the use of **color filters** (Figure 6-72). Within film-recording devices of this type is a very high-quality black-and-white monitor, the screen of which is unusual in that it is extremely flat, to avoid distortion of the image.

Above the monitor is a housing for the film camera. Within it the camera shoots, frame by frame, the images that come up on the special-purpose monitor. The housing around the monitor keeps light out, so that only light from the screen is exposed onto the film.

The recording of each frame is actually a three-step process. In the first step, the red component of the digital image is displayed on the black-and-white monitor as a gray-scale image. Suspended between the monitor and the camera lens is a wheel that holds red, green, and blue filters. When the red component of the image is displayed on the black-and-white monitor, the color wheel automatically rotates so that the red filter is in place over the image. At this point, the software controlling the camera causes the camera to take an exposure. Since the camera sees the black-and-white image on the monitor filtered through the red filter, what is exposed onto the film is the red component of the image, with all the proper shades of red.

Once the red component is finished, the green component of the same image is sent to the small monitor and displayed as a gray-scale image. The color wheel automatically rotates so that the green filter is in place above the monitor, and the camera takes a second exposure. Notice that the film has not advanced. The camera has taken two exposures—a double exposure—onto the same frame of film.

This process is repeated for the blue component of the image. Finally, when all three exposures have been shot to the one frame of film, the frame is fully exposed. At this point, the film is automatically advanced to the next frame, and the whole three-step process, which can take as much as half a minute, begins again for the next image.

Both laser and color-filter film recorders are often designed to accept any of the standard film formats—16mm, 35mm or 70mm. And both require that you carefully set all of the standard photographic parameters. That is, you must decide upon the **shutter speed**, the **f/stop**, and the **color balance**.

Because of image-quality issues, film is still the medium of choice for big-budget, feature-length films. The higher resolution of film will be less important, however, as **high-definition television** (HDTV) becomes more commonly available. Since the resolution of HDTV is approximately 2,000 × 1,000, the difference between video resolution and film resolution will be far less significant.

CHAPTER 7
Advanced Animation

7.1 Introduction

Chapter 4 of this book introduced the basic concepts and techniques of computer graphic animation. There are a great many additional techniques, and this chapter focuses on the most important of those. Many of the newer, more advanced animation techniques are still evolving, but all of them build on the underlying concepts and principles presented in Chapter 4. If you have not already done so, you should study the material in that chapter before proceeding here.

7.2 Animated Fillets

In traditional machining and industrial design applications, a **fillet** is a surface that smoothly blends between two other surfaces. In Figure 7-1 the curved surface between the cylinder and the flat block is a fillet. Figure 7-1a shows these two forms without the fillet. Figure 7-1b shows a fillet between these two forms. Figure 7-1c shows a smooth-shaded rendering, illustrating how the curvature of the fillet blends smoothly with the walls of the cylinder and surface of the box.

In animation, the **animated fillet** technique is analogous to the traditional fillet of industrial design and, like it, creates a new surface between, and attached to, two other surfaces. Figure 7-2a shows the two original surfaces, in this case, two cylinders, and Figure 7-2b shows the new fillet surface, represented here in wireframe, created between them.

As with a standard fillet, an important feature of an animated fillet is that it is defined so that it blends smoothly and without any visible seam with the

(a)

(b)

(c)

Figure 7-1. A fillet surface blends smoothly with its adjacent surfaces.

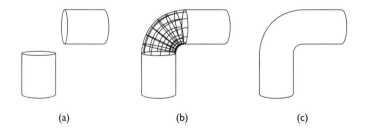

(a)   (b)   (c)

Figure 7-2. A blended surface seamlessly connects two other surfaces.

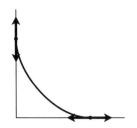

Figure 7-3. The curvature of a fillet is tangent to the adjacent surfaces at the points of contact with them.

(a)   (b)

Figure 7-4. To create a blended surface, you select end contours on each object, untwisting the blended surface if necessary.

(a)   (b)

Figure 7-5. A blended surface automatically deforms as its attached objects move about.

other two objects. In more technical terminology, the fillet surface is said to be **continuous** with the two original surfaces. As a result, when rendered as a shaded surface, the three objects—the two originals plus the blended surface—appear as a single, continuous object (Figure 7-2c.)

The reason a fillet is continuous with the other surfaces is because its curvature is **tangent** to that of the other surfaces. If the curvature of the fillet is represented as a Bezier spline, the tangent handles at the endpoints of the fillet align with those of the adjacent surfaces (Figure 7-3).

Another critical feature of an animated fillet—the one that makes it so valuable for animation—is that the shape of the fillet is automatically recalculated and updated whenever either of the two original objects moves. In other words, if either of the two original objects is animated, the animated fillet changes shape appropriately, always remaining, at every frame, continuous with its two end objects.

In defining an animated fillet, you typically begin by selecting a curve on the surface of each of the two original objects (the bold lines in Figure 7-4a). You then create a default fillet surface. This surface may be twisted, as in Figure 7-4b, if the two curves you selected run in opposite directions—for example, one clockwise and the other counterclockwise. The fillet surface may also be twisted if the starting points of the two curves are out of alignment. In either case, this twisting occurs as the blended fillet tries to connect the points of one curve to the points of the other curve. To correct this, the software allows you to to "untwist" the blended surface, usually by dragging the mouse cursor in one direction or the other.

Once you have defined the fillet between your two objects, these two objects can be animated by moving them or deforming them, and the animated fillet surface will adjust to always remain tangent to the two objects (Figure 7-5).

The animated fillet technique can be useful when you have surfaces that otherwise do not blend together, but should during your animation. An example is the animation of human eyelids. This can be a challenging problem for the animator. On the one hand, modeling the face and eyelids of your character as a single surface can make it difficult to control the deformations of the eyelids. On the other hand, modeling the face as a separate surface from the two eyelids leaves a visible crease between the eyelid and the face, which may not be desirable. The animated fillet technique can provide you with the desired surface continuity while still permitting you to operate on the eyelids as separate objects (Figure 7-6).

Animated fillets can very effectively solve the problem of smoothly connecting two animated surfaces. However, recalculating the fillet surface at every frame so that it is continuous with each of the other surfaces is mathe-

(a)   (b)   (c)

matically complex and can slow down your software, especially if there are
several animated fillet surfaces. You should take this into account in your use
of them.

Figure 7-6. An animated fillet automatically changes shape as the position or shape of its adjacent surfaces change.

7.3 Limits and Constraints

LIMITS

With any animation, whether a single object, a hierarchical model, or an
inverse kinematic model, it is often useful to restrict the range of the model's
motion. One way of doing this is to **limit** its motion. You can define limits for
any of a model's three basic transformations—translation, rotation, scale.
They are most commonly used, however, for translation and rotation. Let us
first consider **rotation limits**.

In some situations you know beforehand that your model should only
rotate in certain ways. Consider the rear wheels of a car. They should be able
to rotate about the axis of the car's rear axle (call it the X axis), but not about
any other axis (unless something breaks)! The front wheels of the vehicle are
a little more complicated (Figure 7-7). In addition to rotating about the X axis
of the axle, they must also be able to rotate about the Y axis, so that the
vehicle can turn. Their rotations about Y, however, will be limited—perhaps
to ± 60 degrees. They will not be able to rotate about the Z axis at all. Defining limits for the rotations of your wheel can help you avoid accidentally
rotating the wheels in ways you do not want.

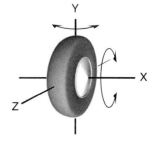

Figure 7-7. The front wheel of a car has rotational limits.

Rotational limits become especially important when you animate complex
articulated figures, such as humans, other limbed animals, and robots,
because our joints have natural, physiological rotational limits. Our knees,
for example, can rotate in only one direction. If a leg model is aligned as
shown in Figure 7-8a, it will not be able to rotate at all about the Y axis or the
Z axis. The only axis about which it can rotate is the X axis. If you define limits for the knee rotations according to these naturally occurring limits, you
can force the leg model to behave as a real leg would. Typically, the way you

	MIN	MAX
x	0	130
y	0	0
z	0	0

Figure 7-8. The joints of animal bodies have naturally occurring rotational limits.

(a)   (b)

	MIN	MAX
x	-120	30
y	-20	10
z	-70	25

Figure 7-9. The rotational limits for a shoulder joint need to be specified around all three axes.

(a)   (b)

define limits is by selecting the model you want to work on and then selecting a menu for defining rotational limits for it. Within this menu, you select the specific joint you are interested in (in this example, the knee joint), and then, for each axis of that joint, you specify the minimum and maximum rotations in degrees. Specifying the minimum and maximum rotation values can be done either explicitly by typing them in, or interactively by positioning your model and saving whatever rotation values it has in that position. Typical values for a human knee joint are as shown in Figure 7-8b.

To fully define the rotation limits of a complete human figure, you go through this process for each joint. Many human joints are more complex than the knee joint used as the example. The shoulder joint in Figure 7-9a, for example, might have the indicated rotation limits.

Carefully defining the rotational limits of each joint of a complex model like the human figure can be a time-consuming process, because every joint, both left and right, must be defined for all three axes. Because of this, some software packages offer higher-level primitives (section 5.10) of human-figure IK skeletons, complete with predefined limits for every joint (Figure 7-10). If your package does not do so for you, taking the trouble to define joint limits yourself can result in a model that is much more easily animated.

Figure 7-10. When an inverse kinematic skeleton has rotational limits on each joint, it behaves in a very natural way.

Sometimes, in fact, such a model behaves with almost uncanny realism. For example, if the rotational limits have been well defined, lifting the hand straight out to the side and then in an arc across the body will cause the arm to rise and bend in a very natural motion. First, the arm rises up with no bending. When the shoulder joint reaches its rotational limit in Z, it automatically begins to rotate around X, to permit the hand to continue to rise. Next, when the shoulder's X rotation has also reached its limit, the elbow joint begins to rotate. Finally, when the elbow has rotated as far as it can, the wrist rotates.

In addition to limiting the rotations of a model, you can also limit its translations. This is usually referred to as **positional limits**. Imagine, for example, a truck with sliding doors (Figure 7-11). By limiting the translations of each door, you can ensure that the motion of the doors will be accurate and easy to animate. If the doors are oriented as in the illustration, each door should be able to translate a small amount positively in X. The rearmost door should be able to translate a little less than the width of the door in the negative Z direction. The other door should be able to translate the same amount positively in Z. Neither door should be able to translate at all in Y.

CONSTRAINTS

In addition to limiting a model's transformations, you can also **constrain** them. Constraining a model means associating its transformations with the transformations of a second model. There are three common types of constraint: position, rotation, and direction.

A **position constraint** constrains the translation of an object. Figure 7-12a shows two objects, a cone and a cube, in their original positions. The cube is shaded to indicate that it is the controlling, or constraining, object. When the cone's position is constrained to the cube's position, the cone snaps to the location of the cube, as in Figure 7-12b. More specifically, the cone's local origin, indicated by the crosshairs, snaps to the cube's local origin. Now, wherever the cube goes, the cone will also go, as if the two were "joined at the hip"—except that they are joined at the local origin.

Not only can you constrain models to each other, you can also constrain entities which do not have any visible surfaces—for example, the effector of an inverse kinematic skeleton, or a dummy null node. When constraining objects to an IK effector, however, you must be aware of a curious effect. The distance an IK effector can translate is restricted, since it must always remain attached to its skeleton. If the effector is constrained to an object that moves farther away than the effector can follow, the effector's skeleton will "reach" towards the constraining object.

You must take this effect into account when constraining effectors. However, it can also be used to good purpose, as illustrated in Figure 7-13. Here an inverse kinematic model is animated, with the hand effector of the

Figure 7-11. Positional limits can be very helpful for some models.

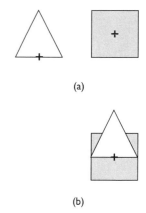

(a)

(b)

Figure 7-12. A position constraint forces one object to stick to another.

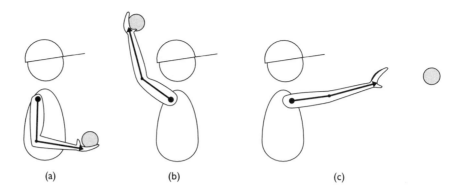

(a)   (b)   (c)

Figure 7-13. Constraining the hand effector to the ball forces the arm to "reach" for the ball.

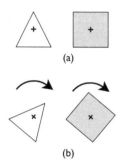

(a)

(b)

Figure 7-14. A rotation constraint forces one object to follow the rotations of another.

(a)

(b)

(c)

Figure 7-15. A direction, or aim, constraint forces one object to point toward another.

ballplayer constrained to the ball (so that he will never, *ever* miss). Given the effect just described, it is quite easy to animate a throwing motion for this player. By simply translating the ball, you can cause the player to "throw" the ball. The hand and ball will move together (Figure 7-13a and b), but when the ball has been translated too far to the right, the hand will "reach" towards the ball, simulating a throwing motion (Figure 7-13c).

A **rotation constraint**, also called an **orientation constraint**, constrains the rotation transformations of one object to that of another. In Figure 7-14 the rotation of the cone is constrained to that of the cube, ensuring that however the cube rotates, the cone will rotate exactly the same way.

A **direction constraint**, also called an **aim constraint**, forces an object to point, or aim, toward its controlling object. In Figure 7-15 the cone is constrained in the direction of the cube, with the result that wherever the cube goes, the cone will adjust its rotation; it always points toward the cube.

In setting up a direction constraint, you must pay attention to the local coordinate system of the object to be constrained—the cone, in the example. This is because a directional constraint forces a particular axis of the constrained object (the cone) to point toward the local origin of the constrainer (the cube). In some software packages, you can select which axis of the constrained object's local coordinate system will be used. In others, the axis is fixed, and you must realign the constrained object's local coordinate system as necessary before implementing the constraint.

Aim constraints are frequently used to control the direction of a character's gaze. If a character's eyeballs are constrained to always aim at an animated object in your scene, the character will always be looking at that object. For example, if his eyeballs are aim-constrained to a fly buzzing about the room, he will always look at the fly. This could be humorous, but it is also not realistic, as we do not fix our gaze that mechanically on anything for very long. More usefully, you can define and animate a dummy node, constraining the eyeballs to always look at that (Figure 7-16). Since a dummy node (section 2.9) has no geometry, it will not render. By keyframing the location of the dummy node, represented as a crosshairs icon in most systems, you can easily animate the direction in which your character is looking.

For all three types of constraint—position, rotation, and direction—the critical point to which the constraint attaches or rotates or points is the local origin of the constrainer. A position constraint snaps to the local origin of the constrainer; a direction constraint points toward the local origin of the constrainer, etc. What do you do if you want to constrain to some other point? One solution is to once again use a null dummy node and constrain to that null node. Since a null node has no geometry, it is invisible when your scene is rendered. If necessary, the null node can be made a child of another object. Constraining to a null, therefore, permits you effectively to constrain to any point in space.

Another approach is to define your constraint in relation to some vertex or control point on the surface of your model. This becomes especially useful if your model is deforming. Remember first that all constraint operations constrain to the local origin of an object. Now recall that when a model deforms, its local origin does not move—only its surface points do so. Thus, if you want something to be constrained to the surface of a deforming object, you must constrain it to a point on that surface—not to the object itself. We see an example of this in Figure 7-17. The flower on the dancer's dress is a model constrained to a surface point of the dress; as the dress deforms with the dance, the flower adheres to a point on the surface of the deforming dress (see section 7.9 for a discussion of the cloth dynamics used for the animation of the dress.)

Figure 7-16. Aim-constraining a character's eyes to a null object, and then keyframing the null, is an easy way to control the direction of the character's gaze.

(a)   (b)

Figure 7-17. An object can be position-constrained to a point on the surface of a deforming model. (Korean dancer, courtesy, Yi-Sul Yoon.)

7.4 Metaballs

One of the most challenging modeling tasks in 3D computer graphics is the naturalistic modeling of human and animal forms, because the variability and subtlety of those forms is extremely difficult to match. Using a hierarchical collection of rigid body parts (section 2.9) can successfully produce robotic or mechanical-looking creatures. Skinning an envelope surface around an inverse kinematic skeleton (sections 4.9 and 7.13) allows you to achieve a deformable character model, but does not directly reflect the musculature of the human animal.

Simulating the muscle masses of an animal and how those muscle masses smoothly flow into one another while still remaining distinct is indeed a difficult modeling problem. The **metaball** technique can be effective for this sort of modeling because it creates surfaces that automatically blend together. When you use this technique, models consist entirely of primitive shapes, most commonly spheres, of a special sort. These spheres, which also may be scaled into ellipsoids, are something *beyond* ("meta" means "beyond") normal spheres. Metaball spheres are not defined as having an explicit spherical surface, as would be the case in the standard surface-modeling techniques described throughout the rest of this book. Instead, they are defined to consist of a variable **density field**. Wherever the density is of a certain value, called the **threshold**, a surface exists. What you see, therefore, when you look at a metaball is the **implicit surface** that follows the contours of the density field, at whatever density value you have defined to be the threshold of visibility. Since the surfaces of a metaball exist wherever the density values are the same as the threshold, these surfaces are referred to in technical literature as **isosurfaces** ("iso" means "same").

An analogy from the world of physics might make this concept clear. If a tiny metal ball were electrically charged and suspended in the air, the charge from that ball would emanate evenly in all directions, creating a spherically shaped electric field. The electric charge would be greatest at the center of this field and would decrease farther away from the center of the field. The metaball technique is based on a similar idea, except that instead of a decreasing field of electricity, you have a decreasing field of density. The density of a spherical metaball is, like the electric charge, greatest at the center of the metaball and decreases, again like the electrical charge, farther away from the center. When the density of the metaball reaches the threshold value, a surface is drawn implicitly.

In Figure 7-18, the concentric rings represent several different density levels of a single metaball. The small ring at the center is the most dense, and each successive ring, moving outward from the center, is less dense. The visibility

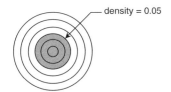

density = 0.05

Figure 7-18. The surface of a metaball is defined to exist wherever the density field of the metaball achieves a certain threshold value.

threshold for this metaball has been set (more or less arbitrarily) to 0.05. Since the density of the metaball decreases uniformly away from the center, the visibility threshold of 0.05 has a spherical configuration, as if a thin film of 0.05 density surrounded the center of the metaball. Wherever this 0.05 density exists, a surface, represented in the illustration by the shaded circle, is defined implicitly. Notice that the visibility of a metaball is an all-or-nothing issue: the metaball does not become invisible gradually as the density decreases, but becomes invisible abruptly at the 0.05 threshold. This abruptness effectively creates the appearance of a surface defined at that threshold.

The power of the metaball-modeling technique is a result of the fact that if two metaballs are placed close enough to each other, the density fields of each will overlap (Figure 7-19a). Wherever the density fields of two metaballs overlap, the density values from the two different balls add up, creating a new density value in a process called **fusion**. If this new density value is greater than the visibility threshold, the overlapped area between the two metaballs is also visible (Figure 7-19b). This extension of the area of the implicit surface creates a viscous, dripping look which has inspired one of the more whimsical names for metaballs, **blobby molecules**.

In most systems you can control both the density of the field and the visibility threshold of each metaball. Some software packages also allow you to adjust additional, hybrid parameters that control some combination of density and threshold. These parameters may variously be called **weight**, **range**, or **influence**. Whichever parameters a specific package offers, adjusting them allows you to cause the metaballs to fuse in a wide variety of ways. Figure 7-20 shows two metaballs that remain the same size and in the same location in each case. The different configurations were created solely by adjusting the parameters that control some combination of the density field and the visibility threshold.

By carefully positioning a number of metaballs and adjusting the densities and thresholds, you can model some very subtle forms (Figure 7-21). The fusion effect of the metaballs automatically produces a smooth transition between balls, effectively mimicking the way masses of human flesh flow smoothly into one another.

(a)

(b)

Figure 7-19. When the density fields of neighboring metaballs overlap, a fusion of density values occurs. The surface that results is a blobby melting of the two spheres into one another.

Figure 7-20. Adjusting the parameters that control density and threshold can cause the metaballs to fuse in a wide variety of ways.

Figure 7-21. This human figure, modeled with the metaball structure seen on the right, exemplifies the subtlety and sophistication possible with this technique. (*Eccentric Dance*, Artist: Eiji Takaoki, © META Corporation Japan.)

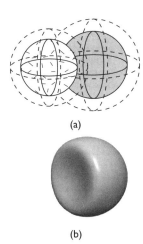

(a)

(b)

Figure 7-22. A metaball can have negative density that subtracts from the density field of its neighbors and produces a concavity.

You can also alter the density field of a metaball in order to create **negative density**. That is, rather than adding to the densities of other metaballs, this field subtracts from them. This approach is very useful when modeling concavities in a surface. Figure 7-22 shows two metaballs. The larger one has a normal positive density; the smaller one has a negative density. Since the density of the smaller metaball is negative, it subtracts from the density field of the larger metaball when the two fields combine, producing the concavity seen in Figure 7-22b. The metaball diagram in Figure 7-21 shows another example of negative density. Here, the ellipsoidal metaball protruding where the navel would be is a negative metaball. The density field of this metaball subtracts density from the metaballs that comprise the belly of the figure, and the result of this subtraction is an abrupt concavity, or navel.

A further refinement of the metaball technique permits you to redistribute the density of a given metaball in a way that is not perfectly spherical. With this approach, known as **eccentric density distribution**, the density of a ball might fade off more quickly on one side of the ball than on another. In Figure 7-23a the density of the metaball drops off normally in a circular pattern to the left of the center, but much more slowly on the right side, producing a bowed look to the rings of the density field. Figure 7-23b shows this metaball as it would look rendered.

Figure 7-23. The density field of a metaball can be distorted to produce an eccentric density distribution.

(a)

(b)

(a)   (b)   (c)   (d)

Figure 7-24. Metaballs can be made more or less hard-edged along any of the three axes.

A variation on the concept of eccentric density provides a method of modifying the shape of a metaball away from its standard spherical shape with **hard-edged** metaballs. Using a slider, you can adjust numbers that control how hard-edged, or squared, the metaball will be along each of the three axes. Figure 7-24 shows the original, spherical metaball (a), the metaball made a bit more square along all three axes (b), made more square yet (c), and squared up but only along one axis, producing an approximately cylindrical blob (d).

Some software systems provide a simplified selection of hard-edged metaballs, which they call **metaball primitives**. The metaball in Figure 7-24c, for example, would be a "cube" metaball. A flattened version of that same shape might be available as a "plane" metaball. Figure 7-24d would be the equivalent of a "cylinder" metaball. A few systems provide metaball primitives in the elongated and tapered shape of human muscles.

When modeling with metaballs, you usually organize them into a special hierarchical structure called a **metaball system**. This functions like a normal hierarchy, allowing you to translate, rotate, or scale entire collections of metaballs as a group. In addition, a metaball system structures the way metaballs blend, or fuse, with one another. Typically, all metaballs within a given system blend with each other (assuming, of course, they are close enough for the sum of their densities to exceed the threshold). Figure 7-25a shows a wireframe representation of a metaball system. Notice that in the hierarchical diagram (Figure 7-25b) there is a single metaball system; all four of the metaballs are members of that system. Figure 7-25c shows the rendered result of this system, with all the metaballs fusing together.

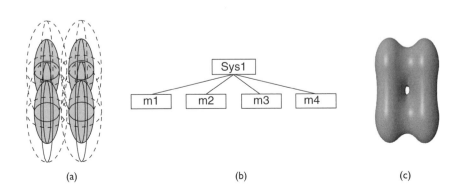

(a)   (b)   (c)

Figure 7-25. Metaballs within a single system blend together.

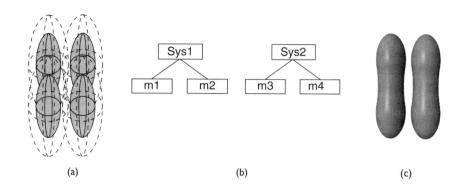

Figure 7-26. Metaballs in different systems do not blend together.

(a)   (b)   (c)

When metaballs are in separate systems, by contrast, they typically do not blend with each other (Figure 7-26). The hierarchical diagram (Figure 7-26b) shows that there are two distinct systems, each with two metaballs. The metaballs of *Sys1*, on the left, do not blend with those of *Sys2*, on the right (Figure 7-26c).

In some situations, however, the use of metaball systems will not provide all the control you need over the blending of metaballs. If you are modeling a human hand, for example, all the metaballs need to be in a single system so they can all be transformed—that is, moved, or rotated, or scaled—as a unit. However, if the metaballs are all in a single system, they will blend with each other by default. The fingers will fuse together, creating the sort of webbing shown in Figure 7-25c.

You can solve this problem with **blending groups**, or **fusion groups**, which allow you to define, both within a system and across a system, how metaballs will blend. First you define the members of each group—that is, which metaballs are in the group. Then you specify which other groups each group does or does not blend with.

Figure 7-27a is the wireframe representation of a single metaball system with five blending groups, G1 through G5. In this simple example, each group has been defined to consist of only a single metaball; in a more complex model, there would normally be many metaballs in each group. The chart (Figure 7-27b) lists each group and the names of all the groups it blends with. Notice that group G1, at the top of the model, blends with the top-left and top-right metaballs of the the "arms." Continuing down the list, group G2, the top-left metaball, blends with G1, the top, and also with G3, the lower part of the left arm. Notice that G2 does *not*, however, blend with any of the groups that comprise the right arm. This arrangement keeps the two arms separate and unfused. The metaballs of the right arm are similarly grouped. Figure 7-27c shows the rendered result of this grouping structure.

A blending structure similar to that of Figure 7-27 would be appropriate for many segments of a human or animal character. A hand, for example,

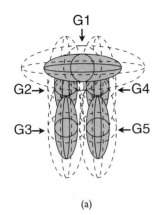

G1

G2→   ←G4

G3→   ←G5

(a)

GROUP	BLENDS WITH
G1	G2 G4
G2	G1 G3
G3	G2
G4	G1 G5
G5	G4

(b)

(c)

Figure 7-27. Blending groups define the blending of metaballs within a system or across several systems.

would consists of a palm (analogous to the top metaball of Figure 7-27) and several fingers protruding from it. A foot would be structured the same way. An entire body would consist of a central object, the torso, with limbs protruding from it.

Recall from the beginning of this section that when you create metaballs, you are not explicitly defining surfaces, as you are with most other modeling techniques. Instead, metaballs create implicit surfaces at certain density thresholds. Because metaball surfaces are only implicit, they must be converted into explicit surfaces before rendering. When a system of metaballs is about to be rendered, it is automatically converted into polygons, and it is this new polygonal surface that is actually rendered. The number of polygons created determines how accurately the polygonal surface approximates the implicit metaball surface: more polygons yield a better approximation; fewer polygons yield a cruder approximation. This issue of **polygon resolution** is illustrated in Figure 7-28. Figure 7-28a shows a simple metaball system; Figure 7-28b, the polygonal structure and rendering of that system using a low polygon resolution; and Figure 7-28c, the same system with a high polygon resolution.

It is important to understand that once a metaball model has been converted into a polygonal model, it loses all its metaball capabilities. Surfaces no longer blend together, and metaball parameters such as density threshold, weight, and influence no longer exist.

The animation of metaball models involves techniques already familiar to you. For example, you can transform individual metaballs using the keyframing approach. That is, you can translate, rotate, or scale each metaball just as you would any other object in a three-dimensional animation, define a keyframe for these transformations, define another keyframe for another set of transformations, and then generate an interpolated set of frames between the two keyframes. You also can hierarchically group a collection of metaballs and transform the entire group with keyframing. Alternatively, you can create an inverse kinematic skeleton to control your metaball model.

(a)

(b)

(c)

Figure 7-28. A metaball system can be converted into a polygonal surface with a lower or higher polygon resolution.

Figure 7-29. Metaballs can produce stunning results, especially in the modeling of human and animal figures. (Courtesy, Jin Wan Park.)

You can also animate the densities and the density distributions of the metaballs. This technique provides a mechanism for animating shape changes and also permits certain shape changes that would be extremely difficult, if not impossible, to accomplish without the metaball approach. We saw an example of this approach in Figure 7-20.

Whichever animation technique you use, complex metaball models can be slow to work with. The calculations required to fuse the metaballs together and to create their implicit surfaces can slow down your software. For this reason it is sometimes easier to use metaballs only as a modeling technique. Having created the metaball model, you instruct the computer to create a static polygonal model from it. You then animate the polygonal model with any of the standard shape-deformation techniques. You might, for example, use metaballs to model a human character. Then you could create a polygonal model from that metaball model and apply the deformable envelope technique (sections 4.9 and 7.13). Such an approach takes advantage of the ability of metaballs to model smoothly blending surfaces, but avoids the time-consuming calculation of new implicit metaball surfaces at each frame of your animation.

In Figure 7-29, a striking example of metaball modeling and animation, both the human head and hand were modeled with metaballs. Careful use of blending groups kept the lips and fingers from fusing in unwanted ways. The head was modeled and animated as a metaball model. The hand was modeled with metaballs, then converted to polygons before it was animated with inverse kinematics and envelope deformation.

7.5 Expressions and Driven Keys

EXPRESSIONS

In certain situations it may be best to think of the animation of a specific object in terms of a mathematical formula, or expression, that describes its motion. For example, if you wanted to move an object along a path in the shape of a standard sine curve, as in Figure 7-30a, you could try to draw a path in the exact shape of a sine curve, but a more accurate way of getting this motion would be to tell the animation system to use the mathematical function, Sine.

Another situation in which it might be easier to produce an animation by thinking in terms of mathematical expressions is when the motion of one object depends on the motion of another. Here, the relationship between the two objects can frequently be described most clearly as a mathematical relationship between the two objects. For example, the sphere in Figure 7-30b moves in the opposite direction and twice as fast as the cube.

Defining an object's motion by specifying mathematical formulae or expressions in this way is referred to as using **expressions**. This is a text-based technique—that is, you type in the text of the mathematical expressions. It is very similar in principle to programming, although much simpler in practice. In fact, the software packages that offer this technique go to great lengths to make expressions accessible to and usable by the average animator. Programming experience is not necessary to make good use of expressions.

Nonetheless, some of the basic principles of programming also apply to expressions. Writing expressions, for example, entails using a specific "language." The syntax and vocabulary of that language vary from one 3D software package to another, but they are all language-based. As in programming, it is important that anything you type be exactly in accordance with the rules of your package's expression language. If it is not, you will get an error message.

Whatever package and language you use, you begin by typing or selecting the name of the object you want to control. You next specify which parameter of that object you want to control. Together, the intended object and its intended parameter are considered the **target**. For example, to specify the translation in X of an object called "cube" as the target, you might type something like *cube.TX*. (Here, and in all subsequent ecamples of this section, I use a hypothetical expression syntax.) Similarly, an object called "Head" might have its rotation around Y specified by *Head.RY*, and its scale along the Z axis by *Head.SY*.

Once you have indicated your target object and parameter, you type in the mathematical expression that will control it. The complexity of the expression varies depending on the animation's requirements and your own mathematical skills.

As a simple example, imagine a set of interlocking gears, as in Figure 7-31, with the highlighted central gear, Gear1, being animated through standard keyframing techniques. The motion of the other gears—both their speed and direction—will be a function of *Gear1*'s motion. Because the gears all interlock, this is an ideal candidate for the expression technique.

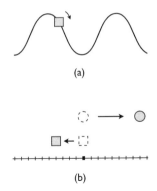

(a)

(b)

Figure 7-30. The motion of some objects can be easily described by a mathematical expression.

Figure 7-31. The motion of Gear2 and Gear3 can be written as simple mathematical functions of the motion of Gear1.

This animation could be produced without expressions, but it is much easier to produce it by taking advantage of the direct mathematical relationships among the gears. (The benefit of using expressions would be even greater if there were dozens or hundreds of interlocking gears!) Consider first the relationship for just one of the dependent gears, *Gear2*. You can see from the illustration that *Gear2* has to rotate in the opposite direction from *Gear1*: if *Gear1* rotates clockwise, *Gear2* must rotate counterclockwise, and vice versa. You can also see that they will have to move at exactly the same speed, since *Gear1* and *Gear2* are the same size (which you can confirm by counting the number of teeth on each gear). In other words, however much *Gear1* rotates, *Gear2* will rotate the same amount, except in the opposite direction. This can be expressed mathematically as:

$$Gear2.RZ = Gear1.RZ * -1$$

That is: "The rotation in Z of Gear2 is equal to the rotation in Z of Gear1 times –1". The reason you multiply by –1 is to negate the value of the rotation, thereby making the gear turn in the opposite direction.

Gear3's motion can be written similarly. Again looking at the illustration, you can see that *Gear3* must rotate in the opposite direction from *Gear1*. The speed of *Gear3*, however, will not be the same as that of *Gear1*. Since *Gear3* is only half as big (count the teeth), it will rotate twice as quickly. In short:

$$Gear3.RZ = Gear1.RZ * -2$$

The multiplication by –2 doubles the speed and reverses the direction of the Z rotation.

In the gear example above, you already made use of one of the **arithmetic operators** that are a standard feature of expressions. These arithmetic operators include the familiar +, –, *, / of programming languages—that is, *add, subtract, multiply, divide*.

All packages that offer expressions also offer a library of standard **mathematical functions** to help you write more complex expressions. These functions are similar to the standard mathematical functions that are part of any programming language. They include sine, cosine, minimum, maximum, square root, absolute value, random number, and others. Usually these functions are referenced, or **called**, by abbreviated names derived from the names of the same functions in the C programming language—for example, *sin( )*, *cos( )*, *min( )*, *max( )*, *sqrt( )*, *abs( )*, *rand( )*.

In addition to standard math functions, expressions also use the **logical operators** of programming languages, with the syntax of the C programming language again the most common. These operators include:

==	is equal to
!=	is not equal to
>	is greater than
<	is less than
>=	is greater than or equal to
<=	is less than or equal to

And to build more complex expression statements, there are also the standard **boolean operators**:

| && | and |
| || | or |

By using a combination of these syntactical elements, you can write some very powerful expressions.

An additional syntactical element, the **conditional** statement, extends the power of expressions quite a bit (just as it does in programming), by defining the conditions under which an event takes place. This requires some sort of *if . . . then . . . else* statement in your expression. The syntax for such a statement varies from one software package to the next, but the concept is the same: "If something is true, then do such and such; otherwise, do something else."

For example, suppose you want the eyelids in Figure 7-32a to open—that is, to rotate about X—when the fly gets very close to the face—that is, when the fly crosses into the positive X half of the coordinate system. You could write an expression for each eyelid that uses a conditional: Figure 7-32b shows such an expression for the right eyelid. This expression, translated into English, says: "If the fly's X translation is greater than 0, then the eyelid's X rotation is −30 degrees (that is, open); otherwise, the eyelid's rotation is 20 degrees (that is, closed)."

A more sophisticated test of whether the fly is "very close" to the man would be to measure the distance between the fly and the man's head, rather than simply to test if the fly has crossed into the positive X half of coordinate space. Many software packages include a function that will do just this, calculating the distance between two objects—more specifically, calculating the distance between the local origin of one object and the local origin of another. Because distance is usually calculated from one local origin to another, you normally indicate the name of the two objects, but not any parameters, when you call the function. Modifying the fly example above, you might therefore write a new expression as shown in Figure 7-33b. In English this reads: "If the distance between the fly and the man's head is less than 2, then the eyelid's X rotation is −30 degrees (open); otherwise, the eyelid's rotation is 20 degrees (closed)." With this new, more robust expression, the eyelid will open

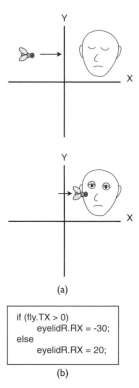

(a)

```
if (fly.TX > 0)
      eyelidR.RX = -30;
else
      eyelidR.RX = 20;
```

(b)

Figure 7-32. Conditional statements can make an object's motion dependent upon some event.

```
if (distance(fly, eyelidR) < 2.0)
      eyelidR.RX = -30;
else
      eyelidR.RX = 20;
```

Figure 7-33. Expression languages allow you to call library functions as you would in programming.

and close no matter where the man is or where the fly is, so long as they are close enough to each other. With the eyelids controlled in this way by expressions, you can now concentrate on the animation of the fly and the man's head, knowing that the eyelids will automatically open or close as necessary.

When referencing an object's location in space as in the fly example, you must be careful to pay attention to whether each parameter is in the **global space** of the whole world or in the **local space** of that particular object. This becomes an issue when you are working with hierarchical models.

As you saw in section 2.9, when one object is the child of another in a hierarchy, the child node inherits the transformations of the parent node above it. Thus, in a hierarchical arm model like that shown in Figure 7-34a, if you rotate the whole arm at the shoulder (Figure 7-34b), all the children of the *WholeArm* node will also rotate.

This presents a curious problem when you want to write expressions that reference the location of the children nodes of such a hierarchy. Suppose, for example, that you want to write an expression that uses the location—that is, the translation values—of the hand. In the example illustrated in Figure 7-34, the hand, even though it is clearly in a different location, has not actually translated. The hand has moved because it has inherited the transformations of all the nodes above it in the hierarchy, but within its own local coordinate system it has not translated at all. Consequently, if you reference the hand's translation in your expression by saying, for example, *Hand.TX*, the value of this parameter will be zero. No matter how much you rotate the *WholeArm* and cause the hand visibly to move, *Hand.TX* will always remain zero (unless you specifically translate the hand away from the arm by operating on the *Hand* node directly).

The solution to this problem is that, rather than referencing the hand's translation within its own local coordinate space, you need to reference its translation within the *global* space of the whole world. In global space, the hand has clearly moved. In local space, it has not.

Most software packages provide a function to permit you to do this. The name and syntax of the function vary, but the effect is the same—to provide global coordinate readings of an object's transformation. Suppose that you have a function called *global( )*. If you simply specify *Hand.TX* in your expression, you will get the local translation of the hand, which in the example is zero. But if instead you type *global(Hand.TX)*, you get the global translation of the hand, which might, for example, be +7.5 in the illustration.

The examples so far have referred only to the nine basic transformation parameters—translation XYZ, rotation XYZ, and scale XYZ. But any parameter of any object can be controlled by an expression. Lighting parameters and shading parameters can also be controlled by expressions. For example, you might want the color of an object to change as the object scales larger.

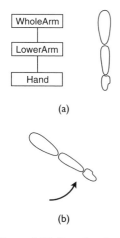

(a)

(b)

Figure 7-34. Even though a transformation on a parent node may cause a child node to move in global space, the child may not move within its own local space.

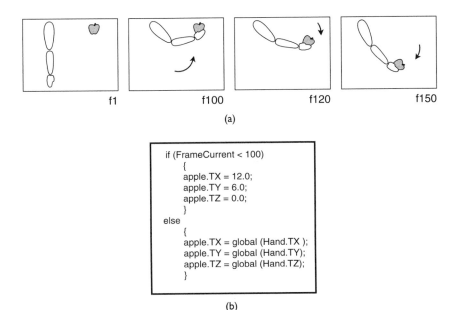

(a)

```
if (FrameCurrent < 100)
    {
    apple.TX = 12.0;
    apple.TY = 6.0;
    apple.TZ = 0.0;
    }
else
    {
    apple.TX = global (Hand.TX );
    apple.TY = global (Hand.TY);
    apple.TZ = global (Hand.TZ);
    }
```

(b)

Figure 7-35. A predefined variable referencing the current frame number can be used to cause events to happen at certain moments.

Or you might cause the intensity of a light to dim as the camera recedes from it. You can use expressions to control the location of specific control points and vertices. For example, you could cause the eyeballs of the man in Figure 7-33 to bulge whenever the fly approaches by using expressions to translate some of the eyeballs' control points in an automated fashion.

In addition to all these parameters, there are also certain standard, predefined variables that allow you to reference other parameters of your animation. One of the most basic is the **current frame** number. As your animation plays, the current frame number is constantly rising, or **incrementing**. You can use this number to make events happen at a specific moment in time. Suppose, for example, that the hand in the previous example is going to reach up and, at frame 100, grab an apple. From that point on, the apple should remain in the hand. By writing an expression that will cause the translation of the apple to attach to the global translation of the hand after frame 100, you can do this very easily (Figure 7-35). Assume, for this example, that before it is picked the apple's X translation is 12.0, its Y translation is 6.0, and its Z translation is 0.0. Also assume that in the software package the current frame number is referenced by a variable called *FrameCurrent*. The expression would be as shown in Figure 7-35b. Notice that more than one expression has been applied to the apple—specifically, one expression for each of the axes of translation. Each of the expressions is similar. The first, for example, translates this way: "If the current frame is less than 100, then the apple's X translation remains at 12.0; otherwise it becomes whatever the global X location of the hand is." By doing this for each of the three translation values, you cause the apple to stick to the hand from frame 100 onward.

DRIVEN KEYS

As we have seen, expressions are very powerful, and frequently not difficult to write. However, in an effort to make the power of expressions even more accessible, some software packages offer the technique of **driven keys**, which automatically write expressions for you, allowing the animator to focus on the visual relationships of objects rather than the syntax of expressions.

As with expressions, you begin by defining a target parameter, here called a **driven** parameter. Rather than typing text as you do with expressions, you define your target through a set of menu selections. The driven parameter is what will be controlled. To use a simple example, you might use the menus to specify that the scale in Y of a cone will be driven (Figure 7-36). You next use the menu to define what is the **driver**—that is, the controlling object/parameter combination. In our example, the driver is the translation in X of the cube.

Once you have defined the driven and driver, you visually position both and use a menu selection to save a **driven keyframe** for that relationship. This means that when the driver's parameter is at the value you see before you, the driven's parameter is at its value, just as you see it. Having defined this first driven keyframe, you repeat the process, repositioning both the driver and the driven, and saving a second driven keyframe for this new relationship.

In Figure 7-36a, we see the driver and driven in their first driven key position. The cube is at 0,0,0, and the cone's scale Y value is 2.0. We see the second driven key in Figure 7-36b, where the cube has been moved to the right to 5,0,0 and the cone has been scaled in Y to SY = 6.0. Having set these two driven keys, the software writes an (unseen) expression for you. The effect of this expression is that as the cube translates from 0 to 5 in the X direction, the cone scales from 2 to 6 in the Y direction.

The driven key software not only writes this hidden expression for you, it also produces a slider interface. By adjusting the position of the slider bar, you translate the cube and simultaneously scale the cone. At any given frame, you can keyframe the position of the slider bar, allowing you to create keyframed animation of the two objects' movements, with each object's movement dependent on the other.

The example just given was deliberately simplified for clarity. In practice, the driven-key technique becomes most useful when it controls more complex motions. One such situation is automating the closing of a hand model. If your hand model has an inverse kinematic skeleton within it, closing the hand will entail translating each of the effectors at the tips of each of the fingers (Figure 7-37). Rather than do this for each finger each time you want to close the hand, you could create a driven key slider. The two extremes of the slider would correspond to "open" and "closed". Sliding the slider bar would translate all of the fingers' effectors simultaneously, closing the hand.

(a)

(b)

Figure 7-36. A driven key sets up a relationship between parameters of different objects.

CloseHand

Figure 7-37. A single driven key can control a more complex set of actions, such as the closing of a hand.

Another situation in which the driven key technique can be useful is in fine-tuning the deformations of a skinned surface on your character model. As we discuss in sections 4.9 and 7.13, skinning surfaces onto an inverse kinematic skeleton causes the IK skeleton to control the deformations of the surfaces. If the deformations that result aren't quite satisfactory, one possible solution is to make the position of an IK effector the driver, and the positions of several surface points the driven. With such a driven key defined, you could keyframe the IK effector of your character, and then keyframe the slider bar of your driven key to adjust the deformation of the surface to suit you.

Expressions and driven keys provide powerful tools for producing animations that might otherwise be difficult to create. Still, the capabilities of these techniques are quite simple compared to those of a full-blown programming language. To approach that level of programming power, you must work with a related technique called procedural modeling and animation, discussed in section 5.4.

7.6 Motion Dynamics: Principles, Rigid Bodies

In certain situations the movement of an object, such as a ball falling from a height and bouncing on a surface, can be predicted very precisely. Physicists have studied this sort of phenomenon for a long time and have developed very accurate mathematical formulae to describe what happens in this situation. Knowing the effect of gravity and various properties of the ball and of the surface, they can calculate, using the laws of physics, how quickly the ball will fall, as well as how high and how often it will bounce.

This sort of mathematically precise and detailed study of the motion of objects is called **motion dynamics** and can be of great use to animators. The ball dropping straight down and bouncing off a flat surface is not very difficult to animate using standard keyframing techniques, but a more complex situation, such as a box being dropped and bouncing down a stairway (Figure 7-38), is very difficult to animate in a naturalistic way using keyframing.

Figure 7-38. The motion of some objects can be calculated precisely according to the laws of physics.

Figure 7-39. Motion dynamics applied to rigid bodies can produce an animation that would be quite difficult to do with keyframing. (© 2001 Sophia Rotchko.)

To estimate realistically how far the box bounces with each bounce, how much and in what directions the box rotates as it flies through the air, which edge or corner of the box strikes the surface of the stairs first, and so on, is a *very* complicated piece of animation. The physical laws of motion dynamics, however, are precise enough for you to calculate the motion of the box.

3D animation packages include this sort of motion-dynamics capability and provide user interfaces that make the technical complexity of the underlying calculations transparent. Typically you use a mouse device to open a menu and make several selections. These selections define the various parameters that control the motion of the object to be animated. Once you have defined these parameters, you make a selection that instructs the system to perform the calculations and play back the resulting animation on the screen. This result is called a **simulation**, because it simulates, or mimics, the behavior of objects in a real-world situation behaving under the influence of real-world physical laws.

Motion dynamics calculations can be applied to many kinds of animation problems, as we will see later in this chapter. In this section we present the basic principles common to all motion dynamics applications, and examine their simplest application: the movement of **rigid bodies**, nondeformable objects whose movement is calculated by motion dynamics. Figure 7-39 is an example of the power of motion dynamics as applied to rigid bodies. In this sequence of animation frames, the first frame shows a collection of books and other objects. In the middle frame, the vase on the highest shelf has fallen and hit the pile of books, causing them to fall in turn. In the last frame, nearly all the objects have fallen to the floor. One hundred percent of this animation was calculated as a motion dynamics simulation of rigid bodies. In subsequent sections we will discuss motion dynamics as applied to soft (deformable) bodies (section 7.7), to particles (section 7.8), and to cloth (section 7.9).

PHYSICAL PROPERTIES

In setting up a simulation you first define the **physical properties** of the object to be animated. That is, the motion-dynamics system must know certain characteristics of the object in order to calculate the simulated movement of the object. For example, a ball made of solid iron bounces much differently than does a ball made of balsa wood.

In physics—and in motion dynamics—one of the most basic physical properties of an object is **mass**. Mass is related to, but not quite the same as, weight. That is, the weight of an object is the result of gravity pulling down on the massiveness of the object. On Earth, gravity is effectively the same everywhere, so mass and weight have a direct, one-to-one correspondence. However, since weight is linked to gravity, the weight of an object *can* change—for example, if the object were in outer space—although the mass of the object remains the same wherever the object is. An object with a large mass is very difficult to start moving and very difficult to stop once it begins moving. This is why astronauts approach docking with a space station very slowly. Even though both the space vessel and the space station are weightless, they are extremely massive and could cause great damage to each other if moving too fast when they make contact.

This same property of mass directly affects how an object moves in a motion-dynamic simulation. For example, if you roll a massive ball down a ramp and onto a level surface, the ball tends to keep rolling for a long time because the massiveness overcomes the forces that otherwise would make the object stop (Figure 7-40a). If you roll a less massive ball down the same ramp, it tends to stop much more quickly on the flat surface (Figure 7-40b).

What makes the one ball more massive than the other is not merely the size of the objects but also the density of the materials from which they are made. A balsa-wood ball is less massive than an iron ball because balsa wood is less dense than iron. A solid clay ball of the same size is more dense and more massive than a balsa-wood ball, but less dense and less massive than an iron ball.

Size does play a role, however, in determining mass, which is a function of both the density and the size (more exactly, the volume) of an object. A small iron ball (Figure 7-40c), even though it has the same density as a larger iron ball (Figure 7-40a), has a smaller mass because it has a smaller volume. Consequently, the little, less massive ball does not roll as far as the larger, more massive ball (Figure 7-40b).

Since the mass of an object depends on both volume and density, most people cannot readily estimate it. Consequently, some systems allow you to define mass indirectly by specifying density. By thinking in terms of material (iron, wood, clay, etc.) you can readily give the system a density parameter value—larger numbers for more dense materials, smaller numbers for less dense materials. The software then automatically calculates the volume of the object and then, from the combination of volume and density, the mass.

The density of an object also is important to consider when simulating objects lighter than air. A gas-filled balloon, for example, rises into the air because the gas inside the balloon is of a very, very low density. This causes the total mass of the balloon to be so little that gravity will not even keep it on the ground.

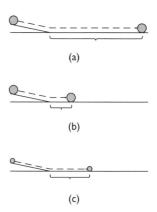

(a)

(b)

(c)

Figure 7-40. The mass of an object plays a key role in how the object behaves as it moves. Mass is a function of both the density of the material and the size of the object.

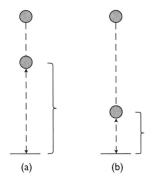

Figure 7-41. The elasticity of an object is a measure of how much the object bounces when it hits a surface.

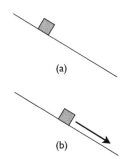

Figure 7-42. The static friction of an object is a measure of how readily the object, when stationary, will start to move after being subjected to some force.

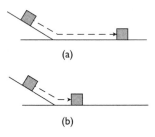

Figure 7-43. The kinetic friction of an object is a measure of how easily the object, when moving, can be stopped by some resisting force.

Another important physical property of objects, called **elasticity**, reflects the way objects bounce. Imagine that two balls have exactly the same mass, but that when you drop these balls, one ball bounces much higher than the other one does (Figure 7-41a and b). A solid rubber ball, for example, tends to bounce much higher than a solid plastic ball—even though, as in this example, the masses of the balls happen to be exactly the same—and a glass marble dropped on a concrete floor bounces much higher than you might expect. Objects that have a high degree of elasticity, such as the solid rubber ball and the marble, tend to bounce a lot. Objects with lower elasticity bounce less.

The term "elasticity" can be a bit misleading, however. In day-to-day usage, the word describes objects easily stretched or deformed. A rubber band and a soft rubber ball that you can squeeze between your fingers are elastic in this sense. As it is used in motion dynamics, however, "elastic" means something different. A glass marble is extremely elastic because it bounces very high, even though it is very hard and does not deform between your fingers at all. In motion dynamics, elasticity refers to the amount of energy retained or lost when an object makes contact with something else. If an object is very elastic, very little energy is lost and the object bounces a lot. If the object is very inelastic, a great deal of energy is lost and the object therefore bounces only slightly.

You must also define the **friction** created by an object. Since friction is a function of how smooth or rough a surface is, this property is sometimes referred to as **roughness**. There are two distinct types of friction. The first is **static friction**, which prevents stationary objects from sliding down inclined planes. It is called "static" because it refers to nonmoving, or static, objects. If, for instance, the static friction of a box placed on a ramp is very great, the box will not slide at all (Figure 7-42a). If you decrease the static friction, the box will begin to slide (Figure 7-42b).

The second type of friction, **kinetic friction**, causes moving, or kinetic, objects to come to a stop. For instance, suppose you place two boxes identical in mass on two ramps identical in slope. What causes one box to stop sliding after only a short time is the kinetic friction, or roughness, of the surface of the box (Figure 7-43b). If the other box is made of some very slickly polished material and has very low kinetic friction, it will continue sliding for a longer distance (Figure 7-43a).

Static friction and kinetic friction function independently and therefore can be adjusted independently in most systems. For example, if you set the static friction of a ball rolling on a surface to zero, the ball will slide, rather than roll, along the surface. At the same time, you can adjust the kinetic friction of the ball up or down. If you increase the kinetic friction, the ball will slide (because the static friction is set to zero) and stop quickly (because the kinetic friction is high). If you decrease the kinetic friction, the ball will slide (because the static friction is still zero) and come to a stop slowly (because the kinetic friction is low).

FORCES AND FIELDS

So far, we have discussed a number of physical properties important for a motion-dynamics calculation. In order to complete the definition of motion dynamics for an object, however, you also need to describe the **forces**, sometimes also called **fields**, that act upon the object. What causes the object to move in the first place?

The most common force that motion dynamics takes into account is the force of **gravity**. Except in very rare circumstances, gravity affects all objects. Even if no other forces cause an object to move, gravity will keep it on the ground. Technically speaking, gravity is the attraction between two objects, caused by the masses of the objects and the distance between them. A ball falls to Earth because the mass of Earth is so much greater than the mass of the ball that the ball is attracted to Earth. This is why a ball in Antarctica will fall "upward" toward the Earth.

From the point of view of most animation, however, you can think of gravity in simpler terms—as a force pulling all objects downward. Consequently, most motion-dynamics systems define gravity as a simple force that pulls all objects downward at a specific rate in the negative Y direction. This force usually exists by default (just as it does on Earth) and affects all objects equally and automatically. Thus, even if you define no other forces and define no other animation, a ball that starts out suspended in the air at frame 1 of a simulation immediately begins falling in frame 2 because of gravity.

The fact that gravity causes objects to fall at a specific rate affects the dimensions you use when modeling objects in a motion-dynamics system. Because the speed at which an object falls is measured in terms of the distance the object travels per second, the measurements of distance you use in the modeling process must be consistent with the measurements of distance used by the motion-dynamics calculations for gravity. If the software you use measures gravity in feet per second, then the units of measurement for your models must also be feet. If gravity is measured in meters per second, then your models must be modeled in metric units. Normally, a motion-dynamics software package sets up default units of measurement, so that the units are consistent in both the modeling and simulation sections of the software. However, if you change the units of measurement, the gravitational force of the motion-dynamics system will not pull objects downward at a physically accurate rate.

Many animators are less interested in physically accurate simulations than in visually interesting animation, and motion dynamics can be used to good

Figure 7-44. Motion-dynamics systems require you to define the forces, such as gravity and wind, that act on objects.

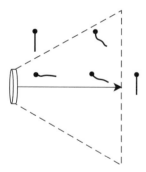

Figure 4-45. Unlike wind, which is omnipresent, a fan force has a limited range.

effect for this. If, however, you do want to create a physically accurate simulation, you must use physically accurate numbers for gravity. On Earth, gravity causes falling objects to **accelerate**—that is, gain speed—at a rate of 9.8 meters per second, which is equivalent to thirty-two feet per second.

In addition to gravity, another force that many systems allow you to define is **wind**, which can be very useful, for example, in animating a curtain blowing in a breeze, or the branches of a tree bending slightly in the wind. These are subtle kinds of movement, difficult to model convincingly with keyframing techniques. A wind force is usually defined as a vector having a location, a direction, and a strength. In Figure 7-44, the arrow pointing to the right represents the wind force. The arrow pointing downward is the default gravity force. The curtain model has been defined to have a certain mass. When the wind force hits the curtain, it tends to push the curtain to the right. At the same time, however, the gravity force tends to pull the curtain straight down. Both of these tendencies are affected by the mass of the curtain itself. The result of these forces pushing and pulling against each other is that the curtain rises and falls and flaps "in the breeze."

A wind force is defined in most systems to affect an entire scene equally from a given direction. For example, several curtains in a scene, each located some distance from the others, are affected to the same degree by the wind.

A variation on the wind concept is a **fan** force. Unlike wind, it is possible to limit both the distance over which a fan force will carry and the radial area that it will affect. In Figure 7-45, the fan force is represented by the cylindrical form on the far left. The arrow emanating from the center of that form and traveling to the right represents the distance over which the force of the fan will carry. At the base of the arrow—that is, at the cylindrical fan icon itself—the force of the fan is strongest. This is why the string close to the base of the arrow is being blown quite a bit. As the force of the fan travels down the arrow, the strength of that force decreases, which is why the next string is not being blown as much as the first. Beyond the tip of the arrow, the force of the fan dies out completely and the string does not move at all.

The force of the fan not only fades as it travels in the direction of the arrow; it also fades as it moves radially away from the center of the fan. The dotted lines emanating from the fan icon demarcate the radial range of effectiveness. The string at the top left, which is completely outside the radial range of the fan, is not moving at all. The string directly to the right lies just inside the radial limit and therefore is being affected slightly. Notice, however, that this string is not being affected as much as the string directly below it, which, even though it is at the same horizontal distance from the fan, is closer to the radial center of the force field.

Turbulence, another force offered by most packages, pushes objects in random directions. The amount of randomness is usually controlled by several

Figure 7-46. Several forces can be applied to each object. Here, vortex, turbulence, and gravity forces are applied to the swirling papers.

noise parameters, while a **magnitude** parameter controls how strong the turbulence is. You can also set an **attenuation** parameter controlling how quickly the force fades with distance. Being at the center of the turbulence subjects you to much more force than being farther away, at its edge. And if you are far enough away, the turbulence will not affect you at all.

Many packages also offer a **vortex** force, which moves objects in a spiraling whirlwind pattern. As with turbulence, you can control the magnitude and attenuation of the force. You can also control the **direction** of spin.

In setting up a motion dynamics simulation, you typically define several forces, some of which, such as gravity, might affect all objects, while others might affect only certain objects. To avoid unnecessary calculations, you **link** each force to specific objects. For example, in Figure 7-46, the papers blown about on the left side of the frames are affected by three forces—a vortex force spinning them in a rising circular pattern, a turbulence force which adds randomness to their motion, and a gravity force which pulls them back to earth. At a later moment in the animation, boxes falling out of the back of the truck are affected by the same gravity force, but are linked to neither the vortex nor turbulence forces (Figure 7-50).

A final force that can be very important in setting up a motion-dynamics simulation is the acceleration an object has as the result of some keyframed action: **keyframed acceleration**. Acceleration is a measure of how fast the speed of an object changes, and the most basic way of giving an object some sort of speed or movement in a three-dimensional animation system is keyframing (described in Chapter 4).

All software packages allow you to combine keyframed animation movements with motion-dynamic simulation. Thus, you might keyframe an animation of a ball translating from one position to another over ten frames (Figure 7-47). This operation involves the standard keyframing techniques of setting a keyframe for the ball as it appears in frame 1, then setting another keyframe for the ball as it appears in frame 10. Having defined the keyframed animation from frame 1 to frame 10, you then direct the simulation software to take over the calculations from frame 11 through frame 40. When the simulation takes over, two forces are at work: the default gravity force, and the acceleration that

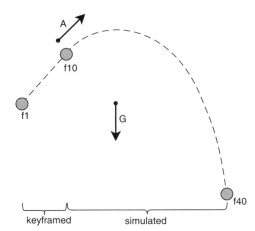

Figure 7-47. Some systems allow you to combine standard keyframed motion with motion-dynamics simulation. Here, the keyframed acceleration of an object is calculated into the motion dynamics.

the ball has as a result of being translated from the position at frame 1 to the position at frame 10. The combination of this keyframed acceleration and gravity causes the ball to continue rising for a while and then to fall.

COLLISIONS

One of the areas in which motion dynamics can be most useful is in simulating **collisions**. The reason the animation of a box falling down a flight of steps (see Figure 7-38) is so complex, for example, is that the box collides with the steps and bounces off them when it does. It is the precise calculation of these collisions, called **collision detection**, that makes a simulation of this animation so effective.

The calculation of collisions, however, can be extremely time-consuming for a computer system, and most motion-dynamics systems therefore allow you to elect whether or not to calculate collisions for a given object. If you know that an object, such as an isolated curtain (see Figure 7-44) won't hit anything in a particular animation sequence, you can turn off collision detection for that object.

If you want to calculate collisions for your model, however, most systems offer several options, all intended to minimize the amount of calculation necessary for a successful simulation. The first option is to define which other objects in the scene might be **obstacles**—that is, which objects the animated object might collide with. When the software does the collision-detection calculations, it will consider only these defined obstacles.

For example, suppose you add a lamppost to the scene in which the box falls down the steps (Figure 7-48). Given the position of the lamppost behind the steps, the box will never collide with it, so you can eliminate it from the list of obstacles that the motion-dynamics software needs to consider in collision-detection calculations. Only the steps, floor, and wall need be considered obstacles.

Figure 7-48. Only those objects that the falling box might hit need to be defined as obstacles for that box. This reduces the calculations necessary for collision detection.

Another area in which most systems offer collision-detection options is in the shape of the objects involved. The collision calculations for a complex shape—a telephone, for example—are more complicated than the calculations for a simple shape, such as a box. Consequently, many systems allow you to use a simpler shape as a stand-in for the purposes of collision calculations. Assuming that a falling telephone is shaped like a simple box, for example, greatly speeds up the collision-detection calculations, although you still see the actual telephone falling. In many animations, the accuracy of the collisions calculations does not need to be exact in order to be visually convincing.

Among the number of simplifying shapes that motion-dynamics systems permit is the **bounding box**, or the smallest rectangular box into which an object will fit (Figure 7-49a). If you use the bounding box of the telephone for collision-detection calculations, the resulting motion is similar to what it would have been if you had used the actual shape of the telephone, since the shape of the bounding box and the shape of the telephone are similar. Likewise, some objects can be conveniently and fairly accurately approximated with a **bounding sphere**, or the smallest sphere into which they will fit (Figure 7-49b).

Bounding boxes and bounding spheres may be used to simplify either the colliding object itself or the obstacles with which the object will come into contact. Sometimes it is possible to use a **bounding plane** as a simplification technique for obstacles. A flat surface that extends infinitely in all directions, a bounding plane could successfully approximate a bumpy surface, for example (Figure 7-49c).

To control the precision with which your software performs collision detection calculations, you can adjust a **collision tolerance** parameter. The smaller this number, the more precise the collision calculations. More precise calculations, of course, slow down the software.

Obstacles are sometimes stationary, as they are in the staircase example of Figure 7-48. Sometimes, however, you want an **animated obstacle**. In Figure 7-50, the animated truck bed has been defined as an obstacle for each of the boxes. As the truck bed rises, gravity pulls the boxes down, colliding them with the rising bed, and eventually sliding them off the back.

(a)

(b)

(c)

Figure 7-49. Bounding boxes, bounding spheres, and bounding planes—all represented by broken lines in this illustration— can be used to simplify collision-detection calculations.

Figure 7-50. Obstacles can be animated with keyframing. Here, the passive-body truck bed rotates upward, causing the active-body boxes to tumble out.

In some motion dynamics simulations, there may be a great many objects colliding with each other, as in the dump truck animation of Figure 7-50. Not only does each of the boxes collide with the truck bed and the ground, but each box can collide with every other box. Collision detection calculations for such a scene can become quite complex and time-consuming, even when the objects are limited, as here, to nondeformable rigid bodies.

In an effort to minimize the complexity of these calculations, most software packages offer a distinction between two types of motion dynamics objects. A **passive body** is one that contributes to the motion dynamics calculations, but itself is not moved by them. Examples of this are the truck bed and ground of Figure 7-50. As passive bodies, both of these objects are obstacles and are therefore contributing significantly to the simulation calculations. Neither of them is affected by those calculations, however. The ground object is not moved at all when the boxes bang into it. The truck bed is moving, but all of its movement is a result of standard keyframed animation, not of motion dynamics calculations. By contrast, an **active body** is an object that not only contributes to the simulation calculations, but itself can be moved by them. In our dump truck example, each of the boxes is an active body. All the movement of each box is purely the result of the motion dynamics calculations. Also, and very importantly, each active body is automatically an obstacle to all other active bodies. Thus, each box can collide with any other box.

ALGORITHMS AND PLAYBACK ISSUES

Motion dynamics algorithms are based on precisely defined principles of physics and mathematics. These have important consequences for the user of motion dynamics software, and it is important to understand several aspects of the underlying science of motion dynamics. Whereas in the real world time is continuous, so that there is no break between one instant and another, in motion dynamics time is treated discretely. That is, time is broken up into a fixed number of measurable increments—for example, thirty increments per second, or one hundred increments per second. These increments are called **time steps**. The smaller the time steps, the more closely they approximate the continuous nature of time, and therefore the more accurately they simulate time n   time n+1

Figure 7-51. If the time step is too large, a fast-moving object might pass through an obstacle in the interval between one time step and the next.

an animated scene. However, smaller time steps also mean more calculations. Consequently, you can define the size of the time steps, giving you the option of trading off accuracy of simulation for speed of calculation if necessary.

The size of the time step becomes especially critical when you have objects that are moving extremely fast and should collide with an obstacle (Figure 7-51). If the time step is too large, the object might be on the left side of the obstacle at time step *n*, and have passed right through it as of time step *n + 1*. Not only does this look incorrect, of course, but it can also cause the software to freeze, since interpenetrating objects are impossible according to the physics of motion dynamics. The solution to this situation is to decrease the size of the time step until the calculations succeed. In extreme situations, the time step may have to be decreased so much that the calculations become impractically slow. In this case, you may have to redesign your animation to avoid the problem in the first place.

Because of the mathematics of motion-dynamics calculations, two simulations of a given scene that use different time steps will not produce the same motions. The path of an object can differ substantially when calculated under two different time steps. For this reason you may not find it useful to define a larger time step to sketch out a preliminary version of an animation, with the intention of switching to a smaller time step for the final animation.

Another important issue in motion dynamics algorithms is **time interdependence**, the dependence of every moment on the preceding moment. What an object will do in the next instant depends on what it is doing now. Imagine two situations, as illustrated in Figures 7-52 and 7-53. In both situations the large ball is in exactly the same location at frame 100—just in front of the character's face. In Figure 7-52, the ball is also moving forward very quickly toward the character as of frame 100. In 7-53, although it is in the same location, the ball is stationary at frame 100, hovering in the air. The subsequent actions of the two balls will therefore be very different. The ball that had been moving quickly toward the character in Figure 7-52 will continue to do so because of its **momentum**—the tendency of a moving object to keep moving unless something stops it—and will crash into the character's face in frame 101. By contrast, the ball that had been hovering in mid-air in Figure 7-53 has no such momentum, and will begin dropping straight down at frame 101.

f 100

f101

Figure 7-52. An object's momentum at one moment contributes to how it behaves in the next.

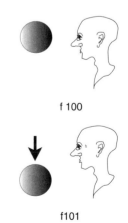

f 100

f101

Figure 7-53. The movement of an object at any one moment is dependent upon what it was doing the previous moment.

The dependence of one simulated moment on the previous simulated moment has important implications for **playback** of a motion dynamics simulation. In order for motion dynamics software to know the positions of objects at frame 101, it must know where they were, and how fast and in what direction they were moving at frame 100. But in order to know that for frame 100, it must first know the same information for frame 99. In short, in order to know the positions of simulated objects at any given frame, the motion dynamics software must go all the way back to frame 1, and recalculate the simulation from the beginning each time.

Different software vendors offer different ways around this problem, as we will see in a moment, but the implications are significant in any motion dynamics software. One implication is that you cannot drag your frame counter through your timeline to view a given frame. If you do so, you will skip some frames as you drag, and the calculations will be inaccurate. Also, when playing back your animation, you cannot force the playback to synchronize to a specific playback rate—for example, video or film. If you do, the playback will skip some frames, and therefore cause inaccurate simulation calculations. And finally, when rendering your frames, you cannot pick a frame in the middle of your sequence and start rendering there. You must always start at frame 1 and render every frame in sequence from there.

Clearly, these restrictions are extremely inconvenient for the animator. As a consequence, motion dynamics packages offer several solutions. One solution is to create temporary **cache data** in RAM. The word *cache* means to hide or store, so cache data is data that has been stored for future use. When you turn on this option, your software will take longer to calculate the simulations the first time through, because it will also be storing this information in RAM. Once the simulations have been calculated, however, the cache data allows you to view your simulation as if it were a normal animation—that is, you can scrub through the timeline, and you can play back the animation, synching it to a particular playback rate. If you make any changes to your simulation setup, however, your must delete the old cache data and calculate new data. For example, if you reposition one of your objects, or change the mass of another object, you must delete the old cache data and recreate it.

A related issue is that, since cached data is stored in RAM, it is not saved permanently with your files on your hard drive. This means that when you return to work on your file the next day, the cache data will have been lost and will have to be recalculated. It also means that if you try to render your frames in several stages—for example, starting at frame 1, then restarting the next day at frame 600—you will have the same problem. To address this, most packages allow you to create a **permanent cache**, sometimes also called, rather picturesquely, a **baked simulation**. In this case, cache data is written to the hard drive and saved with your scene file.

Permanent cache data stores the positions of every object at every frame as **raw data**—that is, as a keyframe at every frame. This can result in data files that are quite large. There are several advantages to creating such permanent cache data, however. Once you have created permanent cache data, you can, if you choose, delete all your motion dynamics elements—forces, physical properties, and so on—because the permanent cache data has stored the positions of every object at every frame. Very importantly, you can also view the raw data curves in your parameter curve editor (section 4.4), where you can thin the curves and then edit them as you would any other parameter curve.

All the motion-dynamics techniques discussed in this section are very powerful and can yield stunningly realistic simulations of an event. Sometimes, however, the most effective thing you can do is to combine the more standard, keyframe-based animation techniques with these sophisticated motion-dynamics calculations. For example, the human figure in Figure 5-13 was animated using standard keyframing and hierarchical animation. The bowling balls, on the other hand, were animated using motion dynamics to achieve a high degree of realism as the balls flew through the air and bounced on the ground about the feet of the character.

7.7 Soft-Body Dynamics

In the previous section we discussed the principles and concepts common to all motion dynamics, and focused on how they are applied to rigid bodies, objects whose shapes do not deform. When motion dynamics calculations are applied to an object whose shape can deform, such an object is called a **soft body**. For a soft body, as for a rigid body, you define physical properties such as mass and elasticity. You also define forces such as gravity or wind, as well as friction and collision obstacles. In addition to all these parameters, there are also several other important issues related specifically to the deformability of soft bodies. We focus on these issues in this section.

Soft-body dynamics can be used for many applications. One example is a soft rubber beach ball falling under the force of gravity, colliding with a surface, and deforming as it bounces (Figure 7-54). Another example is a flag waving in the wind, with the wind and gravity causing the fabric of the flag to ripple in the breeze. A third example of soft body dynamics might be a modeled lock of hair on a CG character's head, with the up and down movement of his walk causing the lock of hair to bounce up and down.

We saw in section 7.6 that when a rigid body moves in a simulation, the motion dynamics calculations act upon the object as a whole. If a cube is bouncing down a stairway, as it is in Figure 7-38, the motion of the entire

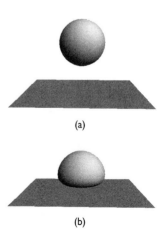

(a)

(b)

Figure 7-54. A soft body is a deformable object moving under motion dynamics.

Figure 7-55. A soft body deforms because its surface points move nonuniformly.

Figure 7-56. Without a structure, the surface points of a soft body can go anywhere, even permitting the object to pass through itself.

(a)

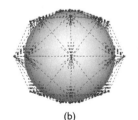

(b)

Figure 7-57. A system of spring forces connecting each surface point is one way to impose a structure on soft bodies.

cube as a unit is simulated, and the entire cube as a unit bounces off the stairs. By contrast, when a soft body moves in a simulation, the forces, friction, and collisions act upon the individual **surface points** of the object (Figure 7-55). When these surface points move nonuniformly, the object deforms. When the ball strikes the surface in Figure 7-55, the surface points at the bottom of the ball react to the collision, while those at the top of the ball keep moving downward.

In some software packages, the calculations of a motion dynamics simulation are performed directly on the surface points of the soft-body object. In others, the software creates a **particle system** (discussed in more detail in section 7.8), attaching each particle to exactly one point on the object's surface. When a given particle moves, its associated surface point moves; when the surface points move, the surface deforms.

In the real world, a soft object has a coherent shape. Although it may deform, it has a **structure** that causes it to maintain its basic configuration. The beach ball we mentioned earlier may squash when it hits something, but it quickly returns to its original, spherical shape. The flag waving in the wind, however much it ripples, retains its basic rectangular structure.

Motion dynamics software must somehow retain the structure of a soft-body object by restricting the movement of its surface points. If it does not do so, the points could go anywhere, causing the object's shape to deform wildly, or even pass through itself (Figure 7-56).

SPRING SYSTEMS

There are two approaches to maintaining the structure of a soft-body object, the first being **springs**. With this approach, the user defines a system of spring-like forces connecting all the points of the object together, as if each pair of points were connected by a rubber band (Figure 7-57).

An important parameter in any spring system is **stiffness**. To continue the rubber band analogy, stiffness controls how flexible the rubber bands are. A stiffness of 100 percent means that there is no flexibility at all, and the object cannot deform at all. If such an object collides with an obstacle, it behaves exactly as if it were a rigid body. By contrast, a stiffness of 0 percent means that the points of the object can go anywhere. This is the same effect as having no springs at all. In setting the stiffness parameter for your springs, you must experiment in a trial-and-error fashion to find the appropriate amount of stiffness.

Another important parameter of springs is **damping**. This controls how quickly adjacent points return to their original positions—how quickly the rubber band snaps back, for example. If damping is 100 percent, the points snap back immediately and stop moving immediately. If damping is 0 percent, the points never stop moving—they bounce and jiggle forever.

Figure 7-58. Defining the springs' parameters on a per-spring basis allows you to cause the soft body to deform differently in different sections of the model.

Both stiffness and damping can be adjusted either globally, for the entire spring system, or on a per-spring basis. The ball in Figure 7-54 had a spring system whose stiffness was defined **globally**, giving every spring equal stiffness, and causing the ball to always return to its original spherical shape. The object in Figure 7-58 has stiffness adjusted on a **per-spring** basis. The springs at the bottom of the object have extremely little stiffness. Those a bit higher up have a little more stiffness, but still not much. The springs in the top portion of the object all have equal stiffness. The result is that when this object collides with the floor, the bottom section, with very little stiffness, collapses and flattens out, while the top section retains its original form.

GOAL OBJECTS

A second approach to maintaining the structure of a soft-body object is to use a **goal object**. With this approach, the software creates a duplicate model of your object, this duplicate becoming the soft-body object, and the original becoming the goal object. Whenever the goal object is moved or deformed, the soft-body object tries to return to the position and shape of the goal object—that is, to its original configuration. More specifically, each surface point of the soft body strives to return to the position of the corresponding surface point on the goal object.

Paralleling the stiffness and damping parameters of springs, goal objects have a **goal weight** parameter, which determines how closely the soft-body object will try to adhere to the goal object. A goal weight factor of 100 percent means that the soft object will adhere exactly to the goal at all times. In this case, the soft body and the goal object are indistinguishable, since they move and deform exactly the same at all times. A goal weight factor of 0 percent means that the soft object does not adhere at all to the goal—that is, it will not follow the goal at all. Intermediate weight values cause the soft body to mimic the goal object more or less.

Imagine the simple case of a soft-body cube, with an identical cube as its goal object, and a goal weight of 50 percent. If you animate the goal cube to move suddenly straight down as in Figure 7-59, the soft-body cube will drop also, trying to catch up to it, because each point of the soft-body cube is trying to catch up to each point of the goal cube. When the goal cube suddenly stops, the soft-body cube will overshoot it, and then bounce back and forth several times, eventually settling down on top of the goal sphere.

Figure 7-59. Defining a goal object is another way to impose structure on a soft body. The soft body object tries to imitate the position and shape of the goal object.

The scenario just described assumed a single, global goal-weight number for the entire cube. As with spring systems, parameters for goal objects can be adjusted either globally or locally. Local goal weights assign different goal weights to individual points. For example, a cube could have a different goal-weight value for each of its six points. If we apply a turbulence force to the soft cube, its points will be pushed about by the turbulence, but keep returning to their original positions as defined by the goal cube. Since each point of the soft-body cube has a different goal weight, however, the corners of the cube will wiggle about in a random way, each one adhering differently to its corresponding goal point.

SECONDARY MOTION

An important concept in traditional animation is that of **secondary motion**. Frequently, as an object or character moves, its large-scale primary motion is accompanied by smaller, secondary motions. If a character suddenly turns around, for example, the primary motion is the action of turning around. Secondary, accompanying motions might include the shaking of his hair as he turns, the flapping of his coat as he turns, a slight wobble of his head, and a blink of his eyes. Some of these secondary motions can be readily animated with soft-body dynamics. Of those mentioned in our example, both the shaking hair and the flapping coat could be animated in this way.

We saw in section 7.6 that moving objects have **momentum**, the tendency to keep moving until they are stopped. A corollary of momentum is **inertia**, the tendency of a stationary object to remain stationary unless something moves it. The combination of these two phenomena causes the secondary motion of our character's hair and coat. As he swings around, the hair and coat initially lag behind because of inertia. Once they are moving, they tend to keep moving because of their momentum, even though his body has stopped turning.

A common way to implement this effect is to combine soft-body dynamics with forward kinematics (section 2.9). If we model a deformable, soft-body lock of hair and make its goal object a child of our character's head, forward kinematics causes the goal hair to inherit the transformations of the parent head (Figure 7-60). If we have adjusted the goal weights of our soft hair so

Figure 7-60. Placing the goal object of your soft body within the hierarchy of a model causes the goal object and its soft body to inherit the motion of the parent object.

those surface points closer to the head deform not at all and those at the tip of the lock deform more, we will achieve the swinging motion we want.

Figure 7-61 shows another example of soft-body secondary motion. Here the character's entire body—torso, arms, head, antennae, cup—are a single surface. As the character jumps up and down, his arms and antennae flop up and down with the inherited motion of his jumping. By defining the character as a soft body with a goal object and adjusting the goal weights of individual points, the animator freed himself to concentrate on the primary jumping motion, while motion dynamics automatically calculated the secondary flopping motions.

Figure 7-61. Carefully adjusting the goal weights of your soft body can produce effective secondary motion. Here, the soft-body arms and antennae flop up and down automatically as the character moves. (Copyright 2001, J. Adam Burke.)

INDIRECT SOFT BODIES

All our examples so far have involved directly defining the models in question as soft-bodies—the cube, the ball, the lock of hair. However, it is frequently helpful to create a soft body of some intermediate object that indirectly controls the shape of your model.

An example would be a **lattice**. Recall from section 4.9 that a lattice is a box-like structure defined around your model. Each of the relatively few points on the lattice controls a larger number of points on the model. By moving a lattice point, you deform a section of your model. Defining your lattice to be a soft body allows you to apply motion dynamics to the lattice, which in turn deforms your model (Figure 7-62).

Another example of indirect control over a model is the **IK spline** technique we saw in section 4.7. With this technique, your model is bound as a skin to an inverse kinematic skeleton, which is in turn controlled by a spline curve. Changing the shape of the spline curve causes the IK skeleton to change shape, which then causes the model to deform.

Figures 7-63 and 7-64 show an example of this approach. In Figure 7-63 we see our character model, rendered here as transparent, with a simple inverse kinematic skeleton running through him from toe to head. The geometry of the model is skinned to this skeleton. Control of the skeleton itself comes from a spline curve drawn next to it. Defining this spline curve to be a soft body gives you indirect motion-dynamics control over the model.

Figure 7-62. Defining a lattice as a soft body allows you to indirectly control the motion of your model through the soft-body lattice.

Figure 7-63. The curve of an IK spline controller can be defined as a soft body.

Figure 7-64. If the goal curve
moves quickly, the soft-body IK
spline controller deforms,
causing the model to deform.

Figure 7-64 shows frames from an animation created with this approach. The goal spline curve (not shown here) has been keyframed to move quickly to the right and then abruptly stop. Its partner, soft-body spline curve has goal weights adjusted locally, with the points at the top of the curve having a lesser weight and those at the bottom having a goal weight of 100 percent. As the goal spline curve jumps to the right, its soft-body equivalent tries to catch up. The bottom of the soft-body curve adheres to the goal curve 100 percent, but the top lags behind because of inertia, causing the character to lean backward. After the goal curve abruptly stops, the soft-body curve overshoots it because of momentum, causing the character to bend forward. The soft-body curve and character wobble back and forth a bit, finally coming to rest in the last frame.

COLLISIONS

Like rigid bodies, soft bodies can collide with objects. With a soft body, however, it is the individual surface points of the object that collide with the obstacle, not the entire object itself. It is because of this that a soft body deforms when it hits an obstacle. When the ball of Figure 7-54 strikes the floor, it deforms because the points on the bottom of the ball hit the floor before the points on the top do. Since the bottom points have collided, they stop. The top points have not yet collided, so they keep moving. The result is the squashed ball we see in the illustration.

Collision calculations have an even bigger impact on computation time with soft bodies than with rigid-bodies. With rigid bodies, it is a single entity, the rigid body, whose collision must be calculated at each time step. For a soft body, the collision of every surface point on your model must be calculated at every time step. Instead of calculating one potential collision per object per time step, you might have to calculate dozens—or hundreds!

This can be one very good reason for using an indirect soft-body controller, as described above. Imagine your model has one thousand surface points. If you put a lattice with only twenty points around your model and make that lattice the soft body, your software will have fifty times fewer collision calculations to do.

It is also possible to collide two soft bodies with each other. The accuracy of collision detection calculations in such a situation can be more problematic, however, since the surfaces of the two obstacles are themselves changing shape. For the same reason, you cannot use bounding objects as stand-ins for your soft obstacles.

7.8 Particle Systems

Many phenomena, including such ephemeral phenomena as smoke, gas, steam, fire, and clouds, cannot be modeled easily as surfaces. In the case of fire, for example, the "surfaces" of fire (if you even can conceive of them in this way) are really molecule-sized particles, so minuscule and myriad that modeling them is impractical. You can sometimes use transparency mapping to simulate fire and other similar phenomena (see section 3.8), but this technique provides only a crude approximation of the phenomena. You have also seen that volumetric lights can be very effective for creating certain atmospheric effects (see section 6.2). Volumetric lights, however, also have limitations because they are restricted to geometrically regular volumes such as cubes, cones and spheres.

Another important characteristic of phenomena such as smoke, fire, and clouds is the way they move. Because the tiny molecules that comprise them are so lightweight, their motion is largely or wholly in reaction to forces such as wind, air currents, gravity, and momentum—in short, the forces of **motion dynamics** that we discussed in section 7.6.

The **particle system** technique handles ephemeral phenomena like these both in terms of the absence of surfaces and the presence of motion dynamics forces. Using this technique, you do not model individual surfaces. Rather, you define the number of three-dimensional "particles" in the system. You also define the forces acting upon these particles, including gravity, wind, and collisions. Finally, you define how each particle or group of particles will be rendered. Since the particles are defined as fully three-dimensional, when the software renders your frames, the particles are rendered within the three-dimensional space of your scene.

EMISSION PARAMETERS

Particle systems can be tremendously complex, with a myriad of parameters for controlling how the particles move, where they come from, how they are rendered, how they interact with the environment, and so on. Each software package has its unique collection of parameters, but certain key parameters

Figure 7-65. The quantity of particles in a system is controlled by the rate at which they are emitted, usually specified as the number of particles per second.

Figure 7-66. The lifetime of particles controls how long they remain visible before dissipating into the atmosphere.

are shared by all packages. One such parameter is the quantity of particles, usually specified as the **emission rate**. Since the particles of a particle system are emitted continuously over time (the flame continues to burn, the rocket exhaust continues to be expelled), the most convenient way to specify how many particles should be in the system is to specify the number of particles emitted per second. This number usually ranges from a few hundred to several thousand. In Figure 7-65a the system represented is emitting relatively few particles per second. In contrast, that of Figure 7-65b is emitting particles at a much higher rate, thereby creating a much denser collection of particles.

Another parameter you can control is the **speed** of the particles. The blast of exhaust coming out of a rocket emits particles that move through space extremely quickly. The particles of a cloud system, by contrast, drift very slowly.

However many particles there are and however quickly they move, some particles remain visible longer than others before dissipating into the atmosphere. The sparks emitted from a sparkler last only a moment, perhaps half a second. The particles of a slowly rising curl of smoke may be visible for several seconds as they waft upward. The parameter, usually measured in seconds, that controls this phenomenon is the **lifetime** of the particles; we speak of the particles "dying" after this amount of time. The two systems in Figure 7-66 are emitting particles at the same rate and at the same speed. The one in Figure 7-66b has a much shorter lifetime than that of Figure 7-65a, however, so its particles dissipate more quickly, resulting in a shorter column of particles.

In defining a particle system you must also specify where the particles are coming from—that is, their **source**. In some systems the source can be defined as an invisible geometric entity that has no actual surface. You might, for example, have an invisible rectangular source hovering above your scene in order to create rain particles, or a spherical source at the tip of a candle to create a candle flame. Some systems also permit you to define a light as a particle source. Thus, you might place a spotlight pointing upward at the base of a water fountain, using it simultaneously to create a spray of water particles and to light them from below.

Frequently, however, you want the source of particles to be a segment of one of the models in your three-dimensional scene. For example, you might want particles to emerge from the spherical tip of a sparkler or the exhaust nozzle at the back of a rocket or a tiny disk at the end of a rifle barrel (Figure 7-67). There are two approaches to achieve this: select a specific surface as the particle source or, as some systems allow, define a shader to be particle-emitting and then assign that shader to the surface in question.

Having defined where the particles are coming from, you must also define where they are going, by specifying the **direction** in which they are

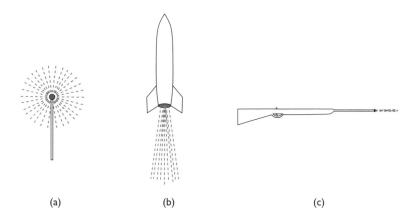

(a)   (b)   (c)

Figure 7-67. The source of particles is frequently associated with a specific surface in your scene.

moving. If the source of the particles is an invisible geometric element or a light, the direction is specified by rotating the icon for that element or light. If the particle source is a surface, the direction is frequently defined by the normals of that surface. Recall from section 3.5 that the normal of a surface is effectively a line perpendicular to the surface at a particular point. Figure 7-68 shows two particle-emitting surfaces, with their normals—and therefore the direction of particle emission—indicated by arrows. The normals of the sphere in Figure 7-68a point outward equally in all directions; the normals of the flat disk in Figure 7-68b all point upward in the same direction.

Frequently, you want the emission of particles to follow a specific direction, but to fan outward a bit as in the rocket and rifle examples (Figures 7-67b and c). Outward fanning is controlled by a parameter usually called **spread**, specified in degrees. The rocket has a spread angle of about 20 degrees; the burst of particles from the rifle barrel has a narrow spread of only a few degrees.

Any of the parameters discussed so far may be adjusted additionally by adding **randomness** to them. For example, you may want to vary the direction of particles by spreading them outward, but not all by exactly the same amount. Or you may want the speed of the particles to vary somewhat, to avoid having every particle moving at exactly the same speed. Some packages allow you to control randomness through a **jitter** value, which alters a parameter by plus or minus a certain amount. For example, if the particles' spread is set to 20 degrees, with a jitter of ± 5, the spread of any given individual particle will range from 15 degrees to 25 degrees. Another way of introducing randomness is through a **noise** factor. Larger noise factors mean more randomness applied to that parameter; smaller noise factors mean less. In Figure 7-69, both the spread and the speed of the particles have been randomized.

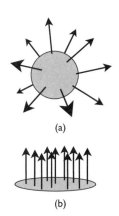

(a)

(b)

Figure 7-68. The surface normals of a particle system's source geometry can be used to specify the direction of emission.

Figure 7-69. Randomness can be applied to any of a particle system's parameters. Here, it is applied to both the speed and the spread of the particles.

RENDERING PARAMETERS

A large number of parameters control the rendering of a particle system. One of these is the **color** of the particles, a parameter often animatable as well. For example, you can make the color of a fire particle change as it moves away from the center of the flame. The licking flames of a burning log might be a hot orange color at the source of the flame, change to a darker red at the top of the flame, and finally change to black (no fire) as they move farther away and "cool." Specifying the animation of the particles' color is typically done by selecting a color at the beginning of the particles' lifetime, another at the end of their lifetime and, optionally, intermediate colors at intermediate points.

You can also define and animate the **transparency** of the particles. Some particles—for example, a gentle mist—would be rendered as quite transparent. Others, such as dense smoke belching from a smokestack, would be rendered as more opaque.

Most particle systems also allow you to control how much the particles **blur** when rendered. A system simulating the sparks that flash from an axe when it strikes a stone should have little or no blurring, to keep the sparks distinct. Smoke, on the other hand, is much more amorphous and its particles therefore should be rendered as blurring to the point that none is individually distinguishable.

A particle's **trail life** is related to blurring. As a particle moves through space, it may leave a visible trail behind. The longer the life of such a trail, the longer the trail itself will be and the more visible. Trail life is normally measured in seconds.

Glow makes particles look incandescent by increasing both their brightness and color saturation. Figure 7-70a shows a rendering of rocket exhaust without glow; Figure 7-70b is exactly the same particle system with glow. Glow fuses the particles together, much like blurring, and simultaneously gives them an intense, fiery look.

In most packages, any of the rendering parameters mentioned so far can also be defined by applying a **texture** to them. Fractal textures (section 6.3) become especially useful in this context. For example, the color of a particle might be defined as coming from a fractal texture, causing each particle to render as an irregular area of color, rather than as a single color. Simultaneously applying a fractal texture to control the particles' transparency will cause the transparency of each rendered particle to vary over the rendered area of that particle. This combination can be very effective, as we see in Figure 7-71, where two different fractal textures were applied, one controlling color and the other controlling transparency. The result is that the rendered particles produce a convincingly smokey look.

(a)

(b)

Figure 7-70. Glow is one of the many parameters that control the rendering of particles.

Figure 7-71. Applying fractal textures to particles can yield effective renderings of smoke and other natural phenomena.

All rendering parameters can be defined for the particle system as a whole, with all particles in the system receiving the same values for those parameters, or on a **per-particle** basis, varying the parameter values for individual particles.

To help you manage the large number of rendering parameters and all their possibilities, many systems provide predefined collections of parameter settings that yield a particular look. Stored in a particles **library**, these can be retrieved and modified to suit a specific purpose. For example, one library particle system might give you a very wispy, transparent look suitable for smoke. Another might produce clouds. Still another might give you a more opaque, almost blobby look. In Figure 7-72, the particles have been rendered with a very dense, opaque, almost tangible spherical look to simulate the billowing thickness of an explosion's flame and smoke.

Figure 7-72. Predefined settings to create specific effects may be stored in a particle library, to be retrieved and modified by the user.

As noted at the beginning of this section, particle systems are defined three-dimensionally, and herein lies much of their strength for 3D computer rendering and animation. When you look at a rendering of a particle system, you are seeing only one point of view of a fully three-dimensional "model." Like any other 3D model, it can be turned around, viewed from another angle, moved to another location, and so on. You could, for example, "fly" your camera into the particle-system clouds in Figure 7-73, going through them and coming out the other side.

High-end particle systems also react to light in a fully three-dimensional way. Where there are fewer particles, light passes through more easily, as at the edges of the clouds in Figure 7-73. If there are a great many particles, light does not pass through. Particle systems will also cast shadows onto other objects. A plane flying between the viewer and the clouds in Figure 7-73 would at some point have the shadow of the cloud cast upon it. You can also define particles to be **self-shadowing**—that is, to cast shadows upon themselves. Both the explosion in Figure 7-72 and the clouds in Figure 7-73 were rendered with this feature.

Figure 7-73. Particle systems create fully three-dimensional models that exist in a fully three-dimensional space.

It is also possible to attach a special kind of picture called a **sprite** to a particle. What differentiates this technique from a standard texturing technique is that the software forces the sprite image to always face the camera. Since the sprite image is always perpendicular to the camera's line of sight, we never see the sprite edge on. The particles, with sprites attached, can move in any direction, and we will always see the full sprite images.

When attaching a sprite image to a particle, you can also apply a transparency map to that image to hide portions of it. If you have an image of a cow, for example, you can attach that image as a sprite to a particle, along with a transparency map that hides everything except the cow portion of the image (Figure 7-74). Rather than seeing a rectangular picture attached to each

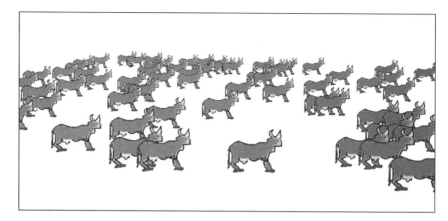

Figure 7-74. Sprite images attached to particles always face the camera. A sprite image with an alpha channel or transparency mask yields a cut-out figure.

Figure 7-75. Three-dimensional models, including hierarchically-organized models, can be attached to particles. If the original model animates, all its instances animate as well.

particle, you now see a cut-out cow attached to each particle. Some systems allow you to achieve this same effect by using a single image that includes an alpha channel (section 8.2). The alpha channel cuts out the figure from the ground in the same way as does a transparency map.

You can further enhance this technique by applying a sequence of animated images as your sprite, rather than a single still image. If you have a sequence of frames of a walking cow, applying them as a sprite to your particle gives the effect of a walking cow attached to your particle. The principle application of this technique comes when you apply animated sprites with transparencies to a large number of particles. By introducing some randomness into your parameters, you can achieve a very reasonable simulation of a herd of creatures.

You can also create particles with **attached geometry**. The model attached to the particles can be as simple as a cube or as complex as a full hierarchically organized machine (Figure 7-75). When a model is attached to a number of particles, it is replicated as an instance (section 2.9), with each instance attached at its local origin to the X, Y, Z location of the particle.

Wherever the particle goes, the model will go with it. If your model is animated, all the instances of it will animate as they move with the particles. One motivation for using this technique is to take advantage of the facility with which particle systems create large numbers of instances. Another motivation is to take advantage of the motion-dynamics controls of particle systems. We turn our attention to that topic now.

MOTION DYNAMICS

As mentioned at the start of this section, another important feature of particle systems is that they incorporate the simulation features of **motion dynamics** (see section 7.6). Thus, the particles of a particle system can be made to react to **forces** such as gravity or wind. The water of a fountain sprays upward and then is pulled back down by gravity. It may simultaneously be blown to the side by a strong wind, causing some of the particles to spray in that direction.

Figure 7-76. Particle systems can be subject to gravity, wind, and turbulence forces.

Since particle systems frequently simulate ephemeral phenomena that are subject to slight shifts in air currents, a **turbulence** force can be especially useful. Many of the particle system renderings illustrated in this section make use of a turbulence force to introduce randomness into the movement of the particles. Figures 7-71, and 7-72 through 7-77 are examples. A significant part of the animator's skill in working with particle systems lies in fine-tuning motion dynamics forces such as turbulence, wind and gravity, to achieve just the right movement of the particles.

In section 7.6 you saw that **collision detection** permits objects to collide, bouncing off each other in physically accurate ways. The same is true of particle systems. When defining the parameters of your system, you can elect to turn collision detection on, specifying which models in the scene are to be considered obstacles: whenever a particle encounters one of these obstacles, it reacts appropriately. How it reacts is determined by parameters you set to make the particles bounce off the obstacle, split into several smaller particles, or stop altogether. In addition, you can set parameters to control how fast or how far the particle will bounce. In Figure 7-77 the rocket's exhaust particles, thrust downward, collide with the ground and radiate outward.

Figure 7-77. Particles may collide with other objects in the scene, bouncing off them, splitting into smaller particles, and changing color.

Most particle systems also allow you to define how the rendering characteristics of a particle change upon collision. In Figure 7-77 the particles change from a very bright, incandescent, flamelike rendering to a dull, smoky rendering as soon as they hit the ground.

PARTICLE-LIKE FUNCTIONS

In addition to the true particle systems just described, some advanced 3D packages offer particle-like modeling functions. These functions operate on actual surfaces, but manipulate surfaces in ways that are particle-like. The most com-

Figure 7-78. Explosion functions manipulate tiny surfaces in a particle-like way.

mon of such functions is an **explosion** function, in which each surface model is broken into many small surfaces (Figure 7-78a), and these small surfaces are made to expand outward in an exploding pattern (Figure 7-78b). This technique is not a true particle system, since it operates on definable and discernible surfaces, usually on polygon models. Remember that any polygonal surface may be broken down into a collection of triangular polygons (see section 2.2). When a polygonal model "explodes," each of the triangles that form the surface is animated outward to create the effect. Since the exploding triangles actually come from the surface of the polygon, the number of exploding pieces is a function of the number of polygons that make up the original sphere. That is, if the model is defined to consist of a 6×6 mesh of polygons, the few triangles exploding outward are quite large. A much denser mesh, say 100×100, produces a great many, and much smaller, triangles.

Some software systems allow you additional control, however, over the size of the exploding pieces. In these software packages, you may decide whether the exploding pieces will be individual triangles or clusters of triangles. If you choose the latter, you also may define how large the largest clusters will be. For example, the largest exploding clusters may consist of ten triangles, and this means that the surface of the sphere will be broken up into pieces the largest of which will comprise ten adjacent triangles (Figure 7-78c).

As with all particle and particle-like techniques, randomness plays a significant role in explosion functions, and you can specify a randomness factor to ensure that not all of the exploding pieces are of a uniform configuration. Other important animation parameters that you can specify include the starting location of the explosion, the strength of the explosion, whether a gravitational force will pull the pieces back down, and how strong this gravitational force is.

A technique related to both particle systems and explosion techniques is known as **flocking**. As the name implies, flocking is designed to simulate the movement of large numbers of creatures in flocking, herding, or schooling patterns. It is most appropriate, for example, for the animation of groups of birds, animals, or fish. In fact, in its most sophisticated implementations, it includes parameters for controlling the behavior of these creatures in realistic ways. One example is **collision avoidance**. Each member of a flock, herd, or school normally moves in such a way as to avoid colliding with its fellows. Sophisticated flocking software incorporates this behavior. Because of the large number of members in a typical flock, however, this can be quite a complicated, and thus slow, calculation. Some advanced flock software also offers controls over species-specific behavior. Pigeons, for example, flock in different patterns than swallows.

Even if the flocking software available to you does not include such sophisticated controls, it can still be extremely useful in simplifying the process of animating large numbers of similar entities. For instance, if you are animating

Figure 7-79. Flocking techniques are designed to simulate the movements of birds, animals, and fish. They also can be used to mimic particle and particle-like functions such as explosions or streams.

pigeon models, then even a flocking function with limited behavioral controls goes a long way to making your models appear to flock like pigeons.

When using the flocking technique, you begin by modeling the element to be flocked, such as a fish (Figure 7-79). The flocking technique will replicate this element as many times as you specify. For example, having modeled a single fish, you might specify that you want a school of fifty fish, and the flocking function will automatically create forty-nine copies.

Having defined the core element, you then indicate how you want the flock to move. Most often you do this by modeling some shape at the location where the flocking animation is to begin and another shape at the location where the flocking is to end. The flocked elements (say, ten fish) are positioned at frame 1 of the animation in such a way as approximately to fill the starting shape. For example, if the starting shape is a cylinder, the fish are arranged to fill a roughly cylindrical shape at frame 1. The words "approximately" and "roughly" are important here, because randomness plays a key role in this sort of function. Fish arranged in a perfectly regular cylindrical pattern are not convincingly flocklike.

Just as you position the flock elements at the start of the animation to fill the starting shape, you position them at the last frame of the animation approximately to fill the ending shape (in Figure 7-79, a sphere). The starting and ending shapes determine the arrangement of the flock elements at the first and last frames, but they do not necessarily indicate how the elements move from the one to the other. By default, the elements of a flock move in an approximately straight line between the starting shape and the ending shape. Once again, the word "approximately" indicates that some degree of randomness is introduced into the path of each element. Usually, you control a randomness parameter, which increases or decreases the amount that each element deviates from the default straight-line path. If you intend the flock to move in some path other than a straight line, you can animate the location of the ending shape. This change causes the flock to "pursue" the ending shape, changing the path of the flock over the course of the animation as the flock tracks the moving target (see Figure 7-79).

7.9 Cloth Dynamics

Figure 7-80. The complex folds of cloth present a difficult modeling problem.

One of the hardest problems of 3D computer graphics has historically been modeling and animating **realistic cloth**. This is because of the complexity of the folds and deformations of cloth. Using one of the standard modeling techniques—polygons, patches, or subdivision surfaces—to model even a simple cloth (Figure 7-80) would be very difficult, requiring you to painstakingly position and reposition numerous surface points to get the desired form. The modeling would be made even more difficult because such surfaces can be stretched infinitely in any direction, whereas cloth has an internal structure that prevents it from stretching too much.

All of this becomes yet more complex if the cloth is animated. As the cloth deforms over time, it would have to be laboriously remodeled with each frame. Using one of the deformer tools we saw in section 4.9 would help, but would not permit the subtlety of folding and creasing characteristic of cloth. Moreover, as the cloth animated, it would almost certainly pass through itself.

The solution to these problems is **cloth dynamics**, which employs the capabilities of motion dynamics (section 7.6) to simulate the draping, folding, and movement of cloth. In a dynamic cloth model simulation, the cloth reacts to gravity, momentum, and other forces, and collides with obstacles. A cloth defined in this way is a type of soft-body (section 7.7.), and as such has an internal spring structure that causes it to retain its form. This prevents the cloth from stretching unrealistically as it deforms.

The process for creating a dynamic cloth model is illustrated in Figure 7-81. First, you define a set of **co-planar curves**—that is, curves all lying in a flat plane. These define the perimeter of a flat surface. With a menu selection, you instruct the software to create a polygonal cloth object from that flat surface. You next define any obstacles the cloth is likely to collide with, making sure the cloth hovers just above the obstacle object. In Figure 7-81a, we see the tablecloth hovering just above the table.

The next step is to **drape** the cloth over the obstacle. To do this, you run a brief simulation in which the cloth drops under the force of gravity and collides with its obstacle object (Figure 7-81b). As it does so, it deforms. Notice in our illustration how, as the cloth drops, the deformation retains the size

Figure 7-81. To give a dynamics cloth model form, you drape it over an obstacle object.

(a)   (b)   (c)   (d)

and structure of the original square cloth. This is because of the internal spring structure that is part of the cloth definition. Finally, when the cloth has draped sufficiently over the obstacle, the simulation is finished, and your cloth is modeled (Figure 7-81d).

Once the cloth is draped, any movement of the obstacle object will cause the cloth to deform. When the table moves in Figure 7-82, it pulls the cloth with it. All the forces operative in the real world—the acceleration of the table, the static friction of the cloth, the flexibility of the cloth, inertia, momentum—function here as well, causing the tablecloth in our illustration to deform a great deal as the table scoots to the right.

When creating a cloth simulation, there are a great many parameters controlling how the cloth behaves. The **polygon resolution** in the cloth object controls how precisely the surface can deform: a cloth with fewer polygons can only approximate the smooth deformation we normally associate with cloth; a cloth with a great many polygons provides a much more accurate modeling of the cloth. As always, larger quantities of data result in slower calculations.

Another important parameter is the cloth's **flexibility**, or **softness**. This permits you to capture the different behaviors of various textiles—for example, the difference between denim and silk.

The collection of parameters defining the characteristics of the cloth are often combined into a **cloth definition**, which can be stored in a **library** and reused for other cloth models. For example, a denim cloth definition, with all the appropriate parameters predefined, can be retrieved from the library and applied to a character's trousers.

Another set of parameters controls the precision of the simulation calculations. One of these is the **minimum collision offset**. Since CG surfaces do not have true thickness, simulated cloth must be kept a slight distance above the surface of its obstacle, to prevent the cloth from intersecting with the obstacle. The minimum collision offset parameter allows you to define this minimum allowable distance between the cloth and its obstacle.

As with all motion dynamics, cloth simulation calculations are performed at a certain **time-step** frequency, typically many times per frame. The more frequently they are performed, the more accurately they reflect the continuous nature of time in the real world. A smaller time step results in a greater number of calculations per frame and more accurate simulations, but at the cost of slower calculations.

As we saw in sections 7.6 and 7.7, the time step becomes especially important for objects that are moving quickly. If the time step is too large, an obstacle might pass through its cloth in the interval between one calculation and the next. This happens in Figure 7-83b. By forcing the software to do its calculations at smaller time increments, this problem can be avoided, as illustrated in Figure 7-83c.

(a)

(b)

Figure 7-82. If a cloth's obstacle object moves, the cloth moves with it, subject to all the forces of motion dynamics.

(a)

(b)

(c)

Figure 7-83. If the time step is too large, an obstacle can pass through its cloth.

Figure 7-84. For a complex and very fast moving cloth, the time step interval may have to be quite small to avoid distortions and self-penetrations of the cloth.

We see another example of this in Figure 7-84. In (a), the kerchief is stationary. In (b), the top of the kerchief has moved downward very quickly, causing the cloth to deform a great deal and very abruptly. In (c), the kerchief abruptly moves up again, causing another radical deformation of the cloth. With the software's default time-step setting, the kerchief stretched and passed through itself very noticeably. To achieve an accurate simulation, the number of calculations per frame had to be increased substantially.

Even with a small time step, however, it remains possible for an obstacle to penetrate a cloth in some circumstances. If it does so, the simulation software can become confused and attempt to solve the same penetration calculation forever. To avoid this, a **maximum collision depth** parameter is usually defined. This tells the software that, if a cloth penetrates an obstacle by more than the amount specified, the software should stop trying to solve those penetration calculations and allow the cloth to remain intersected with the obstacle.

Another important parameter is **self-collision**. Since collision calculations are expensive for any simulation software, you want to minimize them. If you know that your cloth will not collide with itself, this parameter can be turned off. An example would be a curtain very slightly blowing in a breeze. For a curtain flapping in a strong breeze, however, it would be important to turn self-collision on, so that different portions of the curtain do not pass through each other.

One of the common applications of cloth dynamics is **clothing** for animated characters. The techniques for modeling clothing mimic those used in the real world of garment manufacture, and such a cloth object is in fact frequently referred to as a **garment**. As with any cloth, you begin by drawing the set of co-planar curves defining the perimeter of a surface. Since clothing usually needs to enclose a volume, you normally draw several sets of curves in different planes. In Figure 7-85a we see the first set of curves for a shirt. In (b) these curves have been copied to a plane farther back in space. You then instruct the software to create a planar surface for each set of curves. Once these surfaces have been created, you attach them at the appropriate edges. The terminology here is again derived from real-world garment manufacturing, with the surfaces being **stitched** together at their **seams**.

Figure 7-85. To model a cloth garment, you draw co-planar curves and attach them at the appropriate seams.

(a)   (b)   (c)

(a)   (b)

Figure 7-86. As with any cloth, a garment is first draped onto its obstacle object, here the character model. When the obstacle moves, the garment deforms.

Once created, the garment is draped over the character. This process is identical to what we saw in the tablecloth example at the beginning of this section. The cloth garment is modeled so that it hovers just above the character model, which is defined as an obstacle. Running a simulation then causes the cloth to drape over its obstacle character, as in Figure 7-86a. The character can then be animated using any of the standard character animation techniques. As the obstacle character moves, the cloth garment moves with it. In Figure 7-86b the shirtsleeves drop down with the arms of the character, and the shirtwaist creases as the character bends forward.

When creating a cloth garment, is usually helpful to position your model in a **drape pose** with arms and legs spread, as in Figure 7-87a. This allows you to draw the garment curves in a way that produces a fully extended cloth garment. Once again, this echoes real-world garment manufacturing in which flat patterns of cloth are assembled into the final garment. After draping the garment over the character model, you then position the character in the first pose of the animation (Figure 7-87b). With the cloth draped over the character in this way, you define this to be the **initial cloth state**, the configuration the cloth will have at the start of the animation. This step permits the software to avoid recalculating the animation of the cloth as it

(a)   (b)

Figure 7-87. In working with cloth for characters, you first define a drape pose. You then define an initial pose for the first frame of the animation. (Courtesy, Yi-sul Yoon.)

Figure 7-88. The points of a cloth garment can be position-constrained to points on the surface of the obstacle.

Figure 7-89. A cloth can be constrained to an invisible null node. (Hand model, © Kaori Watanabe, 2001.)

Figure 7-90. Cloth dynamics produces a literal realism, sometimes including unwanted, if logical, errors. (Korean dancer, courtesy, Yi-sul Yoon.)

moves from drape pose to the character's starting pose each time you run the animation.

Colorplate 7 shows this same dancer figure in a sequence of frames from an animation. The movements of the dancer were animated very naturalistically and beautifully, using standard inverse kinematics and keyframing to replicate a traditional Korean dance. As the dancer moves, the movements of her dress are calculated with cloth dynamics, without which the complex and subtle movements of the cloth would be virtually impossible.

We saw in section 7.3 that it is possible to force one object to follow the position of another by means of a **constraint**. The same is true of cloth. One situation in which this might be necessary is when gravity would otherwise cause a garment to slide off its obstacle character. In Figure 7-88, the points around the top row of the skirt geometry have been constrained to points on the mannequin, forcing the skirt to stay attached to the mannequin's waist.

Another situation in which a constraint can be useful occurs when you want to attach a cloth to a moving nonobstacle object. In Figure 7-89, the hand model is the parent of an invisible null node at the tip of its forefinger. As the hand moves about, therefore, this null node moves with it. At the same time, the points at the top of the cloth kerchief are constrained to this null node. The result is that, as the hand moves about, the cloth follows it, attached to its fingertip.

Cloth dynamics can be a great deal of fun to work with, and can produce stunning animations. You should be aware, however, that cloth calculations can be very time-consuming. As a cloth deforms, calculations—including collisions, self-collisions, and the effects of forces—must be performed for each of the perhaps hundreds of points defining the surface. As a result, cloth simulations can take a very long time. To alleviate this problem, most cloth packages provide the same **caching** capability we introduced in section 7.6, allowing you to store the results of your simulation calculations either in RAM or on your hard drive. This allows you to view the simulated animation repeatedly without having to recalculate it each time you play it.

You should also be aware that, as with all motion dynamics, cloth simulations yield a **literal realism**. This may or may not be appropriate for the look of your animation. Many animations will be more successful with animated clothing that is "eye-balled" by the animator, rather than simulated. If realism is desired, however, you should be aware that the literality of the simulations may yield unintended, and sometimes quite undesirable, results. In Figure 7-90, the author mistakenly set parameters causing the dancer's left hand to catch on and lift her dress, resulting in a very inelegant and unintended exposure of flesh. The realism of cloth dynamics is part of its appeal, but also can require extensive fine-tuning.

7.10 Motion Capture

Animation typically involves making your characters—whether human, mechanical, vegetable, or animal—behave similarly to the way they behave in the real world. The animation may be deliberately exaggerated or modified to achieve specific effects, but the model for the motion is the real-world behavior of real-world objects and creatures.

ROTOSCOPING

In those cases where you may want to mimic these motions extremely accurately, you can replicate them using one of several physically accurate techniques, which collectively are called **motion capture**. The oldest of these, dating from the days of hand-drawn cel animation, is **rotoscoping**. In its cel-animation implementation, rotoscoping consists of taking photographs of real-world motions and using these photographs as templates on top of which the hand-drawn animation frames are traced. Using a series of such photographs, the animator can trace a corresponding series of keyframe drawings.

Figure 7-91. In rotoscoping, you align your computer model to the figures in a sequence of real-world images. (Photographs from *The Human Figure in Motion* by Eadweard Muybridge, New York: Dover, 1955.)

Applied to 3D computer animation, rotoscoping still involves a series of real-world images, now produced either as photographic still images or as a videotaped sequence. In the latter case, the video sequence is frequently digitized frame-by-frame to produce the necessary still images. These are read into the 3D computer animation program and displayed as background pictures on your computer screen. Using these as templates, you position your three-dimensional model to correspond to the position of the character in the background image (Figure 7-91). Notice how lifelike the model looks, even though it is composed solely of rectangular boxes. Even greater precision can be achieved if photographs or video are shot of the real-world subject from several angles. By carefully aligning your computer model with the pictures in each of several windows—Front, Left, Top, etc.—you can accurately reproduce a fully three-dimensional motion.

Using video as your rotoscoping source has the advantage that it also automatically records the timing of your motion. For example, if your video is the standard NTSC video used in the United States (see section 6.11) every thirty frames of video represents one second of motion. Photography can have the same timing accuracy if special steps are taken to shoot at precise and regular time intervals.

CHANNEL ANIMATION

Computer technology provides even more accurate and thorough motion capture techniques than rotoscoping, however. In its fullest implementation, this approach is called full motion capture, discussed later in this section. In its simpler implementations, it is frequently known as **channel animation**. The principles and concepts underlying channel animation also apply to full motion capture, and so we begin here with a discussion of those as applied to channel animation.

Channel animation introduces a radically different and extremely powerful way of defining an animation sequence. With this technique, you generate an animation sequence in real time, without keyframes, by manipulating one or more input devices.

For example, imagine that you want to make a character nod its head repeatedly at irregular intervals, as if the character were listening to a conversation and saying, "Yes. Yes. I understand. Um-hum. Yes." You could do this with keyframing by rotating the character's head around the appropriate axis—say, the X axis. You also have seen, however, that creating this sort of animation with keyframing requires a substantial amount of trial and error in order to get the details of the movement just right. How quickly should the head move with each nod? How far should the head move? How much time is there between each nod? And so on.

If the system you are working with offers channel animation, however,

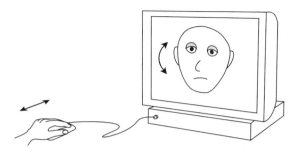

Figure 7-92. Channel animation allows you to create and save animation in real time by manipulating an input device.

you can produce this same animation very easily and quickly and with very precise control. First, you define a linkage between the X rotation of the character's head and the mouse device. (You will see specifically how this is done in a moment.) Once you have defined this link, any movement of the mouse causes an immediate and equivalent rotation of the character's head. For example, if the mouse moves up a lot, the head will rotate up a lot. If the mouse moves quickly, the head moves quickly. And so on. With the linkage defined, you then create the actual animation sequence (Figure 7-92).

Suppose the animation is going to be ten seconds long. The system shows a countdown to the start of the animation sequence, and then, for the ten seconds of the running length, the linkage you defined becomes active, and you move the mouse up and down to control the nodding of the character. At the end of the ten seconds, the animation is complete. Whatever head nodding you produced by moving the mouse has been saved and has become the definition of the animation. In other words, you now have a head-nod animation that can be played back and viewed just like any other animation. If you don't like the result, you can either edit the parameter curves of this new animation or completely regenerate the sequence by repeating the channeling process—that is, start a new countdown, move the mouse for ten seconds, and stop.

The link you describe between the input device (in this example, the mouse) and the animation parameter (*rotation x* of the head) is called a **channel**. The first step in making a channel animation is to define any channels you will use. In order to define a channel, you specify (usually through a series of menu selections) several pieces of information. First, you tell the system which input device you will use for this channel. Sometimes you do this indirectly by indicating the name of the **device driver**, which is a program that manages the input and output of a device. The driver for a mouse device, for example, is referred to as the mouse driver.

Next, you specify which information from that device you will use. A mouse device, for example, produces a constant stream of two pieces of information: location of the mouse in X and location of the mouse in Y. Consequently, in the head-nod example, you have to indicate whether you want to use the X or the Y readings—that is, the horizontal or the vertical movement—from the mouse.

Once you have specified the device and the device information, you must indicate which transformation parameter of which object this incoming information will be channeled to. In the head-nod example, which involves a single channel, you channel the incoming information (vertical movement) from the mouse to the *rotation x* parameter of the head.

It is possible to define and use more than one channel for a single animation, but the number of channels you can have at any one time is limited by the input devices you use. The number of values a device provides is referred to as the **degrees of freedom** of the device. A mouse device, as mentioned above, generates two numerical pieces of information: the horizontal, or X, location of the mouse, and the vertical, or Y, location of the mouse. These two values usually are called *mouse_x* and *mouse_y*. You can use either one or both of these two mouse parameters in a channel. In the example used above, the *mouse_y* parameter made the head of a character nod. If you want that character also to shake its head back and forth sometimes as if saying "no," you can define a second channel using the *mouse_x* parameter. This linkage makes it possible for you to create both nods and shakes of the head in one pass, by moving the mouse either vertically (nod) or horizontally (shake).

Normally, in order to produce meaningful numbers for a given transformation parameter, you must **scale** the values that will be coming in from the input device. For example, many mouse devices produce numbers ranging from zero to one. If you use these numbers directly, as is, for the *rotation x* of the character's head, the head rotates anywhere from zero degrees around X to a maximum of one degree around the X axis. In other words, the movement of the head is almost imperceptible. In order to correct this, you specify in the channel definition that the incoming *mouse_y* values be scaled by a factor of, say, forty. Thus, the zero-to-one range of *mouse_y* values that the mouse device produces is changed by this scaling into a more useful zero-to-forty range of rotation values.

Depending on your animation, you may also have to **offset** the values coming out of your input device. In the example just given, the original values output by the mouse range from zero to one. When multiplied by a scale factor of forty, they range from zero to forty, which translates into a motion that ranges from looking straight ahead (*rotation x* equals zero) to looking down a bit (*rotation x* equals forty). But a head nod should also involve a slight rotation of the head upwards—that is, negatively—before its downward rotation. If you specify a negative offset to the values coming out of the mouse device, you can solve this problem. An offset of negative ten, for example, subtracts ten from any value coming out of the mouse. A zero-to-forty range of numbers therefore becomes a negative ten-to-thirty range of numbers. With

Device	Parameter	Scale	Offset
mouse_x	Head.RZ	60	−30
mouse_y	Head.RX	40	−10

Figure 7-93. Each value from the input device is associated with one parameter of the model, scaling and offsetting the value as necessary.

these numbers, you can achieve a slight upward (negative) rotation of the head before it rotates downward (positively) a maximum of thirty degrees.

All the information defining an animation channel is usually specified through a menu structure. Figure 7-93 shows how this might look for a head-nod and head-shake channel animation as described above. In addition to a rotation around X to make the head nod up and down, you have also defined a rotation around Z to make it shake left and right, scaling the rotation by sixty and offsetting it by thirty so that its values range from negative thirty to thirty.

Once you have defined your channel setup, you do the channel animation, moving your input device to create animation in real-time. As soon as you have done so, a complete parameter curve exists for each specified transformation parameter. At this point, the parameter curve is like any other parameter curve and can be edited with any of the standard parameter-curve editing techniques (see section 4.4).

The parameter curve written by the channel animation is unusual, however, in one very important respect—it has no interpolated values. Every frame is a key frame. Such a curve is often called a **raw** parameter curve to indicate that there has been no processing or interpolation of the data (Figure 7-94). Here each keyframe is indicated by a dot on the curve. Notice that even in those sections of the curve where there is no change—that is, where the curve is flat—there is still a keyframe at every frame. This over abundance of data can be a problem, and most software systems allow you to **thin** the raw curve, converting it into a spline curve which approximates it. (Thinning is discussed in more detail in section 5.3).

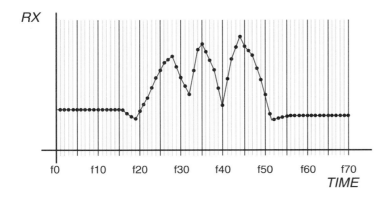

Figure 7-94. The parameter curves produced by channel animation are raw, without interpolated values.

In principle, you can use any device that produces a stream of numbers in digital format as your input device for channel information. The mouse is probably the most common input device on animation workstations, but other devices include joysticks, tablets, and 3D digitizers. If an **audio** device produces digital output, you can channel that output to the animation in the same way that you channel the output of a mouse. You can make a character jump up and down according to the volume of an audio stream, for example.

Even with just a single mouse device, with only two input channels, it is still possible to produce very complex channel animations involving a large number of channels. You do this by creating several channel animations, in sequence, one after another, and adding each one to the previous ones. For example, suppose you want to create that nod-shake-blink-snuffle animation, but you have only one ordinary mouse with two ordinary degrees of freedom. You first define two channels: *mouse_y* = *rotation x* of head (nod), and *mouse_x* = *rotation y* of head (shake). You then create the nod-shake animation sequence using these channels. When you have produced a satisfactory nodding and shaking animation, you delete the channel definitions you have been using and define two new ones. Now you channel *mouse_x* to *rotation x* of the eyelids (blink), and *mouse_y* to *scale y* of the nose (snuffle), then create a second animation of the blinking eyes and the snuffling nose. The nodding and shaking of the head still exist and are not overwritten, because you are creating parameter curves for a different pair of transformation parameters.

When used on an inverse kinematic model, channel animation can be particularly effective. If you have a model of the human body, for example, modeled as a collection of inverse kinematic skeletons (as described in section 4.7), you can define two channels to control the X and Y locations of the effector at the end of one arm. Since the effector controls the positions and angles of all the joints in the arm, moving the effector under channel control moves the entire arm in real time.

A great advantage of channel animation over standard keyframing, in fact, is the immediacy of channel animation. You look at the screen, move the input device, and generate animation "on the fly," in real time. There is a sense, therefore, in which channel animation is more like puppetry than like traditional frame-by-frame animation. Unlike puppetry, however, channel animation allows you to save, repeat, and even edit the actions you create. If the animation is perfect except for one small detail, you can alter the parameter curves written by the channeling to fine-tune the result.

FULL MOTION CAPTURE

The rotoscoping and channel animation techniques discussed so far are methods of capturing motion, but the term "motion capture" usually refers to a particular and very powerful extension of channel animation, **full motion**

Figure 7-95. The actor on the stage has been wired with a motion-capture system. Input from each sensor is channeled into the animation system to control the movement of a computer-generated character. (Courtesy R/Greenberg Associates, Inc. Created by R/Greenberg Associates, MTV, and SoftImage; directed by David Lane of Savoy Commercials for MTV's *Enough Is Enough* campaign.)

capture. In channel animation, a single input device produces real-time data to control a few parameters of a model. In **motion capture**, a collection of many input devices, often called **sensors**, is used to simultaneously control a large number of parameters on a model.

Each input device in a motion-capture system has three degrees of freedom, producing either three-dimensional translation data or three-dimensional rotation data. These devices are attached to a **human actor** (Figure 7-95) and the output from them is channeled to the joints of a computer model, or **virtual actor**. As the human actor moves around, the attached sensors send data to the computer model, controlling its movements and generating, in real time, parameter curves for the entire animation. In other words, at the end of a motion-capture session, the computer model of the character will have the exact same motions that the human actor just performed. If the animation doesn't look right when played back, the actor can repeat the scene, in just the same way that an actor on a movie set would do another "take."

In practice, of course, motion-capture systems are much more complex than the brief description here suggests. All the issues that must be addressed for a single input device in channel animation must be addressed for each of the many input devices of motion capture: each device's output values must be linked to a specific parameter of the model, each value must be scaled and offset, and each resulting parameter curve must be thinned. In addition, anomalies, or **noise**, in the stream of input data coming from each device can cause the quality of the captured data to deteriorate, producing erratic and jerky motions in the virtual actor model. Sophisticated motion-capture software provides procedures for eliminating this noise.

Two broad approaches to motion capture are commonly used. The first approach employs a set of **magnetic devices** attached to the body of the human actor. Each device emits a magnetic pulse. When the actor moves within a field of sensors, each magnetic device—and by implication, the part of the actor to which it is attached—can be located. The second approach is **optical** and uses reflective markers, rather than magnetic devices, on the body of the actor. The location of each marker as the actor moves about is determined by a network of cameras that record the light bouncing off the reflectors.

Each of these techniques has advantages and disadvantages. The magnetic approach requires that a series of cables, almost like umbilical cords, be attached to the actor. The optical approach requires no cables, and so permits greater freedom of movement for the actor. Depending on the posture of the actor, however, some of the reflective markers may be hidden from the view of some of the recording cameras, and this blockage can create problems in the acquisition of the original data. In contrast to this, magnetic sensors, no matter what the posture of the actor, continue to emit pulses and to produce recordable data.

Both approaches require that the actor move within a confined arena, because the recording devices, whether magnetic or optical, are set up in a network and have a limited range. This consideration need not be overly constricting, though, since the recordable arena for many systems can be as broad as five or six meters square.

The specific placement of the 3D sensors on the human actor is important. Typically, they are placed at the main joints—elbows, knees, ankles, shoulders, etc. In addition, several are also usually placed at other locations, such as the chest, abdomen, forehead, and chin, to capture the orientation of those parts of the body (Figure 7-96). The more sensors used, the more accurate the captured data, and the more detailed the motion can be. More sensors, however, also produce more data, which may necessitate very powerful computers.

The structure of the model of the virtual actor is also important and must correspond to the structure of the human actor. This usually requires either a detailed hierarchical model or a detailed inverse kinematic model. More than one model may receive the captured motion data, however. The same data generated by a single motion-capture session can be applied to several different models; the data are scaled and offset as necessary to correspond to the proportions of each model.

Figure 7-96. Motion-capture sensors must be placed at specific locations on the human actor. (Photograph from *The Human Figure in Motion* by Eadweard Muybridge, New York: Dover, 1955.)

In any motion-capture situation, the number of sensors necessarily limits which motions can be recorded. With the configuration of sensors in Figure 7-96, for example, the motion of the actor's individual fingers will not be recorded, since there are no input devices there; there is only a single device at the end of each middle finger to give the overall orientation of the hand.

The motions of the fingers, in this situation, would have to be animated "by hand," using keyframing or one of the other techniques discussed in this chapter and Chapter 4.

A similar issue arises with the facial expressions of the actor in Figure 7-96. Only the general orientation of the head will be recorded by the input devices as they are set up here. For specialized animation situations like **human facial animation** (section 7.14), more detailed configurations of motion sensors can be used to capture the expressions of the human face. Placing a collection of sensors around the lips and mouth, for example, captures the movements of those parts of the body (Figure 7-97). Channeling the data from these sensors to points or controllers on a flexible surface model would permit you to animate a virtual "speaker." For this sort of application, it is also common to record and store a large number of individual facial expressions, associating each with a particular spoken sound and saving each as a pose in a library. As discussed in more detail in section 7.14, by interpolating between these key facial expressions, you can animate a naturalistically speaking computer "talking head." For example, selecting the poses for the "bay" sound and then the "bee" sound would yield a character saying "Baby!"

Figure 7-97. An array of sensors can be placed on a speaker's face to record human facial expressions and speech movements.

Any motion-capture system produces large quantities of data. Remember that in a keyframe-based system, only selected frames are defined as keyframes. The rest of the frames are calculated through an interpolation process, which produces data economically. With motion capture, as with channeling, however, *every* frame is a keyframe. There is no interpolation. All of the animation data is raw data. Motion-capture systems produce data from numerous channels simultaneously and consequently can produce huge quantities of data, which only sophisticated systems can handle.

The argument for motion capture, of course, is that it is precisely the lack of interpolated data that makes it so striking. When humans move, their limbs and joints almost constantly change position in very irregular and subtle ways, and the generalization of movement that results from an interpolated-motion curve often does not convey the idiosyncratic "human-ness" of that movement.

On the other hand, it is possible to overuse motion-capture capabilities and to make an animated character too realistic. If an animated character moves *exactly* like a real human, and especially if that character is modeled and rendered very realistically, it may lose all visual and aesthetic interest. Character animation, like any art form, is interesting to the viewer because it is an *interpretation* of the way we behave. If an animation replicates our behavior too exactly, it may lose the appeal of animation and become a dry simulation. Sometimes, a literal simulation is precisely what you want—for example, if you are producing a crash or crime simulation, or attempting to substitute a virtual CG actor seamlessly into a live-action film. Frequently, however, it is precisely the interpretive eye of the animator that interests us.

Whether through a single input device such as a mouse or through a complex set of motion-detecting sensors, channel animation and motion capture effectively allow you to use your own body to perform the action of an animation. Instead of creating keyframes visually, you define a physical "dance," even if this dance is limited to the movements of one hand on a mouse device. The physicality of your body itself becomes a tool. Many talented animators think this way anyhow. If you ask an animator to show you the timing or movement of some portion of an animation, he or she may spontaneously mime it for you. "It goes like this," the animator will say, and then move his or her hands or arms to show you the rhythm and shape of the motions. Channel animation and motion capture allow you to take advantage of this kind of intuitive physical representation of action and timing.

7.11 Camera-Motion Matching

When working with animation, it is not uncommon to combine live-action footage with your computer-generated scenes and animation. This is especially so in big-budget feature films, in which computer-generated effects have become an integral part of many films. Some rendering aspects of this approach were discussed in section 6.7.

It is also important when combining live-action and animation to take into consideration the movement of your camera. If the camera is moving in your live-footage, your virtual CG camera must move exactly the same way in order for your models to match up with background imagery from frame to frame. The process of calculating the appropriate camera motion is called **camera-motion matching**, or sometimes **camera-motion tracking**.

The first step in this process is to shoot or acquire your **live-action footage**. Figure 7-98 shows three representative frames from a live-video shoot of a street scene. In it, the camera dollies in and rotates left as it moves across the intersection and down the side street. As we discuss the principles of camera-motion matching in this section, you will see that it is important to

Figure 7-98. Camera-motion matching begins with live footage shot with a moving camera.

understand the whole camera-motion matching process before shooting your footage, so it can be shot (or chosen, if you are not shooting it yourself) to maximize the accuracy of the motion-matching calculations later.

Motion-matching software tracks specific points in the two-dimensional frames of your live footage as these points move from frame to frame as a result of camera motion. Extrapolating from these tracked two-dimensional points, the software calculates the animation of a virtual camera through the three-dimensional virtual space of your scene.

The information necessary for these calculations includes certain **camera parameters** of your video or film equipment—for example, whether you used an NTSC video camera, a 16mm camera, or a 35mm film camera. This information is critical because it influences the way your camera sees the space in front of it, and consequently the appearance of each frame.

The points the camera tracks are called **tracking points** and are associated with specific objects in the live-action scene. For example, a tracking point might be defined at the corner of a parked van. As the camera moves through the scene, the van and its tracking point will appear in different locations of the frame, depending on whether the camera has moved in closer, rotated to the left, and so on. Figure 7-99 shows one of our street-scene frames with four tracking points indicated. By tracking a collection of such points, the software can extrapolate from the two-dimensional data of the frames to three-dimensional camera-motion data.

Not all points in a frame can be successfully tracked, however. There are several criteria to keep in mind as you select tracking points. Some points may pass behind other objects in the scene and therefore be **occluded**, or hidden, for part of the sequence. To the extent possible, you should choose points that are visible at all times throughout the entire sequence. Frequently, of course, not all points will be visible at all times. Other objects may occlude them, or they may pass **out of frame** during certain portions of the sequence. In our example, the point at the top corner of the white van is not visible in

Figure 7-99. It is important to carefully define tracking points for the software to follow from frame to frame. The points must satisfy several strict criteria if the software is to succeed in tracking them.

the first frame of the sequence. Selecting points that remain visible in as many frames as possible improves the chances of accurate motion-matching calculations.

You should also choose tracking points representing **stationary objects**—for example, a wall, or a parked car—rather than a moving object. If the object associated with a tracking point is stationary, the software can assume that any movement of that point in the two-dimensional space of the frame is caused by camera movement, rather than by movement of the object itself.

Similarly, the **shape constancy** of the object is important. An object whose shape is changing—for example, a flag rippling in the wind—presents the same problems to the software as a moving object.

The **distance** of your tracking points from the camera is also significant. Selecting a variety of points at a variety of distances from the camera—for example, close-up, middle distance, and far away—facilitates the motion-matching calculations. In some cases, objects at an extreme distance, such as a cloud or distant mountaintop, can be especially helpful.

The mathematics of the motion-matching calculations involves a process called **convergence**. There is always more than one possible camera movement that could produce the pattern of moving points tracked by the software. Consequently, the software evaluates the data, and makes several guesses of possible camera movements. It then re-evaluates the data, and refines its guesses. After several passes of increasing refinement, it converges on the best guess.

An implication of this process is that the more points the software tracks, the more accurate its guesses will be. Consequently, it is important that you define a number of tracking points. Many scenes require between ten and twenty tracking points for successful motion-matching calculations.

In attempting to track each point from frame to frame, the software performs **image-analysis** calculations. Within a small rectangular area around each defined point, the software searches for contrast in the pixel values. This means that a point will be most successfully tracked if it corresponds to an area of **high contrast**—for example, the corner of a light object against a dark background. Areas of insufficient contrast will cause the tracking calculations to fail at many of the frames. Notice that in Figure 7-99, all of the tracking points have been placed at points of significant pixel contrast—the corner of the van, the intersection of the white lines painted on the street, and so on.

Another important set of input data that can help the motion-tracking software is **real-world measurements** from the live-footage site. These are sometimes called **site data** or **survey data**. In our example footage, site measurements might be taken for the length of the car parked at the corner, or the height of one of the building's windows. While not critical, this information can significantly help the software track points more accurately.

Once you have input camera parameters, tracking points, and site data, the motion-matching software calculates the motion of your camera corresponding to the motion of the real-world camera. No matter how carefully you have chosen your tracking points, however, it is unlikely that all of them will be tracked successfully for the entire sequence. One point might be occluded for a certain range of frames, another might lose contrast in the tracking point area. This is why numerous tracking points are defined. As long as several points are successfully tracked at each frame, the camera motion can be calculated.

With the motion of your camera calculated, you next insert your computer-generated **stationary models** into your scene, displaying the live-footage imagery in the background as you do. For example, we might insert a CG model of the white van in our scene, aligning it with the live-footage image of the same van. If the calculated camera motion is accurate, your CG models should remain aligned with their real-world counterparts throughout the sequence. If they do not, you will need to provide more precise input data to the software, and repeat the calculations.

The process of making models that fit accurately into your scene is greatly simplified if you use the same **real-world site data** you collected to assist the tracking calculations. In our example, the measurements we took for the length of a car could also be used to model an accurately proportioned car. This can then be scaled as necessary to fit into the scene. Once correctly positioned, your models will remain in alignment throughout the scene.

With the camera motion calculated and your stationary models inserted, you are now ready to add your animated CG models. The renderings of your computer-generated models can be composited with the live action footage using any of the compositing techniques discussed in section 8.2. Figure 7-100 shows an animated character moving through the street scene we have been discussing.

Figure 7-100. Once the software has calculated the motion of your virtual camera, you insert your CG models. Since the motion of the virtual camera now matches that of the live-action camera, CG models and real-world models align throughout the animation.

The accuracy of motion-matching techniques depends very much on the data you input to the system. Even with accurate data, however, there are some camera operations that this approach can not successfully handle. Changing the zoom of your camera over time is one of these. Nonetheless, camera-motion matching is an extremely powerful technique that greatly extends your ability to combine live-action and animated footage.

7.12 Character Rigging: Movement Controls

Character animation is one of the most popular forms of animation, and plays a central role in animation history. In Chapters 2 and 5, we discussed a variety of techniques that might be used to model the geometry of your character. In Chapter 4, we introduced some of the techniques that can be used to animate a model. In this section and the next, we discuss in more detail techniques specifically designed for animating a character model.

Once the geometry for a character has been modeled, the next step is **character rigging**, sometimes simply called **rigging**, and consists of defining the controls that will be used to move and then deform the geometry of the character.

The complexity of a character's rigging depends on two factors—first, the complexity of the model, and second, the complexity of its behavior. A model of a toy robot will be fairly easy to rig, since it has relatively few moving parts and all of them move in a rigid fashion. A model of a science-fiction movie robot will have many more moving parts, and its rigging will be correspondingly more complex. A realistic human figure is more complex yet, since, in addition to many moving parts, all of its parts must deform in specific ways as they move.

The complexity of rigging can be such that in large production companies, character rigging is frequently a full-time job, with specialists called **riggers** devoting all of their time to this task.

Rigging a character model can involve a wide range of techniques, as we are about to see, with the choice of techniques depending on what your character will need to do. Before beginning, therefore, it is important to think about exactly which motions your character will need to make, as well as how his geometry will need to deform as he moves. For example, the rigging of a character whose only action will be to turn his head and scratch his nose, will be radically less complex and will involve fewer techniques than that of a character who will need to run, jump, somersault, and sword fight.

Figure 7-101. The first step in character rigging is usually to define an inverse kinematic skeleton for your model. (Character model, courtesy, Helen J. Koo.)

Rigging usually consists of two stages—defining how the character moves, and defining how it deforms. In this section, we will examine **movement controls**.

The first step in rigging a character model is usually to develop an **inverse kinematic skeleton** for it. The basic concepts of this technique were introduced in section 4.7. In developing your skeleton, the model is first posed in such a way that the skeleton can be easily drawn within it. This is called the **initial pose** and is usually with the arms extended straight out to the sides. We see an example of this is Figure 7-101. Positioning the arms in this way allows you the greatest flexibility in the eventual range of arm motion. However, it can also sometimes create deformation problems in the area of the shoulders, as we will see in section 7.13. Consequently, if you know in advance that your character will have only a very restricted range of arm movement—for example, the character will simply walk, with its arms swinging at its sides—it may be easier to create an initial pose in which the arms begin in their natural resting position at the character's side.

The techniques for drawing the IK skeleton vary from one software package to another, but they all involve careful placement of the **joints** of the skeleton. Notice in Figure 7-101 that the spine joints have been defined with a slightly rounded curvature, to correspond to the rounded back of the old woman's figure. The spine of a young woman's figure would have a very different curvature. Also in our example, the joints for the head and neck are drawn to capture the forward thrust of the character's head and neck, again, consistent with the age of the character.

After defining the skeleton, you next decide what controls you will use to move that skeleton into different poses. We saw a number of these in section 4.7. The most common technique is to define an **end effector**, also called an **IK handle** in some packages. Defining and then moving an effector at the ankle, for example, causes the knee and hip joints of the skeleton to rotate. We see this illustrated in Figure 7-102.

Another technique is to define an **IK spline** control, a curve drawn to correspond to the curvature of a section of the skeleton. Figure 7-102 shows a spline curve positioned next to the spine. Changing the curvature of the

forward kinematic rotation

IK spline control

IK effector

Figure 7-102. The movement of the IK skeleton can be controlled with a variety of techniques. (Character model, courtesy, Helen J. Koo.)

Figure 7-103. For actions that occur automatically, such as a toe-roll when walking, expressions are often the best technique. (Foot animation by William Sayer.)

curve by moving its CVs changes the configuration of the joints in that area of the IK skeleton.

Finally, there are some situations in which it is easiest to control a portion of a skeleton by directly rotating a joint with **forward kinematics** (see section 4.6). In Figure 7-102 we do this for the single joint in the head area that controls the tilt of the old woman's head.

Another pair of techniques that can be used to control the movement of a skeleton is **expressions** and **driven keys**. As we saw in section 7.5, expressions are a way of defining animation through a simplified programming language. The related technique of **driven keys** allows you to create expressions in a visually intuitive way. Both of these techniques are very commonly used as character movement controls, especially when one movement is a function of another.

A good example is the bending of the toe area as a walking foot touches or leaves the ground, as in Figure 7-103. Since this bending motion is caused automatically by the positioning of the foot at each step, it is possible to create an expression for it, rather than explicitly keyframing the toe-roll motion with each footstep. This allows the animator to concentrate on the walking or running motion of the character, without thinking about the toe roll at all.

A toe-roll expression is a good example of an expression requiring **conditional statements**. As a foot first touches the ground, the first point of contact is the heel, and the foot therefore pivots about the heel. A moment later in the footstep, as the foot starts to leave the ground, the pivot point switches to the ball of the foot. This shift of the pivot point from the heel to the ball can be encoded as a conditional statement in an expression.

A more complex example of expressions controlling a skeleton is **footstep-driven** animation, sometimes also called **bipedal** animation (Figure 7-104). This approach uses the position of the feet to automatically determine the overall position and posture of the character. In the real world, moving a person's foot changes his center of gravity, and he will automatically and intuitively adjust his stance to avoid falling over. For example, picking his foot up and placing it thirty inches in front of him, as in Figure 7-104b, will cause him to shift his body forward, centering himself relative to the new position of his two feet.

The foot-body relationship just described can be encoded in an expression, in which the translation of the whole figure is the average of the translation values of the two feet. If the character is moving along the X axis, an expression for his translation X would be:

$$\text{all.tx} = (\text{footLeft.tx} + \text{footRight.tx}) / 2$$

Similar expressions can control the translations in Y and Z.

(a)   (b)   (c)

Figure 7-104. Bipedal software incorporates complex sets of inter-related expressions, all dependent on the position of the character's feet. Animating the position of the feet automatically changes the posture of the character.

Rotations of the torso could be similarly controlled by the foot positions. If the left foot is lifted straight up in the air as in Figure 7-104c, not only will the center of gravity shift so that it is over the character's right foot, but the torso will rotate to the left to permit this motion. An expression could be written to capture this relationship. However, such an expression would have to be more complex than to merely associate the Y translation of the foot with the Y rotation of the torso. For example, if the foot is lifted up, but is also extended far enough outward in front of the character, the torso does not rotate. A useful set of bipedal expressions, in short, can become quite complex, and many software packages therefore offer a bipedal approach to character animation as a separate module. In this case, not only the torso, but also the swing of the arms and the rotations of the head might be related by expressions to the positions of the feet.

The bipedal approach just described is a sophisticated example of a **higher-level control**, a control which performs a complex combination of operations—for example, "make the character walk." Expressions and driven keys lend themselves to the creation of higher-level controls. Controls that perform very specific operations—"move the ankle," or "rotate the head"— are called **low-level controls**. An example of a **mid-level control** would be the closing or opening of a hand, as described in section 7.5. This movement involves the translation of an IK effector at the tip of each of the five fingers. To simplify the movement of all five fingers, you could create a driven key having a single parameter, *CloseHand*, that translates all five of the finger effectors simultaneously (Figure 7-37).

In Figure 7-105, we see the same character with which we started our discussion, now in an animated pose. In addition to some of the controls described above, this character's rigging also made use of **constraints** (section 7.3) in order to force the aluminum walker to remain attached to each of the old woman's hands. This allowed the animator to animate the movement of the walker by lifting the character's hands, as would happen in real life.

Figure 7-105. A final rigging can combine a great many techniques to allow you to control the movement of your character. You can also constrain objects to parts of your character model. (Courtesy, Helen Koo.)

7.13 Character Rigging: Deformation Controls

In section 7.12, we discussed a number of techniques for controlling the movement of a character model. Once all the controls for the movement of the skeleton have been defined and tested, the next step in character rigging is to define how the geometry of your character will deform as the character moves—that is, the **deformation controls**. Some of these were introduced in section 4.9. We discuss them in more detail here.

If a character consists solely of rigid parts—for example, a mechanical robot—there is no issue of deformation. As the inverse kinematic skeleton of the robot moves, each section of his robot body moves rigidly with the appropriate skeleton joint. This is usually accomplished by defining a hierarchy in which the parts of the robot are children of the corresponding inverse kinematic joints (see section 4.9).

In most character animation, however, the geometry of the character must deform as it moves. In a human figure, when a character bends its leg, the shape of the leg changes. When I lift my arm high in the air, the shoulder muscles bulge. If a fat character squats, the flesh of his belly bulges in certain directions. Defining and controlling all these deformations are part of the character-rigging process.

The most basic way to deform the geometry of a character is to define the geometry as an inverse kinematic **skin**, or **envelope**. This technique was introduced in section 4.9. Remember from that section that skinning involves associating each CV of the geometry with the various joints of the skeleton. The rotation of a joint causes its associated CVs to translate, which in turn causes the skinned geometry to deform.

There are two broad approaches to skinning geometry to a skeleton, each of which can be applied either to the entire skeleton of a character, or to portions of a skeleton. With the first approach, sometimes referred to as an **inclusive skin**, or a **smooth skin**, every CV of the geometry is affected by every joint of the skeleton. The amount of effect a given joint has on a given CV is a function of proximity, but every joint affects every CV at least somewhat. This results is a very smooth deformation of the surface CVs as the skeleton moves. If a character is wearing a voluminous dress, the dress might be attached as an inclusive skin to the leg joints of the skeleton, causing the dress to deform in a very smooth, uniform way as the character moves.

In the second approach to skinning, specific CVs of the geometry are controlled only by specific joints of the skeleton. This is in contrast to an inclusive skin, in which every CV is controlled by every joint. This second, more restricted assignment of CVs to joints is therefore sometimes referred to as a

(a)　　　　　　　　(b)　　　　　　　　(c)

Figure 7-106. Binding a model as a "skin" to your inverse kinematic skeleton can be done as a restrictive skin or an inclusive skin.

restrictive skin (it is also sometimes referred to as a "rigid" skin, which can be misleading, since the geometry does not deform rigidly). This approach is well suited to the limbs and extensions of a character—the arms, legs, and head. Since CVs in restrictive skinning are not controlled by all joints, the CVs of one portion of the model can deform without any influence from other parts of the model. For example, limbs can deform without any deformation of the torso.

We see an illustration of the difference between inclusive and restrictive skinning in Figure 7-106. In (a) we see a head model, with a skeleton inserted into it. In (b), the model has been skinned to the skeleton with a restrictive skin. When the jaw joint is rotated downwards, only the jaw portion of the model deforms. In Figure 7-106c, the same model has been skinned onto the skeleton with an inclusive skin. Now, when the jaw joint is rotated the same amount, the entire face deforms. For a more natural animation in which the character opens and closes his jaw, the restrictive skin of (b) would be preferable. For a more cartoonish animation, we might prefer the inclusive skin of (c).

With a restrictive skin, it may be important to adjust the assignment of the CVs to their respective joints. When geometry is initially skinned to a skeleton, a default assignment of CVs to joints is made based on the proximity of the CVs to the joints. It is assumed that CVs close to a joint should be controlled by that joint. Usually, this default assignment works very successfully. Occasionally, however, a CV in one area of the geometry is mistakenly assigned to a joint that happens to be nearby. We see this in Figure 7-107. The

(a)　　　　　　　　(b)　　　　　　　　(c)

Figure 7-107. When skinning, the surface points of your model are controlled by specific IK joints. If the default assignment of points to joints does not work, you can reassign the points to other joints.

CV on the lower rim of the character's right trouser leg has been mistakenly assigned to the lower joint of his left leg. This causes an unwelcome deformation of the right trouser leg when his left leg moves (Figure 7-107b). By reassigning that CV to the proper joint, the deformation is corrected (Figure 7-107c).

Whether a skin is restrictive or inclusive, each CV on a model's surface may be controlled by more than one joint, and it can become important to adjust the amount of control each joint exercises over each CV. In order to achieve a particular deformation of the surface, you may need a given joint to exercise most of the control over that CV, while a nearby joint exercises partial control. The parameter that controls these relative levels of control is usually referred to as the **CV weight**.

CV weight is represented either as a percentage or as a fraction of 1.0— 1.0 implies 100 percent control by that joint; 0.0 implies 0 percent control. Adjusting the weight of a given CV might involve assigning 70 percent of the control to one joint, 20 percent to another, and 10 percent to another. Figure 7-108 illustrates a situation in which this might be necessary. As the character's arm lifts upward, the shirt must deform in the underarm area. By adjusting the weights of the CVs in that area, you can control how much of the shirt deforms in reaction to the arm's motion. In Figure 7-108b, CV weights in the armpit area have been assigned to give more control to the joints of the upper arm, with the result that the armpit material deforms a lot when the arm is lifted. In Figure 7-108c, less control has been given to the upper arm joint, with the result that the shirt deforms less as the arm is lifted.

In some circumstances, the weighting of the CVs may need to change over time. For example, when the arm is raised a certain amount, the weight of this CV should be 40 percent, but when the arm is raised a great deal, the deformation may look best when that CV has a weight of 20 percent. In this situation, the weighting of CVs can be combined with the **driven key** technique (section 7.5). In the shirt example above, we could define a driven key

Figure 7-108. Adjusting the CV weight of your surface points allows you to control how the surface will deform in a particular area.

(a)　　　　　　　　　(b)　　　　　　　　　(c)

relationship between the height of the arm and the deformation of the CVs. Using a driven-key approach in this situation, rather than explicitly defining numerical CV weights, allows you to think more visually.

Human limbs frequently present special deformation challenges. When you bend your arm at the elbow, the inner side of the mid-arm area creases, while the outer side, the elbow, bulges in a very specific shape. There are several ways to replicate this. As we saw in section 4.9, some software packages offer **crease controls**. These adjust the amount of surface area affected by the joints, effectively changing the CV weights. By decreasing the amount of surface area, a crease can be created. At the same time, the crease control may allow you to push the surface outward above and below the crease.

A more powerful technique for achieving this effect is a special kind of **lattice**, frequently called a **flexor**. A flexor is a special-purpose lattice designed specifically for the limbs of character models, making use of many of the capabilities of a driven key. Unlike a normal lattice, but like an IK skeleton, a flexor has an initial pose. Like a driven key, the rotation of an IK joint is linked to the flexor, causing the flexor to deform whenever the joint is rotated. Exactly how the flexor deforms is determined by the animator, who positions the joints, then adjusts the settings of the flexor to get the desired deformation for that position.

In Figure 7-109a we see a leg model with an inverse kinematic skeleton inside it, and the geometry of the leg skinned to the skeleton. We also see a flexor, represented by the lattice-like box, around the knee. As the skeleton and leg bend at the knee (Figure 7-109b) the flexor adjusts to deform the knee area in a very natural way. When the joints are rotated back into their initial pose (Figure 7-109c) the flexor also goes back to its initial pose, and the knee area resumes its initial deformation.

Flexor lattices can be adjusted to deform the geometry in a variety of ways. In Figure 7-109, the flexor causes a **crease** on the inside of the knee, while at the same time causing a knee-shaped **bulge** on the outside.

(a)   (b)   (c)

Figure 7-109. Joint flexors combine the features of lattices and driven keys, allowing you to define how a surface will deform in the area of an IK joint. (Copyright 2001, Misook Song.)

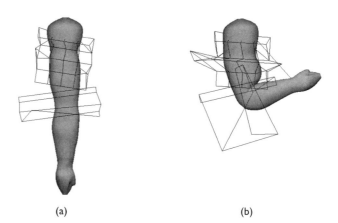

Figure 7-110. A bone flexor can control the deformation of your model in the area between two joints.

(a)   (b)

A second variety of flexor lattice allows you to associate a flexor with the **bone** of a skeleton—that is, the area between two joints. This permits you to create bulges in areas of **muscle**. Figure 7-110 illustrates this. In addition to a joint flexor at the elbow, a bone flexor has been defined on the upper-arm bone to create a bulging in the area of the bicep muscle.

On a complex character model, there may be a variety of flexors applied simultaneously, along with any of the other rigging techniques we have discussed. In Figure 7-111, two flexors are defined for each arm—one in the area of the elbow, another in the shoulder area. In addition, a standard, non-flexor lattice has also been defined in the area of the collarbone and neck.

There are a great many techniques and subtleties involved in character rigging. For a complex model with complex motions, character rigging can become quite involved. For good character animation, however, effective character rigging is indispensable. At a minimum, it vastly simplifies the animation of your model. In many cases, it makes animation possible that would have been impossible otherwise.

Figure 7-111. Some character models require a number of flexors at both joints and bones. (Copyright 2001, Misook Song.)

7.14 Facial Animation

The animation of human **facial expressions** plays a critical role in many animations. This is because so much of our interpretation of human behavior and human motivation comes from our reading of a person's facial expressions. In real-world interactions, the slightest rise of an eyebrow, furrowing of a forehead, or curl of a lip can completely change the meaning of a situation. This is true of facial animation as well, and because of this, facial animation can be one of the most challenging and most satisfying aspects of animation.

Expressive facial animation does not require complex models. The example seen in Figure 7-112 illustrates this. Here, the facial model consists solely of a handful of geometric primitives—a sphere for the head, spheres for the eyes and mouth, and cylinders for the eyebrows. Moreover, none of these forms is deformed; all are simply rotated or scaled. In spite of the simplicity of the model and the technique, the three heads illustrated here are quite expressive. This is because the animator was able to capture the essentials of these facial expressions—for example, the angled eyebrows and flattened mouth of the angry face in (a). The key to good facial animation is the animator's ability to see and record in his mind's eye the movements and changes that comprise a given human facial expression. With this visual reference in mind, the animator can turn even the simplest cartoon facial model into a wonderful, very human face.

In practice, of course, most facial models involve more subtle geometry than in Figure 7-112. Moreover, we usually want to deform this geometry to simulate the shape changes of the facial muscles and flesh—for example, the pursing of lips, the wrinkling of a nose, or the swelling of cheeks. For these situations, the most frequently used technique is the **blended keyshape** technique introduced in section 4.9. Applied to facial animation, this means creating a number of keyshapes for the entire face (Figure 7-113). Once these keyshapes are defined, you define keyframes by blending two or more of the keyshapes together to yield your final facial expression at that frame. The software interpolates the facial shapes in between the keyframes, yielding the final animation.

There are a number of details of the blended keyshape process that can greatly facilitate the process when applied to keyshaped facial animation.

First, it is usually advisable to break each facial expression down into several, **modular expressions**. Rather than creating a single keyshape for an angry face, it is better to create several sub-keyshapes, each capturing one element of the angry facial expression—for example, left eyebrow down, right eyebrow down, left corner of mouth down, right corner of mouth down. We see this in some of the keyshapes of Figure 7-113. The bottom row shows

(a)

(b)

(c)

Figure 7-112. Even with simple models, a skilled animator can produce effective facial animation. The key is observation—being able to see how humans move and react.

360   A D V A N C E D   A N I M A T I O N

Figure 7-113. The blended keyshape technique is the most commonly used technique for facial animation, permitting you to build a library of facial expressions. (© 2000, Keith Reicher.)

four different aspects of mouth deformation. This approach gives you more flexibility in assembling your final facial expressions, effectively giving you a vocabulary from which you blend them together to create the final facial expression. If desired, you can then save some of these final facial expressions as their own keyshapes, thereby building a library of progressively higher-level keyshapes.

A second helpful tip is the creation of keyshapes which are **exaggerations** of the expressions you might be interested in achieving. Since the blended keyshape approach allows you to take percentages of each shape, it is advisable to have more than you need of a given expression, rather than less. For example, rather than creating a keyshape of exactly the smile you want to achieve, you should create one for an exaggeratedly large smile. When you do the final animation, you can select only 70 percent of that exaggerated smile, giving you the more natural smile you originally wanted. Because your keyshape was defined with exaggeration, however, you also have the option of creating a more extreme smile, without having to define a new keyshape to achieve it.

A third useful tip is that most software packages permit you to insert **in-between keyshapes** into your keyshape library. This becomes important if the interpolation from one keyshape to another doesn't give you quite the

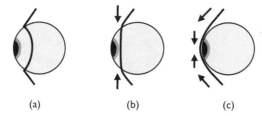

(a)   (b)   (c)

Figure 7-114. When making blended keyshapes, you may need to make in-between keyshapes.

animation you intended. An example of this might be the closing of an eyelid (Figure 7-114). Recall that the interpolation from a keyshape *A* to a keyshape *B* entails the interpolation of the X,Y,Z coordinates of each point on the surface of *A* to their new X,Y, Z positions in *B*. The movement of each point, from *A* to *B*, therefore, is in a straight line. In some cases, this straight-line interpolation will cause problems. In our example of the eyelid, it would cause the eyelid to pass through the eyeball, as in Figure 7-114b. By creating an in-between deformation of the eyelid halfway between A and B, as in (c), this problem can be solved.

In addition to blended keyshapes, you can also use **inverse kinematic skeletons** to deform a model's geometry for facial expressions. In section 4.7 we saw how IK skeletons can be applied to a variety of models. In sections 7.12 and 7.13 we investigated how they can be applied to move and deform human character models. It is also possible to create an IK skeleton within a head model to help control the facial animation. In Figure 7-115, we see a simple skeleton inside the model of an old man's head. Coming up from the neck to the base of the skull, the skeleton branches off—one direction going toward the top of the head, and the other going toward the jaw. The geometry of the head model is then skinned to the entire skeleton.

The result of this rigging is that when the jaw joint of the skeleton is rotated up and down, the character's jaw goes up and down, deforming as it does. In Figure 7-115a, we see the character with no jaw rotations; in (b) the jaw bone has been rotated upward slightly to give the appearance of an old man's toothless mouth closing; and in (c), the jaw bone of the skeleton has been rotated downward to lower the jaw and open the mouth.

Combining the inverse kinematic technique with the blended keyshape technique can be particularly effective. We see this illustrated in Figure

(a)   (b)   (c)

Figure 7-115. An inverse kinematic skeleton inside a head model can control the jaw movements.

(a)   (b)   (c)

Figure 7-116. You can combine inverse kinematics and blended keyshapes in one model. (Courtesy, Bill Burg.)

7-116. Here, an inverse kinematic skeleton moves the boy's jaw up and down. At the same time, other elements of his face—such as his eyebrows, eyelids, and lips—are deformed through blended keyshapes.

A specialized application of blended-keyshape facial animation is **sound synching**, in which the deformations of the mouth are animated to synchronize with spoken speech (Figure 7-117). In general, the same principles apply here as they do in keyshaped facial animation. First, it is important to make sure that the geometry of the mouth area has enough surface points to permit the kind of deformation needed. That geometry is then deformed and saved as keyshapes. The mouth animation is produced by creating keyframes at frames corresponding to the speech in the soundtrack, and allowing the software to interpolate between the key mouth shapes.

The mouth keyshapes chosen should correspond to the **phonemes** of the language spoken. These are a set of critical sounds, and in English include such sounds as *ah*, *iy*, *sh*, etc. For a simplified cartoon-style animation, only nine or ten phonemes might be necessary. For a more realistic mouth animation, a more complete set of phonemes would be selected, with a keyshape developed for each. When developing mouth keyshapes for selected phonemes, it is common for an animator to use a mirror to very carefully analyze the shape of his or her mouth as he pronounces each sound. In Figure 7-117, we see six of the phonemes used by the animator for his model. In all, he developed some thirty phoneme keyshapes.

Once the phoneme keyshapes are defined, the next step is usually to read into your animation software an **audio file** of the dialogue. Most 3D software packages provide a graphic representation, called an **audio waveform,** of this audio. We see one such waveform in Figure 7-118. When you play your animation, you not only see the animation, but also hear and see the soundtrack. By dragging the timeline of your animation to the precise moment when a sound begins, you can determine the exact frame at which your phoneme keyshape should occur.

Mouth keyshapes do not exist in isolation, of course. Rather, they are combined with the other facial-expression keyshapes you have already

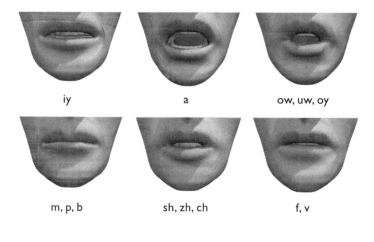

iy   a   ow, uw, oy

m, p, b   sh, zh, ch   f, v

Figure 7-117. For lip-synched animation, you develop blended keyshapes for the mouth positions of specific phonemes. (© 2000, Keith Reicher.)

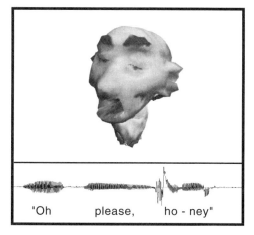

"Oh   please,   ho - ney"

Figure 7-118. Viewing the waveform of your audio track allows you to synchronize your mouth animation to the dialogue.

defined. This permits you in one instance to create an animation of a happy character laughing, "Oh please, honey!", and at another to create a sad character sighing, "Oh please, honey."

Yet another critical aspect of facial animation is **head gestures**. Frequently, inexperienced animators focus too exclusively on the facial deformations that comprise a facial expression, at the expense of the overall orientation and movement of the head. In fact, a great deal of facial expression is conveyed purely through the movement and position of the head. A downward-looking head sends one signal, a head with chin uplifted in the air sends another, and a head tilted to the side yet another. Try this experiment: Stand behind someone and study their head movements as they engage in conversation. You will be surprised at the amount of head movement of the average person, even in the course of a normal conversation. You may also be surprised to find how much variation there is from person to person. All of these slight head movements and poses are meaningful to us, and must therefore become part of any good facial animation.

(a)   (b)   (c)

Figure 7-119. A critical aspect of human facial expression is the angle and tilt of the head.

We see an example of this in Figure 7-119. In this sequence, we reuse the same model we saw in Figure 7-115. Neither its facial features nor its texture map is animated, other than a slight up/down movement of the jaw. Each pose, however, involves a tilt of the head. In our example, this is accomplished by rotating the group of IK joints that include the jaw and upper-head joints (see Figure 7-115 for a diagram of the skeleton). In spite of the simplicity of the technique, the result is quite striking. Each of the poses conveys a distinctly different feeling, a different interpretation of the old gentleman's state of mind.

A specialized application of facial animation is **hyperrealism**. The goal here is to produce models and animation of human characters so naturalistic as to be indistinguishable from the real. One of the industries especially interested in this approach is the film industry, where CG characters of this nature are sometimes called **synthetic actors**. The hope among some in the industry is that these will eventually (and more cheaply) replace real human actors.

Applied to facial animation, hyperrealism begins with the creation of a very realistic head model. This is usually done either with polygons, or with subdivision surfaces. We see an example of this is Figure 7-120. In addition to accurately capturing the shape of the head, it is also important to structure

Figure 7-120. Hyperrealism in facial animation combines extremely naturalistic modeling, rendering, and animation. (© 2001, Alceu Baptistão/Vetor Zero Brazil)

(a)   (b)

its geometry in a way that will later permit naturalistic facial animation. This typically involves arranging the polygons of the surface to align with the muscles of the face. Notice in the wireframe version of our example (Figure 7-120a) that the polygons conform to the shape of the cheek, lip, eye, and neck muscles. In Figure 7-120b, we see this model with realistic textures and lighting applied. A full-color image of this model can be seen in color plate 1.

Once the model has been built, any of the facial animation techniques described in this section can be used to animate it. Since the goal is hyper-realism, **motion capture** may be combined with a selection of other techniques. As discussed in more detail in section 7.10, motion capture for facial animation involves placing sensors at various locations on the face of an actor. A device then reads the position of each sensor as the actor talks and changes facial expression. The positional data is input to software that applies it to a CG model of a head. The complexities of handling the raw data read from the sensors are significant and usually require special-purpose software devoted to that task. The results, however, can be an uncanny realism of movement.

However it is accomplished, facial animation can be a rich, engaging, and sometimes amusing (Figure 7-121) aspect of animation.

Figure 7-121. Facial animation can be one of the most engaging aspects of the animator's art. (Courtesy, Soon-woo Kwon.)

7.15 Nonlinear Animation

Animators have long been aware of the powerful features of **digital video editing**, also known as **nonlinear editing** (see section 8.3). These include the ability to easily insert a video segment, or **clip**, at any point in the total sequence, as well as to slow that clip down, speed it up, or cross-dissolve it with another clip.

Based on the paradigm of digital video editing, **nonlinear animation** is a technique incorporating many of the same capabilities, as well as several additional ones. It allows you to cut and paste clips of animation, repeat them, change their speed, and even cross-dissolve them with other animation clips.

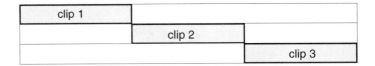

The interface to nonlinear animation software usually mimics that of a digital-editing program, and is equally intuitive to use (Figure 7-122). The user drags icons representing animation clips into a time bar, and then positions, stretches, and otherwise modifies those icons, which in turn modifies the animation clips they represent.

When you perform an operation on a clip, the software interpolates numbers for the **animation parameters** used by that clip. A simple clip might consist of a cube rotating and translating across the screen. When you perform an operation on this clip—for example, making it twice as fast—the software alters the values for the translation X,Y,Z and rotation X,Y,Z of the cube.

Since nonlinear animation software operates on the parameters of the models in your clip, the first step in using this technique is to define what those parameters will be. The collection of parameters that will contribute to a clip is sometimes called a **clip set**. (It is also sometimes called a *character set*, although this name can be misleading, since the models used for clips need not represent characters.) To define a clip set, select all the parameters of the model or models you are working on, and make the designated menu selection. Once defined, the clip set becomes a selectable node, just like any other node in your scene.

The process of defining a clip set is similar to that of defining a pose set for pose-based animation (section 4.12). In fact, in packages offering both pose-based animation and nonlinear animation, clip sets and pose sets may be defined by a single operation.

Once the clip set has been defined, you begin animating your model, saving keyframes for that clip set, which in turn saves keyframe information for all the parameters in the clip set. Once animation for your clip set has been keyframed, you make a menu selection to define that animation as a **clip**.

There are a variety of operations you can perform on your clip once it has been defined. One is to **repeat**, or **cycle** it. In Figure 7-123, we see three repetitions of the clip called *Walk*. When you cycle a clip, you can elect to have each cycle begin either at the position of the original clip, or where the previous cycle concluded. In the latter case, this will **offset** the parameter values of each cycle by the concluding values of the previous cycle. This becomes especially important for any clip in which the model is translating. Imagine a walk clip in which the character is at X = 0 on frame 1 of the clip, and at X =

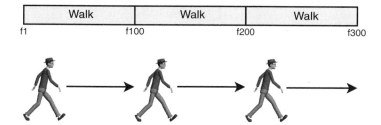

Figure 7-123. An animation clip can be repeated and offset with each repetition, to yield a continuous animation of your model moving through space. (Character model, courtesy, Bill Burg.)

10 on the last frame of the clip. For the cycling to be effective, the character should start the second repetition of the clip at X = 10, not at the original X = 0 position. Telling the software to offset the clips when cycling solves this problem.

Another basic clip operation is **scaling**, which makes a clip play faster or slower. This is accomplished either visually, by dragging the edge of the clip icon right or left, or numerically, by typing in a value. Scaling the one hundred-frame clip in Figure 7-124a by a factor of 1.5 will turn that clip into a slower, 150-frame version of the same animation (Figure 7-124b).

You can also **offset** a clip to make the animation occur either sooner or later in time. Again, this is accomplished either visually, by clicking and dragging the clip left or right along the timeline, or numerically, by typing in a number. In Figure 7-124c we see our original, one hundred-frame *Walk* clip offset by fifty frames, so that it now starts at frame 50. At the same time, it is scaled by 300 percent, making it 300 frames long and ending at frame 350.

Clips can also be used at more or less than 100 percent of their full **strength**, or **effect**. This is possible because the nonlinear-animation software, recall, is operating on the individual animation parameters in your clip set. If a character moves his hand to a particular X,Y,Z location, the three

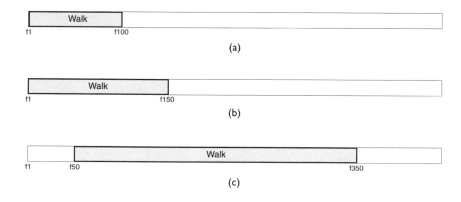

Figure 7-124. A nonlinear animation clip can be scaled to speed it up or slow it down, as well as offset in time to make the clip occur sooner or later.

X,Y,Z values can be multiplied to give more or less of the same movement. Setting the strength parameter to 50 percent would cause the character to move his hand only half as far.

One of the most powerful features of nonlinear animation is the ability to **cross-dissolve** two clips. Since nonlinear animation is based on a software interpolation of the parameters defined in the clip set, the parameter values in one clip can be averaged with those in a second clip, as long as these two clips share the same parameters.

As an example, imagine a clip set for an animated human figure. This clip set might include such parameters as the translation X,Y,Z of the left ankle effector, the translation X,Y,Z of the right ankle effector, the rotation X,Y,Z of the neck joint, and so on. With this clip set, we make three animation clips— one of the character walking, a second of him running, and a third of him jumping. We then insert these into our nonlinear animation software (Figure 7-125). To increase the duration of each action, we also cycle some of the clips.

To create our first cross-dissolve, we position the first *Run* clip along the timeline so that its beginning overlaps the end of the second *Walk* clip. The larger the time overlap between the two clips, the slower the cross-dissolve. We then use a menu selection to tell the software to create a cross-dissolve between the end of *Walk* and the beginning of *Run*. The result of this cross-dissolve is that the character begins by walking, then (during the cross-dissolved section) makes a gradual transition from walking to running, and then runs.

The nonlinear animation we see in Figure 7-125 is a good illustration of the power of this technique. The result of this nonlinear animation is that the character walks across the floor, gradually starts running, runs at full speed, jumps, lands, continues running, and finally slows down from a run to a walk, and then to a slower walk. All of this was accomplished by repeating, offsetting, scaling and cross-dissolving a total of only three distinct clips.

Figure 7-125. One of the most powerful features of nonlinear animation is the ability to cross-dissolve between two clips, causing the model to gradually transition from the action of the first clip to that of the second. (Character animation, courtesy, Bill Burg.)

In addition to the easy creation of cross-dissolve transitions from one clip to another, most nonlinear animation systems offer **graphic editing** of a transition's curves. Any cross-dissolve transition is initially created with the software's default interpolation—usually, a spline interpolation. That interpolation can be represented as a curve, and that curve can then be edited, using all the standard parameter-curve editing techniques we saw in section 4.4. For example, the first transition from walking to running could be modified to use an ease-in-ease-out interpolation.

A major advantage of nonlinear animation is the **modularity** illustrated in Figure 7-125. A small number of clips can be repeatedly reused to build up a variety of more complex animations. It is common for an animator or animation team to develop a **clip library**, adding clip sets and clips to it over time and selecting and sharing them as needed.

For some applications, it can be useful to use this modular capability to decompose animations into more elemental movements, so that these lower-level movements can be mixed and matched to create new, more complex animations. For example, the walk clip we have been using in our discussion could itself have been built from several more elemental clips.

Figure 7-126 shows four figures representing four clips. In clip (a), the character translates across the floor, with no arm or leg movement. In clip (b), the only motion is his arms swinging back and forth. Clip (c) consists of him walking in place, with no arm motion and no translation. Clip (d) consists of the character standing in place and squatting, with neither arm nor leg motion. By combining, overlapping, and cross-dissolving these clips (Figure 7-127), we could produce an animation of the character swinging his arms but not walking, then walking with arm swing, then squatting as he walks and swings his arms, then walking and swinging his arms in his normal, upright position again.

Notice in Figure 7-127 that, in order to get the various lower-level motions to combine properly, the clips are placed under one another, without

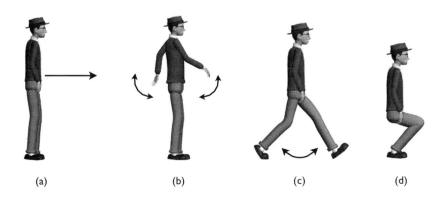

(a)   (b)   (c)   (d)

Figure 7-126. Nonlinear animation is modular and can make use of decomposed motions as the basic vocabulary of your animation. (Character model, courtesy, Bill Burg.)

Translate				
Arms	Arms	Arms	Arms	Arms
	Legs	Legs	Legs	Legs
			Squat	

Figure 7-127. Combining and cross-dissolving modular clips allows you to build up more complex actions. (Character model, courtesy, Bill Burg.)

cross-dissolve. This causes their movements to add together: the *Translate* clip is added to the *Legs* clip which is added to the *Arms* clip, producing a character walking across the floor swinging his arms. The exception to this is the *Squat* clip, which is cross-dissolved with the others to create a gradual transition from upright to squatting and back again.

How much modularity is appropriate for your clips depends on the animations you expect to eventually produce. At some point, defining ever smaller and smaller modular clips creates more work for the animator than it saves. The principle remains, however—the modularity of nonlinear animation is one of its essential strengths, and building a library of reusable clips can greatly enhance your animation capabilities.

A final and very powerful capability of nonlinear animation is the ability to apply the animation from one clip to **multiple character models**. Recall that nonlinear animation manipulates the set of parameters defined in the clip set. If two models have identical parameters, the animation stored in a clip originally developed for character *A* can be applied to the parameters of character *B*. Thus, a running animation originally developed for the thin man in Figure 7-128a can be applied to the very different character in Figure 7-128b. To work properly, however, each of the two characters must have an identical IK skeleton structure, with identical parameters controlling it.

The capabilities of nonlinear animation are powerful and varied. Knowing what they are and designing projects with them in mind can greatly facilitate an animator's work. This becomes especially true in large projects or team situations, where animation clips can be reused in different circumstances and to different effects.

(a)

(b)

Figure 7-128. If two models share the same clip set of parameters, an animation clip of one can be applied to the other. (Character model, courtesy, Bill Burg.)

CHAPTER 8
Postproduction

8.1 Introduction

While it is often possible to render final, ready-to-record frames of an animation, it is sometimes not possible and frequently not desirable to do so. It is often to your advantage to render each frame in pieces and to assemble the pieces later. For example, you might create a background image and a foreground image separately and then combine these images later to make the final frame. This process of assembling various pieces of an image is called **compositing**. Additionally, you might render several sequences of animation, and then assemble them, possibly altering the order or length of the sequences, defining transitions between sequences, or adding a soundtrack. This process is called **editing**.

Together, compositing and editing comprise **postproduction**, which we introduce in this section. Be forewarned that postproduction is a very large topic, with entire books written on aspects of the process. Only a brief introduction is presented here. It will behoove you to study the capabilities of both compositing and editing in much more detail, as they are integral parts of the animation pipeline.

8.2 Compositing

Combining and processing images in various ways is known as **compositing**. Because of the complexity of compositing software, it usually runs as a separate, stand-alone package outside of your 3D animation software. The various compositing operations you perform with this software can be applied either to individual still images, just as you would with a 2D imaging program, or, more importantly for the animator, to entire animation sequences.

Why not, you might think, just render your frames in one pass and be done with it? A first answer is that it is almost impossible to "just render the frames in one pass and be done with it." That is, only rarely will you render all the frames perfectly the first time. Even after you have completed all the rendering tests, the chances are that, given the complexity of most animations, somewhere you will have made a mistake and have to rerender some portion of your work. The experienced animator assumes this and considers it part of the process. When it does happen, it is often much easier and faster

Figure 8-1. It is often advisable to break a rendered frame into component elements—for example, the foreground and background portions of this scene. These components are then composited to form the final frame. (City-scape, courtesy Steve Rittler. Robot, courtesy Steven Lin.)

to correct mistakes and rerender if the frames have been broken down into component images.

Imagine, for example, a sequence of frames in which a three-dimensional character (in Figure 8-1, a robot) walks in front of a complexly modeled three-dimensional cityscape, as the camera pans slowly by. Imagine further that you have rendered these frames and found some rendering error on the character. The rendering of all the buildings is fine, however. In a frame such as the one described, it might take the computer five minutes to render the buildings and thirty seconds to render the character. If you have set up the rendering so that the building models in the background and the character model in the foreground are rendered separately and composited later, you now will be in a position to take advantage of this fact and rerender only the foreground character model. This can save a tremendous amount of time. If this segment of the animation is thirty seconds long and is being recorded at the standard thirty-frames-per-second video rate, in fact, you will have just saved yourself seventy-five hours of rerendering time (30 seconds × 30 frames = 900 frames × 5 minutes per frame for background buildings = 4,500 minutes ÷ 60 minutes per hour = 75 hours)! Even calculating in the time needed to do the compositing of all the frames, which might be one or two hours, you will have saved three full days of machine time!

Even if you make no rendering errors, using a compositing approach as part of your rendering process provides flexibility. To continue with the previous example, suppose that upon seeing the rendered frames you decide to change the walk of the character slightly. If you have set up the rendering in the foreground-background composited fashion, you will be able to make this change in about one-tenth of the rerendering time it would have taken if you hadn't, since you have to rerender only the figure itself. A difference of this magnitude makes it more likely that you actually will make such an improvement. If you know that you will have to spend three additional days rerendering the scene, you are more likely to decide that the animation is good enough as is, even though in reality it still could be improved.

This kind of flexibility becomes especially important in production situations where decisions have been made about one portion of the animation but not yet about another. If the rendering is organized appropriately, final rendering of those portions that have been decided upon—say, the background buildings—can proceed even as the details of the other components are being worked out. If the rendering is being done in a noncomposited, all-in-one-pass fashion, all rendering must be postponed until all design decisions have been made. The result of this, of course, is that decisions are often made hastily, and badly.

A final motivation for using a composited approach to produce your final frames is that sometimes there is simply no other way, for example, when 3D computer animation must be combined with live-action footage. Another example would be where some special two-dimensional effect is to be added as a post-process to the rendered frames. In both of these cases, the animation is necessarily in the realm of compositing. The three-dimensionally rendered frame becomes one element, the live-action frame or two-dimensional effect another, and the final frame is the result of compositing the two in some fashion.

All of this is not to say that all animation sequences should be rendered in a composited manner. If there will be no significant advantage to breaking the final frame into component pieces, and if there are no special two-dimensional effects, there may very well be nothing gained by using a composited approach. Very often, however, there is a significant advantage.

The most common compositing operation, called **matting**, is the capability of combining a foreground image and a background image, as described in the previous section. The word "matte" here means a mask—something that blocks out, or hides, something else.

Suppose that your foreground picture is a robot, rendered against a plain black background (Figure 8-2a). A matte, or mask, of that image is a black-and-white cutout in the shape of the robot (Figure 8-2b). This matte picture is derived from the original picture. The background color in the original becomes black in the matte picture; everywhere else, the matte picture is white.

In most systems, this matte picture is produced automatically at the same time that the rendered image (the robot, in this example) is calculated. Some software packages store the matte image as a separate picture file. More commonly, however, the matte information is stored within the same file that stores the picture's Red, Green, and Blue color information. In this case, the matte information is referred to as the **Alpha channel** of the picture, and the picture itself as RGBA (Red, Green, Blue, and Alpha).

(a)

(b)

(c)

(d)

Figure 8-2. A matting operation. The robot (a) is copied through the matte (b) onto the background image (c) to produce the final image (d).

Now suppose that you also have a separately rendered background picture of some buildings (Figure 8-2c) on top of which you want to put the robot. Doing so consists of copying the foreground picture through the matte onto the background picture. If you imagine placing the matte picture over the foreground picture, and if you imagine that the black areas of the matte are opaque and the white areas transparent, then you can understand how this process works. The matte picture blocks out those portions of the robot picture that lie behind the opaque, or black, areas of the matte. Only those portions of the robot picture that lie within the transparent, white areas of the matte go "through" the matte, and the result is a composited picture (Figure 8-2d).

More technically, a matting operation is calculated in terms of pixel values. For a simple matte operation such as the one just described, the computer tests the value of each pixel in the matte picture. If the value at a pixel is 0 (black), the pixel of the foreground picture at the same location is not copied on top of the background picture. If, on the other hand, a pixel value is 255 (white), the color of the corresponding pixel in the foreground picture is copied on top of the background image, overwriting the old color of the pixel (that is, the pixel color of the background image) at that location.

A problem would arise, however, if matting were reduced to this sort of all-or-none, black-and-white situation. Recall that most three-dimensional renderings are produced with anti-aliasing, to conceal the staircasing effects that can be so distracting in computer graphics (see section 3.10). Since the edges of an anti-aliased model are a blurred combination of the model's color and the background color, an all-or-none matte will not work. If the white areas of such a black-and-white, or **hard-edged**, matte are large enough to include the anti-aliased pixels, they form a dark halo around the composited model. If the white areas of the matte are small enough to crop off the anti-aliased pixels, it recreates the jagged edges that the anti-aliasing had eliminated.

The answer to this problem, a **soft-edged matte** makes use of intermediate gray values, as well as pure black-and-white values, to determine which portion of a foreground picture will pass through the matte picture onto the background picture. Notice (in Figure 8-3, a blowup of a portion of the matte in Figure 8-2b) that the interior of the robot still translates into white in the matte image, and that the background portion of the original robot image still translates to black in the matte. However, the anti-aliased edges of the robot now translate into shades of gray in the matte, producing a soft edge. When the foreground picture of the robot is copied through this matte, a *percentage* of the color is copied through at these gray pixels. The darker the matte pixel, the less of the original goes through. The lighter the matte pixel, the more of the original goes through. In the center of the robot, for example, the color of the matte is pure white (the pixel value is 255), so 100 percent of the fore-

Figure 8-3. A close-up of a soft-edged matte, showing the intermediate values of gray around the edge of the matte.

ground image passes through the matte. Along the edge of the robot, a given matte pixel might have a value of 128. Since 128 divided by 256 equals 0.5, 50 percent of the color of the robot at that pixel will go through the matte. This color is combined with 50 percent of the color of the background image at the same pixel location. The result is that the robot image blends properly with the background image.

The matting we have described so far is the simplest kind of matte, a **straight** alpha matte, and consists of only black and white information in the alpha channel governing how much of the background color should show through the matte. Some software packages offer a modified version of matting, called a **pre-multiplied** alpha matte. This variation, like a straight matte, has transparency information stored in the alpha channel. However, it also incorporates percentages of your image's background colors directly into the RBG information of your color image, specifically in those areas of partial matting around the edges of your objects. This sort of matte can produce a very clean masking operation if the compositing software also has information about the colors of the background. When compositing with alpha mattes, therefore, it is important to first determine whether your 3D software is producing a straight matte or a pre-multiplied matte. It is then important to tell your compositing software that you are using either straight or pre-multiplied mattes. And finally, if you are using pre-multiplied mattes, you need to give your compositing software information about the original background colors against which your models were rendered.

So far we have been discussing a single matte operation for a single still image. When you use a sequence of mattes for a sequence of animation frames, the operation is called a **travelling matte**. One of the most common and powerful uses of such a matte is to combine computer graphics, or **CG**, footage and **live-action** footage. Television advertisements, newscasts, documentaries, and even sitcoms use this technique regularly. But nowhere is it more common than in the production of Hollywood films, where all manner of wondrous CG monsters, ghosts, tornadoes, explosions, and spaceships are seamlessly matted in with live-action footage of our favorite actors.

Combining CG footage and live action has become an enormously sophisticated art unto itself, involving much more than simply the rendering of 3D models and matting them onto film. In order for the effect to be believable, the **lighting** in both the live-action scenes and the computer-generated scenes must match exactly. Figure 6-24 in section 6.4 is a good example of this sort of matching.

Registering your computer model to the live-action scene is another issue that comes up when you combine computer imagery and live-action footage. For animated creatures, this is often done with **stand-in actors**. For example, if a computer-generated monster is to run down a hallway and jump on the back of the fleeing hero, a human actor might play the part of the monster as the scene is being shot. Once shot, the film is digitized frame by frame and the computer-generated monster matted into each frame on top of the human stand-in. The new digital frames are then recorded back to film.

When dealing with live action, you must also carefully match the camera motion of the computer animation to that of the live footage. One way of doing this is with camera-motion matching software described in section 7.10. Another is with a **motion-tracking device**, in which the film camera is mounted on a mechanical device whose movements are controlled by a computer program. This enables you to reshoot the scene as many times as you want with exactly the same camera motion, and also to replicate the exact same camera motion in the virtual space of a 3D computer animation program.

Finally, convincing matting of CG over live-action requires careful matching of **reflections**. No matter how carefully a computer model is registered to the scene's action, no matter how well-matched are the lighting and camera motion, if the model does not have the reflections our eyes tell us it should have, something will seem amiss. Here the most useful technique is reflection mapping (see section 6.9). Special software can analyze the digitized frames of the live-action footage, producing appropriate reflection maps for the computer model.

Another important film application of many of these same matting techniques is the **digital replication** of elements, whether computer generated or live-action. Rather than the "cast of thousands" that was trumpeted by film producers of another era, film producers today often take advantage of the computer's matting capabilities to turn a cast of a few dozen into what seems like a cast of thousands. If a scene calls for a band of horsemen to

Figure 8-4. This image combines a number of techniques. The ring and fire were modeled and rendered three-dimensionally. The fish are a single two-dimensional image that was manipulated and matted after the rendering. The lightning was painted digitally, frame by frame. (*The Absolute Contingency*, © 1993 Brett D. Gardy.)

ride up the hill, it is frequently now much cheaper to hire only a few actors, digitize the footage of them, extract their images from the digitized frames, and replicate those few horseman across the hillside in a cut-and-paste fashion.

In addition to the matte operation, compositing systems provide **image-processing** functions that operate either on single images or combinations of images. Some of the different image-processing functions you might find in compositing software include changing the brightness of an image, changing the contrast of an image, increasing or decreasing the color saturation of an image (for example, by pulling down all the red values, or pulling up all the blue values), blurring an image, rotating an image, and magnifying an image. The list also includes the myriad image-processing **filters** you find in image-retouching software packages. All these operations, in combination with matting and many others, comprise the field of **special effects**, a field complex enough that numerous special-effects companies and special-effects professionals devote themselves uniquely to these concerns.

A final special-effect technique that is very effective but often overlooked by computer animators is the **hand-painting** of individual frames. In certain situations, if the number of frames is not too great, the best way to get an unusual effect (such as a flash of lightning, a puff of smoke, or an explosion of light) on your already rendered three-dimensional frames is to retouch the images by hand, frame by frame. Once the frames have been rendered, like any other picture, they can be read into a digital paint program, retouched or added to, and then resaved.

Computer animators, especially those who are less experienced, tend to take a rather purist approach to the production of their animation frames. The feeling is that if it is not done in 3D, it is "cheating." In fact, however, the final criterion in animation is not how was it done, but how it looks. Whether your frames were produced entirely through three-dimensional rendering, or through some combination of two-dimensional special effects and compositing is ultimately insignificant. If it looks good, it looks good. There is no such thing as "cheating."

A good example of this principle is the frame seen in Figure 8-4. In this animation, the ring, the mapped image within it and the fire around it were all rendered three-dimensionally. The school of fish was produced in a two-dimensional image-processing program and then matted on top of this rendered image. Finally, the lightning was hand-drawn frame by frame on top of the composited image to produce the final frame.

8.3 Editing

Although it is outside the scope of this book to discuss video and audio editing in any detail, it is worthwhile to look into the capabilities of these processes, because these capabilities are substantial, easy to implement, and used very commonly. These capabilities are used so commonly, in fact, that they usually—and rightly—are treated as an integral part of the process of producing computer animation.

Video exists in two broad categories: digital and analog. Until several years ago, all video was **analog video**, and the video we watch on our TVs and home movies still is. Analog information runs in a continuous stream, without discrete subdivisions. Examples of such information include the sounds you hear and the light you see. There is, for example, no dichotomy between the shade of yellow light entering a window and the slightly whiter shade of yellow a bit to one side of that light. These colors progress smoothly and continuously from one to another. Physically, analog information of this sort is created by light waves and sound waves, and usually is represented as smoothly curving waveforms, to capture the continuous nature of the information. Analog video records visual information as a sequence of continuous analog signals onto a magnetically charged videotape. When played back through the proper equipment, these continuous analog signals appear as moving imagery.

Digital video, by contrast, handles imagery in the same way that the computer graphics techniques you have seen throughout this book handle imagery. The smooth, continuous information of the visual world is broken down into tiny, discrete elements. Since each of these pieces of information can be represented as an individual number, the information is referred to as "digital." Instead of representing visual information as a series of analog wave-forms, digital video represents information as collections of discrete, digital "bits" of information, which can be stored either on disks or on tapes.

Digital information has the advantage over analog information of being completely unambiguous. In the digital world, a particular element either does or does not have a certain numerical value—it either is or is not a certain color, for example. With analog information, things are never this clear-cut. A particular analog color is always "this color plus or minus a little."

When working with digital video, you normally begin by recording animation frames onto a special digital disk or tape. As of publication of this book, the most common medium is **miniDV** tape.

Today, all video editing is done with digital video. Unlike the older analog video, digital video provides perfect image reproduction when you make copies or modifications of your video. Making either copies or modifications is known as going down a **generation**, since the new video is once removed from the original. Digital editing also permits random access of your video, in contrast to the sequential, or linear, access required by the older analog technology. For this reason, digital editing is also called **nonlinear editing**.

The process of editing video with a digital, non-linear system combines approaches from digital image compositing, discussed in the previous section, with approaches from traditional analog video editing. Digital editing programs, however, vary in complexity significantly depending on whether you are working on a low-end system suitable for small production environments or on a full-scale, high-end system suitable for feature-length films. Some of the most salient features of all digital video editing systems are summarized here.

When you work with a digital video-editing system, the visual material is organized into **clips**, segments of either computer-generated or live-action imagery that may range in length from a few frames to several minutes. Segments of sound are also referred to as clips. Clips of imagery are **video clips**; clips of sound are **audio clips**.

You begin by reading into your editing system the clips you will be using. Within the system are **tracks**, usually represented graphically as horizontal bars, the horizontal direction of the track representing time. Using a cut-and-paste approach, you define the sequence in which clips should occur by selecting a clip and dragging it to a particular track. By sliding it horizontally left or right, you define where in time the clip should occur. You then select the next clip and position it in one of the tracks, either the same track or one of the other tracks.

Figure 8-5. Digital editing systems allow you to define the sequence of events by visually positioning both video and audio clips in tracks.

Figure 8-5 shows a typical interface of such a system, with two video clips inserted on the first video track, V1, and a third video clip inserted on a second video track, V2. Below them are two audio tracks, with a single, long audio clip in audio track A1, and two short clips in audio track A2. Audio clips are normally represented as waveforms, the graphs seen in tracks A1 and A2. At the top of the screen is a timeline, in seconds, indicating that the total running time of this example is twenty-five seconds.

It is not necessary to use the entire length of a clip. You may elect, for example, to use only seven seconds of a ten-second clip, cropping off one second from the beginning of the clip and two seconds from the end. In this example, the starting point, or **in-point**, of the clip would be one second into the clip; the ending point, or **out-point**, would be two seconds from the end. The in-point and out-point are collectively known as **edit points**. Adjusting the edit points can usually be done either visually, by dragging a marker along the length of the clip, or numerically, by typing in the exact frame number at which you want the clip to begin or end.

Once you have specified the sequence in which clips will occur, you specify the **transition** between the clips, or how the end of one clip interacts with the beginning of the clip that follows. In the simplest transition, a **cut**, one clip abruptly begins just as another abruptly ends. The clips in Figure 8-5 all have cut transitions between them: as soon as clip A ends, clip B begins; as soon as B ends, C begins.

Because there are many types of transitions, video editing moves beyond the mere sequencing of imagery and becomes a form of image compositing. One of the most common transitions is the **cross-dissolve,** in which two images are blended together (Figure 8-6). When performing a digital cross-dissolve, you somehow must indicate how much of each picture is to end up in the final blend. You often do this by specifying a number between zero and one for the first of the two images. Zero means that none of the first image will be used, which in turn implies that all of the second image will be used. A blend value of one means that all of the first image will be used, while none of the second image will be used.

Figure 8-6. A cross-dissolve blends together two images (one the person walking, the other the clown in a coffin). (*Iggy's Dream #74*, © Michael O'Rourke)

The way in which the percentages are applied is very similar to the procedure for the soft-edged matte. Suppose that 20 percent of the first image and 80 percent of the second are to be used. For each pixel of the final image, the three RGB pixel values of the first image are multiplied by 0.2. Then the three RGB values of the same pixel in the second image are multiplied by 0.8. The two results are added together to produce the final color for the new, blended image at that pixel. This process is repeated for every pixel of the image.

Closely related to the cross-dissolve are the **fade-in** and **fade-out** edits (Figure 8-7). A fade-in is a cross-dissolve from a blank black screen to the sequence to be viewed. A fade-out goes in the opposite direction, cross-dissolving from the animation sequence to a black screen.

Another common technique for making the transition between two sequences is the **wipe** (Figure 8-8). In this kind of edit, one sequence slides or "wipes" across the screen, revealing a second sequence behind it as it goes. Depending on the style of wipe, the new sequence can come in horizontally, vertically, or diagonally. Some systems also allow you to bring in the new sequence through an expanding circular pattern, or an expanding square pattern.

In the previous section we discussed alpha channel matting. An alternative approach to masking out portions of an image is **chroma keying**, which is similar to a hard-edged mask in that it is an all-or-nothing operation. Certain color ranges are defined to be transparent, or "keyed," out of an image, and any colors in this range are invisible, allowing the imagery from a second source to show through. The range of colors defined to be the "key"— that is, to be invisible—is controllable by the editor. The most common colors used for this process are specific hues of blue and green, and the process of keying these out from a video image is referred to as **blue screening** or **green screening**.

Figure 8-7. A fade-in dissolves from black to picture. A fade-out dissolves from picture to black.

Figure 8-8. A wipe replaces a scene with a new scene. The new scene slides in horizontally, vertically, diagonally, or through a circular window.

You operate on transitions in the same way as clips. First you select a transition, for example a cross-dissolve, and drag its icon to a transition track. Then you position the transition in time by sliding it horizontally along the track. As with a clip, you can adjust the length of the transition by sliding markers at its beginning or end to the left or right. By placing the transition between two video clips (Figure 8-9), you indicate how you want those two clips to interact and for how long.

One of the great advantages of digital video editing is that you can use transitions to composite any number of video tracks without any deterioration in the quality of color information. (This is true of digital audio as well.) In Figure 8-10, video clip B cross-dissolves with clip A at the same time that clip C fades in and at the same time that clip D mattes in. Because all the

Figure 8-9. Between any two segments of video you can define a transition, adjusting its type and length.

	00:00	00:05	00:10	00:15	00:20	00:25	00:30
V1		A					
T1			Xdis				
V2				B			

Figure 8-10. In digital video, any number of tracks of imagery can be composited together without loss of image quality.

	00:00	00:05	00:10	00:15	00:20	00:25	00:30
V1		A					
T1			Xdis				
V2				B			
T2		Fade-in					
V3		C					
T3	Matte						
V4	D						

information for these clips is purely numerical, there is no loss of image quality as the various images are composited together.

Once you have completed the editing of your work with your nonlinear editing software, you make a **master** copy in digital format on digital media—for example, on miniDV tape. From this master you can make as many duplicates, or **dubs**, as you wish. If your dubs are also in digital video format, there will be no loss of image quality. You can also elect to make dubs in one of the analog formats—for example, VHS dubs for viewing at home in most standard VCRs. If you make analog dubs, you must be aware that copying from your digital master to an analog dub necessarily entails some loss of image quality. The amount of quality lost will depend primarily on the **bandwidth** of your analog medium—that is, how much image information it can contain per unit of time. A beta videotape, for example, has a higher bandwidth than a VHS tape, and therefore provides better quality dubs from your digital master.

Conclusion

In the course of this book you have learned both the basic and many advanced principles and techniques of 3D computer animation. To begin with, you examined the issues involved in preproduction design and planning. Then, since in any 3D animation there must be objects to animate, you saw all the major approaches to "building"—that is, modeling the shape of—an object. You also examined the issues involved in making a picture, or rendering, of a three-dimensional scene: the definition of the surface properties of an object, the lighting, the use of the camera. You then investigated at length the major principles and techniques involved in actually making an object move—that is, animating it—within the computer. Finally, you considered the compositing and editing techniques of postproduction.

You now should be prepared to apply the knowledge you have gained, perhaps pursuing animation as a form of entertainment or as a branch of the fine arts, or perhaps employing it in any one of a multitude of fields, such as television-commercial graphics or the feature-film market. Industrial designers, architects, interior designers, and sculptors are among those professionals who have greatly enhanced their work through the simulation capabilities of three-dimensional computer animation. Biologists, chemists, and medical professionals have found 3D computer animation useful as a means of previewing a situation or of visualizing a scientific model.

You can expect that the applications, and with them the power of computer animation will continue to expand very rapidly. The capabilities of 3D computer graphics are vastly more sophisticated today than they were even as short a time as three years ago. This evolution is partly due to the tremendous growth in the speed and memory capacities of computer hardware, and partly to a delightful dragon-biting-its-tail phenomenon involving the capabilities of the technology and money. As the technology has become more useful to more professionals, they and the institutions they are part of have become more willing to invest in the hardware and software of 3D computer animation. As more money has been invested, more research has been possible. With increased research have come more improvements in the capabilities, and these in turn have attracted more investment, and so on.

Techniques, for example, that at this writing are described as advanced will become standard. As they do, new techniques currently only incubating in research laboratories and hardly conceivable now will replace them. At the same time, the hardware that underlies all of this technology will continue to develop—faster than you can imagine, if the past is any guide. Approaches and techniques that researchers cannot even dream of attempting to implement now, simply because they are physically impossible given the current hardware, will be possible within a few years. And all of this development will, as it has in the past, sift down and (sooner rather than later) become part of the standard, off-the-shelf 3D computer animation packages that you or I or your company or my company can buy.

It is a truly exciting time to be involved in three-dimensional computer animation.

Index